Job Creation in Latin America and the Caribbean

Job Creation in Latin America and the Caribbean

RECENT TRENDS AND POLICY CHALLENGES

Carmen Pagés, Gaëlle Pierre,
and Stefano Scarpetta

A COPUBLICATION OF PALGRAVE MACMILLAN
AND THE WORLD BANK

1818 H Street NW
Washington DC 20433
Telephone: 202-473-1000
Internet: www.worldbank.org
E-mail: feedback@worldbank.org

1 2 3 4 12 11 10 09

A copublication of The World Bank and Palgrave Macmillan.

Palgrave Macmillan
Houndmills, Basingstoke, Hampshire RG21 6XS and
175 Fifth Avenue, New York, N. Y. 10010
Companies and representatives throughout the world

Palgrave Macmillan is the global academic imprint of the Palgrave Macmillan division of St. Martin's Press, LLC and of Palgrave Macmillan Ltd. Macmillan® is a registered trademark in the United States, United Kingdom and other countries. Palgrave® is a registered trademark in the European Union and other countries.

ISBN: 978-0-8213-7623-2 (Paperback)
eISBN: 978-0-8213-8025-3
ISBN: 978-0-8213-7688–1 (Hardcover)
DOI: 10.1596/978-0-8213-7623-2

Library of Congress Cataloging-in-Publication Data
Pagés, Carmen.
Job creation in Latin America and the Caribbean: recent trends and policy challenges / Carmen Pagés, Gaëlle Pierre, and Stefano Scarpetta.

p. cm.—(Latin American development forum series)
Includes bibliographical references and index.
ISBN 978-0-8213-7623-2 (pbk.)—ISBN 978-0-8213-7688-1 (hbk.)—ISBN 978-0-8213-8025-3 (electronic)

1. Manpower policy—Latin America. 2. Manpower policy—Caribbean Area. 3. Unemployment—Latin America. 4. Unemployment—Caribbean Area. 5. Latin America—Economic policy. 6. Caribbean Area—Economic policy. I. Pierre, Gaëlle. II. Scarpetta, Stefano. III. Title.

HD5730.5.A6P34 2009
331.12'0424098—dc22

2009017016

Cover design: ULTRA designs

Printed in the United States.

Latin American Development Forum Series

This series was created in 2003 to promote debate, disseminate information and analysis, and convey the excitement and complexity of the most topical issues in economic and social development in Latin America and the Caribbean. It is sponsored by the Inter-American Development Bank, the United Nations Economic Commission for Latin America and the Caribbean, and the World Bank. The manuscripts chosen for publication represent the highest quality in each institution's research and activity output and have been selected for their relevance to the academic community, policy makers, researchers, and interested readers.

Advisory Committee Members

Other Titles in the Latin American Development Forum Series

China's and India's Challenge to Latin America: Opportunity or Threat? (2009) by Daniel Lederman, Marcelo Olarreaga, and Guillermo E. Perry, editors

Does the Investment Climate Matter? Microeconomic Foundations of Growth in Latin America (2009) by Pablo Fajnzylber, Jose Luis Guasch, and J. Humberto López, editors

Measuring Inequality of Opportunities in Latin America and the Caribbean (2009) by Ricardo de Paes Barros, Francisco H. G. Ferreira, José R. Molinas Vega, and Jaime Saavedra Chanduvi

The Impact of Private Sector Participation in Infrastructure: Lights, Shadows, and the Road Ahead (2008) by Luis Andres, Jose Luis Guasch, Thomas Haven, and Vivien Foster

Remittances and Development: Lessons from Latin America (2008) by Pablo Fajnzylber and J. Humberto López, editors

Fiscal Policy, Stabilization, and Growth: Prudence or Abstinence? (2007) by Guillermo Perry, Luis Servén, and Rodrigo Suescún, editors

Raising Student Learning in Latin America: Challenges for the 21st Century (2007) by Emiliana Vegas and Jenny Petrow

Investor Protection and Corporate Governance: Firm-level Evidence Across Latin America (2007) by Alberto Chong and Florencio López-de-Silanes, editors

The State of State Reform in Latin America (2006) by Eduardo Lora, editor

Emerging Capital Markets and Globalization: The Latin American Experience (2006) by Augusto de la Torre and Sergio L. Schmukler

Beyond Survival: Protecting Households from Health Shocks in Latin America (2006) by Cristian C. Baeza and Truman G. Packard

Natural Resources: Neither Curse nor Destiny (2006) by Daniel Lederman and William F. Maloney, editors

Beyond Reforms: Structural Dynamics and Macroeconomic Vulnerability (2005) by José Antonio Ocampo, editor

Privatization in Latin America: Myths and Reality (2005) by Alberto Chong and Florencio López-de-Silanes, editors

Keeping the Promise of Social Security in Latin America (2004) by Indermit S. Gill, Truman G. Packard, and Juan Yermo

Lessons from NAFTA: For Latin America and the Caribbean (2004) by Daniel Lederman, William F. Maloney, and Luis Servén

The Limits of Stabilization: Infrastructure, Public Deficits, and Growth in Latin America (2003) by William Easterly and Luis Servén, editors

Globalization and Development: A Latin American and Caribbean Perspective (2003) by José Antonio Ocampo and Juan Martin, editors

Is Geography Destiny? Lessons from Latin America (2003) by John Luke Gallup, Alejandro Gaviria, and Eduardo Lora

About the Authors

Carmen Pagés is principal economist at the research department of the Inter-American Development Bank. She was at the World Bank at the time when the background research for this book was undertaken. She has published extensively in the areas of labor economics and institutions. Her research focuses on the determinants of productivity, the effects of labor market institutions and policies on economic outcomes, and the determinants of informal employment. A native of Spain, she holds a MA degree in Economics from the Universidad Autonoma de Barcelona and a PhD in Economics from Boston University.

Gaëlle Pierre is a consultant for the World Bank. Her research has focused on labor markets; she has published work on a range of issues, including labor market regulations, the role of the investment climate in job creation, gender wage differentials, and the design of social policies. Her work in these areas covers Western Europe, Eastern and Central Europe, Sub-Saharan Africa, and Latin America. She has a PhD in Economics from the University of Warwick and a MSc, also in Economics, from the London School of Economics.

Stefano Scarpetta is head of the Employment Analysis and Policy division of the OECD and the editor of the OECD Employment Outlook. He was lead economist and labor market advisor at the World Bank when this book was written. He is a research fellow and the deputy director of the programme of work on Employment and Development at the Institute for the Study of Labour (IZA), Bonn. He has published extensively in academic journals and edited several books in the fields of labor economics and industrial relations, economic growth, and industrial organization. His current research focuses on the effects of labor market policies and institutions on economic outcomes and the role of regulations and institutions for productivity growth, creative destruction, and job reallocation. A native of Italy, he holds an MSC in Economics from the London School of Economics and a PhD from the Département et Laboratoire d'Economie Théorique Appliquée (DELTA) of the Ecole des Hautes Etudes in Science Sociales in Paris.

Contents

Boxes

Figures

TABLES

Acknowledgments

This study was prepared by Carmen Pagés, Gaëlle Pierre, and Stefano Scarpetta, with the contribution and excellent assistance of Erika Molina and Mariano Negri. It draws on background papers by a number of researchers, including Reyes Aterido, Mary Hallward-Driemeier, Sebastian Galliani, Maurice Kugler, and Alejandro Micco.

This work was supported by the Chief Economist of the Latin American and the Caribbean (LAC) Region and by the Research Department of the Inter-American Development Bank. The study benefited from useful comments and suggestions provided at various stages by Ahmad Ahsan, Omar Arias, Norman Loayza, William Maloney, Pablo Fajnzylber, Guillermo Perry, Jaime Saavedra, and an anonymous referee.

Abbreviations

ALMP	active labor market program
BADEINSO	Base de Estadísticas e Indicadores Sociales (Social Indicators and Statistics Database)
BI	Balassa index
CEDLAS	Centro de Estudios Distributivos, Laborales y Sociales (Center for the Study of Distribution, Labor, and Social Affairs)
CIMO	Programa de Calidad Integral y Modernización (Comprehensive Quality and Modernization Program) (Mexico)
ECLAC	Economic Commission for Latin America and the Caribbean
FDI	foreign direct investment
G7	Group of Seven
GDP	gross domestic product
GGDC TED	Groningen Growth and Development Centre and the Conference Board's Total Economy Database
IC	investment climate
ICLS	International Conference of Labor Statisticians
IDB	Inter-American Development Bank
ILO	International Labour Office
ISIC	International Standard Industrial Classification
IUSA	individual unemployment savings account
JI	job intermediation
OECD	Organisation for Economic Co-operation and Development
PAC	Programa de Apoyo a la Capacitación (Program to Support Training) (Mexico)
PROJoven	Programa de Capacitación Laboral Juvenil (Youth Training Program) (Peru)

SEDLAC	Socio-Economic Database for Latin America and the Caribbean
SITC	Standard International Trade Classification
UI	unemployment insurance
UNIDO	United Nations Industrial Development Organization
UNPD	United Nations Population Division
UNSD	United Nations Statistics Division
WAP	working-age population

Overview

Throughout Latin America and the Caribbean, unemployment and the poor quality of jobs have become two central issues in public debates and in the policy agenda of governments. Almost two decades after the introduction of comprehensive macroeconomic stabilization packages and trade, fiscal, and financial market reforms, growth prospects remain lukewarm, and labor markets show a disappointing performance.

Labor market slack manifests itself in different ways in the countries of the region. For example, open urban unemployment rates vary from under 4 percent in Mexico to 15 percent in Colombia. In addition to open unemployment, the quality of jobs is a major source of concern. For example, the shares of employment in all types of informal nonagricultural work (independent workers, including the self-employed; domestic workers; and workers employed in microenterprises) continue to be high and have increased from an average of 42.8 percent in 1990 to 45.6 percent in 2006 (Perry and others 2007).

These poor labor market outcomes carry a substantial social and political cost. In particular, opinion polls (the annual Latinobárometro survey) confirm that employment is people's primary concern in almost all countries of the region, and a large majority of respondents are "worried" or "very worried" about losing their jobs. A sense of malaise about the inability of structural changes to deliver the expected benefits in terms of employment and welfare is reflected in a decline in support for reforms since the late 1990s (Panniza and Yañez 2006). Creating viable and productive employment is vital for creating and sharing prosperity in the region.

This book strives to better understand the recent labor market trends in the countries of the region and the factors that underlie the failure of many of those countries to create more—but especially more productive and rewarding—jobs. In particular, the book addresses four main questions:

- How well are the Latin American and Caribbean economies doing in terms of growth and job creation compared with other emerging economies? The book shows that jobless growth concerns only a few Latin American and Caribbean countries. In most of the rest, many jobs have been created over the past decade, but their productivity and pay were low.

- Is the weak creation of productive jobs the result of lack of dynamism in the economy? To address this question, the book dives into the behavior of firms. In particular, it looks at how resources are reallocated across firms and sectors. This analysis uncovers that, in most countries of the region, many jobs are created and destroyed, but this activity does not necessarily lead to better allocation of labor to the most productive jobs. Many new and potentially productive firms are small and encounter difficulties in expanding.
- What are the constraints to productive job creation across different types of firms? The book exploits information from a large number of firms in Latin America and the Caribbean regarding their exposure to and the effect of different aspects of the business climate in the region. Particular emphasis is placed on assessing differences across small, medium, and large firms and, when available, contrasting the responses of formal and informal firms. The book shows that small firms tend to be more constrained by lack of access to finance, macroeconomic instability, competition from informal firms, and corruption, while large firms are hampered by an inappropriate regulatory environment.
- What is the relative importance of labor market policies in strengthening the creation of productive jobs in the countries of the region? Firms in the region seldom cite labor market regulations as a major concern, even though those regulations are relatively rigid from an international perspective. The book shows that this apparent lack of concern is mainly because other constraints to firms' operation and expansion are more pressing. It also suggests that as other constraints are lifted, inappropriate labor market regulations become a binding constraint. The book goes on to advocate rethinking social protection systems, shifting protection from jobs to workers, and advancing the design of social security programs and labor market policies. The overarching goals are to protect workers while fostering the creation of more and better jobs.

"Jobless Growth" or "Growthless Jobs"? Long-Term Growth and Employment Performance in the Region

From an international perspective, income per capita growth in Latin America and the Caribbean has been disappointing during the past three decades. Although gross domestic product (GDP) per capita growth has improved since the "lost decade" of the 1980s, available data suggest that in the past 15 years it has been rather modest and has not prevented a continued divergence from other developing regions.[1] In particular, the countries of the region have been outperformed by many countries with which they were at par in terms of income per capita in the 1970s. In the past decade, not only has growth in the region been lower than what was observed in the dynamic emerging economies of East and South Asia, but it has also been lower than the average of the high-income countries of the Organisation for Economic Co-operation and Development (OECD). Moreover, there has been no recent convergence of income within the region, whereas in the 1970s, poorer Latin American and Caribbean countries grew faster than richer ones.

This relatively modest performance is partly explained by the fact that labor productivity, the usual main driver of growth, has grown at a very slow rate (figure 0.1). For example, by 2006 worker productivity in the region was 21 percent of that of the United States, against 30 percent in 1980.

Although productivity has been muted in most countries of the region, much of the modest output growth has been driven by strong—and relatively resilient—job creation. In terms of employment growth, the region has even outperformed many of the comparator countries, where the employment rate growth associated with a given growth in GDP has been higher than in many other parts of the world (figure 0.2). Job creation has gone in pair with the large increase in the labor supply brought about by rising female participation and a growing working-age population.[2] Hence, the employment rate (the share of the working-age population in employment) has remained fairly constant. In some countries, open unemployment increased over the past 15 years.

Countries outside the region that experienced similar growth in their working-age population over the same period showed very different patterns of adjustment. Although they achieved much higher labor productivity growth, they were exposed to more modest increases in participation and employment rates than were countries in Latin America and the Caribbean.

This combination of high employment growth and low productivity growth implies that the quality of created jobs has been fairly low. Among the group of countries for which wage data could be collected, only Bolivia, Chile, and Nicaragua have experienced positive wage growth in the period from 1994 to 2004, while the remaining countries suffered a decline in real wage growth. Moreover, other indicators of job quality, such as the percentage of salaried jobs that are affiliated with social security or the share of workers in medium and large firms, have also declined, hence confirming that the quality of employment fell since the early 1990s. In fact, the share of workers not registered with social security has increased in all but one country for which that measure is available.

Overall, since the early 1990s, only some Latin American and Caribbean countries have experienced "jobless growth"—that is, a lack of job creation relative to the growth of working-age population combined with

Figure 0.1 Growth Decomposition for Latin America and the Caribbean, 1990–2004

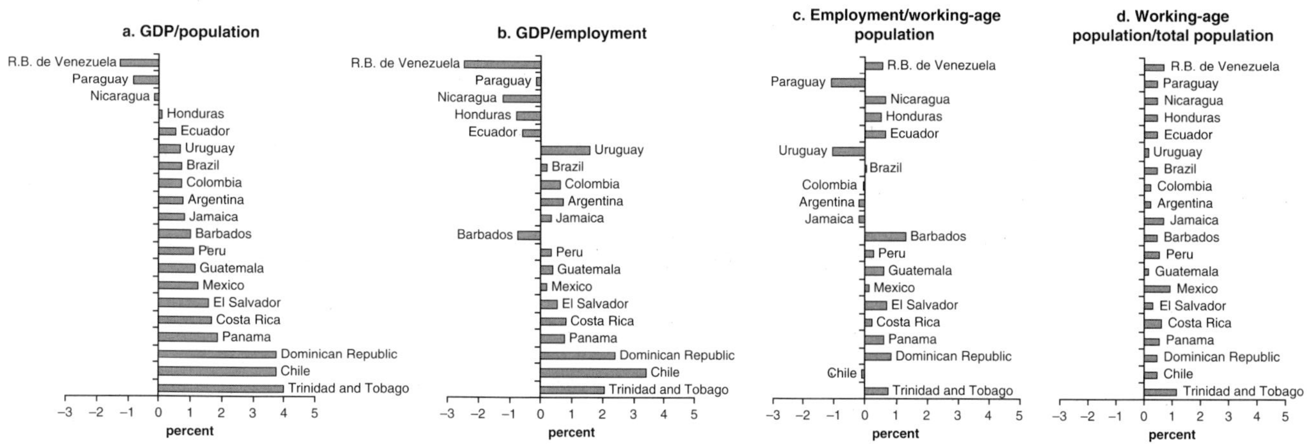

Sources: United Nations Population Division, United Nations Statistics Division, national statistical offices, and Groningen Growth and Development Centre Total Economy Database.

Note: Employment data for Uruguay cover only urban areas. The GDP and employment series were smoothed applying a Hodrick-Prescott filter. GDP per capita growth can be decomposed as the sum of GDP per worker growth, employment rate growth, and growth in the rate of the working-age population over the total population.

Figure 0.2 Change in Employment Rate and Income per Capita, 1980–2004

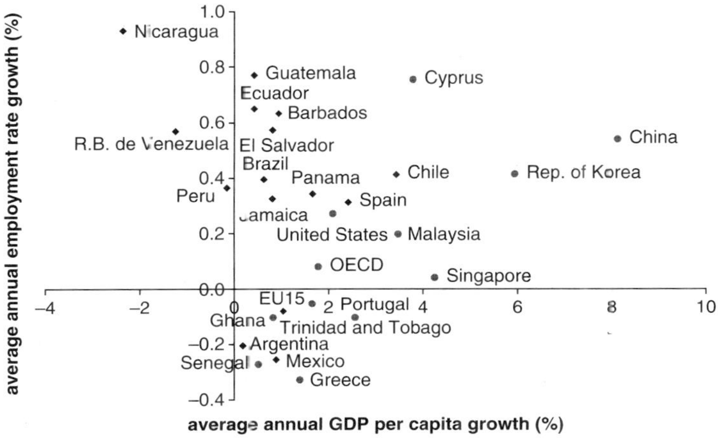

Sources: United Nations Population Division, United Nations Statistics Division, national statistical offices, and Groningen Growth and Development Centre Total Economy Database.

Note: EU15 = the 15 countries that comprised the European Union before May 1, 2004. Employment data for Uruguay cover only urban areas. The GDP and employment series were smoothed applying a Hodrick-Prescott filter.

positive economic growth (figure 0.3). These countries include Argentina, Chile, Colombia, Jamaica, Paraguay, and Uruguay, which had low job creation and stronger productivity growth. The other countries show signs of "growthless jobs"—that is, weak output growth coupled with strong labor supply increases and thus low or even declining labor productivity growth (especially in Barbados, Ecuador, Honduras, Nicaragua, and the República Bolivariana de Venezuela).

The strong labor supply pressure observed in the past decades is likely to ease in the coming years. Working-age population growth appears to have peaked around 1980, whereas its long-term trend suggests that the demographic bulge will recede in the near future. However, easing labor supply pressure should not be a motive for complacency. Strong labor supply growth does not automatically result in higher unemployment, because the economy can expand more rapidly and create more jobs. Similarly, the opposite process does not guarantee an easing of labor market pressures.

The analysis presented in this book focuses on the reasons behind the expansion of low-productivity jobs and the role that governments can play in changing this evolution.

Figure 0.3 Change in Employment Rate and Labor Productivity by Country in Latin America and the Caribbean, 1990–2004

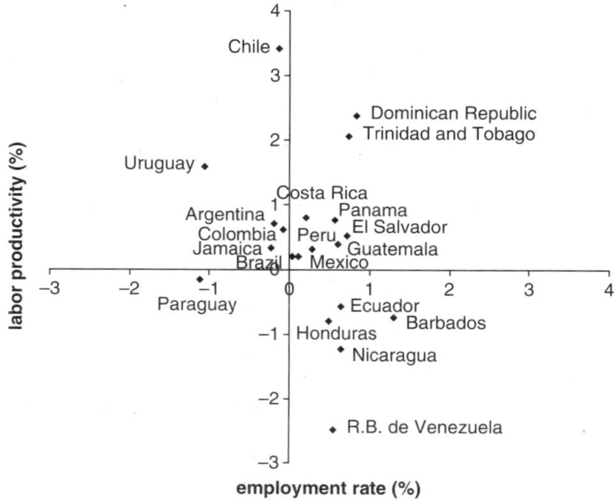

Sources: For GDP data, United Nations Statistics Division; for employment data, national statistical offices and Groningen Growth and Development Centre Total Economy Database; for working-age population data, national statistical offices and United Nations Population Division.

Supply-Side Effects

What lies beneath these employment and growth outcomes? Several supply-side effects can be identified.

Increasing Female Participation

The increase in labor supply in Latin America and the Caribbean has been driven by widespread increases in female participation, which were historically low by international standards. The improvements in women's educational attainment explain about 30 percent of the increase in participation. In addition—and contrary to expectations—the increase in female employment has not been concentrated in the service sector but, with different intensity, has occurred in all sectors. At the same time, a decrease in the employment and participation rates of men has accompanied the increase in female participation and employment rates (figure 0.4). These facts, coupled

Figure 0.4 Change in Employment Rates by Gender and Change in Youth Participation Rate, Early 1990s to Mid 2000s

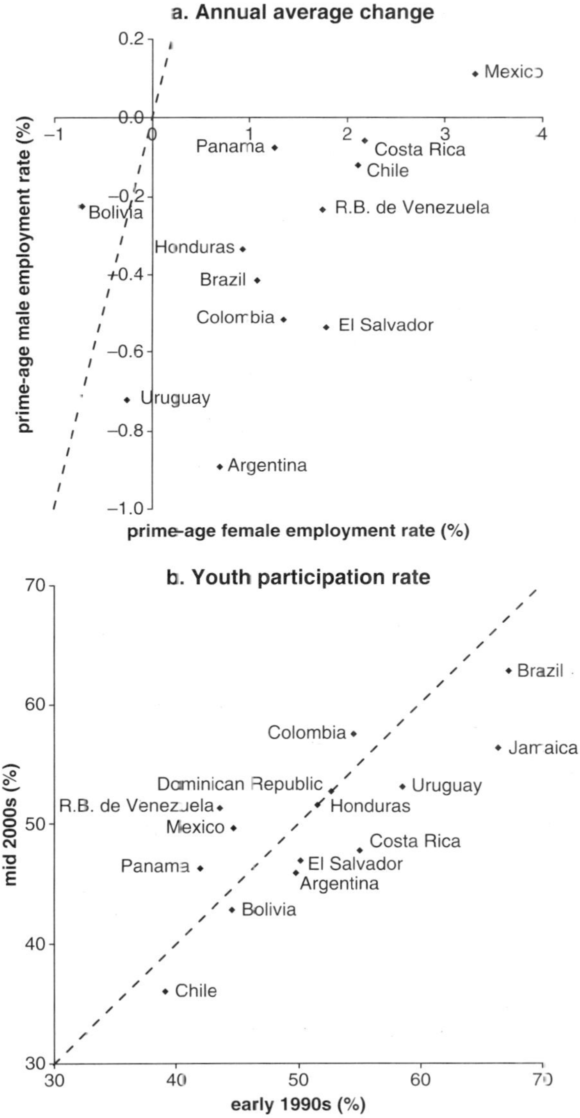

Sources: Employment rates by gender are from Inter-American Development Bank's Sociómetro database; youth participation rates are from the World Bank's Socio-Economic Database for Latin America and the Caribbean.

Note: Prime-age population includes people age 25 to 49; youths include people age 15 to 24. Data for Argentina and Uruguay are urban.

with a declining female wage gap, indicate that female work may have benefited from rising opportunities, perhaps at the expense of men.

However, greater access to jobs for women should not hide that female work segregation has declined only slowly; that female unemployment has increased more rapidly than that of males; and that, in some countries, the proportion of employed women not registered in social security has increased faster than that of males.

A Decline in Participation by Youths

The participation and employment rates of youths ages 15 to 24 also declined in the majority of countries (figure 0.4). This evolution is consistent with a shift in households' labor supply between low-educated women and youths. The latter, perceiving either a demand for higher skills or worsening labor market conditions, seem to have turned to schooling. Indeed, the proportion of youths who were neither in the labor force nor in school also fell during the same period.

Fewer employment opportunities for youths are associated with important social problems. At the same time, low contribution rates to social security for all workers, but particularly for the youths, are an issue of major social and policy concern in most countries of the region.[3] These countries tend to rely on individual capitalization for their social security systems, and contributions of workers at young ages have an inordinate weight in their final pension benefits (Berstein, Larrain, and Pino 2006).

A Shortage of Skilled Workers

One of the factors behind the weak output and productivity growth in the region is the relative shortage of skilled labor. Skill-biased technological change and greater trade openness have increased the demand for skills, but the response of the supply has been slower. This shortage has led to a rise in the returns to education in the region in recent decades (see, for instance, De Ferranti and others 2003, IDB 2003, and the references within those sources). Wages of workers with tertiary education increased at a faster rate than those of workers with secondary education despite the growing relative supply of workers with tertiary education.[4] Similarly, the relative wages of workers with primary and secondary education remained relatively constant, even when the share of population with secondary education increased relative to the share of the population with primary education.

Evidence also indicates that although skills are becoming more valuable, not all workers with tertiary education have skills that are equally valued in the labor market. Despite the rising demand for skilled labor, the unemployment rates of workers with some tertiary education have increased more, in percentage terms, than those of workers with secondary education. In addition, in many countries—most notably Argentina and Colombia—wage inequality among workers with some tertiary education has increased at a faster pace than among workers with secondary or primary education. This trend indicates that far from being ubiquitous, changes in wages are concentrated at the top end of the skilled distribution.[5]

Moreover, on average, firms in Latin America and the Caribbean take longer to fill skilled vacancies than firms in other regions and countries. Interestingly, however, in the region, these shortages are not reported as important obstacles for the growth of firms. This finding is a reflection of the many other obstacles that firms face to operate a business. Skill shortages are more pronounced among firms that are expanding (in terms of jobs), young firms, larger firms, firms that are partly or totally government owned, firms that produce garments, and firms in some high-productivity services like marketing. These features—combined with the fact that perceptions of skill shortages as an obstacle seem to be more acute in countries that have experienced higher economic growth (for example, Chile)—suggest that skill shortages pick up in periods of growth and that they constitute an important obstacle once other constraints are lifted.

Improvements in human capital accounted for a fraction of the overall labor productivity growth of recent decades. However, from an international perspective, educational improvements have been slow, especially when compared with the fast-growing countries of East Asia. It is therefore necessary to undertake simultaneous investments in skills and technology to allow for both higher productivity growth and more equitable distribution of income (De Ferranti and others 2003).

Improving investment in skills starts within the formal education system, but governments can also foster lifelong learning. Although on-the-job training cannot be a substitute for quality formal education, it can potentially bridge the gap between the skills learned at school and the skills that firms require from workers to adopt new technologies and innovations (De Ferranti and others 2003). However, finding the right mode of delivery remains an important challenge for the countries of the region.

In addition, as will be discussed further, active labor market policies are a set of government interventions that have been used in many countries to help groups of workers that have specific difficulties in finding productive jobs.

Structural Changes Across and Within Sectors: Shedding Light on the Sources of Low Productivity Growth

Beyond skill shortage, the weak productivity performance of the countries in the region is also due to the weak investment and innovative capacity of many firms and the lack of efficient allocation of labor and capital to the most productive uses. Evidence from many industrial and emerging economies suggests that productivity growth depends not only on the ability of existing businesses to invest and harness the benefits of new technologies that become available in the international market, but also on the ability to reallocate resources to more productive uses. The slow growth of productivity in the region can be traced to a less dynamic reallocation of resources across sectors and, within each sector, across firms than is found in other fast-growing economies, as well as to the expansion of sectors with relatively low levels of productivity

Low Reallocation of Employment, Which Did Not Always Improve Resource Allocation

As in most market economies, the countries of the region have experienced sizable shifts in resources across the macrosectors of the economy. This process has also been triggered by major macroeconomic and structural policy changes, including ambitious macrostabilization programs, major liberalization of trade and financial markets, and privatization of many state-owned enterprises in key sectors. The sizable process of reallocation of both output and employment across sectors of the economy has had, without doubts, profound economic and social implications. However, from an international perspective, the magnitude of reallocation tends to be smaller than that observed in most of the fast-growing countries in East Asia.

More importantly, in many countries of the region, employment—and in some cases even output—shifted from agriculture and, more importantly, manufacturing toward the service sector (figure 0.5). Shifting resources toward service activities is a common phenomenon in most market economies as they move up the income ladder. However, the magnitude and composition of the changes have specific characteristics in the region and contribute to explain the low-quality job creation. First, the decline in manufacturing employment is comparatively large. As an illustration, the share of GDP in manufacturing in Latin America and the Caribbean was similar to that of East Asia during the 1970s. By 2003, however, it dropped to about 15 percent, whereas it rose to about 30 percent in East Asia. Second, many of the new tertiary jobs have been created in relatively low-productivity and low-wage services, such as retail and wholesale trade or community, social, and personal services. So while, for example, the trade sector accounts on average for 32 percent of employment growth, it accounts for –84 percent of total growth in labor productivity. In turn, manufacturing employment explains only 5 percent of total employment growth and 33 percent of total labor productivity growth.[6]

Even within manufacturing, resources have often shifted from more productive activities to less productive ones, with highly productive industries downsizing instead of investing and expanding. A simple decomposition

Figure 0.5 Changes in the Structure of Output and Employment, Early 1990s to Early 2000s

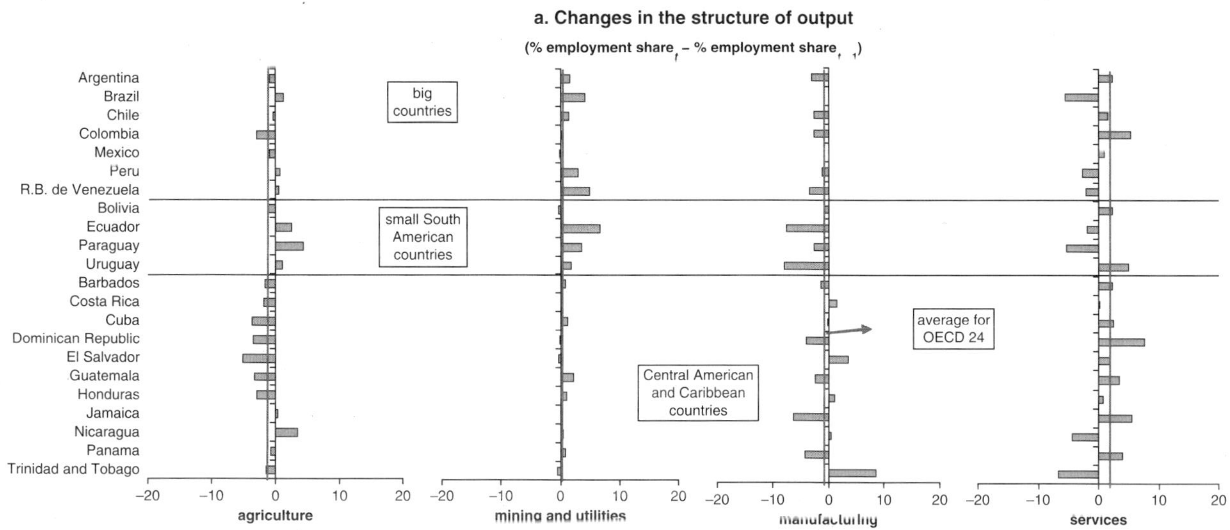

(continued)

Figure 0.5 Changes in the Structure of Output and Employment, Early 1990s to Early 2000s (*continued*)

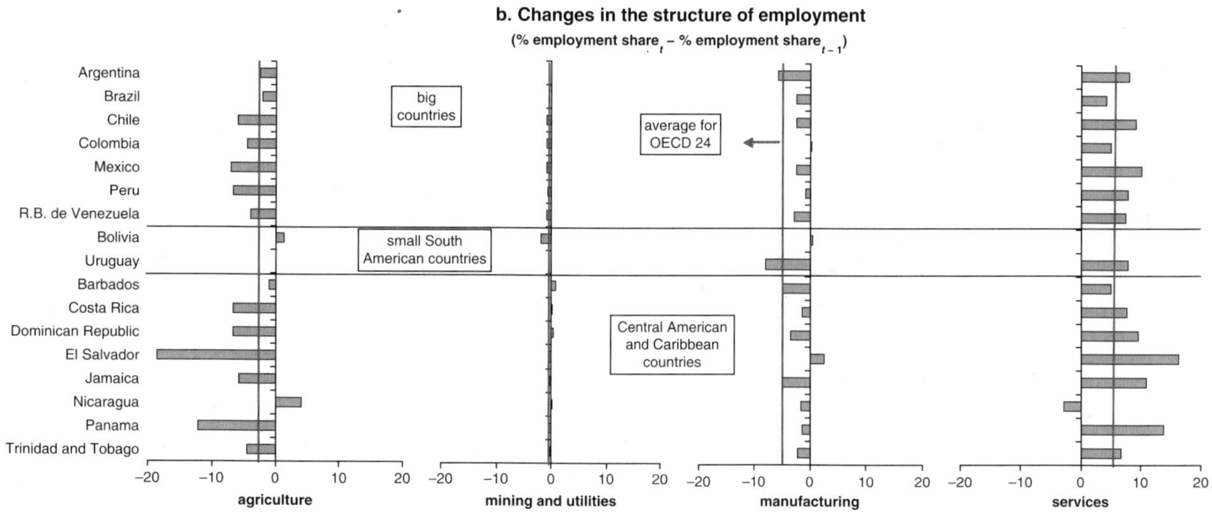

Source: GDP by economic activity at constant 1990 prices, US$, United Nations Statistics Division: employement by economic activity from Statistical Offices of individual countries of the Region.

of productivity growth in manufacturing reveals that in a number of countries employment has shifted toward less productive sectors. In addition, industries that have grown in terms of productivity have downsized employment; that is, they have adopted a defensive restructuring process rather than a strategic restructuring with new investment and job creation.

The evidence also suggests that the countries of the region have reduced their ability to shift resources toward highly dynamic sectors (that is, sectors that account for a large share of the world's trade). Although countries in the region may not have a comparative advantage producing such goods, a deterioration of the ability to cater to world demand may indicate an inability to invest in the development of industries with high world demand.

Moreover, capital-intensive activities with the highest potential to generate productive jobs have been downsized, largely in favor of natural resource–intensive activities—an area where countries of the region have maintained or increased their comparative advantages. The ability of these industries to generate productive jobs in large number is limited.[7] In contrast, in most comparators countries, capital-intensive industries have been gaining share in employment and value added.

There are, however, some exceptions to these general patterns in the region. In particular, Costa Rica, El Salvador, and Mexico all have specialized in manufacturing activities—especially in the assembly industries of electronics, computers, automobile, and textiles that serve primarily the U.S. market. Most of these industries are relatively low technology, operate under the regime of *maquilla*, and use low-skill labor intensively.

The Entry of Productive Firms and the Exit of Obsolete Ones

Unlike reallocation across sectors, job reallocation within industries has been very high in most countries of the region relative to other countries, with around 10 to 15 percent of all jobs being created or destroyed every year on average.[8] Nonetheless, major differences also exist within the region: Argentina is characterized by a fairly low degree of job reallocation, while Brazil and Mexico have higher reallocation rates than most other countries for which data are available.

Firm demographics—the creation of new firms and the destruction of obsolete ones—account for a significant share of the overall job turnover in most countries of the region, generally about 20 to 30 percent of total job creation and destruction. Moreover, evidence from Chile and Colombia, for which longer time-series data are available, suggests that the role of entry and exit in the reallocation of labor has increased in the past decade. But contrary to the case in OECD countries, firm entries play a smaller role in total job creation than exits do for job destruction in most countries of the region, except Mexico. This is because most of the new firms are very small, and many fail in the initial years of life. Although, as in most other regions, firm entry and exit are important for productivity growth, the small size of new entrants and the difficulty even successful new firms face in expanding have limited their role in exerting strong pressure on well-established incumbents to strengthen their efficiency. Indeed, international evidence reveals a strong positive and statistically significant correlation between the net entry contribution in a country-sector (measured using time averages from the country-sector-year data) and the productivity growth of incumbents (figure 0.6). However, this correlation is not found in the region, where firms' dynamics do not seem to affect productivity growth of incumbent firms through the contestability effect.

A Difficult Business Environment for New Firms, Especially Small, Low-Technology Ones

Differences in the nature of firm entry and difficulties for firm survival and postentry employment growth in Latin America and the Caribbean could explain why new firms do not generate enough contestability for incumbent firms. Moreover, much of firm entry in the countries of the region takes place in low-technology industries. Also, much of the creation and destruction of firms observed in the region takes place among micro and

Figure 0.6 Incumbent Productivity Growth versus Net Entry Contribution

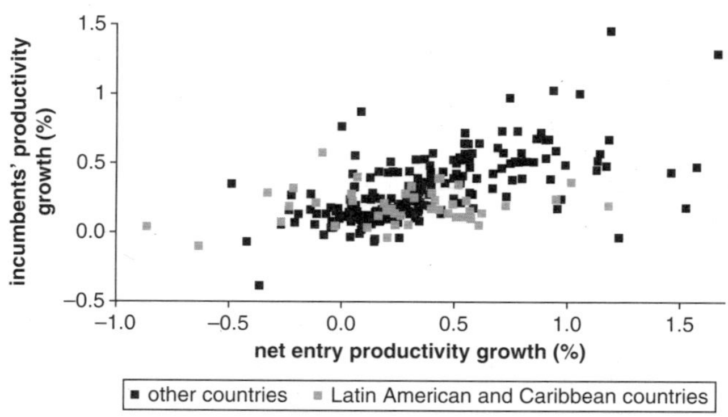

Sources: Bartelsman, Haltiwanger, and Scarpetta 2004 firm level database.
Note: Correlation = 0.58 (statistically significant at 1%).

small businesses These results suggest that most of the dynamism in terms of reallocating resources takes place among small and relatively low-tech activities, whereas larger firms or sectors higher up in the technological ladder face a lower level of dynamism and market selection.

New businesses—even those with successful business plans—also face clear barriers to expansion. Market selection is harsh for new businesses in the region. Argentina, Colombia, and especially Mexico have very low survival rates both in the total business sector and in manufacturing. In Mexico, 75 percent of entrant firms are in the market after two years, 50 percent remain in business after five years, and only about 30 percent are still in business after seven years. Failure rates among young businesses are high in all market economies, but in industrial countries, about 50 to 60 percent of new firms are still in business after seven years. But even for those that survive, the potential for postentry expansion is often limited. Only in Mexico is the extraordinary market selection after entry matched with high opportunities for expansion among the survivors (figure 0.7).

The small size of new entrants, the relatively low surviving rates, and the low postentry employment growth can account for the low incidence of small and medium-size (formal) firms (20–99 employees) in the countries of the region compared with other countries. In all market economies, the overwhelming majority of firms have fewer than 20 employees, and 50 to

Figure 0.7 Average Firm Size Relative to Entry, by Age, Manufacturing

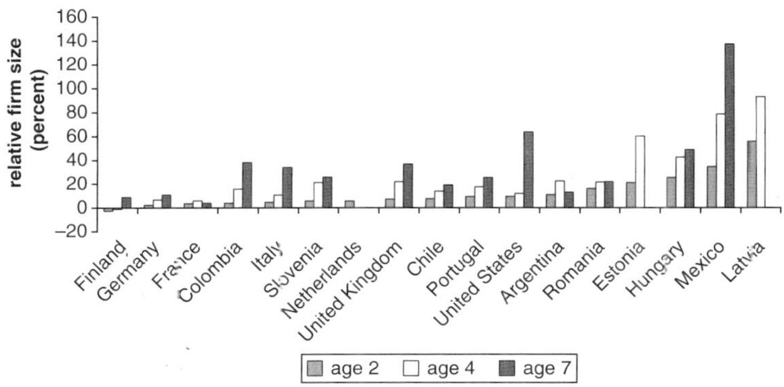

Sources: Bartelsman, Haltiwanger, and Scarpetta 2004, firm level database.
Note: Data for Germany do not include the territory of the former German Democratic Republic.

60 percent—or even more—are micro units with fewer than 10 employees. But the overall share of these firms in total employment is low, often below 30 to 35 percent. The countries of Latin America and the Caribbean are no exception to these trends, which may apply even more to the region considering that many micro firms are in the informal sector and thus not recorded in the official firm-level data. But it is important to note that the share of small and medium-size firms in Argentina, Chile, and Colombia is lower than that observed in a number of industrial countries (figure 0.8), even if one focuses only on formal firms. Their proportion in the total number of firms and total employment would be even smaller if the many small informal firms were taken into account.

The polarization of firms in the region between micro (informal) units and relatively medium to large units, with a missing middle of small and medium-size formal firms, can also be related to the industry structure of each country. A simple fixed effect regression of the share of medium-size firms in the total population of formal firms, controlling for industry effects, suggests that on average the five Latin American countries for which data are available (Argentina, Brazil, Chile, Colombia, and Mexico) have a share of small firms (20–99 employees) that is 5.2 percentage points smaller than the OECD average, and 2 to 3 percentage points smaller than in East Asia or transition economies.[9]

Figure 0.8 The Missing Middle: Share of 20- to 99-Employee Firms in Total Firms

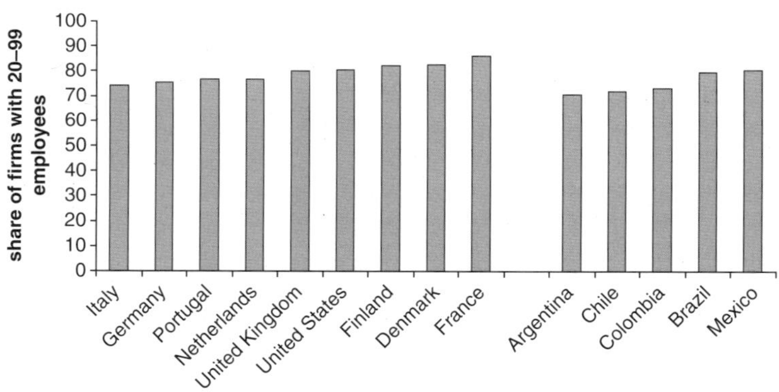

Sources: Bartelsman, Haltiwanger, and Scarpetta 2004 firm level database.

Note: Data for Germany do not include the territory of the former German Democratic Republic.

All in all, the sectoral and firm-level analysis suggests a mixed picture with limited reallocation of labor across sectors but sustained churning within each of them. A number of factors are likely to have contributed to this apparent dichotomy. On the one hand, trade liberalization over the past two decades has helped to raise competition within all tradable sectors, and this heightened competition has been associated with increased churning. This trend has been accompanied by a process of privatization that has allowed for the restructuring of former state-owned enterprises and the release of resources that new private ventures could have used. On the other hand, the real appreciation of the currencies in many countries of the region, as a result of the shift to fixed exchange regimes in the 1990s and, more recently, to the surge in commodity prices, has changed comparative advantages away from certain tradable sectors (such as manufacturing) toward mining (which is capital intensive) and nontradable service sectors (which are labor intensive but have low productivity). The currency appreciation, coupled with trade liberalization, put extra pressure on the firms concerning the productivity gains needed to remain competitive and deepened the process of cleansing of obsolete firms in tradable sectors. At the same time, however, a difficult business environment has made it hard for many private firms to fully exploit their potential and to expand and create productive jobs. Nevertheless, the large churning of firms and workers, particularly within small firms and low-productivity sectors, has had important implications for the welfare of workers, as they have been facing high levels of hard-to-diversify risk. The next section sheds more light on the barriers for firm growth and job creation.

Addressing the Constraints to Productive Job Creation: Improving the Investment Climate

The region's investment climate affects firms' entry, survival, and growth, favoring the proliferation of micro firms at the expense of small, medium-size, and large firms. Notable improvements to the investment climate have been achieved in recent decades through major economic reforms in the countries of the region. However, the region is still characterized by a difficult and uncertain business environment that is driven, among other factors, by costly or uncertain access to finance, a poor regulatory environment, and corruption.

The results from employers' opinion surveys (the World Bank's Enterprise Surveys) conducted among registered firms around the world suggest that firms in the region complain mostly about the risk and uncertainty of doing business. On average, the main obstacles to employment growth are the risks associated with an unstable macroeconomic situation and the instability of economic and regulatory policies (figure 0.9). Importantly, in an international context, macroeconomic and policy risks are more of

Figure 0.9 Main Investment Climate Obstacles in Latin America and the Caribbean

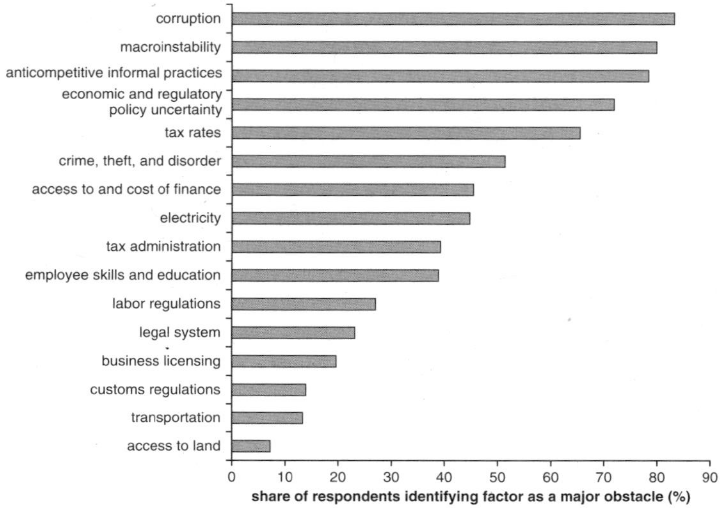

Source: World Bank Enterprise Surveys.

Note: For Brazil, Ecuador, El Salvador, Guatemala, Honduras, and Nicaragua, surveys were conducted in 2003. For Chile and Guyana, surveys were conducted in 2004. For Costa Rica, survey was conducted in 2005. For Argentina, Bolivia, Colombia, Mexico, Panama, Paraguay, Peru, and Uruguay, surveys were conducted in 2006.

an obstacle in Latin America and the Caribbean than in any other region of the world. Issues associated with corruption and the rule of law follow closely. Among factors that affect the cost of production, the cost of and lack of access to finance play the most important role.

Another important insight offered by these surveys is that formal firms tend to view informal firms as unfair competitors. The cost advantage that informal firms derive from not paying taxes or social security contributions seemingly would allow them to compete—on unequal terms—with formal firms. This perception suggests that formal and informal firms are in similar markets and, therefore, informal firms may be taking market share from formal firms. It also suggests that better enforcement of laws could, at least to some extent, contribute to an expansion of formal employment.[10]

Comparing the responses of micro firms with informal firms also yields interesting insights, although unfortunately such comparison is available only for Brazil and Guatemala. It is relevant that informal firms complain less about taxes and regulations, yet other areas of the investment climate, such as macroeconomic uncertainty or access to land, remain relevant for them.

The same surveys also reveal that small and large firms tend to be differently exposed to—and affected by—policy and market failures. This finding lends support to theoretical research that emphasizes the importance of resource misallocation caused by differential treatment across firms in explaining lower productivity levels in developing economies (Hsieh and Klenow 2007; Restuccia and Rogerson 2003). Small firms tend to complain more about access to and cost of financing, about economic and regulatory instability, and about corruption and crime. They also complain more than large firms about the competition from informal firms. This finding is again to be expected if informal firms look similar to small formal firms in aspects other than their law abiding behavior. It suggests that the existence of informal firms hampers the growth of small and micro formal firms. In contrast, large firms report the legal system, regulatory issues (such as customs and labor), and skill shortages as the higher obstacles (figure 0.10).

Figure 0.10 Perceptions about Investment Climate Obstacles: Medium and Large Firms Relative to Small Firms

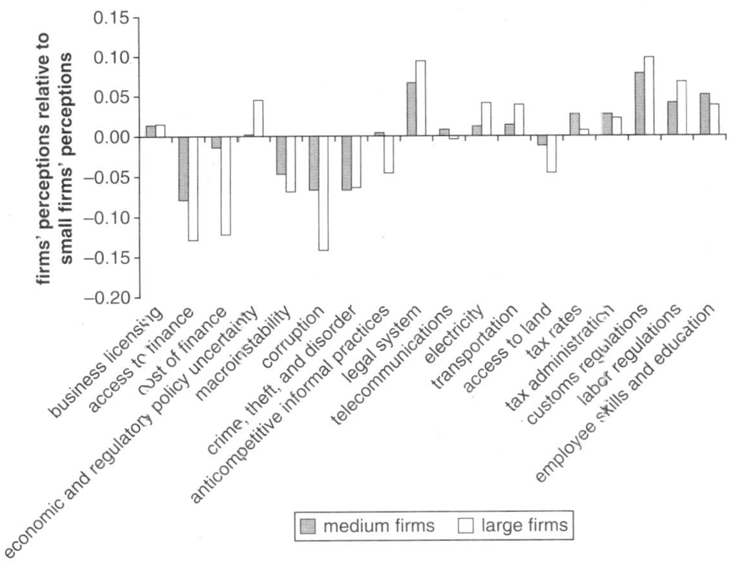

Source: World Bank Investment Surveys in Latin America and the Caribbean.

Note: Sample is as in Perre (2006).

Differences in the effect of the regulatory environment are likely to be driven by uneven enforcement of regulations among small and large firms, which, in turn, responds to the fact that tax collection tends to be more cost-effective in the latter. Enforcement is particularly uneven in Latin America and the Caribbean, where government inspections concentrate more on larger firms than in other regions. The evidence consistently indicates that a predictable regulatory environment and simplified administrative procedures lead to higher growth of all firms. However, uneven enforcement is likely to create unfair comparative advantages for micro and small firms, allowing them to gain market shares at the expense of larger firms. The latter, in turn, become less numerous and less large than they would otherwise be. These results suggest important consequences for aggregate productivity if, as supported by much evidence, larger firms tend also to be the most productive: as labor and capital are allocated to smaller, less productive firms, aggregate productivity declines.

Corruption also creates disincentives for the expansion of micro and small firms into medium and large ones. Across the world smaller firms tend to complain more about corruption (both in terms of existence and value of bribes as a percentage of sales or government contracts) than do larger firms—especially in Latin America and the Caribbean, where higher levels of corruption are associated with lower employment growth in medium-size and large firms.

Consistent with previous employer surveys (IDB 2004), smaller firms interviewed in the Enterprise Surveys are more likely to report being constrained by low access to and high costs of external finance across the developing world than are larger firms, and this finding occurred more often in Latin America and the Caribbean than in other regions. Interestingly, however, objective indicators of access to credit do not suggest such a difference. The results also indicate that although some measures of financial development, such as the incidence of overdraft facilities or the possibility of selling on credit, favor employment growth in the smaller firms, other measures, such as the availability of external financing for investments, are associated with the expansion of small, medium, and large firms.[11]

In sum, large and small firms in the region face different constraints to the creation of formal jobs. Small firms seem to be hampered by insufficient access to and cost of finance, competition from informal firms, and corruption, whereas large firms are constrained by an inappropriate regulatory framework (including labor laws) and skill shortages. High macroeconomic and policy instability are the main obstacles reported by all firms, including the informal ones. This finding suggests that policies that promote a stable macroeconomic and policy environment can do much for productive job creation in the region. Better policies will also allow shifting from a pattern of high reallocation, but with little consequences for productivity growth, to a process of reallocation in which less productive jobs are substituted for more productive ones, with substantive improvements in aggregate productivity.

All in all, the creation of productive jobs rests on the ability of governments to put in place a comprehensive policy framework that goes way beyond the labor market but includes stable macroeconomic conditions, rule of law, access to finance, and sound and predictable regulations in different markets. It is therefore key that governments coordinate their agendas across different ministries so as to pursue consistent policies that promote productive job creation.

Achieving vigorous productive job creation is a necessary condition for improving labor market outcomes in the region, particularly given the high rates of growth of the labor supply. However, job creation alone is not sufficient, because important market failures lead to labor market problems that require specific interventions in the market. The next and final sections of this overview relate the findings regarding the role of labor market policy,[12] its functioning in the region, and the required reforms needed to lead to achieve the objectives of more productive job creation and better worker protection.

Improving Regulation: Shifting to Protecting Workers Rather Than Jobs

As stated previously, the evidence suggests that the countries of the region endure a large amount of job reallocation, although the effectiveness of such reallocation in promoting better matches in the labor market seems to be low. Although part of the turnover is voluntary and can be accommodated with retirements and resignations, evidence indicates that the process of job destruction and creation is lumpy and difficult to accommodate in these ways. Moreover, workers who are not registered with social security are also those more likely to transit from employment to unemployment. Labor reallocation can therefore have large welfare costs on workers. Income loss associated with unemployment is relatively low in the region, especially as the duration of unemployment tends to be relatively short. However, such brief duration is likely to be due to the limited income-support mechanisms available in the region. Workers may therefore be forced to accept any jobs in order to have some income. Hence, the long-term losses of displacement could be quite high, particularly for workers who are forced to accept worse jobs.

Impairment of Employment and Productivity Performance by Job Protection

In a context of large inequalities, employment instability, and poor labor conditions that characterize most countries in the region, governments have used hiring and firing regulations to protect workers against the risk of unemployment by making dismissal more difficult or by mandating a high financial compensation in case of dismissal.[13]

Although there is an intense debate in the literature on the effects of stringent employment protection legislation on the level and quality of employment, recent work suggests that the specific features of employment protection legislation in many countries of the region contribute to explain their weak job performance.[14] This empirical work suggests that aggregate employment, value added, and firm entry are reduced in countries with very stringent hiring and firing regulations. This effect is estimated to be larger when the comparative advantage of countries in the volatile industries is higher. Moreover, this recent work suggests that stringent regulations more severely affect medium and large firms.

Studies also find that high administrative firing costs may be more detrimental for economic activity than is high mandatory severance pay. This finding implies that to some extent the combination of policies often found in the region (such as few administrative restrictions and high firing costs) is potentially less problematic than the one found in other developing countries (for example, India, where mandatory severance payments are low, but administrative costs of dismissal are extremely high). Indeed, except in Peru—and unlike in many countries—the region's administrative dismissal procedures[15] are among the least rigid in the world, whereas firing costs,[16] at an average of 60 weeks of wages, are among the highest.

Overall, protecting jobs rather than workers can have important adverse effects on productivity growth. By impairing the efficiency of job reallocation, job protection has an adverse effect on the level of productivity across time, industries, and countries (Bartelsman, Scarpetta, and Haltiwanger 2004; Foster, Haltiwanger, and Krizan 2002). In addition, because employment protection legislation raises the cost of workforce reorganizations, it reduces firms' capacity to exploit technological opportunities, given the greater potential for adopting technologies available in international markets.

Job protection also affects the structure of employment. Job security regulations tend to reduce the share of workers in wage employment and increase self-employment; they also tend to promote job stability for prime-age males, while reducing job opportunities and lengthening unemployment spells for youths, women lacking work experience, and those with low skills (for industrial countries, see Addison and Teixeira 2003; for Chile, see Montenegro and Pagés 2004).

In addition to its economic costs, protecting workers against unemployment risk through severance payments provides inadequate coverage against this risk. First, severance payments are generally linked to tenure and thus provide low benefits to workers with short employment spells. Second, severance payments tend to be poorly enforced even among formal sector workers: only a fraction of workers are de facto covered by them—often the more educated ones, a factor that also makes severance payments regressive.[17]

In sum, shifting from employment protection as the main mechanism to protect workers against unemployment risk toward other mechanisms that target workers themselves and not their job has the potential to reduce the overall risks associated with labor mobility, to increase fairness in the labor market, and ultimately to promote an efficient allocation of labor toward more productive uses and productivity growth.

Improvement of Income Protection Mechanisms

Improving income-support schemes in Latin America and the Caribbean requires progress toward two interrelated objectives:

- Reinforcing insurance mechanisms that help workers cope with the income losses of unemployment
- Extending coverage to include workers who are now employed in the informal sectors and who generally cope with risks after they have occurred, often resorting to unproductive strategies that perpetuate poverty.

Attaining these goals requires making resources available to workers during unemployment spells.

To tackle the shortcomings of severance payments, governments in a number of countries have introduced prefunding in the form of regular contributions toward individual unemployment savings accounts (IUSAs).[18] IUSAs have a number of advantages over severance payments, but it is well known that individual savings are not an efficient way to insure against unemployment risk, because they do not allow pooling risk across a large number of individuals (Blanchard 2004; Ferrer and Riddell 2005). In addition, because the length of contributions is related to job tenure, IUSAs do not adequately protect workers with short tenures or long unemployment spells. Finally, like severance payment mechanisms, IUSAs cover only registered workers.

Public provision of unemployment insurance (UI) can correct for the strong information asymmetries and the moral hazard and adverse selection problems that prevent the development of private UI schemes. It also enhances the ability to pool resources across large groups. However, the implementation of UI is not an easy task because the unemployment status is difficult to observe, particularly for informal sector workers, and because income protection is likely to reduce the intensity of job search unless sufficient resources are available to allow close monitoring of beneficiaries. Hence, implementing UI requires efficient monitoring and strong administrative capacity. In fact, only eight countries in the region have UI schemes—Argentina, Barbados, Brazil, Chile, Colombia,

Ecuador, Uruguay, and the República Bolivariana de Venezuela—and in these countries coverage tends to be low and beneficiaries are disproportionately from the richer segment of the population. Moreover, current UI systems lack the strict eligibility requirements—as well as the capacity to enforce them—that ensure that beneficiaries have the means and incentives to go back to gainful employment.

Two countries, Chile and Ecuador, combine UI with IUSAs. These systems are interesting because UI can take over in the case of workers who face repeated unemployment spells and, having run down their IUSA funds, are left without income support.

UI programs do not cover informal workers, many of whom are from the poorer population groups. Thus, in periods of crisis, governments in the region have often resorted to workfare programs to reduce the costs of unemployment for the poor. These often harried responses have led to poorly designed and implemented programs (Márquez 2000). Although workfare programs are a way to provide income support to the poorer workers, extending social protection to all workers requires understanding each country's circumstances and the structure of informal employment. Because of the nature of informal employment, the relevant systems of protection have to be noncontributory (that is, funded with general revenues). However, if they are based on separate mechanisms that are not well integrated with the mechanisms for formal workers, noncontributory schemes for informal sector workers mixed with contributory schemes for formal sector workers may increase informality because formal workers may want to switch to informal jobs so that they do not have to make contributions (Levy 2008).

As the history of developed countries shows, at this stage of development most countries of the region can afford some level of social protection. Moreover, income support can compensate workers for necessary reforms to make labor and other regulations less constraining for firms.

Rethinking Social Security

Policies to improve the quality of jobs represent a main component of a comprehensive strategy to ensure that the labor market produces equitable and efficient outcomes. Governments may intervene in different ways but each of the instruments needs careful evaluation. For example, although advances in mandatory benefits tend to be viewed as advances in workers' welfare, it is also the case that excessive and burdensome regulations lead to poor job creation, particularly in higher-paying firms (see chapter 5). For this reason, governments need to walk the fine line between legislating better work conditions and assessing whether such conditions are appropriate given the level of development and labor productivity of a country. Care is particularly important when enforcement capabilities are weak and inappropriate regulations lead firms or workers to opt out of such higher standards and work under informal and often substandard conditions.

Social security programs are a good example of a social policy instrument that needs careful evaluation. They are aimed at improving the lot of workers, but their costs and uneven enforcement create important distortions in the labor market. Social security affiliation rates are very low and in most cases declining in the countries of the region. They are also unevenly distributed, with very low rates of affiliation among unskilled and young workers. This pattern seems to be driven by a combination of two main factors (Auerbach, Genoni, and Pagés 2005):

1. A low valuation for the benefits (health insurance and particularly old-age pensions), which leads to a low willingness to contribute and, other things equal, to a preference for jobs with low enforcement
2. The presence of some rationing, which is driven by the presence of firms that are not registered and that would face costs beyond actual contributions if they were to enroll workers in social security and therefore emerge from their unofficial status.

Low valuation, in turn, may be associated with insufficient anticipation of the consequences of being underinsured (particularly in regards to old-age pensions), of tapping into alternative means of informal insurance (assistance from relatives), or of relying on the state as the ultimate purveyor of assistance.

Low willingness to pay for social security contributions implies that workers and employers will perceive nonwage costs as a tax whose incidence depends on the relative elasticity of labor demand and supply. However, to the extent that jobs in formal and informal firms are similar and workers can switch to informal jobs, the incidence of the tax will fall mostly on formal firms, with important consequences for formal employment creation. The limited existing evidence lends credit to this hypothesis: Heckman and Pagés (2004) estimate that an important part of the cost of social security falls on employers.

Although financing social security out of labor income is likely to generate important distortions in the labor market and to imply low coverage, countries can consider various options to improve their systems.[19] Tax rebates for low-wage workers could provide an important stimulus for registered employment, particularly in countries where minimum wages are binding. (This approach is used in some European countries, including France.) The shortfall in revenues could be financed by slightly higher value added taxes. But beyond tinkering with the contribution rate, governments can use other reforms to improve coverage and reduce labor market distortions. Unbundling contributions for different types of benefits could be an option, for example, that would provide the basic benefits that are most valued by the less affluent workers and would allow for higher contributions (and possibly higher benefits) for higher-income workers. Better still, countries could consider the feasibility of financing social security benefits (or some subcomponents of it) through general revenues. Delinking social security provision from the labor market would eliminate the disincentives for creating and accepting informal sector jobs.

Addressing the Needs of Vulnerable Workers by Increasing the Effectiveness of Active Labor Market Policies

Active labor market programs (ALMPs) can usefully supplement income-support schemes, and provide specific help to the most vulnerable workers. Even if they tend to have limited effects on aggregate job creation, active labor market policies, when well designed, properly targeted, and run efficiently, can improve the functioning of the labor market in a cost-effective way. They facilitate workers' job searches and employers' recruitment (job intermediation); they enhance workers' skills and their employability (training); and, in some specific cases, they contribute to job creation through job subsidies and direct job creation.

Job intermediation is currently largely underdeveloped in the region (see Mazza 2003; for Brazil, see Ramos 2002). However, the limited available evidence suggests that it can be efficient in improving the quality of the jobs that are found by job seekers (see Flores Lima 2006; Ramos 2002). Moreover, advances in information technology mean that basic services can be established relatively cheaply. It has therefore been argued that the countries of the region should investigate the potential of such opportunities and design quality services that will attract both employers and job seekers.

Training and retraining for the unemployed aim to provide job seekers with marketable skills that potentially increase their employability and earning capacity. Evidence on the effects of training in developing countries is patchy, but the results suggest positive effects both on the probability of employment and on the quality of job accessed (Rosas Shady and Ibarrarán 2008). The results also suggest that the effects may be larger for some groups, such as women. Two elements appear crucial in ensuring the success of training. First, the quality of training is important in explaining subsequent labor market outcomes. The few evaluations that take this dimension into consideration show that it makes a big difference in the outcomes of participants (see, for example, Chong and Galdo 2006 for Peru). Second, evidence suggests that involving employers (as occurred in Colombia) or private providers in the training is beneficial to trainees. In particular, demand-driven approaches are found to be more efficient.

Since the 1990s, emphasis on promoting job creation in the private sector has increased, but workfare and public works programs still play an important role in the overall expenditure on active labor market policies in the region. The available evidence indicates that even when public works programs successfully target the poor, they do not improve subsequent earnings or employment probabilities (see Betcherman, Olivas, and Dar 2004; for Argentina, see Jalan and Ravallion 2003). As such, these programs are best considered income-support tools rather than skill-transfer programs and can be useful devices to *temporarily* transfer resources to workers or households in need when other mechanisms of targeting are not available. Improving the training content of tasks and linking them to job intermediation services may improve their effect on earnings and postprogram employment outcomes. To ensure that transfers are self-targeted, programs must enforce work requirements. In addition, payments need to be below market to preserve workers' incentives to leave the program for better jobs.

Wage and employment subsidy programs aim to cover the initial cost of training new workers, so that by the time the subsidy ends, their productivity is high enough for the employer to have a strong incentive to keep them. The available evaluations, which have mostly been carried out in developed countries, show that, in practice, subsidies lead to substantial employment creation but at the expense of large deadweight losses and substitution effects (Marx 2005). Few countries of the region have used such subsidies, and apart from the Proempleo program in Argentina, they have been small and their coverage has been low. The evaluation of the Proempleo program shows some positive short-term employment effects but no positive effects on future earnings. Moreover, because of the costs and administrative procedures involved for firms, take-up was quite low (Galasso, Ravallion, and Salvia 2004).

There may be a case for employing wage subsidies to remedy the disemployment effects created by high social security taxes or binding minimum wages when reforms addressing these obstacles are not viable. Combining subsidies with other active labor market policies, such as training or job searches, may improve future earnings outcomes.

Microenterprise development, which combines financial assistance with technical services such as training, counseling, and assistance in business plan development, can successfully increase the productivity of beneficiaries and, by extension, improve the viability of microenterprises. This type of intervention is particularly important in the region given that microenterprises employ a large proportion of the labor force, mostly in the informal sector (Orlando and Pollack 2000), and, as previously shown, face specific difficulties surviving and expanding in many countries of the region. These programs, however, need to be better evaluated.

The evaluations that have been carried out, both in developed countries and in the region, are encouraging. They suggest that microenterprises that have benefited from these programs have better chances of survival (see Betcherman, Olivas, and Dar 2004 for developed countries; Ramos 2002 for Brazil; Samaniego 2002 for Mexico; Tan and López-Acevedo 2005 for Mexico). However, an important weakness of most of these evaluations is that they do not provide information on the net effect of these programs (see Betcherman, Olivas, and Dar 2004 for developed countries; Ramos 2002 for Brazil; Samaniego 2002 for Mexico) or they poorly choose the control group (see Tan and López-Acevedo 2005 for Mexico). An exception is a Chilean pilot study, which finds that the probability of bankruptcy is lower and the probability of expansion is higher among microenterprises that benefited from the program than among firms in a control group (Bravo, Contreras, and Crespi 2000).

Overall, microenterprises seem far from having reached their potential in the region, and there is scope for developing such interventions (Auer, Efendioglu, and Leschke 2005). Providing integrated services to would-be entrepreneurs or existing firms tends to lead to better outcomes.

Improving the Administrative and Enforcement Capacity of Labor Authorities

The effect of labor regulations and policies on employment and productivity depends significantly on the capacity of countries of the region to enforce the law. Whether the objectives that rules and regulations are meant to achieve ultimately prevail depends on the way they are implemented on the ground.

Evidence indicates that the administrative capacity is relatively low in the region and tends to affect employers negatively. Analysis based on the World Bank's Enterprise Surveys suggests that employers in the region do not trust their governments' efficiency or regulatory quality. They also report being adversely affected by weak rule of law. Given limited resources, involving the private sector and using technological advances can make program administration more efficient. Countries of the region can improve the quality and delivery of social services at relatively low costs by applying technological advances, such as magnetic or electronic cards, mobile computing, automated teller machines, or solar technology. Unions can also facilitate and monitor the implementation of labor regulations.

As previously stated, enforcement is patchy and uneven across firms. This situation may create strong incentives for remaining small and invisible. However, evidence also shows that improving labor regulations is necessary to avoid the strong negative employment effects of better enforcement. Thus, though increased enforcement could help some small and medium firms to gain market share from informal ones, higher enforcement is also likely to magnify the strong adverse effects of regulations on formal employment that have been found in the literature.

Countries need to develop reforms within the framework of a social dialogue that brings in all the interested stakeholders and is responsive to the needs of the economy. A lack of productive cooperation may lead to additional costs for employers if disputes occur more often and unions use regulations as a confrontation tool instead of as a means to protect workers from unfair treatment. Having a fruitful social dialogue remains a challenge in many countries, developed and developing alike, and especially in Latin America and the Caribbean, where labor relations have overall been confrontational and marred by lack of trust (IDB 2003). However, examples of successful dialogue between government officials, employers, and workers' representatives exist in the region (for example, in Barbados and Panama, as described in Fashoyin 2004).

The judiciary system has often been called on to fill the gap in enforcement. Yet the implementation of labor law in courts is likely to affect its economic results. The empirical and theoretical evidence currently available on this topic is limited and based on court case studies. These studies identify several types of issues that can arise when the judiciary is involved in labor relations, all of which affect its eventual effect on labor market outcomes. Judges may make idiosyncratic decisions that have wider impacts; judges may not be independent or accountable; finally, excessive judicialization of labor relations may lead to increases in case loads and eventually to delays. The evidence for several countries of the region shows that conciliation is generally cheaper and less time consuming. Nevertheless, there is often a lack of emphasis on conciliation.

The effect of labor courts may differ across types of firms. Evidence indicates that large firms are more likely to see laid-off workers contest the firing through a tribunal, and once started, court procedures last longer for large firms than for other firms.

In sum, to improve on the current, mostly disappointing labor market outcomes of the region requires, among other steps, improving the efficiency and quality of labor market regulations and institutions. What are the steps to be taken?

Before a process of reform of the labor market in a given country, it would be useful to take stock of the strengths and limitation of the country's current income protection systems, as well as the effectiveness of active labor policies. This effort implies assessing the nature and magnitude of uninsured unemployment risk, as well as redundancies and overlaps in social protection schemes.

The next step is to devise ways to move from job protection to income protection. In countries with restrictive administrative procedures for dismissal (for example, Ecuador, Panama, and Peru), a reform should consider streamlining administrative procedures for dismissal. In countries where more than one program covers registered workers (for example, Brazil, where registered workers are covered by mandatory severance pay, UI savings accounts, and UI), reforms should envision consolidation into fewer but perhaps more efficient and better designed systems.

Finally, only after designing effective and quality programs and improving government efficiency in delivering services, governments should turn to improving the enforcement of regulations and policies.

Summary and Directions for Further Analysis

This book provides a comprehensive review of labor market developments in Latin America and the Caribbean over the past 15 years and sheds light on factors that are behind the generally poor creation of productive jobs in the region. The book reviews economic and labor market developments up to 2004 or 2005. Since then, a number of countries in the region have experienced strong economic growth, with some improvements in the labor market, not only in terms of a reduction in unemployment, but also in terms of the creation of more productive jobs. These developments are good news and underline that strong and sustainable growth is a necessary—albeit not sufficient—condition for better outcomes in the labor market. But the structural issues identified in the book are all pertinent today. Sustaining the process of economic growth and better sharing it across the different groups in the labor market require tacking these structural issues, many of which have a clear policy lever.

It is difficult to draw general policy conclusions for the region as a whole, given the significant heterogeneity in the performance of the individual countries and in their respective policy and institutional settings. But a common theme that emerges in the book is that poor job creation is largely the result of the difficulties private firms have in operating in a market in which they face stronger competition from abroad but also a bumpy and uncertain domestic regulatory and institutional environment that tends to discourage risk taking. This theme suggests that promoting the creation of more and better jobs requires a comprehensive strategy that goes well beyond the labor market. It requires a level playing field in which all private economic agents have their chance. Many of the barriers to job creation identified in this book have to do with macroeconomic instability, opacity of regulations, corruption, and lack of access to finance. However, a lot can and should be done in the labor market to contribute to an environment that is more conducive to the creation of more and better jobs. Stringent regulations that are not enforced—or cannot be enforced—do not help even formal sector employment, whereas the lack of social protection instruments does not help workers cope with labor mobility or seek more productive, but perhaps more challenging, jobs. Labor reforms are often difficult to pass, especially when labor market conditions are tough.

A stronger and less confrontational role of the social partners in the design and implementation of reforms would be an asset.

The book provides a comprehensive review of labor demand conditions in the region and highlights a number of policy challenges. But further analysis is warranted in each country and from a cross-country perspective. For example, the book focuses largely on the formal sector, and while a recent World Bank publication (Perry and others 2007) provides a comprehensive review of the informal economy in the countries of the region, much remains to be done to assess the interactions between firms and workers in the formal and informal sectors. In any event, it is clear that informality will remain an issue for many years to come, even if economic growth is maintained. So the key challenge is how labor market policy can reach out to the many people who are currently unprotected without necessarily raising the incentives for employers and workers not to declare their labor contract. More should also be learned about the political economy of labor market reforms in the region. After major efforts in opening up to international trade and reforming the financial and product markets, reforms of the labor market seem the natural follow up. Yet it is proving overwhelmingly difficult to reform the labor market in most countries of the region, despite its widely recognized incongruence with the requirements of dynamic market economies. Although there is growing interest in the so-called flexicurity approach of the labor market—with relatively lax job protection and effective income support to workers affected by labor mobility—as promoted in a number of industrial countries, it remains to be seen how the main principles of flexicurity can be translated in the labor market context of the region, which has shown limited administrative capacity to handle benefits, activate unemployed job seekers, or facilitate matches between demand and supply. These questions are just some of those examined in this book that deserve further in-depth analytical work.

Notes

1. Obtaining comparable statistics on GDP and productivity growth at the aggregate and especially at the sectoral level is very difficult for most countries of the region. This problem is largely attributable to the presence in all countries of a sizable informal sector and to the different capacity of statistical instruments to capture its different features. See annex 3.A in chapter 3.

2. Some countries experienced growth rates in labor supply of about 4 percent a year (about 20 to 25 people for each 1,000 population). Most countries experienced growth rates between 2 and 3 percent. Such high growth was fueled by high growth of the working-age population and, in most cases, by positive and substantial increases in labor force participation.

3. The increase in informality that has been observed in the region in recent years is feared to have slowed down growth and social development and to have threatened the integrity of society. This book mainly covers the formal sector,

providing pointers to the links and interactions between the formal and informal economies as needed. Perry and others (2007) provide an extensive study of the root causes and reasons for the growth of informality in Latin America and its implications.

4. The Heckscher-Ohlin and the Stolper-Samuelson theorems of international trade predict that trade openness increases the price of the factor that is more abundant in a country. Under the hypothesis that Latin America has abundant unskilled labor, these theorems would predict that trade openness leads to an increase in the price of unskilled labor and a decline in the returns to education.

5. Attanasio, Goldberg, and Pavcnik (2004) noted this trend for Colombia.

6. Averages were computed for the 12 largest countries in Latin America plus the Dominican Republic.

7. The industries of raw material processing and foodstuffs typically use automatic plants, which are intensive in capital and natural resources but require few high-skill workers (Katz and Stumpo 2001).

8. This measure of job turnover may also underestimate overall worker mobility, because it considers only job creation and destruction across firms and not labor movements within firms and because it does not include movement in and out of unemployment or in and out of the labor force.

9. These differences are statistically significant at the 1 percent level.

10. Latin American countries seem to differ from other developing countries in this respect. La Porta and Schleifer (2008), using the same data but for a sample of low-income countries mostly in Africa and Asia, find no evidence that anticompetitive practices from informal firms are an issue in their sample. Instead, La Porta and Schleifer (2008: 34) conclude that "formal firms appear to be very different animals than informal firms" and that there is no evidence that informal firms predate on formal ones.

11. Aghion, Fally, and Scarpetta (2007), using firm-level data for a sample of industrial Latin American and transition economies of Eastern Europe, find evidence that lack of financial development has a particularly negative effect on the entry of small firms and on postentry growth of successful new businesses.

12. These policies are defined as those that directly intervene in the labor market, as opposed to the ones previously mentioned that require interventions in other areas.

13. Botero and others (2004) find that countries with a longer history of leftist governments have more extensive regulation of labor.

14. A large body of literature assessing the effect of such legislation on labor market variables, mostly on the basis of analysis of data for industrial countries, has had ambiguous results. The lack of conclusive results arises in part because regulations change very infrequently and tend to be applied at the national level for all workers. Two new empirical studies (Haltiwanger, Scarpetta, and Schweiger 2006; Micco and Pagés 2006) use a new methodology that potentially overcomes these problems. Micco and Pagés (2006) estimate a difference-in-difference model to explore the effects of labor regulations across different industries with different intrinsic volatility. The hypothesis is that industries that are intrinsically more volatile will be more affected by hiring and firing regulations. Haltiwanger, Scarpetta, and Schweiger (2006) extend the methodology used by Micco and Pagés (2006) to explore the effects of labor regulations across industry and firm-size cells. Their assumption is that hiring and firing regulations are likely to be more binding on the industry and firm-size cells that have the greatest propensity for reallocation.

15. These procedures include requesting the permission of officials, consulting with unions, or finding alternative placements for workers.

16. These costs include severance pay obligations, advance notice requirements, and associated penalties (see World Bank 2006).

17. For more on this topic, see Blanchard (2004), IDB (2003), Jaramillo and Saavedra (2005), and Mondino and Montoya (2004). De Ferranti and others (2000) argue that when Latin American countries had little exposure to foreign competition, the effective pooling of unemployment risk offered by severance pays was spread over a greater population, because consumers often subsidized potentially bankrupt firms by paying higher prices. However, this possibility has declined rapidly as countries have embarked on trade liberalization and reforms aimed at fostering domestic competition.

18. Such countries include Chile, Colombia, Ecuador, Panama, Peru, and the República Bolivariana de Venezuela.

19. See Perry and others (2007) on informality for a more elaborated discussion on social security reforms.

References

Addison, J., and P. Teixeira. 2003. "What Have We Learned about the Employment Effects of Severance Pay? Further Iterations of Lazear et al." IZA Discussion Paper 943, Institute for the Study of Labor, Bonn, Germany.

Aghion, P., T. Fally, and S. Scarpetta. 2007. "Credit Constraints as a Barrier to the Entry and Post-entry Growth of Firms." *Economic Policy* 22 (52): 731–79.

Attanasio, O., P. Goldberg, and N. Pavcnik. 2004. "Trade Reforms and Wage Inequality in Colombia." NBER Working Paper 9830, National Bureau of Economic Research, Cambridge, MA.

Auer, P., U. Efendioglu, and J. Leschke. 2005. *Active Labour Market Policies around the World: Coping with the Consequences of Globalization.* Geneva: International Labour Office.

Auerbach, P., M.-E. Genoni, and C. Pagés. 2005. "Social Security Coverage and the Labor Market in Developing Countries." Research Department Working Paper 537, Inter-American Development Bank, Washington, DC.

Bartelsman, E. J., J. Haltiwanger, and S. Scarpetta. 2004. "Microeconomic Evidence of Creative Destruction in Industrial and Developing Countries." IZA Discussion Paper 1374, Institute for the Study of Labor, Bonn, Germany.

Bartelsman, E. J., S. Scarpetta, and J. Haltiwanger. 2004. "Distributed Analysis of Firm-Level Data from Industrial and Developing Countries." Institute for the Study of Labor, Bonn, Germany.

Berstein, S., G. Larrain, and F. Pino. 2006. "Chilean Pension Reform: Coverage Facts and Policy Alternatives." *Economia* 6 (2): 227–79.

Betcherman, G., K. Olivas, and A. Dar. 2004. "Impacts of Active Labor Market Programs: New Evidence from Evaluations with Particular Attention to Developing and Transition Countries." Social Protection Discussion Paper 0402, World Bank, Washington, DC.

Blanchard, O. 2004. "Designing Labor Market Institutions." Lecture presented at the Seventh Annual Conference of the Central Bank of Chile on Labor Markets and Institutions, Santiago, March 28. http://econ-www.mit.edu/files/687.

Botero, J., S. Djankov, R. La Porta, F. López-de-Silanes, and A. Shleifer. 2004. "The Regulation of Labor." *Quarterly Journal of Economics* 199 (4): 1339–82.

Bravo, D., D. Contreras, and G. Crespi. 2000. "Evaluating Training Programs for Small-Scale Entrepreneurs: A Pilot Study." Universidad de Chile, Santiago.

Chong, A., and J. Galdo. 2006. "Training Quality and Earnings: The Effects of Competition on the Provision of Public-Sponsored Training Programs." Research Department Working Paper 555, Inter-American Development Bank, Washington, DC.

De Ferranti, D., G. E. Perry, I. S. Gill, J. L. Guasch, W. Maloney, C. Sánchez-Páramo, and N. Schady. 2003. *Closing the Gap in Education and Technology*. Washington, DC: World Bank.

De Ferranti, D., G. E. Perry, I. S. Gill, and L. Servén. 2000. *Securing Our Future in a Global Economy*. Washington, DC: World Bank.

Fashoyin, T. 2004. "Tripartite Cooperation, Social Dialogue, and National Development." *International Labour Review* 143 (4): 342–71.

Ferrer, A., and W. Riddell. 2005. "Unemployment Insurance Savings Accounts in Latin America: Overview and Assessment." In *Improving Severance Pay: An International Perspective*, ed. R. Holzmann and M. Vodopivec. Washington, DC: World Bank.

Flores Lima, R. 2006. "El Servicio de Intermediación Laboral como instrumento para promover la inclusión social y de género en el mercado laboral en México." Centro de Investigaciones sobre Economía Laboral y Gestión del Conocimiento, Mexico City.

Foster, L., J. Haltiwanger, and C. J. Krizan. 2002. "The Link between Aggregate and Micro Productivity Growth: Evidence from Retail Trade." NBER Working Paper 9120, National Bureau of Economic Research, Cambridge, MA.

Galasso, E., M. Ravallion, and A. Salvia. 2004. "Assisting the Transition from Workfare to Work: A Randomized Experiment." *Industrial and Labor Relations Review* 58 (1): 128–42.

Haltiwanger, J., S. Scarpetta, and H. Schweiger. 2006. "Assessing the Job Flows across Countries: The Role of Industry, Firm Size and Regulations." IZA Discussion Paper 2450, Institute for the Study of Labor, Bonn, Germany.

Heckman, J., and C. Pagés. 2004. "Introduction." In *Law and Employment: Lessons from Latin America and the Caribbean*, ed. J. Heckman and C. Pagés, 1–108. Chicago: University of Chicago Press.

Hsieh, C.-T., and P. Klenow. 2007. "Misallocation and Manufacturing TFP in China and India." NBER Working Paper 13290, National Bureau of Economic Research, Cambridge, MA.

IDB (Inter-American Development Bank). 2003. *Good Jobs Wanted: Labor Markets in Latin America—2004 Report on Economic and Social Progress in Latin America*. Washington, DC: IDB.

———. 2004. *Unlocking Credit: The Quest for Deep and Stable Bank Lending—2005 Report on Economic and Social Progress in Latin America*. Washington, DC: IDB.

Jalan, J., and M. Ravallion. 2003. "Estimating the Benefit Incidence of an Antipoverty Program by Propensity-Score Matching." *Journal of Business and Economic Statistics* 21 (1): 19–30.

Jaramillo, M., and J. Saavedra. 2005. "Severance Payment Programs in Latin America." *Empirica* 32 (3–4): 275–307.

Katz, J., and G. Stumpo. 2001. "Regímenes sectoriales, productividad y competitividad internacional." *Revista de la CEPAL* 75 (December): 137–59.

La Porta, R., and A. Schleifer. 2008. "The Unofficial Economy and Economic Development." NBER Working Paper 14520, National Bureau of Economic Research, Cambridge, MA.

Levy, S. 2008. *Good Intentions, Bad Outcomes: Social Policy, Informality, and Economic Growth in Mexico*. Washington, DC: Brookings Institution Press.

Márquez, G. 2000. "Labor Markets and Income Support: What Did We Learn from the Crises?" Research Department Working Paper 425, Inter-American Development Bank, Washington, DC.

Marx, I. 2005. "Job Subsidies and Cuts in Employers' Social Security Contributions: The Verdict of Empirical Evaluation Studies." Paper presented at the conference on Changing Social Policies for Low-Income Families and Less-Skilled Workers in the E.U. and the U.S., University of Michigan, Ann Arbor, April 7–8.

Mazza, J. 2003. "Labour Intermediation Services: Lessons from Latin America and the Caribbean." *CEPAL Review* 80 (August): 159–75.

Micco, A., and C. Pagés. 2006. "The Economic Effects of Employment Protection Laws." IZA Discussion Paper 2433, Institute for the Study of Labor, Bonn, Germany.

Mondino, G., and S. Montoya. 2004. "The Effects of Labor Market Regulations on Employment Decisions by Firms: Empirical Evidence from Argentina." In *Law and Employment: Lessons from Latin America and the Caribbean*, ed. J. Heckman and C. Pagés, 351–400. Chicago: University of Chicago Press.

Montenegro, C., and C. Pagés. 2004. "Who Benefits from Labor Market Regulations? Chile, 1960–1998." In *Law and Employment: Lessons from Latin America and the Caribbean*, ed. J. Heckman and C. Pagés, 401–34. Chicago: University of Chicago Press.

Orlando, M. B., and M. Pollack. 2000. *Microenterprises and Poverty: Evidence from Latin America*. Washington, DC: Inter-American Development Bank.

Panniza, U., and M. Yañez. 2006. "Why Are Latin Americans So Unhappy about Reforms?" Research Department Working Paper 567, Inter-American Development Bank, Washington, DC.

Perry, G., W. Maloney, O. Arias, P. Fajnzylber, A. Mason, and J. Saavedra-Chanduvi, eds. 2007. *Informality: Exit and Exclusion*. Washington, DC: World Bank.

Ramos, C. 2002. "Las políticas del mercado de trabajo y su evaluación en Brasil." Macroeconomía del desarrollo 16, Economic Commission for Latin America and the Caribbean, United Nations, Santiago.

Restuccia, D., and R. Rogerson. 2008. "Policy Distortions and Aggregate Productivity with Heterogeneous Plants." *Review of Economic Dynamics* 11 (4): 707–20.

Rosas Shady, D., and P. Ibarrarán. 2008. "Evaluating the Impact of Job Training Programs in Latin America: Evidence from IDB Funded Operations." Working Paper, Office of Evaluation and Oversight, Inter-American Development Bank, Washington, DC.

Samaniego, N. 2002. "Las políticas de mercado de trabajo en México y su evaluación." Macroeconomía del Desarrollo 18, Economic Commission for Latin America and the Caribbean, United Nations, Santiago.

Tan, H., and G. López-Acevedo. 2005. "Evaluating Training Programs for Small and Medium Enterprises: Lessons from Mexico." Policy Research Working Paper 3760, World Bank, Washington, DC.

World Bank. 2006. *Doing Business 2007: How to Reform*. Washington, DC: World Bank.

Part I

Employment Dynamics in Latin America and the Caribbean

Throughout Latin America and the Caribbean, unemployment and job creation have become two central issues in public debates and in the political agenda of governments. The first part of this book examines labor market dynamics in the region, both at the aggregate level (chapter 2) and for particular sociodemographic groups (chapter 3). The evidence presented suggests that labor market developments have been shaped by at least three interrelated factors: (a) low growth of labor productivity, (b) fast growth of labor supply, and (c) slow improvements in human capital coupled with growing demand for skilled labor. In many countries, supply pressures—led by demographics and a rapid increase in female participation—were met by strong job creation, particularly when the modest pace of growth in the gross domestic product is taken into account. The combination of low income growth and relatively strong job creation is mirrored in very low productivity growth and often a declining quality of jobs in many countries in the region. By most measures, the share of labor in informal jobs increased, while a higher share of workers found themselves in jobs that did not pay enough to lift them and their families out of poverty. In some countries, job creation was not able to accommodate the strong increase in labor supply, leading to significant increases in open unemployment. All in all, in many countries of the region, the experience was not of "jobless growth," but rather of "growthless jobs"; therefore, increasing the quality of jobs constitutes one of the most important policy challenges of the region.

1

Jobless Growth or Growthless Jobs?

Job Creation Challenges from a Macroperspective

More than a decade since the introduction of comprehensive macroeconomic stabilization packages and trade, fiscal, and financial market reforms, growth prospects remain disappointing from an international perspective, and labor markets show lackluster performance. This chapter thoroughly examines labor market trends in the Latin America and the Caribbean since past decades and assesses the role that labor demand and labor supply factors have played in shaping these outcomes. It also places this performance in the wider context of the world experience. The performance of particular sociodemographic groups is examined in the next chapter.

The data used in this and the next chapter were obtained from a number of different sources: time-series data on employment were obtained from national statistics sources, the International Labour Office (ILO), and the Groningen Growth and Development Centre and the Conference Board's Total Economy Database (GGDC TED). For industrial countries, data from the Organisation for Economic Co-operation and Development (OECD) were also used. Working-age population (WAP) data were obtained from national statistics offices and the United Nations Population Division (UNPD). Gross domestic product (GDP) data were obtained from the United Nations Statistics Division (UNSD). A major effort was made to ensure the consistency of the different sources of data in terms of geographical and age range coverage and across countries. A large number of indicators, particularly those disaggregated by gender, education, and age, were obtained from the Socio-Economic Database for Latin America and the

Caribbean (SEDLAC), produced by the Center for the Study of Distribution, Labor, and Social Affairs (Centro de Estudios Distributivos, Laborales y Sociales, or CEDLAS) of the National University of La Plata (Universidad Nacional de La Plata) in Argentina, in partnership with the World Bank, as well as from Sociómetro, a data set of indicators of socioeconomic conditions in Latin America produced by the Research Department of the Inter-American Development Bank (IDB).[1] Both data sets are processed from the household surveys data bank of the Program for the Improvement of Surveys and the Measurement of Living Conditions in Latin America and the Caribbean, a joint initiative of the World Bank, the IDB, and the United Nations Economic Commission for Latin America and the Caribbean.

Growth Performance in Latin America and the Caribbean since the 1970s

It is useful to start this investigation of growth, productivity, and job creation in Latin America and the Caribbean with a long-term perspective. Many of the disappointing patterns of employment discussed in this book are the results of long-standing problems in promoting growth, technological progress, and ultimately the creation of productive jobs.

Sluggish Growth and Lack of Convergence with Developing Countries

Growth in Latin America and the Caribbean since the 1970s has been low compared with that in other regions of the world. The region's average annual growth rate was just above 1 percent, compared with more than 2 percent in OECD countries. Average income growth in East Asia and the Pacific was close to 6 percent a year, well above that of Latin America. Sub-Saharan Africa and the Middle East and North Africa were the only regions to experience lower rates of growth than Latin America (figure 1.1).

In this discussion, the region is divided in two groups to facilitate analyzing growth performance at the country level. Group A comprises countries that had income per capita above or equal to the regional median in 1970, while group B contains countries with income below the region's median. Both groups of countries went through similar experiences over the past 35 years: income per capita growth rates deteriorated from the 1970s to the 1980s, improved in the 1990s, and worsened again during the early 2000s (see table 1.1).[2]

Intraregional Income Inequality

Income inequality across countries within the region has not declined since the 1970s. Poorer countries—group B—experienced some degree

Figure 1.1 Evolution of Income per Capita Growth by Region, 1970–2005

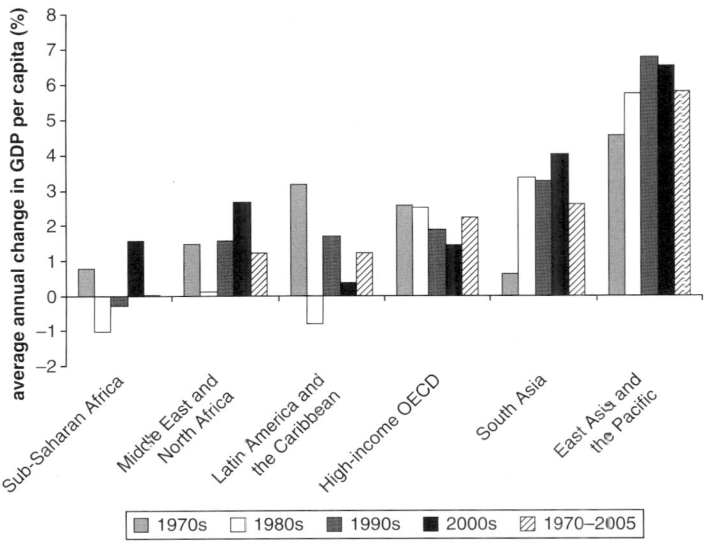

Source: World Bank 2005.

of income convergence toward the richer countries of group A during the 1970s, but the income gap expanded again during the 1980s and 1990s (see table 1.1 and annex 1.A for the individual performance of each country of the region). Not much variation exists in the intraregional income gap in the early years of the 21st century: on average, income per capita grew at a comparable rate in both groups of countries.

Lackluster Growth Performance

Putting the region's performance in perspective with a group of comparator countries is also useful. The selection criteria are countries that had income per capita levels comparable to those of groups A and B in 1970 and are not oil producers or part of the socialist bloc (see annex 1.A for selection criteria). Quite tellingly, all but one of the countries that were chosen with these criteria as comparators for group A performed better than the Latin American and Caribbean countries and are today part of the industrial world (Cyprus, Greece, Malta, Portugal, Singapore, and Spain), while one country (South Africa) had a performance similar to that of group A. No countries in

Table 1.1 Growth Performance in Latin America within Country Groups

	Growth of GDP per capita (%)				*Growth of trended GDP per capita (%)*			
Country	*1970–79*	*1980–89*	*1990–99*	*2000–04*	*1970–79*	*1980–89*	*1990–99*	*2000–04*
Average for group A	1.8	–0.3	2	–0.5	1.3	0.6	1.4	0.5
Average for group B	2.7	–1.1	1.4	0.5	2.2	–0.6	1	0.6

Sources: UNSD; UNPD; United Nations Department of Economic and Social Affairs 2006.

Note: Group A comprises countries that had per capita income above or equal to the regional median in 1970; Group B contains countries with income below the region's median.

GDP per capita is measured in constant 1990 prices in U.S. dollars. Annualized cumulative growth rates are shown. The trended GDP per capita series was smoothed by application of a Hodrick-Prescott filter. The Hodrick-Prescott filter estimates an unobserved trend for time-series variables. It aims at removing low-frequency variation from a time series by representing it as the sum of a smoothly varying trend component and a cyclical component. The trend component is included as the solution to a "penalty function" problem. A parameter λ sets the trade-off between lack of smoothness and data fit. A widely accepted convention is to set this parameter equal to 100 for yearly data. This convention was followed in the study. The Hodrick-Prescott filter was applied to all of the series in an attempt to smooth the effects of the business cycle. The GDP purchasing power parity series from the Groningen Growth and Development Centre and the Conference Board were smoothed starting from the 1960 observation.

the comparator group were outperformed by countries in group A. Similarly, comparator countries for group B include the Republic of Korea, Malaysia, and Mauritius, which have growth rates above or at 4 percent a year, as well as the Arab Republic of Egypt, Ghana, Morocco, Mozambique, Nigeria, Senegal, Thailand, Tunisia, Turkey, Zambia, and Zimbabwe. In both cases, the average performance in the comparator group was significantly better than the performance of the region. The average growth of countries in group A during the period from 1970 to 2004 was 1 percent compared with a growth rate of 3 percent in the comparator sample (table 1.2). Similarly, group B's average growth rate was 0.8 percent a year, against 1.8 percent in the comparator group. Perhaps more important, such gaps are not diminishing: average performance of countries in both groups since 1990 also has been substantially below that of the comparator countries.

Table 1.2 Growth Performance of Comparator Countries

	Growth of trended GDP per capita (%)	
Country	*1970–2004*	*1990–2004*
Average for group A	1.0	1.1
Average for group A comparators	3.0	2.4
Cyprus	3.6	2.9
Greece	1.8	2.1
Malta	5.5	3.2
Portugal	2.6	2.3
Singapore	5.1	3.5
Spain	2.2	2.5
South Africa	0.1	0.5
Average group B	0.8	0.9
Average group B comparators	1.82	1.64
Egypt, Arab Rep. of	2.9	1.9
Fiji	1.6	1.6
Korea, Rep. of	5.9	4.8
Ghana	–0.2	1.9
Malaysia	4.3	3.3
Mauritius	4.2	3.9
Micronesia, Federated States of	1.8	0
Morocco	1.7	1.3
Mozambique	0.9	3.4
Samoa	0.9	1.3
Senegal	0.2	1.2
Solomon Islands	0.4	–1.7
Thailand	4.5	3.2
Tunisia	2.9	3
Turkey	1.9	1.6
Zambia	–2	–1.1
Zimbabwe	–1	–1.8

Sources: UNSD; UNPD; United Nations Department of Economic and Social Affairs 2006.

Note: GDP per capita is measured at constant 1990 prices in U.S. dollars.

Drivers of Growth

A simple way to understand the drivers of aggregate growth is to use a growth accounting decomposition framework in which growth of income per capita is decomposed into the growth of labor productivity, the employment rate, and the share of WAP in total population.[3]

During the period between 1990 and 2004, the region experienced a small increase in income per capita, averaging about 1 percent a year (see figure 1.1). This rise in income was supported by an increase in all three components.

Labor Productivity

As is the case in industrial countries, a strong correlation exists between changes in GDP per capita and labor productivity across Latin America and the Caribbean. This correlation indicates that changes in labor productivity are the main drivers of differences in growth across countries in the region. Yet productivity growth was less than 1 percent a year in all countries but Chile, the Dominican Republic, Trinidad and Tobago, and Uruguay (see figure 1.2, panel b)—well below the rates attained in the fast-growing Asian countries.

Employment Rates and Working-Age Population

A not so common characteristic of countries of the region, at least when compared with industrial countries, is the relatively large contribution of employment rates and the growing share of the WAP to GDP per capita growth. Thus, in all countries but five (Argentina, Colombia, Jamaica, Paraguay, and Uruguay), employment rates increased during the 1990s, in most cases adding between 0.5 and 1.0 percentage points a year in GDP per capita growth (see figure 1.2, panels c and d). As discussed later in this chapter and in chapter 2, much of the growth in employment rates is explained by the fast growth of female participation rates from a relatively low base compared with that in industrial countries. A growing weight of the WAP over the total population also contributed between 0.5 and 1.0 percent in annual GDP per capita growth.

Jobless Growth

The majority of countries in Latin America and the Caribbean experienced a simultaneous increase in labor productivity and the employment rate (figure 1.3), which implies that the region cannot be characterized as one of jobless growth, at least when looking at the overall employment performance. Growth rates in these countries—Brazil, Costa Rica, the

Dominican Republic, El Salvador, Guatemala, Mexico, Panama, Peru, and Trinidad and Tobago—were among the highest in the region (figure 1.2).

Nevertheless, some countries (Argentina, Chile, Colombia, Jamaica, and Uruguay) did suffer what could be labeled as jobless growth because labor productivity increased but the employment rate fell. Among the countries that experienced a trade-off between labor productivity and employment rate growth, those that bolstered productivity fared better in terms of overall income growth. The influence of labor productivity in explaining income growth is supported by the correlation coefficients: the correlation coefficient between income per capita and labor productivity growth is 0.86, whereas the coefficient between income per capita and employment rate growth is 0.27, and the one between income per capita and the ratio of WAP growth is 0.29. Low rates of labor productivity growth, combined with relatively high rates of employment growth, are an indication of the low quality of the jobs created in the region. As discussed later in the chapter, the low quality of the jobs was reflected in an increasing share of workers in low-wage and informal employment in most countries.

Comparing the experience of the years since 1990 to that of the previous decade sheds some light on the nature of growth in the region. During the "lost decade" of the 1980s, income per capita dropped in half the region's countries (Barbados, Brazil, Chile, Ecuador, Jamaica, Mexico, and Panama), while barely growing in the other half (Argentina, El Salvador, Guatemala, Nicaragua, Peru, Trinidad and Tobago, and the República Bolivariana de Venezuela). Consistent with the evidence of the years since 1990, labor productivity outcomes for the most part followed those of GDP per capita during the 1980s. Nonetheless, and quite puzzlingly, the majority of countries experienced growth in employment rates during the 1980s, which, in turn, did not improve in a noticeable way after economic conditions improved in the 1990s (figure 1.4).[4] The simple correlation coefficients estimated for this decade attest to these patterns: the correlation coefficient between income per capita and labor productivity growth is 0.94, whereas the one between income per capita and employment rate growth is merely 0.04.[5] Clearly, the experience of labor markets in Latin America and the Caribbean since the 1980s has not been one of jobless growth but rather one in which employment follows labor supply.

This conclusion is particularly evident when the region's experience is placed in an international context: employment rate growth in Latin America and the Caribbean during the 1990s and early 2000s outperformed that in countries from the comparator sample (see figure 1.5). Employment growth in most countries of the region outpaced not only that of the European Union (EU15)[6] or of the United States, but also that of other developing countries, such as China, Korea, Malaysia, Thailand, or Turkey. At the same time, most of the comparators experienced higher

Figure 1.2 Growth Decomposition for Latin America and the Caribbean, 1990–2004

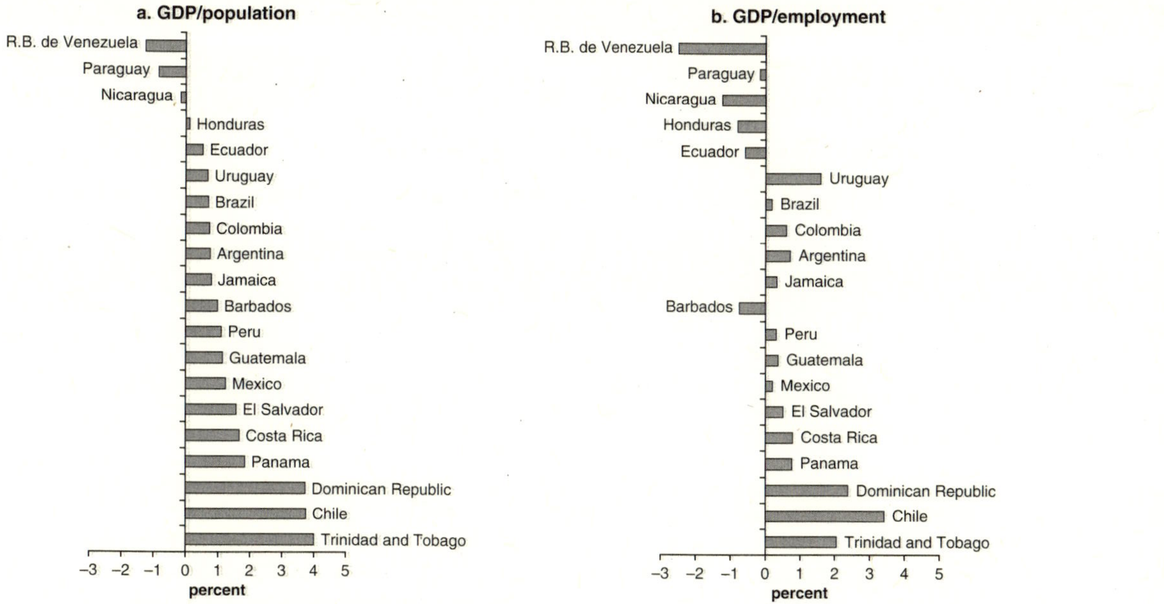

(continued)

Figure 1.2 Growth Decomposition for Latin America and the Caribbean, 1990–2004 *(continued)*

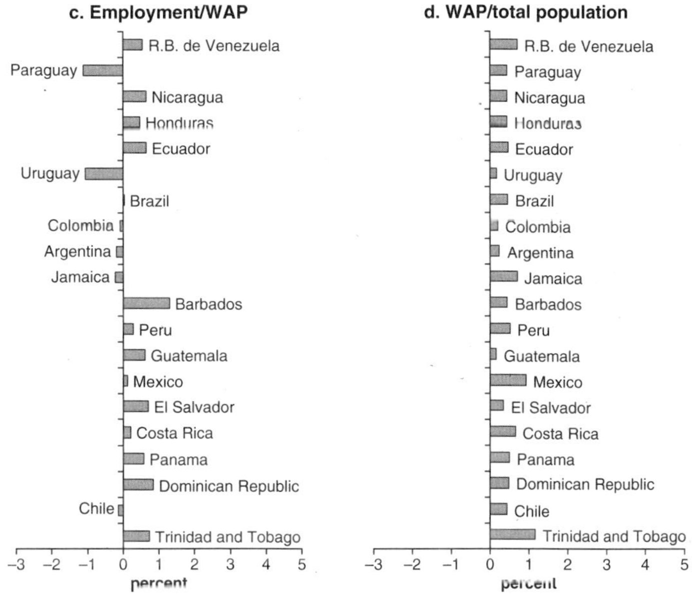

Sources: UNSD; UNPD; national statistics offices; GGDC TED.

Note: Employment data for Uruguay cover only urban areas. The GDP and employment series were smoothed by application of a Hodrick-Prescott filter. For most countries, the period covered is 1990 to 2004, but for some countries, end periods differ slightly. See annex 1.B.

Figure 1.3 Average Annual Change in Employment Rate and Labor Productivity, by Country, in Latin America and the Caribbean, 1990–2004

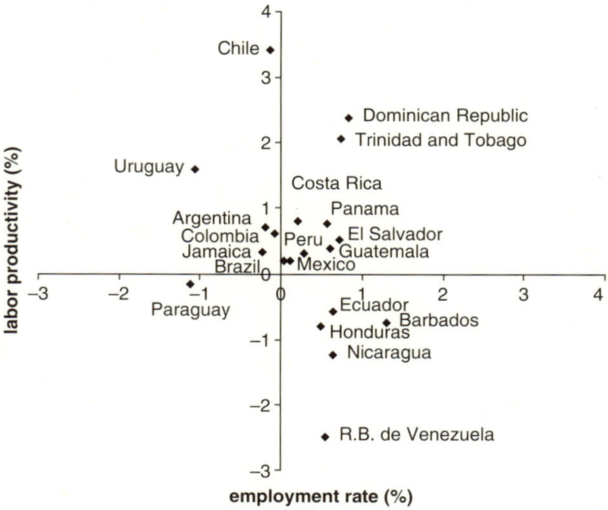

Sources: For GDP data, UNSD; for employment data, national statistics offices and GGDC TED; for WAP data, national statistics offices and UNPD.

productivity growth. The same is evident if comparisons are made in terms of employment rates and GDP growth since 1980 (figure 1.6). With the exception of Argentina, Chile, Mexico, and Trinidad and Tobago, which are in line with the comparators, the rest of the countries in the region had extraordinarily high rates of employment growth given their growth in GDP. Despite the obvious advantages that such strong employment growth implies for labor markets in Latin America and the Caribbean, the lack of productivity growth that accompanied this strong job creation has important implications for the quality of jobs in the region.

Drivers of Productivity

Commonly used measures of labor productivity do not take into account the characteristics of the labor force, yet factors such as age, level of experience, and in particular education affect the resulting productivity of workers. Most countries in the region have experienced an improvement in the human capital of their labor forces. If human capital is measured by

Figure 1.4 Average Annual Change in Employment Rate and Labor Productivity, by Country, in Latin America and the Caribbean, 1980–90

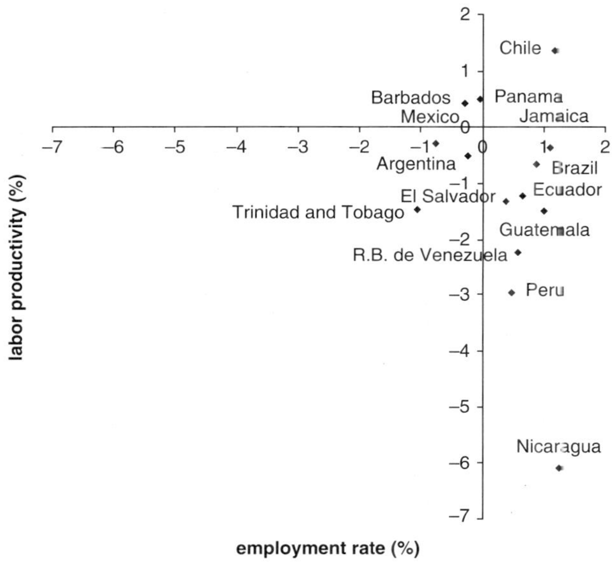

Sources: For GDP data, UNSD; for employment data, national statistics offices and GGDC TED; for WAP data, national statistics offices and UNPD.

education attainment, the share of workers with higher education is seen to increase, and the share of workers with low education attainments fell in all countries analyzed (see table 1.3).

Effect of Human Capital

In understanding how changes in human capital affect labor productivity, constructing an alternative measure of productivity based on a weighted measure of labor input can be useful. By assigning workers different weights depending on their skill level, this measure controls for changes in labor composition (see annex 1.C for details). In table 1.4, the change in the weighted measure of employment (column 3) is decomposed into change in observed employment (column 4) and changes in labor composition (column 5). In all cases but in Mexico, the quality-adjusted measure of employment is higher than the observed employment. In Mexico, the labor composition effect to labor productivity is close to zero. This

Figure 1.5 Average Annual Change in Employment Rate and Labor Productivity, by Country, in Latin America and the Caribbean and Comparator Sample, 1990–2004

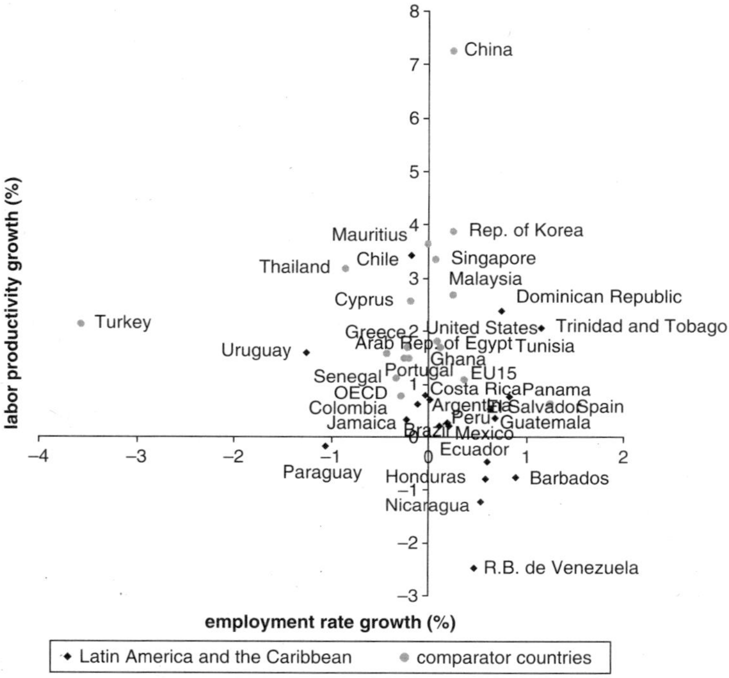

Sources: For GDP data, UNSD and World Bank World Development Indicators database; for employment data, national statistics offices, GGDC TED, and OECD labor force surveys; for WAP, national statistics offices, GGDC TED, and OECD labor force surveys.

outcome can be explained by the fact that since 1990, large cohorts of unskilled workers have entered the labor force in Mexico, counteracting the natural increase in the human capital of the workforce. According to calculations by CEDLAS, adult employment between 1992 and 2000 rose by 18 percent among the less educated population in Mexico, while increasing only 5 percent among workers with higher levels of education. In addition, table 1.4 presents two indicators of productivity growth: one is the mainstream labor productivity measure—labor productivity observed—and the other is output by weighted measure of labor input (column 6), which can be interpreted as the growth in labor productivity when changes in the quality of employment are taken into account. The

Figure 1.6 Average Annual Change in Employment Rate and Income per Capita, 1980–2004

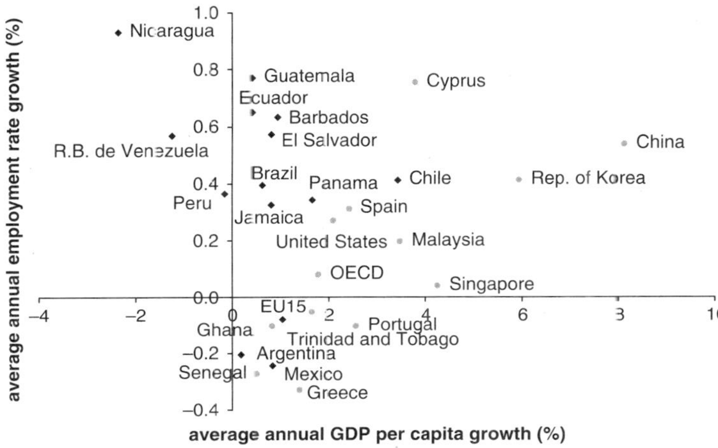

Sources: For GDP data, UNSD; for population data, UNPD; for employment data, national statistics offices and GGDC TED; for WAP data, national statistics offices and UNPD.

Note: Employment data for Uruguay cover only urban areas. The GDP and employment series were smoothed by application of a Hodrick-Prescott filter.

fact that, in most cases, this number is quite small indicates that, within skill categories, productivity absent skill improvements has remained flat. Changes in the skill composition of employment contributed positively to labor productivity growth in all countries analyzed but Mexico (see table 1.4). The composition effect was actually the main driver behind the increase in total labor productivity in Brazil, Colombia, and Peru.[7]

Effect of Low Educational Attainment

Despite recent improvements, the pace of human capital enhancement has been rather modest in the region over the longer run, especially when compared with that of other countries, particularly East Asian economies. In 1960, the average years of education for people age 25 years and older in Latin America were comparable with those of people of the same age group in Korea, Singapore, and Taiwan, China. By 2000, years of education in these Asian economies were between 35 and 75 percent higher than those in Latin America. Moreover, while in East Asia the rate of growth of education from 1980 to 2000 was 1.4 years per decade, in Latin America, it was only

Table 1.3 Structure of Employment by Level of Education

		Level of education (% of workers)					
		Low		*Medium*		*High*	
Country	*Period*	*Starting year*	*Ending year*	*Starting year*	*Ending year*	*Starting year*	*Ending year*
Argentina	1992–2001	39	34	39	38	22	28
Brazil	1990–2001	73	62	19	29	8	9
Chile	1990–2000	40	30	43	48	17	22
Colombia	1992–1999	60	57	26	30	13	13
Costa Rica	1990–2000	56	51	30	32	13	17
Ecuador	1994–1998	62	57	26	29	13	15
El Salvador	1991–2000	65	58	26	31	8	11
Honduras	1990–1999	83	77	13	18	3	5
Jamaica	1990–1999	40	30	54	63	6	7
Mexico	1992–2000	58	48	30	36	12	16
Nicaragua	1993–1998	66	64	28	30	6	6
Panama	1991–2000	48	37	36	41	17	22
Peru	1991–2000	41	39	44	40	14	20
Uruguay	1989–2000	49	37	38	44	14	18
Venezuela, R.B. de	1989–1998	59	51	31	34	11	15

Source: Authors' calculations based on household survey tabulations made by CEDLAS.

Note: Low = 0 to 8 years of formal education; medium = 9 to 13 years; high = more than 13 years.

Table 1.4 Productivity Growth and Decomposition of Labor Input

		Annualized rate (%)				
Country	*Period*	*Total labor input, adjusted for compositional change*	*Total employment*	*Labor composition*	*Labor productivity growth, accounting for composition effect*	*Labor productivity growth, observed*
Argentina	1992–2001	0.86	0.65	0.20	1.19	1.39
Brazil	1990–2001	2.89	2.38	0.51	–0.15	0.37
Chile	1990–2000	2.15	1.97	0.18	3.60	3.79
Colombia	1992–99	2.39	2.05	0.34	0.27	0.61
Costa Rica	1990–2000	3.83	3.62	0.21	0.90	1.11
Ecuador	1994–98	2.73	2.57	0.16	–0.57	–0.41
El Salvador	1991–2000	3.39	3.23	0.16	0.56	0.72
Honduras	1990–99	4.52	4.31	0.20	–1.44	–1.23
Jamaica	1990–99	0.79	0.53	0.26	1.13	1.39

(continued)

Table 1.4 Productivity Growth and Decomposition of Labor Input *(continued)*

		Annualized rate (%)				
Country	*Period*	*Total labor input, adjusted for compositional change*	*Total employment*	*Labor composition*	*Labor productivity growth, accounting for composition effect*	*Labor productivity growth, observed*
Mexico	1992–2000	2.85	2.86	–0.01	0.14	0.13
Nicaragua	1993–98	4.45	4.08	0.38	–1.26	–0.89
Panama	1991–2000	3.19	3.08	0.11	0.85	0.96
Peru	1991–2000	2.92	2.58	0.34	0.01	0.34
Uruguay	1989–2000	–0.20	–0.34	0.15	2.55	2.70
Venezuela, R.B. de	1989–98	4.05	3.55	0.50	–2.32	–1.82
Average		2.72	2.47	0.25	0.36	0.61

Sources: For data on returns to education, national household surveys as processed and tabulated by CEDLAS, http://www.depeco.econo.unlp.edu.ar/cedlas/; for data on structure of the population by level of education, Barro and Lee 2000; for GDP data, UNSD, smoothed using the Hodrick-Prescott filter.

Note: Total labor input refers to the growth of effective employment adjusted by changes in human capital. Series were smoothed by application of a Hodrick-Prescott filter. Differences between labor productivity growth reported in this table and those depicted in figure 1.1 are explained by the use of different time periods for each country. Data limitations prevented constancy in the periods of analysis used. *Labor productivity* is defined as GDP per hour worked. The column labeled "Accounting for composition effect" measures productivity, keeping the composition of employment by skill level constant.

0.75 years (IDB 2003). Furthermore, the performance of Latin American students in internationally comparable tests is much lower than that of students in comparator countries, suggesting the low quality of education may be a key determinant of the lackluster productivity performance.

Dynamics of Employment

The other key factor of the growth accounting decomposition is employment. Here, we present further evidence of what was indicated in the previous section, that is, that job creation was higher in Latin America and the Caribbean than in comparator countries. Even though the quality of many jobs created was rather poor. On average, the region created 12 jobs a year for every 1,000 people of working age. Costa Rica, Honduras, and the República Bolivariana de Venezuela, which created 18 jobs a year for every 1,000 people of working age, had the most dynamic labor markets during the period analyzed, closely followed by Ecuador, Guatemala, and Nicaragua with 17 jobs a year. By the same token, the Southern Cone, Colombia, and Jamaica performed rather poorly, creating fewer than 10 jobs a year.[8] Although some countries experienced a small degree of deceleration in the rate of job creation, this rate did not, for the most part, experience large fluctuations from 1990 to 2004 (figure 1.7).

Figure 1.8 compares performances across Latin America and the Caribbean and the comparator countries. The distribution of employment growth in Latin American countries is undoubtedly more upward skewed (average job creation is depicted in descending order) than that in comparator countries. In addition, the average annual job creation in the sample of comparator countries is only 10 workers for every 1,000 people of working age compared with 12 workers in Latin America.

Low Elasticity of Employment to Output and High Elasticity of Real Wages

The employment performance in Latin America and the Caribbean since 1990 is somewhat puzzling because income is one important driver of employment. As it turns out, however, wages are also an important driver of employment in Latin America (see annex 1.D).

The effect of output fluctuations on the level of employment depends on the effect of output fluctuations on wages. This book's empirical analysis for the period between 1980 and 2004 supports findings by González Anaya (2002) and IDB (2003) that in Latin America, labor markets adjust to output fluctuations through changes in wages rather than through changes in employment rates. The estimated short-run elasticities of employment deviations to output deviations from trend are notably smaller in the region than in OECD countries (see figure 1.9).[9] The average output elasticity of

Figure 1.7 Breakdown of Job Creation in Latin America and the Caribbean per 1,000 Working-Age People, 1990–2004

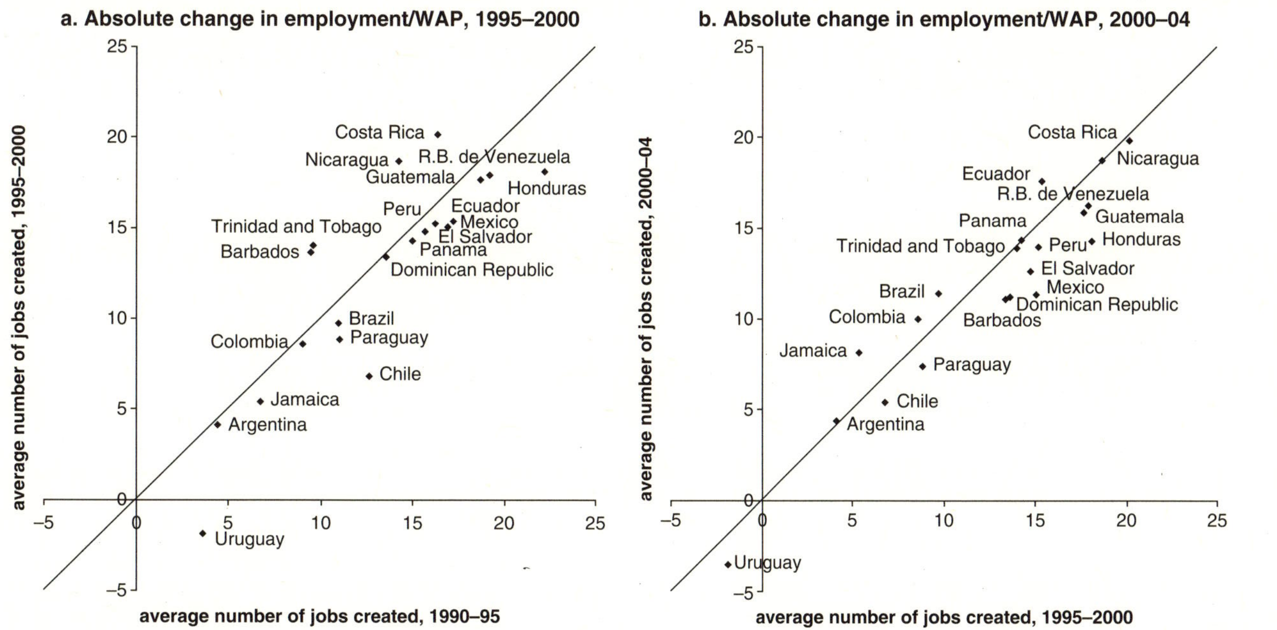

Sources: National statistics offices and GGDC TED.

Note: Employment data for Uruguay cover only urban areas. The employment series was smoothed by application of a Hodrick-Prescott filter. WAP is measured as the average of the initial and last period.

Figure 1.8 Distribution of Countries by Average Annual Job Creation, 1990–2004

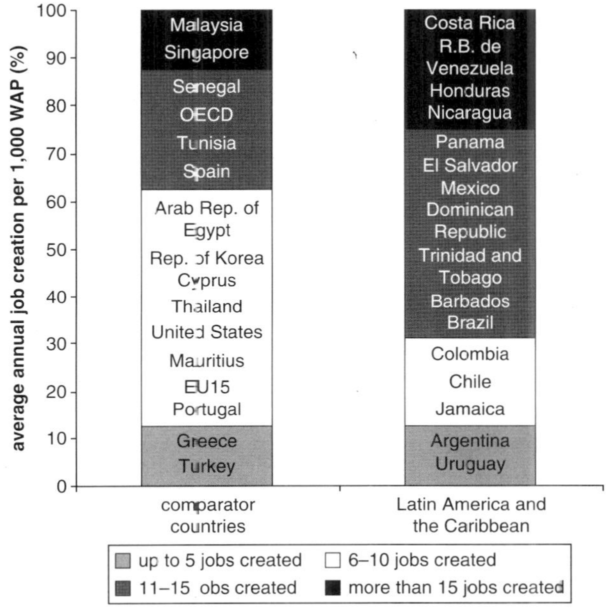

Sources: For employment data, national statistics offices, GGDC TED, and OECD labor force surveys; for WAP data, national statistics offices, UNPD, and OECD labor force surveys.

Note: Employment data for Uruguay cover only urban areas. The employment series was smoothed by application of a Hodrick-Prescott filter. The Hodrick-Prescott filter could not be applied to Senegal's data.

employment for the sample of countries analyzed here is 0.36 in Latin America and 0.72 in OECD countries. Meanwhile, in Latin America, the output elasticity of real wages appears to be noticeably higher than that of employment (see figure 1.10). The calculations suggest that in Argentina, Guatemala, Mexico, and the República Bolivariana de Venezuela real wage deviations from the trend associated with variations in output are larger than employment deviations. Colombia is the only country in the sample studied where the elasticity of real wages was notably lower than that of employment, suggesting that in past decades the Colombian labor market adjusted to output shocks through employment rather than wages. Colombia's behavior is more in line with the behavior of developed countries than with the dynamics of labor market adjustment prevalent in Latin

Figure 1.9 Output Elasticity of Employment

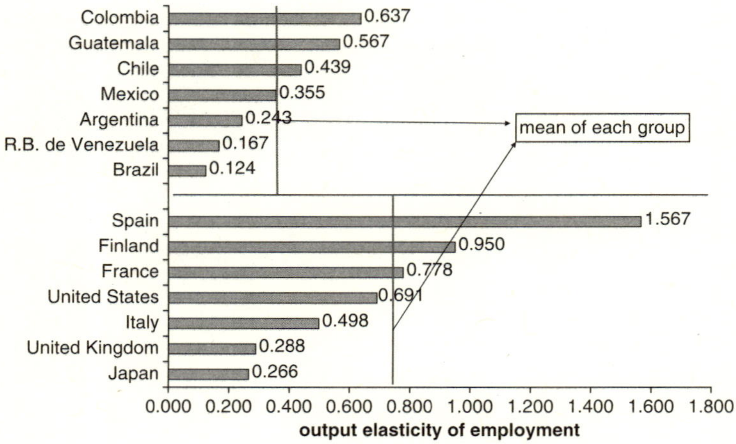

Sources: See annex 1.D.

Figure 1.10 Output Elasticity of Wages

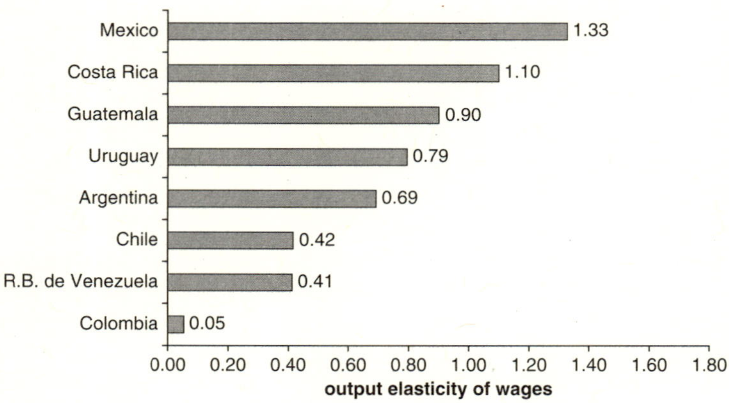

Sources: See annex 1.D.

America. IDB (2003) finds that the average output elasticity of real wages in Latin America and the Caribbean was almost two times larger than that in the average developed country.

Given that real wages tend to reflect labor productivity, high elasticity of wages suggests high elasticity of labor productivity. Since 1990, as well as in the 1980s, sizable changes in income per capita were accompanied by comparable changes in labor productivity amid relative stable employment rate growth. The implication of this conclusion is that the kinds of jobs that the economy generated during times of sluggish economic growth might have been "bad jobs"—low-productivity jobs—presumably with accompanying low labor returns.

Relationship between Wage Growth and Productivity Growth

How well do changes in real wages track changes in labor productivity? Figure 1.11 depicts the evolution of labor productivity and real wage growth rates for nine countries in Latin America. Figures for wages are notoriously difficult to obtain in the region. In most cases, they cover only certain sectors of the economy. Often, they are not comparable across countries because the coverage of sectors or the measurement method differs widely across countries. In other cases, the geographic coverage is limited to the main urban centers. The data presented here suffer from some of these problems. They cover only formal sector workers, and in Peru, data cover metropolitan Lima only. Despite these limitations, the correlation in labor productivity and real wage patterns is apparent in most countries and periods of the data, although the degree of correspondence varies by country. This finding indicates that earnings growth is constrained by the low productivity growth of the region.

Falling Quality of Employment

Although in most countries of the region, job creation has been quite dynamic, particularly when placed in an international context, the ILO-led discussion of decent work has called into question the notion that *any* job creation is positive. The World Commission on the Social Dimension of Globalization (2004) stated that poverty in the developing world is not associated with lack of employment, but rather with the low productivity of existing jobs, and that such low productivity explains the slowdown in the rate of poverty reduction in the 1990s.

A number of approaches can be used to measure job quality. In developed countries, studies tend to focus on identifying bad jobs, mostly on the basis of earnings criteria (see IDB 2007 and the references therein). This approach has also been recently adopted in the context of developing

Figure 1.11 Evolution of Labor Productivity and Real Wage Growth, 1980s to Early 2000s

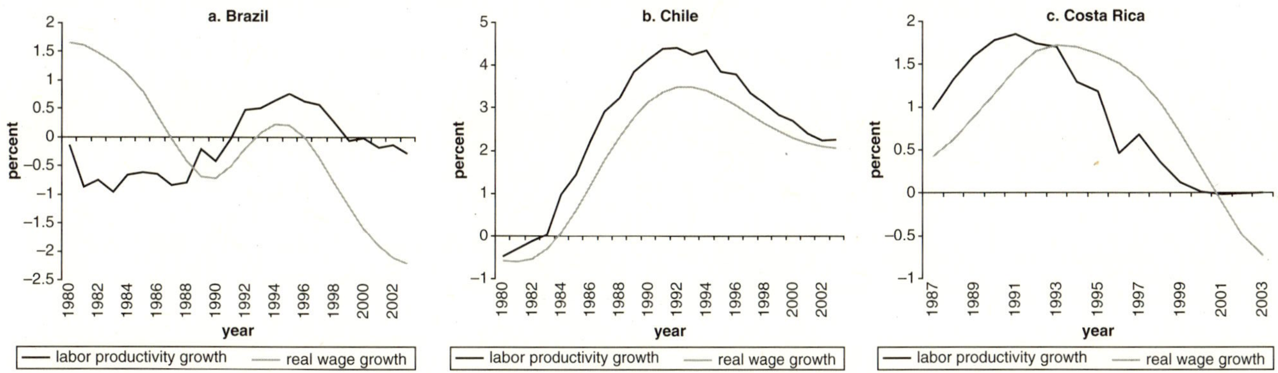

(continued)

Figure 1.11 Evolution of Labor Productivity and Real Wage Growth, 1980s to Early 2000s *(continued)*

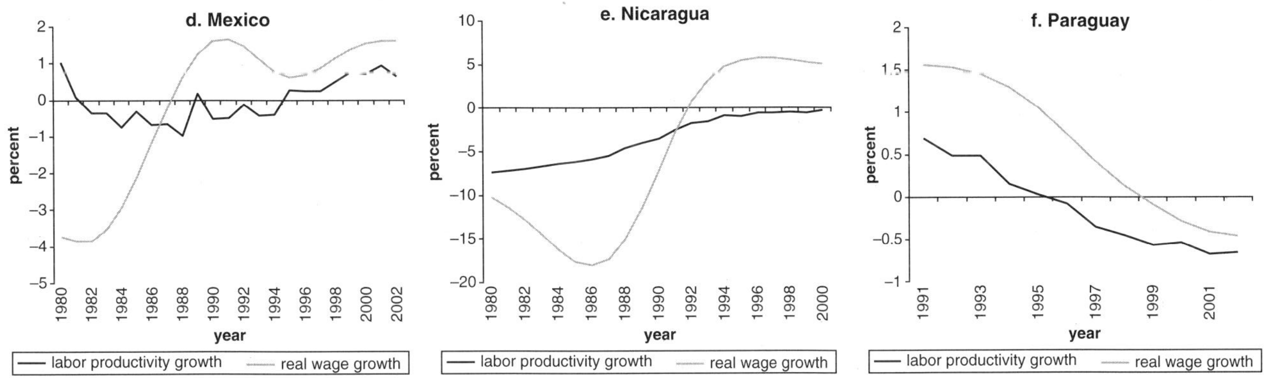

(continued)

Figure 1.11 Evolution of Labor Productivity and Real Wage Growth, 1980s to Early 2000s *(continued)*

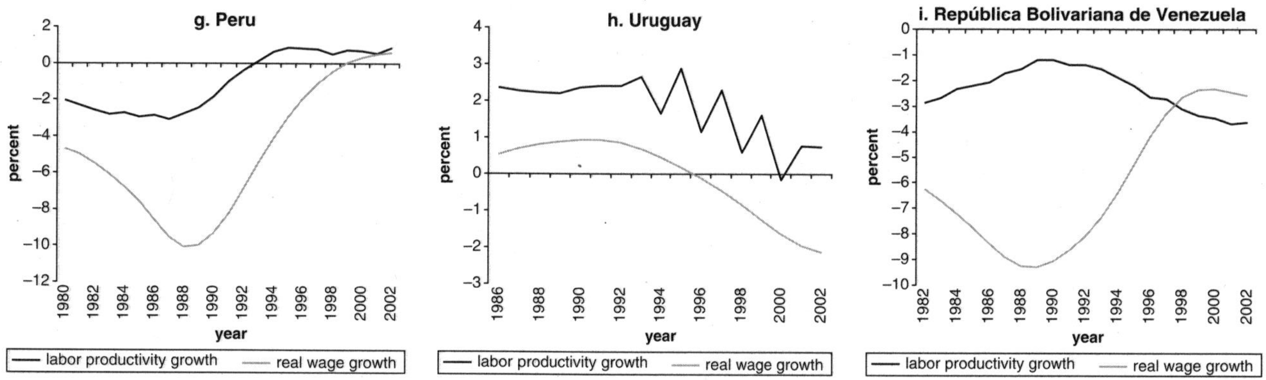

Sources: For GDP data, UNSD; for employment data, national statistics offices and GGDC TED; for real wage data in the formal sector, Economic Commission for Latin America and the Caribbean Social Indicators and Statistics Database (Base de Estadísticas e Indicadores Sociales, or BADEINSO).

Note: Both series were smoothed by application of a Hodrick-Prescott filter.

economies. A method led by the ILO is to compute the share of people in the labor force who are poor (*working poor*)—assuming that labor force participants and non–labor force participants have the same probability of being poor (see Majid 2001). Alternatively, Duryea and Pagés (2003) measure the percentage of workers with low-wage jobs. These, in turn, are defined as those jobs that pay an hourly rate below the level that would allow workers living with a family of average size and participation rate to obtain a per capita income above a threshold of US$2 a day in purchasing power parity terms. The working-poor measure focuses on workers' poverty outcomes, whereas the low-earnings measure focuses on the wage or productivity levels of jobs. Of course, not all working poor, as defined by the ILO, must be employed in low-productivity jobs—they could have high earnings but be supporting a large number of individuals. Similarly, not all workers in low-wage jobs, as defined by the second approach, are poor—they could belong to households with higher-income individuals. Given the focus on the nature of jobs, this book measures "bad jobs" according to the second method, using the US$2 a day as the poverty threshold.

Panel a of figure 1.12 compares the average incidence in low-wage jobs in 1990–97 and 1998–2004 and shows that it increased in most countries.[10] IDB (2007) shows that a high correlation exists between the incidence of low-wage employment and national poverty headcount estimates, suggesting that the evolution of poverty headcounts is largely determined by the performance of the labor market and, in particular, by the evolution of earnings. Factors such as income transfers to poor households, changes in participation patterns, or changes in household formation are less important influences on the evolution of poverty.

The second approach for gauging the extent to which the employment generated in the region falls under the "bad jobs" category looks beyond wage indicators and assesses working conditions and nonwage benefits. This approach is the most widely used in developing countries where wage data are less widely available. Social security affiliation is one of the most common forms of assessing the quality of a job. Under this measure, quite strikingly, in all countries for which data are available but El Salvador, the share of workers affiliated to social security through their jobs declined since 1990 (figure 1.12, panel b).

Another commonly used indicator of job quality is the share of informal jobs, defined according to the job category of a worker. For example, those who are self-employed, who are employers or employees of microenterprises, or who work as unpaid labor are customarily classified as informal workers.[11] Under this classification, the share of informal workers increased in most countries (figure 1.12, panel c).

Discussion continues, however, regarding whether mixing these categories of work into one informal category provides a good description of the heterogeneity of conditions within the informal sector. In

Figure 1.12 Evolution of the Quality of Employment in the Region

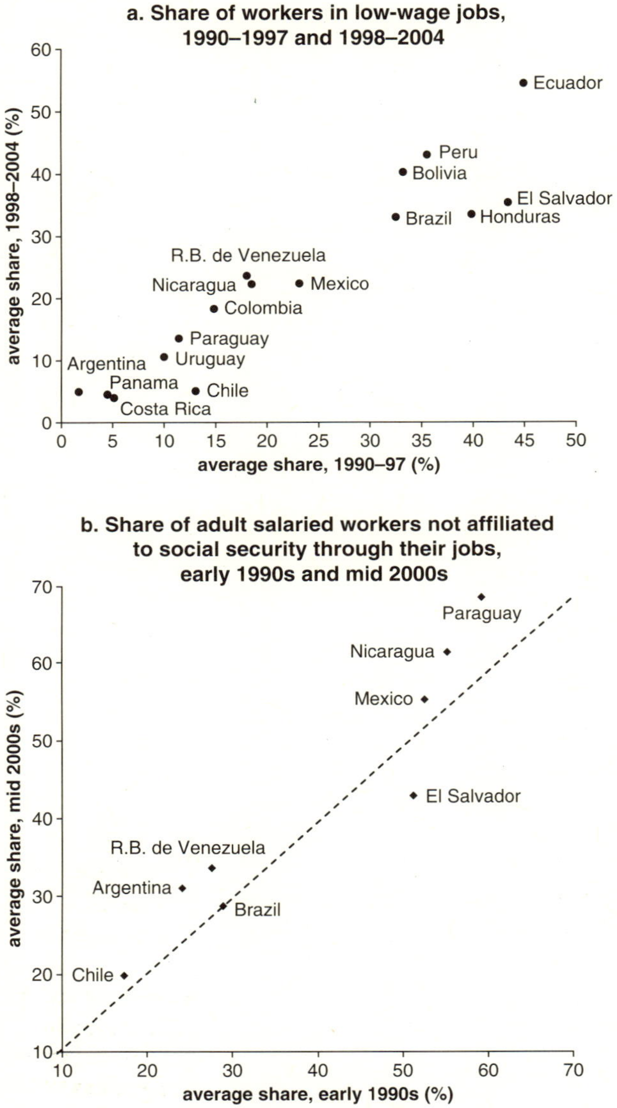

(continued)

Figure 1.12 Evolution of the Quality of Employment in the Region *(continued)*

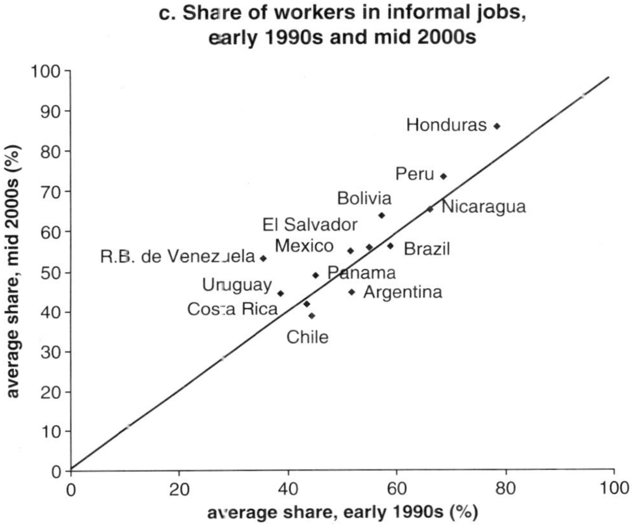

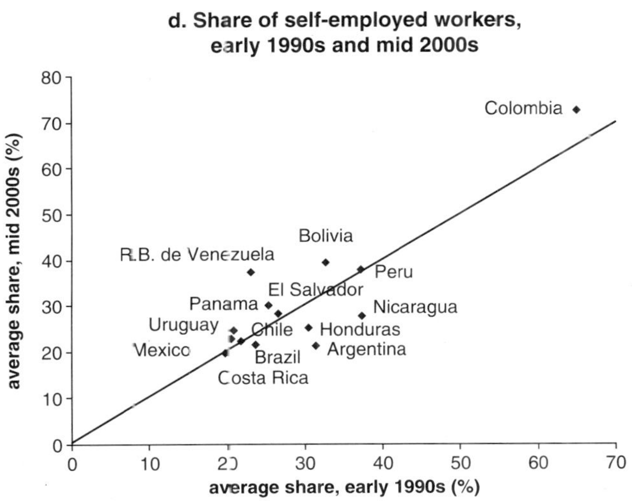

(continued)

Figure 1.12 Evolution of the Quality of Employment in the Region *(continued)*

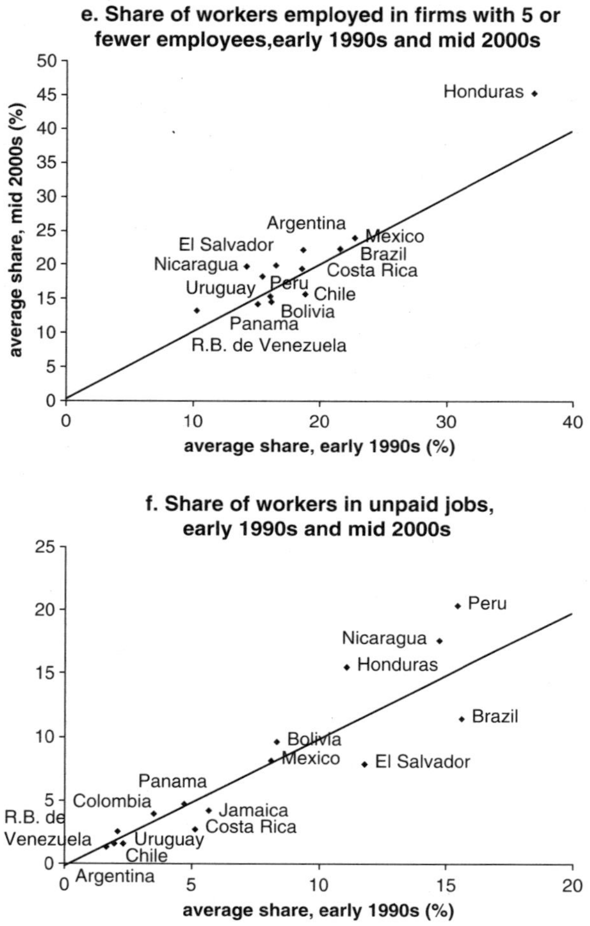

Sources: For panel a, IDB 2007; for data for rest of panels, SEDLAC.

Note: Informal jobs are defined as the sum of self-employment, employment in micro firms, and unpaid jobs.

particular, evidence, summarized in Perry and others (2007), suggests that self-employment may be a quite desirable form of work. A recent study (Madrigal and Pagés 2008a) points in the same direction, finding that a surprisingly large share of workers in salaried work would rather be self-employed while the number of self-employed workers who would prefer being salaried is much lower (table 1.5). Madrigal and Pagés (2008b)

Table 1.5 Workers' Preferences in Selected Latin American Countries

Country	*Share of salaried workers who would prefer being self-employed (%)*	*Share of self-employed workers who would prefer being salaried (%)*
Belize	45	23
Ecuador	59	41
El Salvador	67	48
Guatemala	57	32
Honduras	79	32

Source: Madrigal and Pagés 2008a, based on household surveys from Ecuador (2008), El Salvador (2007), Guatemala (2007), Belize (2007), and Honduras (2007).

further examine this issue and find that measures of job quality based on informality do not yield the same ranking of job quality as workers' self-reported assessments of job satisfaction. The study also finds substantial differences in job satisfaction within different types of informal jobs. Self-employed workers reported high levels of job satisfaction, comparable in many cases to formal jobs. In contrast, salaried employment in micro firms was associated with lower wages and nonwage benefits, higher job instability, and lower job satisfaction.

These results indicate the usefulness of looking at the different components of informal employment separately. Figure 1.12 shows that the share of workers in self-employment decreased in about half the countries considered (panel d), while the share of workers employed in micro firms rose since the early 1990s (panel e). Although it cannot be ruled out that this trend could in part reflect growing employment in small but dynamic start-up firms, the patterns explained previously cast doubts on this interpretation. The share of unpaid workers also increased in some countries, but it declined in a few others (panel f).

In sum, although measuring quality of employment is a difficult and by no means resolved task, combining the evidence on the evolution of labor productivity, average wages, workers with low-wage jobs, and the different components of informality strongly suggests that the share of workers in low-quality jobs has increased since the early 1990s.

Dynamics of Labor Supply

Latin American and Caribbean countries are currently undergoing a demographic transition typical of countries moving up the development ladder. Although a certain degree of variation exists across countries, the region is experiencing an overall increase in the share of working-age population. However, the annual growth rate of the WAP has been declining since the 1980s. It was 2.4 percent during the 1980s, compared with 2.2 percent during the 1990s and 2.0 percent during the early 2000s (see table 1.6). The growth in the share of WAP results from the natural lag between falling mortality rates—attributable to improved health conditions—and the subsequent drop in birth rates, which, however, adjust only gradually as expectations adapt to the evolving health status and changing living habits.

A substantial increase in the share of WAP is expected to translate into rising labor supply. Declining dependency rates create a window of opportunity during which the possibilities for economic and social progress are enhanced. The challenge for countries in this intermediate stage of the demographic transition is therefore to create enough sources of employment to capitalize on this opportunity before the window closes (IDB 2003).

The rising share of WAP did translate into an increase in overall labor supply in the region. To measure the effect of this increase, this study decomposes the absolute change in labor supply into three elements: the change in labor force participation rate, the change in the ratio of working-age to total population, and the absolute change in total population (figure 1.13). In most countries, the three components expanded during the 1990s and early 2000s. Chile, Jamaica, Mexico, Trinidad and Tobago, and Uruguay are the only exceptions to the regional pattern: the rate of labor force participation in these countries declined between 1990 and 2004. In all the countries analyzed here except for Barbados and Trinidad and Tobago, the increase in the overall population was the main driver behind labor supply growth; however, many countries experienced healthy growth of labor participation, which in most countries was at or above 0.5 percent a year.

Increased Female Labor Force Participation

The substantial growth of the labor force was driven by an increase in female labor market participation. In fact, whereas since 1990 prime-age female participation increased in most of the region, prime-age male participation rates dropped (see figure 1.14). This issue is discussed further in chapter 2. The well-documented rise in female labor supply of recent decades has clearly worked to reduce the gender differential in participation rates. Given the increased autonomy and financial stability associated with remunerated work, increased participation can naturally, other things being equal, be considered a positive turn of events. The fact that the rise in female participation was accompanied by falling male participation,

Table 1.6 Population Growth Rates in Latin America and the Caribbean, 1980–2004

	1980s (%)		1990s (%)		Early 2000s (%)	
Country	*WAP*	*Population*	*WAP*	*Population*	*WAP*	*Population*
Argentina	1.65	1.49	1.43	1.22	1.31	0.97
Barbados	1.09	0.32	0.79	0.34	0.56	0.15
Brazil	2.40	2.08	2.11	1.53	1.57	1.42
Chile	2.13	1.66	1.89	1.58	1.93	1.14
Colombia	—	—	1.98	1.59	1.61	1.85
Costa Rica	—	—	3.71	3.11	3.19	2.34
Dominican Republic	2.41	2.13	2.07	1.53	1.86	1.49
Ecuador	3.23	2.58	2.44	1.82	1.93	1.82
El Salvador	1.77	1.09	2.41	2.08	2.26	1.87
Guatemala	2.33	2.41	2.41	2.30	2.71	2.44
Honduras	—	—	3.15	2.93	3.95	2.85
Jamaica	1.03	0.91	1.51	0.86	1.40	0.48
Mexico	3.48	2.16	2.78	1.73	2.05	1.37
Nicaragua	2.96	2.74	3.30	2.86	3.21	2.53
Panama	3.03	2.16	2.57	2.04	2.33	1.35
Paraguay	2.99	3.07	3.04	2.60	2.90	2.41
Peru	2.92	2.30	2.28	1.78	2.12	1.52
Trinidad and Tobago	1.30	1.19	1.78	0.57	1.28	0.33
Uruguay	—	—	1.05	0.74	0.53	0.72
Venezuela, R.B. de	3.17	2.72	2.85	2.15	2.65	1.37
Average	2.37	1.94	2.23	1.69	2.00	1.48

Sources: For WAP data, national statistics offices and UNPD; for total population data, UNPD.

Note: — = not available. Colombia, Costa Rica, Honduras, and Uruguay were not included in the calculation of the regional average.

however, raises some questions on the quality of these improvements. Have women forced their way into an at-capacity labor market by driving some men out of it? Have they achieved labor force entry at the expense of deteriorating working conditions? Chapter 2 explores the dynamic of changes in the composition of the labor force in detail.

Figure 1.13 Decomposition of Labor Supply Growth, 1990–2004

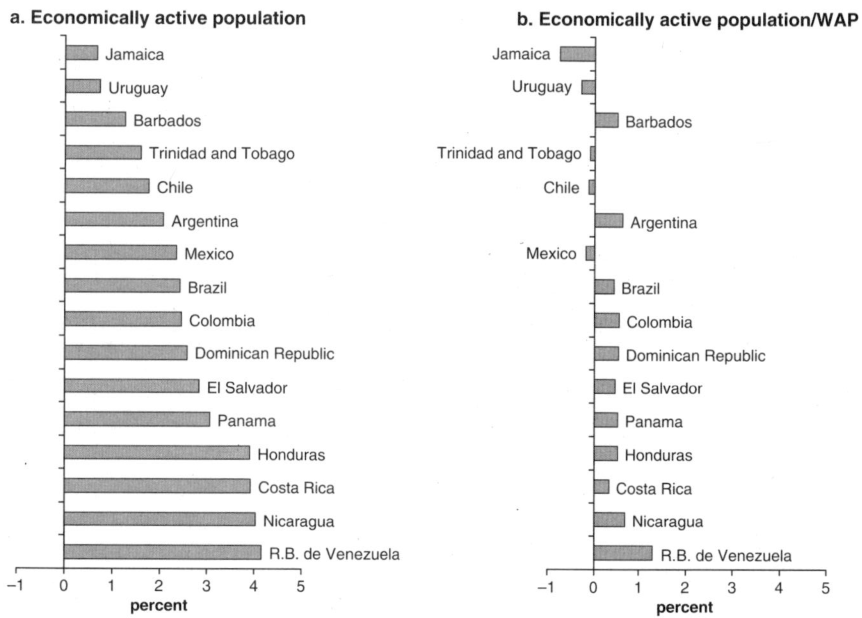

(continued)

Figure 1.13 Decomposition of Labor Supply Growth, 1990–2004 *(continued)*

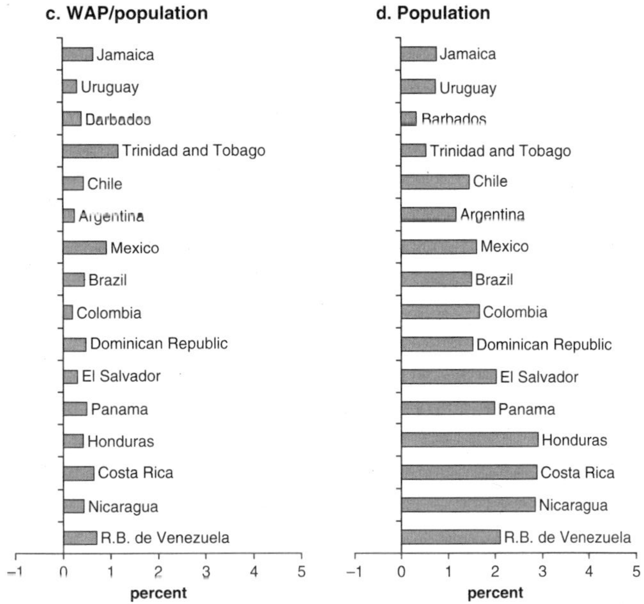

Sources: For economically active population data, national statistics offices; for WAP data, national statistics offices and UNPD; for population data, UNPD.

Note: The economically active population series was smoothed by application of a Hodrick-Prescott filter.

Figure 1.14 Annual Average Change in Prime-Age Participation Rate, by Gender, 1990–2004

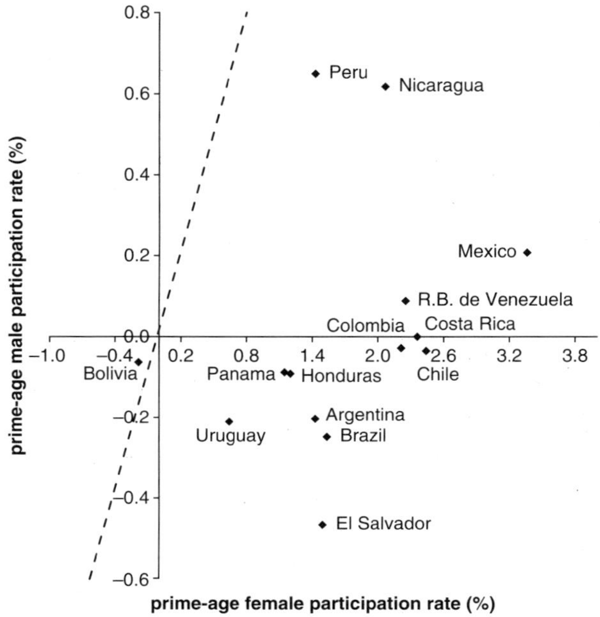

Source: Sociómetro, Research Department, IDB.

Note: Prime-age population includes people 25 to 49 years of age. For a detailed description of endpoint years used by country for this analysis, refer to annex 1.B. Data for Argentina and Uruguay are urban.

High Rates of Labor Supply Growth but Poor Labor Productivity Outcome

As already discussed, job creation was, on average, relatively (to GDP growth) higher in Latin America and the Caribbean than in the sample of comparator countries. Figure 1.15, however, makes clear that labor supply growth was also higher on average than in comparator countries. This finding is evident from the more upwardly skewed distribution of labor supply growth in Latin American countries. The labor force in comparator countries grew at an average rate of 11 individuals for every 1,000 people of working age. The labor force for Latin America and the Caribbean meanwhile expanded by an average of 13 individuals for every 1,000 people of working age.

Figure 1.15 Distribution of Countries by Average Annual Labor Supply Growth, 1990–2004

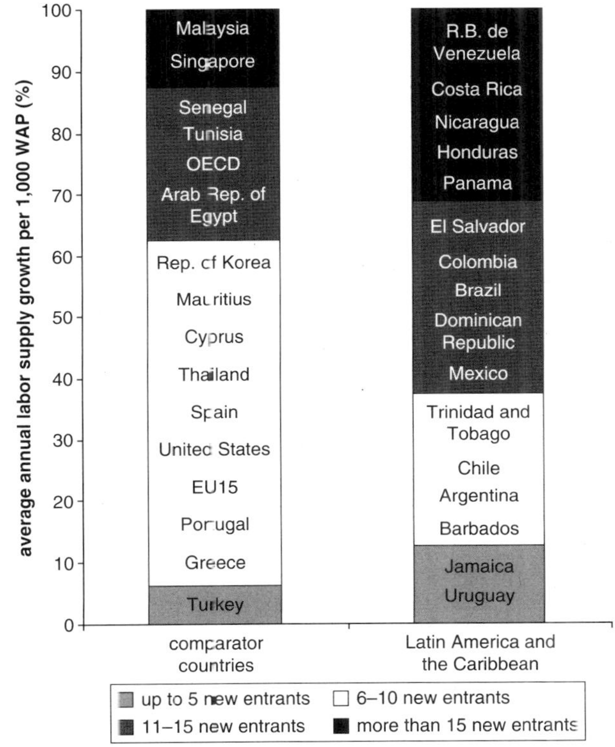

Sources: For employment data, national statistics offices, GGDC TED, and OECD labor force surveys; for economically active population data, national statistics offices and OECD labor force surveys; for WAP data, national statistics offices, UNPD, and OECD labor force surveys.

Note: Employment data for Uruguay cover only urban areas. The employment and economically active population series were smoothed by application of a Hodrick-Prescott filter.

Given the high growth rate of the Latin American labor force revealed in this section, the sluggish labor productivity growth since 1990 could be a "normal" outcome for countries undergoing demographic changes such as the ones currently under way in Latin America and the Caribbean. To analyze this hypothesis, this section compares the labor productivity growth rates of countries in Latin America and the Caribbean with those of countries in the comparator sample that showed analogous WAP growth during the period between 1990 and 2004.

The results show that, even when changes in the demographic variable are controlled for, countries in Latin America and the Caribbean underperformed the comparator sample in terms of labor productivity growth (see table 1.7). Comparator countries that experienced annual WAP growth of 1 and 3 percent showed labor productivity growth rates that are more than double the rates of even the best-performing countries in Latin America and the Caribbean. The same is true for comparator countries that experienced annual WAP growth of 2 percent, with a few exceptions—Chile, the Dominican Republic, and Trinidad and Tobago experienced labor productivity growth rates comparable to those in Thailand and Indonesia, their counterparts in the comparator sample.

Countries outside the region that over the same period experienced similar growth in WAP showed very different patterns of adjustment. Although they managed much higher labor productivity growth, they experienced lower employment rate growth than in Latin America and the Caribbean (table 1.7).

Higher Proportion of Unemployed Workers

Despite high employment growth in many countries, the rapid pace of labor supply implied that, in most countries, the number of workers willing to work grew faster than the number of employed workers, leading to a higher share of unemployed workers in the WAP (see figure 1.16). Given the substantial labor supply growth, however, an increase in the absolute number of unemployed workers does not necessarily imply an increase in the unemployment rate—the ratio of unemployed workers to total labor force participants. Figure 1.17 shows that unemployment rates increased in roughly half the countries studied (Argentina, Brazil, Chile, Colombia, Costa Rica, Honduras, Nicaragua, Uruguay, and the República Bolivariana de Venezuela) while decreasing in the other half (Barbados, the Dominican Republic, El Salvador, Jamaica, Mexico, Panama, and Trinidad and Tobago). High and increasing unemployment rates were bad news, especially for youths, whose unemployment rates soared to, on average, 20 percent of the labor force. The dynamics of the youth labor market are explored in chapter 2.

Increasing Unemployment in Countries with Low or Negative Employment Growth

The analysis so far has shown that in most countries of the region, the increase in the supply of labor has been atypically high. Was the rise

Table 1.7 Labor Productivity and Employment Rate Growth by WAP Growth Rate, 1990–2004

Working-age population annual growth rate (%)	*Sample*	*Country*	*Labor productivity annual growth rate (%)*	*Employment rate annual growth rate (%)*
1	Latin America and the Caribbean	Argentina	0.7	–0.2
		Barbados	–0.7	1.3
		Jamaica	0.3	–0.2
		Uruguay	1.6	–1.1
	Countries in the comparator sample	Korea, Rep. of	3.9	0.3
2	Latin America and the Caribbean	Brazil	0.2	0.1
		Chile	3.4	0.0
		Colombia	0.6	–0.1
		Dominican Republic	2.4	0.6
		El Salvador	0.8	0.7
		Panama	0.3	0.0
		Peru	0.5	0.7
		Trinidad and Tobago	2.1	0.7
	Countries in the comparator sample	Indonesia	2.2	–0.5
		Thailand	3.2	–0.9

(continued)

Table 1.7 Labor Productivity and Employment Rate Growth by WAP Growth Rate, 1990–2004 *(continued)*

Working-age population annual growth rate (%)	*Sample*	*Country*	*Labor productivity annual growth rate (%)*	*Employment rate annual growth rate (%)*
3	Latin America and the Caribbean	Ecuador	–0.5	0.2
		Guatemala	0.3	0.2
		Honduras	–0.8	0.5
		Mexico	0.2	0.1
		Nicaragua	–1.2	0.6
		Paraguay	–0.2	–1.2
		Venezuela, R.B. de	–2.5	0.6
	Countries in the comparator sample	Malaysia	2.7	0.3
		Singapore	3.3	0.1

Sources: For GDP data, UNSD and World Bank World Development Indicators database; for population data, UNPD and OECD Web site; for employment data, national statistics offices, GGDC TED, and OECD labor force surveys; for WAP data, national statistics offices, UNPD, and OECD labor force surveys.

Note: The GDP and employment series used were smoothed by application of a Hodrick-Prescott filter.

Figure 1.16 Labor Market Changes in Latin America and the Caribbean, 1990–2004

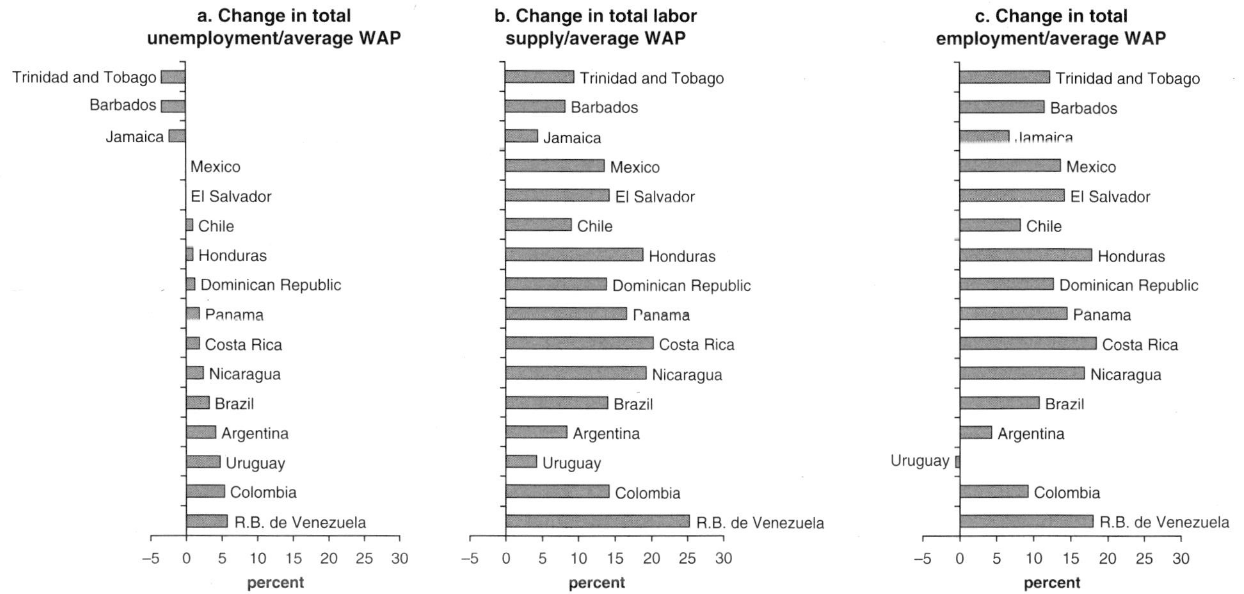

Sources: For unemployment and economically active population data, national statistics offices; for employment data, national statistics offices and GGDC TED; for WAP data, national statistics offices and UNPD.

Note: Employment and unemployment data for Uruguay cover only urban areas. The economically active population, employment, and unemployment series were smoothed by application of a Hodrick-Prescott filter. There was no average annual change in total unemployment divided by WAP in Mexico, while in El Salvador it was 0.09 percent.

Figure 1.17 Unemployment Rate Growth, 1990–2004

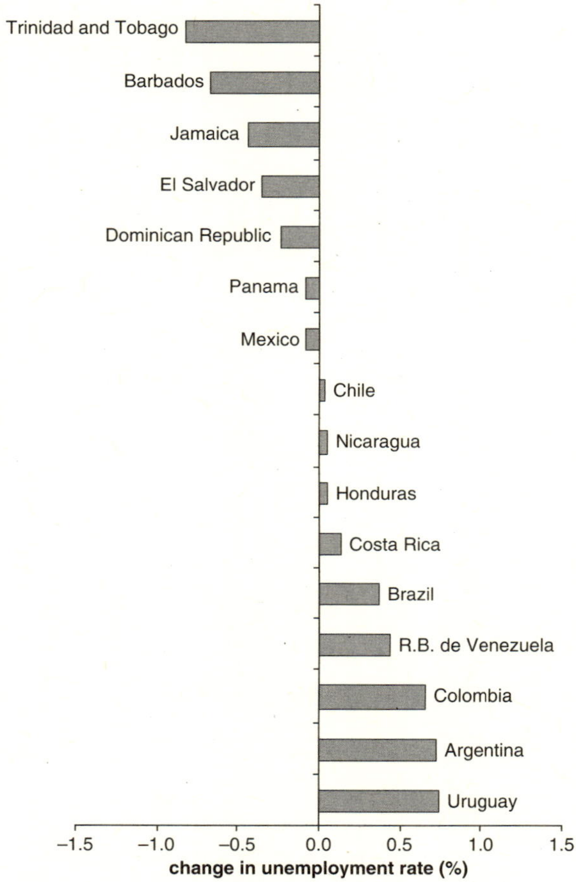

Source: Authors' calculations using data from national statistics offices.

Note: Unemployment data for Uruguay cover only urban areas. The economically active population and unemployment series used were smoothed by application of a Hodrick-Prescott filter.

in unemployment driven by such trends, or rather, did unemployment increase in the subset of countries where the growth of jobs was low?

Table 1.8 summarizes the individual countries' labor market performance over a number of dimensions, classifying each variable's change (either in rate or first difference) from 1990 to 2004 as high, medium, low, or negative (see table notes for the classification criteria). Of the

Table 1.8 Change in Employment and Unemployment Outcomes by Country, 1990–2004

Country	*Growth of employment rate*[a] *(1)*	*Growth of share of WAP*[b] *(2)*	*Growth of labor participation*[c] *(3)*	*Growth of unemployment per 1,000 WAP*[d] *(4)*
Venezuela, R.B. de	**High**	**High**	**High**	**High**
Uruguay	*Negative*	*Low*	*Negative*	*High*
Argentina	*Negative*	*Medium*	*High*	*High*
Colombia	*Negative*	*Low*	*High*	*High*
Nicaragua	**High**	**Medium**	**High**	**Medium**
Brazil	Low	Medium	Medium	Medium
Trinidad and Tobago	High	High	Negative	Negative
El Salvador	**High**	**Low**	**Medium**	**Negative**
Barbados	**High**	**Medium**	**High**	**Negative**
Mexico	Low	High	Negative	Negative
Jamaica	*Negative*	*High*	*Negative*	*Negative*
Panama	**High**	**High**	**High**	**Low**
Honduras	**Medium**	**Medium**	**High**	**Low**

(continued)

Table 1.8 Change in Employment and Unemployment Outcomes by Country, 1990–2004 *(continued)*

Country	*Growth of employment rate*[a] *(1)*	*Growth of share of WAP*[b] *(2)*	*Growth of labor participation*[c] *(3)*	*Growth of unemployment per 1,000 WAP*[d] *(4)*
Costa Rica	Medium	High	Medium	Low
Chile	*Negative*	*Medium*	*Negative*	*Low*
Dominican Republic	High	Medium	High	Low
Ecuador	**High**	**Medium**	—	—
Peru	Low	Medium	—	—
Paraguay	Negative	Low	—	—

Sources: National statistical offices, GGDC TED, and UNPD.

Note: Countries in bold are those with growthless jobs; countries in italics are those with jobless growth. Variables in columns 1, 3, and 4 are smoothed by application of a Hodrick-Prescott filter.

a. Low = 0.0 to 0.2 percent; medium = 0.2 to 0.5 percent; high = greater than 0.5 percent; negative = less than 0.0 percent.

b. Low = 0.2 to 0.4 percent; medium = 0.4 to 0.6 percent; high = greater than 0.5 percent; negative = less than 0.0 percent.

c. Low = 0.0 to 1.0 percent; medium = 1.5 to 2.5 percent; high = greater than 2.5 percent; negative = less than 0.0 percent.

d. Change of number of unemployed/WAP (mean) × 1,000: low = 0 to 2; medium = 2 to 4; high = greater than 4; low = less than 0.

nine countries in which unemployment rates increased during the period (figure 1.17), five were countries in which employment growth was negative (Argentina, Brazil, Chile, Colombia, and Uruguay). Nonetheless, in at least two countries, Argentina and Colombia, an adverse low job creation situation was compounded by a large increase in labor participation. Still, in some other countries, most notably the República Bolivariana de Venezuela, but also Costa Rica and Nicaragua, unemployment increased despite high employment growth, as a consequence of extraordinarily high labor supply growth.

Conclusions

This chapter has examined economic growth and job creation outcomes in Latin America and the Caribbean since 1990, placing them in a historical and wider geographic context. It finds that the common assertion that the region has been experiencing a situation of jobless growth is not an appropriate description of the labor market situation in many countries.

It is true that positive growth in labor productivity during 1990 to 2004 was not accompanied by an increase in employment rates in five countries of the region (Argentina, Chile, Colombia, Jamaica, and Uruguay). It is also a fact that these countries have experienced the highest increases in unemployment rates. However, among these five countries, only in Chile was average GDP per capita growth above 1 percent—arguably the only country with a rate of growth high enough to generate a substantive rise in employment rates.[12]

In fact, in most countries of the region, meager economic growth was the norm, and thus the outcome of low employment growth could have been expected. Quite surprisingly—and atypically when compared to the international experience—in many countries employment growth was robust despite low and unstable GDP growth. This finding is likely to be related to the high real wage flexibility that characterized the labor markets of many Latin American and Caribbean countries. Quantity, however, was not accompanied by quality. In fact, the quality of jobs, as measured by wage levels, registration in social security, or employment in the modern sector (salaried jobs in firms larger than five workers), has deteriorated in most countries.

These findings suggest that the countries in the region can be divided into at least two groups: the "growthless job creation" countries and the "jobless growth" countries

1 *"Growthless job creation" countries.* A low pace of economic growth and relatively strong job creation characterizes these countries. Job creation has been largely driven by the evolution of the labor supply and accompanied by high wage elasticity. Many of the jobs created have been of low productivity and low pay.

2 *"Jobless growth" countries.* These countries have a relatively lower wage elasticity, which, coupled with a situation of low or negative GDP growth, has resulted in low or negative employment growth and a large increase of unemployment. Some of the relatively richer countries of South America (Argentina, Chile, Colombia, and Uruguay) fall into this category.[13]

Annex 1.A: Selection of Comparator Countries

The selection criteria for countries included in the comparator sample were intended to identify countries of particular interest to Latin America for comparison purposes. In this sense, the objective was to compare the region's performance over the past 35 years with that of countries that had similar income levels in 1970, the starting point of the analysis.

First, countries in Latin America and the Caribbean were separated into two groups:

- Group A comprised countries that in 1970 had income per capita above or equal to the region's median.
- Group B comprised countries that in 1970 had income per capita below the region's median.

The 1970 income level of Latin American countries within each of these groups defined two income per capita ranges for the selection of comparator countries. Comparator countries that satisfied this criterion were divided into three groups in the following manner:

- Group + comprised countries that in 1970 had income per capita within the Latin American income range but in 2003 had surpassed the Latin American range for that year.
- Group = comprised countries that in both 1970 and 2003 had income per capita within the Latin American income range.
- Group – comprised countries that in 1970 had income per capita within the Latin American income range but in 2003 had income below the Latin American range for that year.

Transition and oil-driven economies were excluded from the comparator sample of countries. Annex table 1.A.1 shows the final list of comparator countries. The actual countries included in the empirical analysis vary by exercise, depending on the countries for which reliable data are available. Annex table 1.A.2 further shows the growth performance of individual countries in Latin America and the Caribbean from 1970 to 2004.

Table 1.A.1 Sample of Comparator Countries

Latin American and Caribbean countries	*Comparator countries* +	*Comparator countries* =	*Comparator countries* –
Group A	*Group A+*	*Group A=*	*Group A–*
Argentina	Cyprus	South Africa	
Barbados	Greece		
Brazil	Malta		
Chile	Portugal		
Costa Rica	Singapore		
Cuba	Spain		
Jamaica			
Mexico			
Panama			
Trinidad and Tobago			
Uruguay			
Venezuela, R.B. de			
Group B	*Group B+*	*Group B=*	*Group B–*
Belize	Korea, Rep. of	Egypt, Arab Rep. of	Ghana
Bolivia	Malaysia	Fiji	Mozambique
Colombia	Mauritius	Micronesia, Federated States of	Nigeria
Dominican Republic		Morocco	Senegal
Ecuador		Samoa	Solomon Islands
El Salvador		Thailand	Zambia
Guatemala		Tunisia	Zimbabwe
Honduras		Turkey	
Nicaragua			
Paraguay			
Peru			

Source: UNSD.

Table 1.A.2 Growth Performance of Individual Countries in Latin America and the Caribbean, 1970–2004

	Annualized cumulative growth of GDP per capita (%)				*Annualized cumulative growth of trend GDP per capita (%)*			
Country	*1970–79*	*1980–89*	*1990–99*	*2000–04*	*1970–79*	*1980–89*	*1990–99*	*2000–04*
Group A								
Argentina	1.0	–2.6	3.5	–3.5	0.2	–0.8	1.3	–0.6
Bahamas	0.2	1.0	–0.9	–1.0	0.4	1.1	–0.8	0.5
Brazil	5.8	0.2	1.0	0.5	4.9	0.7	0.9	0.7
Chile	0.3	1.2	5.0	2.7	–0.6	2.8	4.5	2.3
Costa Rica	3.6	–0.5	3.0	1.6	2.2	0.3	2.3	2.0
Jamaica	–1.5	1.0	0.6	1.0	–2.3	0.5	1.0	0.3
Mexico	3.3	–0.7	1.3	0.1	3.5	0.2	1.1	1.3
Panama	1.8	–0.3	3.5	1.3	2.4	1.4	2.4	1.8
Uruguay	2.3	–0.2	2.9	–1.0	2.1	1.2	1.7	–0.9
Venezuela, R.B. de	1.3	–2.5	–0.3	–6.5	0.5	–1.2	–0.7	–2.6
Average A	1.8	–0.3	2.0	–0.5	1.3	0.6	1.4	0.5
Group B								
Bolivia	2.0	–2.3	1.4	0.4	0.8	–1.6	1.2	0.5

(continued)

Table 1.A.2 Growth Performance of Individual Countries in Latin America and the Caribbean, 1970–2004 *(continued)*

	Annualized cumulative growth of GDP per capita (%)				*Annualized cumulative growth of trend GDP per capita (%)*			
Country	*1970–79*	*1980–89*	*1990–99*	*2000–04*	*1970–79*	*1980–89*	*1990–99*	*2000–04*
Colombia	3.2	1.2	1.0	0.9	2.8	1.7	1.3	–0.1
Dominican Republic	4.3	1.0	4.5	0.8	3.9	0.9	3.6	2.9
Ecuador	6.2	–0.6	0.0	1.9	5.6	0.1	0.3	0.1
El Salvador	2.1	–1.4	2.7	0.1	0.1	–0.5	2.0	0.8
Guatemala	3.1	–1.9	1.4	–0.4	2.2	–0.9	1.1	0.5
Honduras	2.6	–0.5	0.2	1.1	2.1	–0.1	0.3	0.4
Nicaragua	–3.2	–4.0	1.0	0.5	–2.1	–4.7	0.1	1.5
Paraguay	5.5	0.0	–0.5	–1.2	6.2	0.8	–0.4	–1.5
Peru	0.9	–2.9	2.2	1.4	0.6	–1.9	0.8	1.3
Average B	2.7	–1.1	1.4	0.5	2.2	–0.6	1.0	0.6

Sources: UNSD; UNPD; United Nations Department of Economic and Social Affairs 2006.

Note: GDP per capita is at constant 1990 prices in U.S. dollars. The trended GDP per capita series was smoothed by application of a Hodrick-Prescott filter. For Argentina, Ecuador, Guatemala, Peru, and the República Bolivariana de Venezuela, the fourth column of each variable covers 2000–03.

Annex 1.B: Selection of Analysis Time Frame

Most of the analysis in this chapter focuses on the period from 1990 to 2004. Because 2004 was the latest year for which substantial data were available for the sample of countries used in the analysis, it was chosen as the ending year. There are, however, some exceptions to this time frame. In some countries, reliable data were not available for some particular years, so some adjustments were made to the period studied. The following are exceptions to the 1990–2004 rule:

- 1989–2004: Panama
- 1990–2001: Nicaragua
- 1990–2003: Argentina, Ecuador, Guatemala, Peru, and the República Bolivariana de Venezuela
- 1991–2002: Trinidad and Tobago
- 1991–2003: Honduras and Uruguay
- 1991–2004: Colombia, the Dominican Republic, and Paraguay.

For the countries for which a sufficiently long data series was unavailable, the endpoint years for the period of analysis were chosen so as to try to minimize the effect of the business cycle. For most countries, this procedure was not necessary given that a Hodrick-Prescott filter was applied precisely to smooth the effects of the business cycle. The utility of this method, however, is limited when the data series is too short. Therefore, the endpoint years for the period of analysis were explicitly chosen in the case of Costa Rica (1990–2004), Dominican Republic (1991–2004), Honduras (1991–2003), and Uruguay (1991–2003). For all these countries, the available data series were shorter than 20 years.

Annex 1.C: Labor Input Growth Adjusted for Different Levels of Education

An education-adjusted measure of labor growth was constructed by computing labor input as a weighted sum of workers with different characteristics. Workers were weighted according to their marginal productivity, which was proxied with a measure of wages at each education level. The use of wages as a proxy for labor productivity relies on the strong assumption that firms operate under constant returns to scale in competitive input and product markets. BLS (1993) provides a discussion of deviations from this hypothesis.

The difference between the weighted and unweighted labor input yields the following index for the compositional change of labor input (the quality of labor):

$$\Delta cl = \Delta l(adj) - \Delta n, \tag{1.C.1}$$

where cl = labor composition (that is, the effect of changing labor quality on total labor input); n = the logarithm of the unweighted measure of employment; and $l(adj)$ = the logarithm of the weighted measure of labor input that controls for changes in the quality of the workforce over time:

$$\Delta l(adj) = \sum_j \bar{v}_{j,t} \cdot \Delta n_{j,t}, \tag{1.C.2}$$

$$\text{where} \quad \bar{v}_{j,t} = \frac{1}{2}\left(v_{j,t} + v_{j,t-1}\right) \text{ and } v_{j,t} = \frac{\frac{w_{j,t}}{w_{pi,t}} N_{j,t}}{\sum_{i=1}^{4} \frac{w_{i,t}}{w_{pi,t}} N_{i,c}}.$$

In equation 1.C.2,

- j is an index of the category of workers. There are four categories according to the maximum level of education completed: incomplete primary (base category), complete primary, complete secondary, and complete tertiary. These categories were constructed using the database of Barro and Lee (2000).
- n_j is the level of employment for each category j. The aggregate level of employment, obtained by adding the employment for each category, was rescaled using the employment series of the Overview. These series were smoothed by application of a Hodrick-Prescott filter.
- The wage rate of each educational category was computed relative to the wages of workers in the incomplete primary category (w_{pi}). These relative wages were constructed using the scaled coefficients of education level from a Mincer equation estimated by CEDLAS.

Equation (1.C.1) can be rearranged as follows to yield a decomposition of the overall growth of labor into the unweighted employment growth and the labor composition growth:

$$\Delta l(adj) = \Delta n + \Delta cl \tag{1.C.3}$$

Table 1.4 shows the results of this decomposition.

Annex 1.D: Estimation of Employment and Real Wage Elasticities

The model for the relationship of employment and output was inspired by the simplest specification proposed by Gordon (1993). The dependent variable in the model is the first difference of the logarithm of employment to its short-run trend. This independent variable is regressed on a term constructed by lagging the dependent variable, the first difference of deviations of the log of output from its trend, and an equilibrium correction term.

The model takes this form:

$$(\Delta\ln - \Delta\ln N^{*})_t = c + \beta_1 (\Delta\ln - \Delta\ln N^{*})_{t-1} + \beta_2 (\Delta\ln Q - \Delta\ln Q^{*})_t + EC_{t-1} + \mu, \qquad (1.D.1)$$

where N = employment; Q = output; $EC_t = (\ln N - \ln N^{*})_t - K(\ln Q - \ln Q^{*})_t$ (error correction term); μ = error term; and J^{*} $(J: N, Q)$ = trend of variable J, obtained using a Hodrick-Prescott filter. The ratio $\beta_2/(1 - \beta_1)$ reflects the short-term elasticity of employment deviations to output deviations.

Annex table 1.D.1 presents the results of estimating model 1.D.1 separately on a sample of observations from Latin America and another sample from OECD countries, all in the period between 1980 and 2004.

The evidence in annex table 1.D.1 suggests that the sensitivity of employment to output variability is smaller in Latin America than in developed countries. These results seem to be robust to model specification. Two additional models were estimated to support these results. Equation 1.D.2 regresses the first difference of employment on the first difference of output, and equation 1.D.3 is an Okun regression:

$$\Delta\ln N = c + \beta_1 \Delta\ln Q + \mu \qquad (1.D.2)$$

$$(\Delta\ln N - \Delta\ln N^{*})_t = c + \beta_1(\Delta\ln Q - \Delta\ln Q^{*})_t + \mu \qquad (1.D.3)$$

The results of this exercise are similar to those stemming from Gordon's (1993) model in the implied difference of elasticities across samples. Within each sample, however, there is a difference in the ranking of countries according to their elasticities.

The three regressions estimated here present an inherent weakness in that they do not take into account possible structural breaks that may have occurred in the period analyzed.

A Dickey-Fuller test with two lags—with and without a trend—found that all variables are integrated to the first order. In addition, employment was found to be cointegrated with output in all countries of the sample.

Table 1.D.1 Output Elasticity of Employment

	Argentina	*Brazil*	*Chile*	*Colombia*	*Guatemala*	*Mexico*	*Venezuela, R.B. de*
L.(D.lnEmp – D.lnEmp*)	−0.118	−0.392	−0.498	−0.052	−0.152	−0.164	−0.328
	(0.64)	(1.81)*	(3.09)***	(0.28)	(0.88)	(1.18)	(1.41)
(D.lnGDP – D.lnGDP*)	0.272	0.172	0.658	0.67	0.653	0.413	0.222
	(4.01)***	(1.76)*	(4.81)***	(1.84)*	(3.54)***	(5.90)***	(2.57)**
L. equilibrium correction	−0.597	−0.473	−0.47	−0.444	−0.481	−0.761	−0.744
	(3.08)***	(2.12)**	(2.37)**	(2.89)***	(2.43)**	(4.54)***	(2.29)**
Number of observations	22	22	22	22	22	23	22
R-squared	0.64	0.33	0.64	0.38	0.51	0.71	0.44
beta2/(1 – beta1)	**0.243**	**0.124**	**0.439**	**0.637**	**0.567**	**0.355**	**0.167**
	Finland	*France*	*Italy*	*Japan*	*Spain*	*United Kingdom*	*United States*
L.(D.lnEmp – D.lnEmp*)	0.334	0.312	0.340	0.164	0.099	−0.494	0.231
	(2.23)**	(2.74)**	(2.06)*	(0.75)	(1.38)	(1.96)*	(2.66)**

(continued)

Table 1.D.1 Output Elasticity of Employment *(continued)*

	Finland	*France*	*Italy*	*Japan*	*Spain*	*United Kingdom*	*United States*
(D.lnGDP – D.lnGDP*)	0.633 (7.61)***	0.535 (7.11)***	0.329 (2.66)**	0.222 (3.30)***	1.412 (12.81)***	0.431 (3.76)***	0.531 (11.45)***
L. equilibrium correction	–0.272 (1.21)	–0.330 (1.64)	–0.346 (2.63)**	–0.366 (1.77)*	–0.444 (3.32)***	-1.297 (3.87)***	–0.198 (1.11)
Number of observations	23	23	23	23	23	23	23
R-squared	0.85	0.82	0.65	0.58	0.94	0.82	0.89
beta2/(1 – beta1)	**0.950**	**0.778**	**0.498**	**0.266**	**1.567**	**0.288**	**0.691**

Source: Authors' calculations.

Note: * = significant at the 10 percent level; ** = significant at the 5 percent level; *** = significant at the 1 percent level. Absolute values of *t*–statistics are in parentheses.

For a sample of Latin American countries, the response of wages to output was estimated in a similar manner as for employment. The only difference in these regressions is that the equilibrium correction term in wage model was lagged two periods rather than one. The intention of this practice is to account for rigidities in the response of wages to output deviations that may occur because of institutional characteristics that limit the speed of adjustment, such as collective bargaining of salaries.[14] Annex table 1.D.2 shows real wage elasticities for number of Latin American countries estimated using model 1.D.1.

As a way of comparison, annex table 1.D.3 reports the output elasticities of employment and real wages estimated by González Anaya (2002) and IDB (2003) for similar, though not identical, time frames.

Data sources for this exercise are as follows:

- Employment (N):
  - *Argentina.* Urban participation and employment rates (1980–2003) from the National Institute of Statistics and Censuses (Instituto Nacional de Estadísticas y Censos) were applied to the national working-age population (10 years and older) from United Nations Economic Commission for Latin America and the Caribbean (ECLAC).
  - *Brazil.* Data were from the Monthly Job Inquiry (Pesquisa Mensal de Emprego) of the Brazilian Institute of Geography and Statistics (Instituto Brasileiro de Geografia e Estatística).
  - *Chile, Colombia, Guatemala, Mexico, and the República Bolivariana de Venezuela.* Data for the period from 1980 to 2000 were kindly provided by Ugo Panizza (used in Loboguerrero and Panizza 2003) and were originally from the International Labour Organization. The authors of this study updated this series through 2003 or 2004 using the same source.
  - *OECD countries.* Data are from the GGDC TED, August 2005.

- Real output (Q):
  - *Argentina and Brazil.* Data are from the UNSD.
  - *Chile, Colombia, Guatemala, Mexico and Venezuela.* Data are from the International Monetary Fund's World Economic Outlook Database.
  - *OECD countries.* Data are from the GGDC TED, August 2005.

- Real wage index:
  - *General.* An index of wages in manufacturing deflated by the consumer price index was provided by Ugo Panizza.
  - Argentina and Colombia. Data are from ECLAC.
  - Chile, Costa Rica, Guatemala, Mexico, Uruguay, and the República Bolivariana de Venezuela. ILO data for wages in the manufacturing sector were used.

Table 1.D.2 Output Elasticity of Real Wages

	Argentina	*Chile*	*Colombia*	*Costa Rica*	*Guatemala*	*Mexico*	*Uruguay*	*Venezuela, R.B. de*
L.(D.lnW – D.lnW*)	–0.231 (1.96)*	0.006 (2.01)*	–0.543 (1.99)*	–0.196 (1.17)	–0.300 (1.25)	–0.347 (2.17)**	–0.060 (0.23)	–0.301 (1.06)
(D.lnGDP – D.lnGDP*)	0.852 (2.64)**	0.415 (2.88)**	0.083 (0.29)	1.316 (2.49)**	1.171 (0.53)	1.788 (3.04)***	0.842 (2.78)**	0.538 (1.97)*
L2. Equi. Corr.	–0.714 (3.03)***	–0.367 (1.23)	–0.587 (2.16)**	–0.548 (2.72)**	–0.699 (2.99)***	–0.362 (0.95)	–0.36 (0.95)	–0.557 (1.92)*
Number or observations	19	19	19	19	19	19	19	19
R-squared	0.51	0.38	0.27	0.52	0.38	0.48	0.37	0.33
beta2/(1-beta1)	**0.69**	**0.42**	**0.05**	**1.10**	**0.90**	**1.33**	**0.79**	**0.41**

Source: Authors' calculations.

Note: * = significant at the 10 percent level; ** = significant at the 5 percent level; *** = significant at the 1 percent level. Absolute values of *t*–statistics are in parentheses.

Table 1.D.3 Other Estimations of Output Elasticities of Employment and Real Wages

	Employment		*Wages*	
	González Anaya (2002)	*IDB (2003)*	*González Anaya (2002)*	*IDB (2003)*
Argentina	0.17	0.18	0.84	0.91
Brazil	0.18	0.16	1.15	1.08
Chile	0.36	0.33	0.68	0.10
Colombia	0.52	0.61	0.9	-0.05
Costa Rica	0.22	0.09	0.7	1.48
Mexico	0.12	0.19	2.29	1.42
Uruguay	0.29	0.28	0.91	0.82
Venezuela, R.B. de	0.32	0.29	1.21	0.63

Sources: González Anaya 2002; IDB 2003.

Notes

1. The CEDLAS database is available at http://www.depeco.econo.unlp.edu.ar/cedlas/sedlac/default.html, and the IDB database is available at http://www.iadb.org/res/sociometro.cfm.

2. Two notable exceptions are Colombia and Paraguay, where income per capita growth rates, although positive, declined consistently from the 1970s onward.

3. The definition of WAP varies by country. The calculations in this chapter are based on the criteria set by the source of each country's employment data. Accordingly, WAP covers people who are 10 years old or over in Argentina, Bolivia, Brazil, the Dominican Republic, El Salvador, Honduras, Nicaragua, and Paraguay; people who are 12 years old or over in Colombia and Costa Rica; people who are 14 years old or over in Mexico and Uruguay; people who are 15 years old or over in Chile, Panama, and the República Bolivariana de Venezuela; and people who are between 15 and 64 years old in Ecuador, Guatemala, and Peru.

4. Furthermore, in countries such as Brazil, Chile, Guatemala, Jamaica, and Nicaragua, the rate of employment rate growth declined markedly in the 1990s and early 2000s relative to the 1980s. The unusual case of Argentina is worth noting. This country experienced an average drop in employment rate both during the 1980s and from 1990 to 2004.

5. Additionally, the simple correlation coefficient between income per capita and the ratio of WAP growth is 0.32.

6. The EU15 are the 15 countries that comprised the European Union before May 1, 2004.

7. In the case of Brazil, if not for the change in the skill composition of employment, labor productivity would actually have dropped, possibly a reflection of successful government efforts since 1980 to increase enrollment in primary and secondary education.

8. The Southern Cone is composed of Argentina, Chile, Paraguay, and Uruguay. Employment data for Uruguay cover only urban areas. A Hodrick-Prescott filter was applied to smooth the employment series.

9. The analysis of employment and real wage elasticities was limited by the range and frequency of the available data. Only a few reliable observations could be collected for each country, covering a period of time that is at most 24 years long—20 years in the case of real wages. Consequently, the relative significance of employment and wage elasticities cannot be compared across decades, for example, nor can whether such elasticities vary in different parts of the business cycle be examined. See annex 1.D for an explanation of these calculations.

10. IDB (2007) examines the reasons behind the rise in low-wage employment and documents that increasing unemployment, mediocre economic growth, and rising demand for education, prompted by increasing imports of capital goods and technology, all contribute to increasing the share of low-wage employment. In comparison, the effects of the increasing participation of women in the labor force or the changing structure of employment are small, and in some instances, such as the declining share of agriculture, they have gone in the direction of reducing low-wage work.

11. The definition proposed by the 1993 International Conference of Labor Statisticians (ICLS) is that the informal sector comprises nonprofessional self-employed activities and employees or owners of microenterprises (defined as firms with fewer than 5 or 10 workers). The definition allows flexibility in the inclusion or exclusion of professional self-employed, domestic help, and unpaid workers as part of the informal sector. In 2003, the ICLS proposed a new definition under which informal workers would be those under the 1993 definition plus employees holding informal jobs—that is, all those forms of employment relationships that in law or in practice are not subject to national labor legislation, income taxation, social protection, or entitlement to certain employment benefits.

12. If countries were in full employment, economic growth would not necessarily lead to increases in employment rates but rather to higher wages. Yet given the relatively low employment rates of women in Latin America, there is still room for higher employment rates.

13. Although this text referred to these countries as "jobless growth countries," technically this adjective should apply only to Chile; the rest of the countries suffered from low economic growth, which implied that only sluggish job creation could be expected.

14. See Forslund, Gottfries, and Westermark (2005) for empirical methodologies that are used to estimate wage adjustment.

References

Barro, R. J., and J. Lee. 2000. "International Data on Educational Attainment: Updates and Implications." NBER Working Paper 7911, National Bureau of Economic Research, Cambridge, MA.

BLS (Bureau of Labor Statistics). 1993. *Labor Composition and U.S. Productivity Growth, 1948–90.* Bulletin 2426, Bureau of Labor Statistics, U.S. Department of Labor, Washington, DC.

Duryea, S., and C. Pagés. 2003. "What Human Capital Policies Can and Cannot Do for Productivity and Poverty Reduction in Latin America." In *Latin American*

Democracies in the New Global Economy, ed. Ana Margheritis, 145–72. Coral Gables, FL: North-South Center Press.

Forslund, A., N. Gottfries, and A. Westermark. 2005. "Real and Nominal Wage Adjustment in Open Economies." Working Paper 18, Uppsala University, Uppsala, Sweden.

González Anaya, J. 2002. "Labor Market Flexibility in Thirteen Latin American Countries and the United States: Revisiting and Expanding Okun Coefficients." Working Paper 136, Center for Research on Economic Development and Policy Reform, Stanford University, Palo Alto, CA.

Gordon, R. J. 1993. "The Jobless Recovery: Does It Signal a New Era of Productivity-Led Growth?" *Brooking Papers on Economic Activity* 24 (1): 271–316.

IDB (Inter-American Development Bank). 2003. *Good Jobs Wanted: Labor Markets in Latin America—2004 Report on Economic and Social Progress in Latin America*. Washington, DC: IDB.

———. 2007. *Outsiders? The Changing Patterns of Exclusion in Latin America and the Caribbean*. Washington, DC: IDB.

Loboguerrero, A. M., and U. Panizza. 2003. "Inflation and Labor Market Flexibility: The Squeaky Wheel Gets the Grease." Research Department Working Paper 495, Inter-American Development Bank, Washington, DC.

Madrigal, L., and C. Pagés. 2008a. "The Quality of Jobs in Latin America." Background report prepared for *Beyond Facts: Understanding Quality of Life*, Inter-American Development Bank, Washington, DC.

———. 2008b. "Does Informality Reflect Job Quality? Evidence from Job Satisfaction." IDB Research Working Paper 654, Inter-American Development Bank, Washington, DC.

Majid, N. 2001. "Economic Growth, Social Policy, and Decent Work." Employment Paper 2001/19, International Labour Office, Geneva.

Perry, G., W. Maloney, O. Arias, P. Fajnzylber, A. Mason, and J. Saavedra-Chanduvi, eds. 2007. *Informality: Exit and Exclusion*. Washington, DC: World Bank.

United Nations Department of Economic and Social Affairs. 2006. *World Population Prospects: The 2004 Revision*. New York: United Nations.

World Bank. 2005. *World Development Indicators 2005*. Washington, DC: World Bank.

World Commission on the Social Dimension of Globalization. 2004. *A Fair Globalization: Creating Opportunities for All*. Geneva: International Labour Office.

2

Skills, Gender, and Age Dimensions of Job Creation

Chapter 1 documented how the 1990s and early 2000s have been a period of high employment but low labor productivity growth in many countries. As a result, many individuals are working—but in low-quality, low-earnings jobs. Nevertheless, many other workers found themselves unemployed, because in a number of countries, job creation was not enough to absorb all those who wanted a job. This chapter assesses how different types of individuals fared in the labor market. This analysis is important both to evaluate the welfare consequences of some labor market aggregates and to obtain further understanding of the causes of the observed aggregated trends. In particular, this chapter assesses (a) the growing importance of skill in determining how workers fare in the labor market, (b) the differential performance of women and men, and (c) the problems for youths in finding good-quality jobs.

Improving the employment opportunities of unskilled women and youth workers is crucial for the welfare of society as a whole. The earnings of the unskilled, as well as the earnings and job opportunities of women, are key determinants of poverty rates. At the same time, the lack of employment opportunities for youths increases the occurrence of crime, violence, and other difficult social problems.

Declining Demand for Unskilled Labor

A rapidly expanding literature has documented an increase in the returns to education during the 1990s in Latin America and the Caribbean (see, for instance, De Ferranti and others 2003, IDB 2003, and the references within). Wages of workers with higher levels of education (tertiary) increased at a faster rate than those of workers with secondary education (figure 2.1)

Figure 2.1 Average Annual Percentage Change in Hourly Nominal Wages by Educational Level, Early 1990s to Mid 2000s

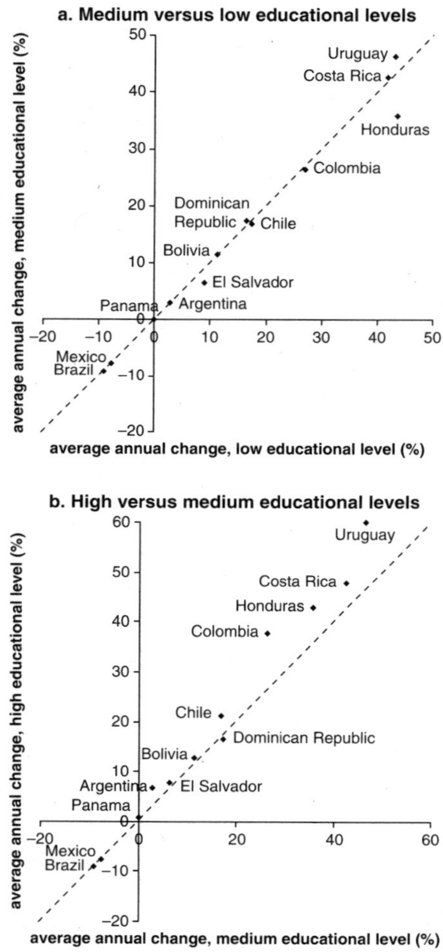

Source: Socio-Economic Database for Latin America and the Caribbean (SEDLAC).

Note: Educational levels: low = 0 to 8 years of formal education, medium = 9 to 13 years, and high = more than 13 years. Hourly wages refer to the main activity and are expressed in nominal local currency units. The figure applies to the population of adults from 25 to 64 years of age. For the selection of periods for each country, see annex table 2.A.1.

despite the relative growth in the supply of workers with tertiary education.[1] At the same time, consistent with a rising demand for skill, the relative wages of workers with secondary education remained constant compared with the wages of workers with primary education, even though the growth of population with secondary education outpaced the growth of population with only primary education. Most studies attribute these findings to an increase in the demand for skilled labor propelled by skill-biased technological change. However, there is an ongoing discussion regarding the extent to which such trends may also be related to increasing trade openness.

The increasing demand for skill is not driven by the reallocation of employment across sectors—as would be the case if changes in the demand for skill were due to trade—but rather to an increase in the demand for skilled labor within each sector (De Ferranti and others 2003; Pavcnik and others 2003; Sánchez-Páramo and Schady 2002). Even if trade cannot directly explain the observed patterns in skill demand, however, a number of studies have found an indirect association between trade and the increasing demand for skill. Industries that are more exposed to foreign competition underwent a faster process of retooling and a much more intense skill-biased technological change.

Adaptation to the Need for Skilled Labor

Labor markets in the region have adapted to changes in the demand for skill—mostly through prices—with little evidence that the employment rates of the less skilled have fallen relative to the supply of unskilled labor. In that sense, little evidence exists of "employment skimming"—that is, the increase of labor productivity at the expense of job opportunities for unskilled workers. Instead, in most countries the upgrading of employment is in line with the changes in the supply of skills. Only in Argentina, Brazil, and Costa Rica did the participation of workers with tertiary education increase faster in employment than in the working-age population (figure 2.2). This finding suggests that, with few exceptions, relative wages have been flexible enough to bring labor demand in line with the supply of skills. This experience contrasts with the experience of many countries of the Organisation for Economic Co-operation and Development (OECD), particularly in continental Europe, where job creation was skewed toward the highly skilled, and many low-skill workers were trapped in unemployment or inactivity (Scarpetta and others 2000). The higher incidence of informal activities, coupled with the more limited coverage of safety nets in Latin America and the Caribbean than in OECD countries, may explain why relative wages adjusted more and why employment rates of the less skilled kept in line with supply in most Latin American and Caribbean countries.

Figure 2.2 Change in the Participation in Employment and Working-Age Population of Population with Tertiary Education

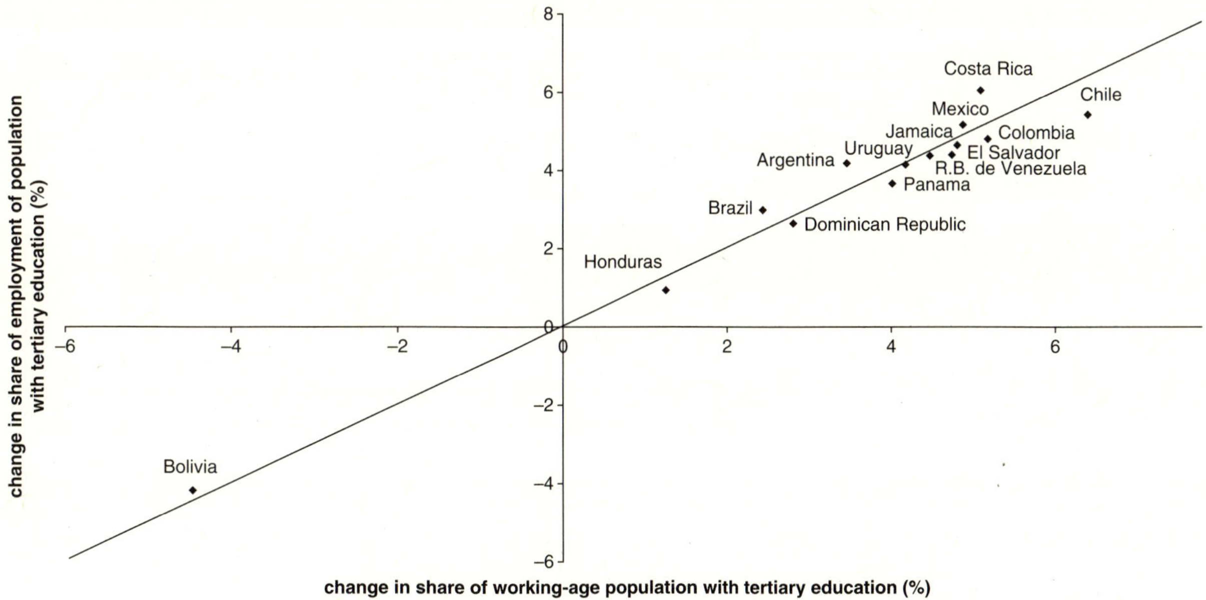

Source: SEDLAC.
Note: For the selection of periods for each country, see annex table 2.A.1.

Deterioration of Working Conditions—Especially for Medium-Skill Workers

In most countries, the proportion of workers with low and medium levels of education holding informal jobs (defined as employees in small firms, nonprofessional self-employed workers, and zero-income workers) increased since 1990 (figure 2.3). In a number of countries, the proportion of workers in informal jobs also increased for workers with tertiary education, but the increase was larger for workers with intermediate levels of education.

The share of workers holding informal jobs may not provide an accurate assessment of the quality of jobs, because for many workers, being self-employed—and in some cases being employed in micro firms—may be choices that provide the best returns given workers' endowments and characteristics (see Perry and others 2007). Thus, another useful, although again incomplete measure of working conditions, is the percentage of salaried workers who are affiliated to the social security system. Although this information is available for only a limited number of countries, the data indicate that the percentage of salaried workers not affiliated to social security increased for all skill levels in all countries, with the exception of El Salvador (figure 2.4). The data also show a larger increase for workers with intermediate levels of education compared with those with higher or lower educational attainment.

Many Workers with Tertiary Education Lack the Appropriate Skills

Some evidence indicates that in a number of countries employers are becoming more selective when recruiting high-skill workers. Despite the rising demand for skilled labor, the unemployment rates of workers with tertiary education (completed or uncompleted) have increased more, in percentage terms, than those of workers with primary or secondary education. The only exceptions to this trend are Argentina, Costa Rica, and Mexico, where the unemployment rates of less skilled workers have increased at a faster pace than those of skilled labor (figure 2.5). Although this trend could also be driven by the fact that when all unemployment rates are up, unemployment is likely to increase more, in percentage terms, for those with lower starting unemployment rates, there are other indications of increasing selection at the top.

Thus, in some countries—most notably in Argentina, Colombia, and Nicaragua, but also in Costa Rica and Mexico—wage inequality among workers with some tertiary education has increased at a faster pace than among workers with secondary or primary education (table 2.1). This finding indicates that, far from being ubiquitous, changes in wages are

Figure 2.3 Average Annual Percentage Change in Share of Adults in Informal Jobs, by Educational Level, Early 1990s to Mid 2000s

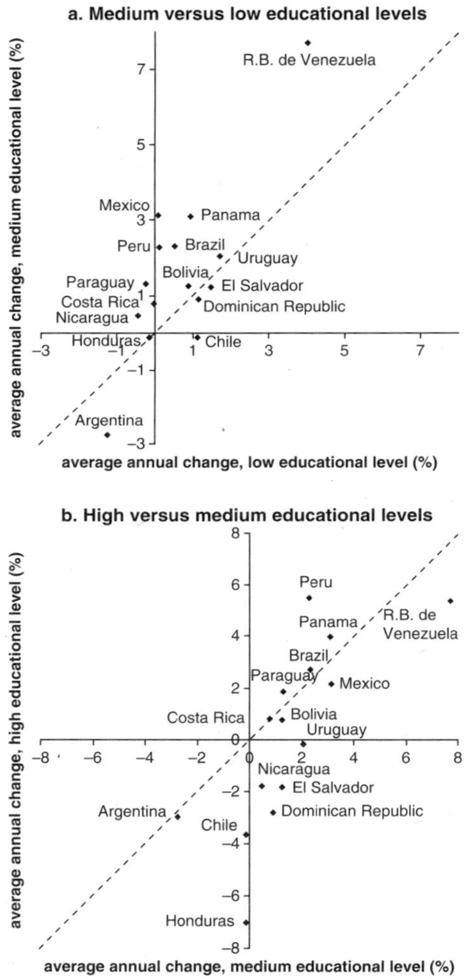

Source: SEDLAC.

Note: Adults workers are between 25 and 65 years of age. *Informal employment* refers to salaried workers in small firms, nonprofessional self-employed workers, and zero-income workers. For the selection of periods for each country, see annex table 2.A.1.

Figure 2.4 Average Annual Percentage Change in Share of Salaried Adult Workers Not Covered by Social Security, by Educational Level, Early 1990s to Mid 2000s

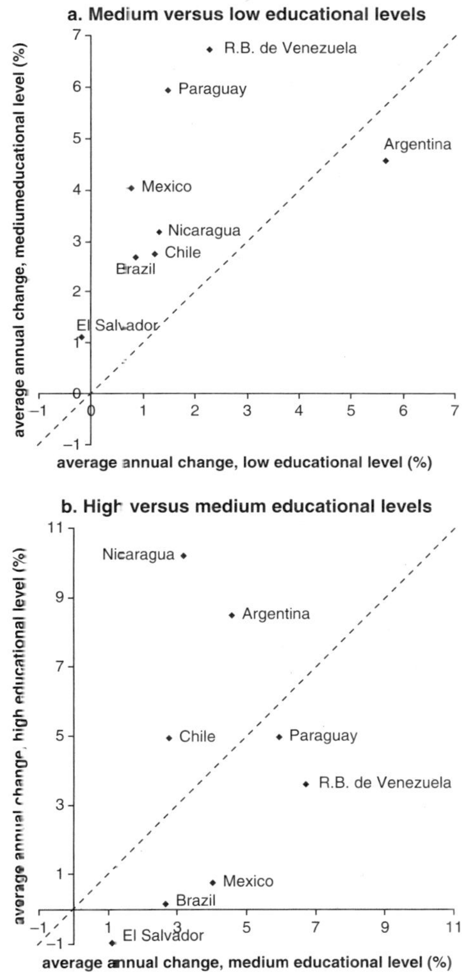

Source: SEDLAC.

Note: Adults workers are between 25 and 65 years of age. For the selection of periods for each country, see annex table 2.A.1.

Figure 2.5 Average Annual Percentage Change in the Unemployment Rate of Skilled versus Less Skilled Adult Workers

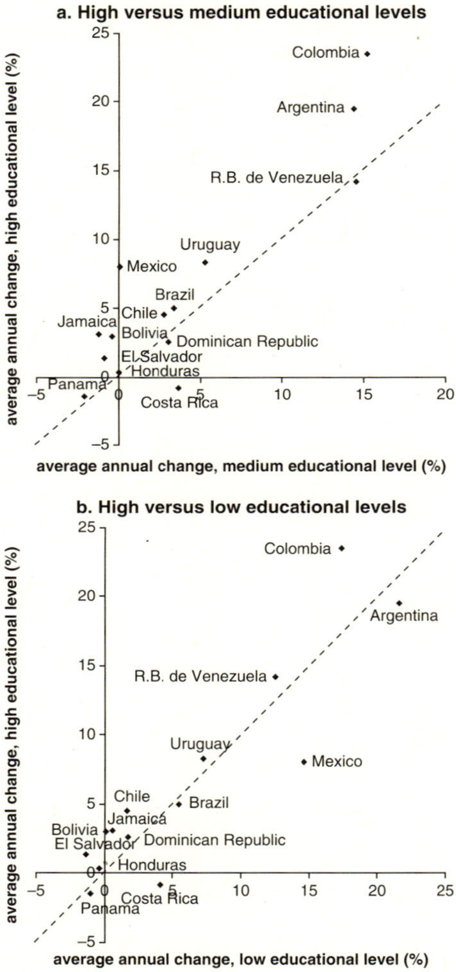

Source: SEDLAC.

Note: Adults workers are between 25 and 65 years of age. For the selection of periods for each country, see annex table 2.A.1.

Table 2.1 Change in the Variance of Earnings by Skill Level

Country	*Period*	*Total*	*Completed primary education*	*Completed secondary education*	*Tertiary education (completed or uncompleted)*
Argentina	**1993–2002**	**13**	**6**	**6**	**11**
Brazil	1993–2003	–22	–18	–15	–4
Chile	1992–2003	–2	1	2	–7
Colombia	**1992–2003**	**–4**	**–17**	**3**	**17**
Costa Rica	**1990–2004**	**–4**	**–9**	**–2**	**3**
El Salvador	1995–2002	15	13	13	11
Honduras	1990–2003	32	19	41	11
Mexico	**1992–2004**	**–4**	**4**	**5**	**6**
Nicaragua	**1993–2001**	**–9**	**–12**	**8**	**16**
Panama	1995–2003	20	24	1	7
Paraguay	1991–2003	43	5	42	33
Peru	1991–2000	66	68	34	29
Uruguay	1992–2003	8	–4	5	–2
Venezuela, R.B. de	1991–2004	13	12	10	9

Source: Authors' estimates based on household surveys.

Note: **Bold** indicates countries where earnings variation among workers with tertiary education outpaced that among other workers at other educational levels.

concentrated at the top end of the distribution of earnings for skilled labor.[2] Greater increase in wage inequality at higher education levels is compatible with a situation in which skills are becoming more valuable, but not all workers with tertiary education have skills that are equally valued in the labor market. Instead, growing differences in the quality of education across educational institutions and in the demand for graduates with different specializations or educational backgrounds are increasing the differences in earnings and employment opportunities among workers with tertiary education.[3]

Insufficient Supply of Skilled Workers

On average, Latin American firms take longer to fill a vacant skilled job than firms in the rest of the world (table 2.2). Some countries—most noticeably Brazil and Ecuador—report very significant shortages compared with those in either the rest of the world or the group of comparator countries.

Table 2.2 Skill Shortages: Time to Fill a Vacancy and Perception of Lack of Skills as an Obstacle for Growth Relative to Other Obstacles

Country (year of data)	*Median time to fill a skilled vacancy (weeks) (a)*	*Median time to fill an unskilled vacancy (weeks) (b)*	*Time to fill skilled versus unskilled vacancy (weeks) (a)/(b)*	*Average time to fill a skilled vacancy (weeks)*	*Lack of skills as an obstacle for economic growth relative to other obstacles[a] (country average)*
Peru (2002)	1.14	0.57	2.00	3.36	–0.66
Bolivia (2000)	1.43	—	—	4.98	—
Nicaragua (2003)	1.43	0.57	2.50	4.51	–0.47
Costa Rica (2005)	2.00	1.00	2.00	3.39	–0.41
Guyana (2004)	2.00	2.00	1.00	4.09	0.72
El Salvador (2003)	2.14	1.00	2.14	3.74	0.11
Honduras (2003)	2.14	0.86	2.50	4.47	–0.15
Guatemala (2003)	3.00	1.00	3.00	5.93	–0.05
Brazil (2003)	5.60	1.40	4.00	8.77	–0.13
Ecuador (2003)	7.00	2.00	3.50	14.32	–0.26
Chile	—	—	—	—	0.38
Latin America and Caribbean average	2.79	1.16	2.41	5.76	–0.09

(continued)

Table 2.2 Skill Shortages: Time to Fill a Vacancy and Perception of Lack of Skills as an Obstacle for Growth Relative to Other Obstacles *(continued)*

Country (year of data)	*Median time to fill a skilled vacancy (weeks) (a)*	*Median time to fill an unskilled vacancy (weeks) (b)*	*Time to fill skilled versus unskilled vacancy (weeks) (a)/(b)*	*Average time to fill a skilled vacancy (weeks)*	*Lack of skills as an obstacle for economic growth relative to other obstacles[a] (country average)*
Portugal (2005)	1.00	1.00	1.00	2.38	−0.09
India (2002)	2.00	1.00	2.00	3.18	−0.22
Korea, Rep. of (2005)	2.00	2.00	1.00	3.42	−0.16
Greece (2005)	2.00	1.00	2.00	2.97	0.02
Spain (2005)	2.00	1.00	2.00	2.81	0.19
China (2002)	2.00	1.00	2.00	5.22	0.32
Mauritius (2005)	2.00	1.00	2.00	4.20	0.47
World average	2.15	1.09	1.97	3.82	−0.15
Germany (2005)	3.00	2.00	1.50	3.70	0.13
Ireland (2005)	3.00	1.00	3.00	3.77	0.39
Thailand (2004)	4.00	1.00	4.00	5.92	0.61
South Africa (2003)	4.00	1.00	4.00	5.04	0.74

Source: Authors' elaboration from World Bank Investment Climate Surveys.

Note: — = not available.

a. Computed as the average of the individual deviation of each firm's response to the skill question relative to the average individual response to a number of questions regarding different obstacles for firms' operation.

Such filling times are not driven by inefficiencies in recruiting all types of workers: a comparison of the relative time to fill a skilled versus an unskilled vacancy indicates that in Latin America, the relative scarcity of skilled labor is higher as measured by the relative time to fill a vacancy in a skilled job.

Interestingly, however, these shortages in the region are not reported as important obstacles for the growth of firms (table 2.2), which may be a reflection of the many other obstacles that firms face in operating a business (chapter 5). On average, firms in the region rate a shortage of skills as an important obstacle—relative to other issues—only slightly above the world average. In addition, in many countries in the region, skill shortages are less likely to be reported as a major concern than in most comparator countries. Quite noticeably, there is very little correspondence in the region between the actual weeks to fill a vacancy and the extent by which a lack of appropriate skills is perceived to be an important obstacle relative to other issues. Brazil and Ecuador, which reported the longest time to fill a vacancy, are among the countries in which skills are seen as less of an obstacle relative to other possible obstacles, such as macroeconomic and policy instability or lack of access to capital. Instead, a much higher correspondence exists between the time to fill a vacancy and the subjective measure in the comparator countries sample.

Skill Constraints in Growing Firms and Growing Countries

A regression of individual firms' valuation of skill shortage as an obstacle for growth (compared with the average of the valuation of all other obstacles) against a number of firm and sector characteristics, as well as country and year fixed effects, indicates that, throughout the world, skill shortages are more pronounced among firms that are expanding (in terms of employment), young firms, larger firms, and firms that are partly or totally government owned, as well as firms in the production of garments and in some high-productivity services such as marketing. The analysis indicates that these patterns also hold for the Latin American and Caribbean sample. However, Latin American and Caribbean firms that are expanding employment report being relatively more constrained than similar firms in the rest of the world. This feature, combined with the fact that the perception of skill shortages as an obstacle seems to be more acute in countries such as Chile (table 2.2), which experienced strong economic growth, suggests that skill shortages pick up when firms grow and that they constitute an important obstacle when other constraints are lifted. A comparison of the perception of skill shortages in Peru in 2002, after a period of stagnant economic growth, and in 2006, after four years of high growth, indicates again that skills shortages are perceived as important constraints after growth is under way and when firms may want to upgrade their production processes (figure 2.6). Skills shortages are also more acute in the fast-growing East Asian and Pacific countries.

Figure 2.6 Skill Shortages in Peru as an Obstacle to Growth, 2002 and 2006

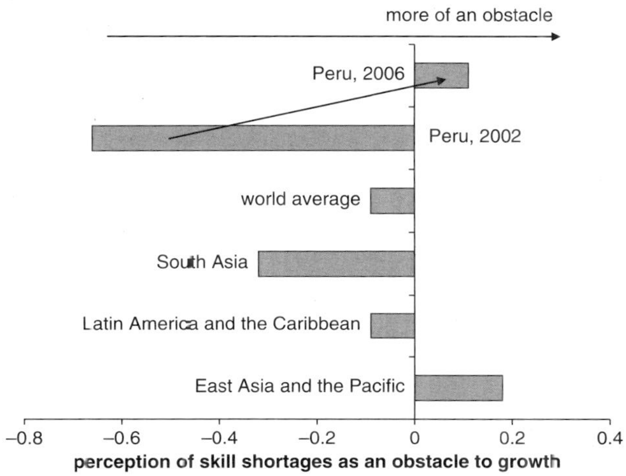

Source: World Bank Investment Climate Surveys.

Note: Units correspond to deviations of the average response of each firm to how much skill shortages are an obstacle for their growth, relative to the average response to other possible sources of obstacles to their growth. A positive number implies that skill shortages are perceived as more important than other obstacles, whereas a negative implies the opposite.

Importance of Enhancing Human Capital While Adopting Measures to Boost Productivity Growth

Advances in human capital accounted for a substantial fraction of the overall labor productivity growth of recent decades (chapter 1). However, from an international perspective, both educational improvements and productivity growth have been insufficient in the region, especially when compared with the fast-growing economies of East Asia. Therefore, simultaneous investments in skills and technology must be undertaken to allow for both higher productivity growth and a more equitable distribution of income (De Ferranti and others 2003).

Thus, the rising price of skill is increasing the already very high levels of income inequality in the region. Moreover, though a higher return to skill increases individuals' incentives to acquire higher levels of education, too many barriers to acquiring an education—particularly an education of good quality—remain. Credit constraints force many families either to withdraw their children from school too early or to put them in low-cost, but also low-quality, schools, where they acquire a degree but not necessarily useful skills. Educational policies need to address credit constraints and the low quality of education so that the historically slow progress in education can be reversed. These policies are particularly needed when a higher demand for skill goes hand in hand with a more than proportional increase in the unemployment rates and the dispersion of wages of workers with higher levels of education. This is because such factors suggest that employers are increasingly demanding real skills, rather than formal degrees.

Large Increase in Female Participation

The last decade of the 20th century has been called a remarkable decade for working women in Latin America (Duryea, Cox Edwards, and Ureta 2001). As shown in chapter 1, women's labor market participation and employment rates grew at a fast pace, often despite the low overall economic growth and, as will be shown, declining male employment rates. Although women have always played an active role in the domestic sphere, their progress in the realm of remunerated work is considered of special importance because of its potential role in raising women's welfare and empowering them as active members of society. It is therefore of particular importance to look more closely at the patterns of inclusion of women in the labor market by trying to disentangle whether these rapid changes were driven by increased economic opportunities—propelled perhaps by changing attitudes toward female work and the division of labor within households—or, rather, were driven by necessity.

Trends in Female Participation and Employment

The large increase in labor force participation rates was driven by increasing female participation, particularly of women with low educational attainment. Female participation in the region increased at a fast pace between the early 1990s and the mid 2000s in all but one country (Bolivia) for which comparable data are available (figure 2.7, panel a). In a number of them (Chile, Colombia, Costa Rica, Mexico, and the República Bolivariana de Venezuela), the rate of growth of participation was above 2 percent a year. Female employment rates show very similar patterns, with increases in all countries but Bolivia (figure 2.7, panel b). These developments contrast with a generalized decline in male participation and employment rates in nearly all countries of the region. The decline in male participation rates was more significant in Argentina, El Salvador, and Uruguay.[4] Notice that the figure refers to the participation rates of adult

Figure 2.7 Change in Participation and Employment Rates by Gender, Prime-Age Workers, Early 1990s to Mid 2000s

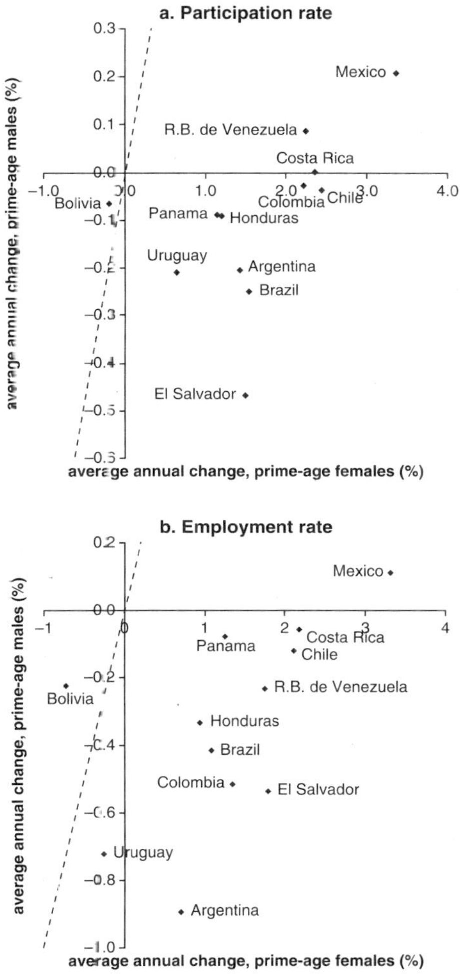

Source: Sociómetro, Research Department, Inter-American Development Bank (IDB).

Note: Prime-age population comprises people 25 to 49 years of age. For a detailed description of endpoint years used by country for this analysis, refer to annex table 2.A.1. Data for Argentina and Uruguay are urban.

workers and that therefore the decline in male participation is not due to higher enrollment of young male individuals in education.

Despite this brisk pace of change, female participation in the region remains low relative to comparator countries. Participation rates are above those registered in Middle East and North African countries or in Turkey but below the averages of North American, Western European, and East Asian countries. Bolivia, Peru, and Uruguay are the countries with the highest participation rates in Latin America and the Caribbean, with rates around 60 percent. At the opposite end, the Dominican Republic and Honduras have the lowest participation rates, oscillating around 40 percent (figure 2.8).

A look at the rate of change in female participation rates, however, indicates that the region has outperformed the growth rates in comparator countries since the early 1990s (figure 2.9). This finding suggests that Latin America and the Caribbean might be experiencing a catch-up effect in terms of female participation.

Increases in female participation and employment rates occurred across all education levels but especially among women with low levels of educational attainment. Employment increased more rapidly for women with primary education than for women with secondary education or more (figure 2.10), except in Brazil and Colombia. Other authors have confirmed these trends. For example, Abramo and Valenzuela (2005) found a larger increase in female participation at the lower end of the income distribution. They present evidence that 1990 labor force participation for low-income women was no higher than 28.7 percent, whereas that of high-income women was 50.7 percent. This gap would have closed considerably by 2000, with 39.3 percent of the low-income and 54.6 percent of the high-income women in employment. These authors also point out that raising female participation among low-income women is more difficult given their lower access to child care and greater obstacles in sharing domestic responsibilities.

Only in Chile, El Salvador, Mexico, and Peru do signs exist of substitutions of unskilled men with unskilled women. Thus, only in these four countries did a simultaneous bias exist toward unskilled labor for female work while the employment of less skilled men declined more (or increased less) than that of more skilled males. In Colombia, Nicaragua, and Uruguay, male employment was also biased toward the unskilled, whereas in Argentina, Brazil, Costa Rica, Honduras, and the República Bolivariana de Venezuela, no evidence of bias exists. Thus, overall trends were less favorable to males, but no across-the-board trends indicated which skill group suffered the highest decline within the male population.

Despite the gains in employment rates already discussed, the full extent of women's employment aspirations was not met. Female unemployment rates increased in most countries. Male unemployment rates increased as

Figure 2.8 Female Participation in Latin American and Caribbean Countries versus Comparator Countries, Mid 2000s

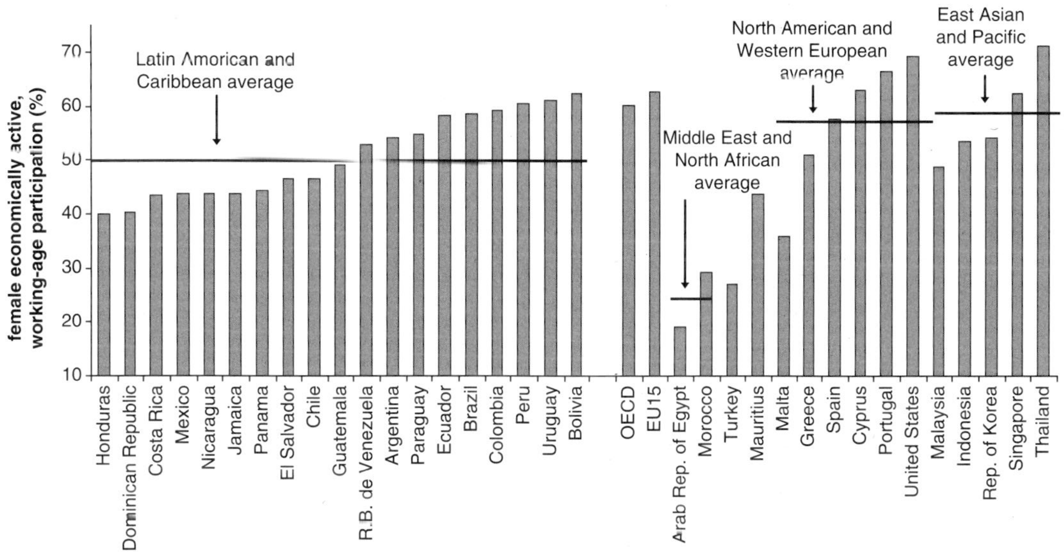

Sources: For Latin American and Caribbean participation rates, Sociómetro, Research Department, IDB; for comparator countries participation rates, International Labour Office (ILO) Bureau of Statistics LABORSTA database, United Nations Population Division (UNPD), national statistics offices, and OECD labor force surveys.

Note: EU15 = the 15 countries that comprised the European Union before May 1, 2004.

Figure 2.9 Change in Female Participation Rates: Latin America and the Caribbean Countries versus Comparator Countries, Early 1990s to Mid 2000s

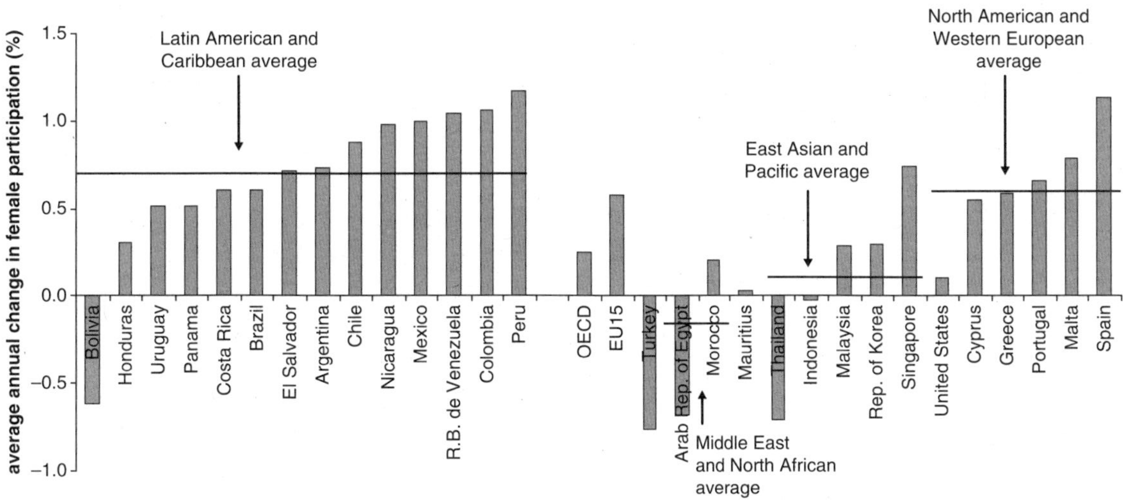

Sources: For Latin American and Caribbean participation rates, Sociómetro, Research Department, IDB; for comparator countries, participation rates were calculated by the author using data from ILO LABORSTA database, UNPD, national statistics offices, and OECD labor force surveys.

Note: EU15 = the 15 countries that comprised the European Union before May 1, 2004. For a detailed description of endpoint years used by country for this analysis, refer to annex table 2.A.1. Data for Argentina and Uruguay are urban.

Figure 2.10 Employment Rate Change, by Gender and Level of Education, Early 1990s to Mid 2000s

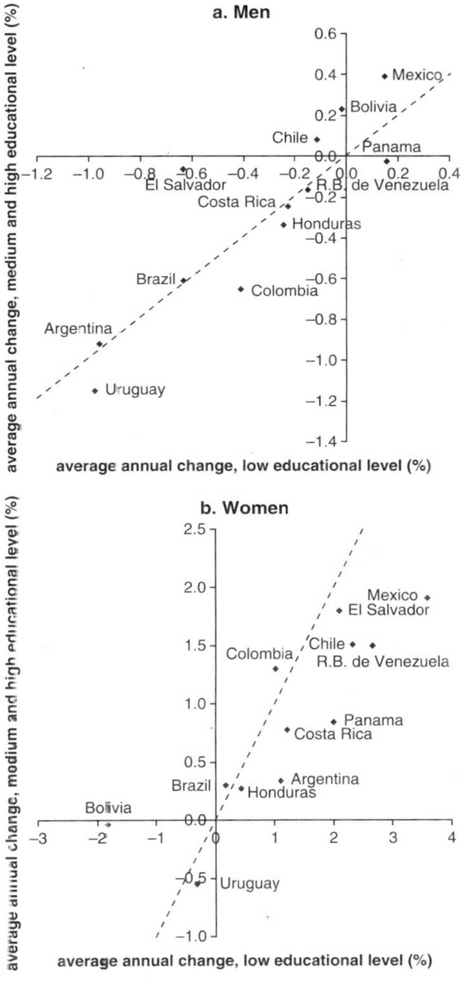

Source: Sociómetro, Research Department, IDB.

Note: Education categories are as follows: low = no schooling to complete primary education; medium = incomplete secondary education to complete secondary education; high = any postsecondary education. For a detailed description of endpoint years used by country for this analysis, refer to annex table 2.A.1. Data for Argentina and Uruguay are urban.

well, but in a majority of countries, the increase in unemployment rate was more pronounced for women (figure 2.11). However, female unemployment and male unemployment are highly correlated, suggesting that changes in both responded to the same driving factors.

Factors That Explain the Increase in Female Participation and Employment

As mentioned before, developments in female participation and employment need to be interpreted quite differently depending on the causes that drove so many women to work. From the purely economic point of view, women's participation is related to the type of jobs and the earnings women can attain in the labor market compared to the benefits of remaining outside paid work. This balancing of options explains why, on average, higher-skill women participate more in paid work. In contrast, access to income other than through women's own work reduces women's incentives to participate. So other things being constant, higher market opportunities or lower household income—for example, because

Figure 2.11 Unemployment Rate Change, by Gender, Early 1990s to Mid 2000s

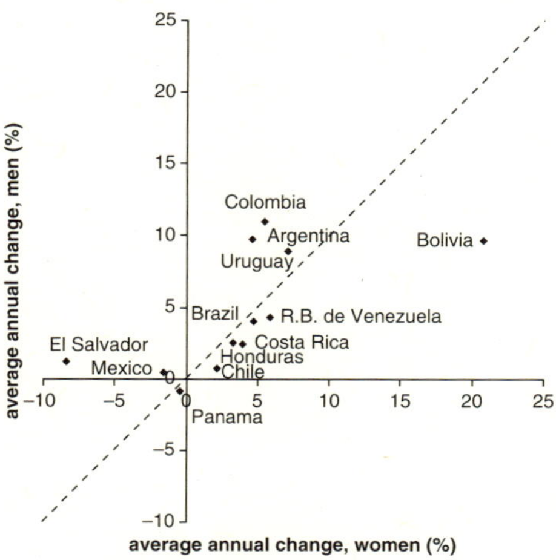

Source: Sociómetro, Research Department, IDB.
Note: For sources and end years, see annex table 2.A.1.

of low earnings or lower employment rates of other members of the household—may each trigger higher participation rates. The number and age of children also affect participation rates because these factors increase the opportunity cost of paid work. Thus, over time, factors such as increasing education and decreasing fertility rates should favor higher female participation because they increase the value of paid work relative to the value of domestic activities.

The noneconomic literature also emphasizes aspects such as new cultural conventions that favor the autonomy of women (Abramo and Valenzuela 2005) and shifting roles within the household. In addition, a changing mindset on the part of employers may have reduced the discrimination toward women at work. Macroeconomic instability has also been mentioned as a factor behind increasing female workforce participation. Cunningham (1998) finds that, in Mexico, many women entered employment during the economic crisis but also remained employed afterward. Repeated and frequent crises, as seen in Latin America, would also lead to increasing participation. The rest of this section assesses the evidence for supply and demand factors that can account for the large increase in female participation.

Supply factors. Education is an important factor in explaining participation rates. Higher education attainment increases expected wages, raising the opportunity cost of household work. Duryea, Cox Edwards, and Ureta (2001) show that schooling attainment for the female labor force increased considerably in all the Latin American countries they analyzed.[5] More recent data for a large number of countries support this finding. Thus, primary completion rates were higher for women than for men in most countries of the region by 2003 (figure 2.12, panel a). Moreover, although among the overall adult population average years of schooling are higher among males than among females in many countries (figure 2.12, panel b), the reverse is true among younger people. For example, among the population 21 to 30 years of age, in all but six countries women's average years of schooling are higher than men's.

Given the changing pattern of schooling attainment, one might expect women's education to explain a large share of the important participation rate increase shown in panel a of figure 2.7. Duryea, Cox Edwards, and Ureta (2001) assess how much of that increase can be accounted for by changes in education.[6] To do so, they decompose participation rate changes into three components: (a) changes associated with improvements in the educational attainment of the women, weighted by each group's participation rate in the early 1990s; (b) increases in participation within each education group, weighted by the initial shares of female population in each education group; and (c) an interaction term that measures whether participation increased the most for the education groups with highest growth. Their results indicate that in most countries the first component—that is,

Figure 2.12 Educational Attainment by Gender

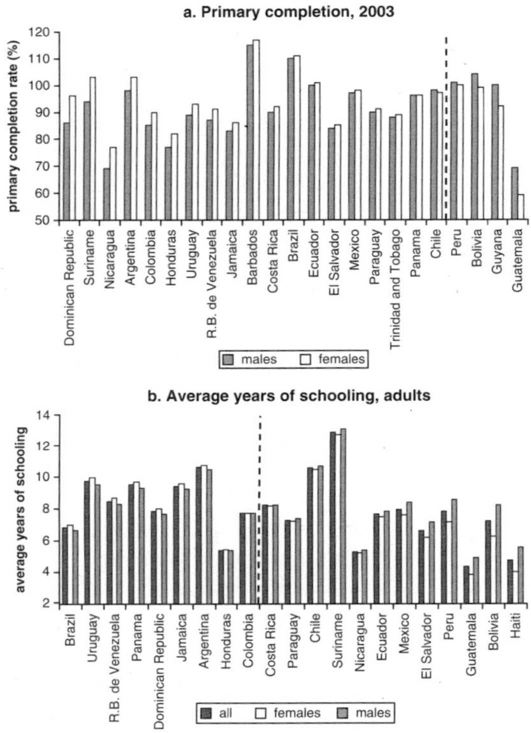

Sources: For panel a, United Nations Educational, Scientific, and Cultural Organization; for panel b, SEDLAC, based on data from household surveys.

Note: For panel a, primary completion rate is the percentage of students completing the last year of primary school. It is calculated by taking the total number of students in the last grade of primary school, minus the number of repeaters in that grade, divided by the total number of children of official graduation age. Countries are ranked according to the difference between male and female completion rates in descending order. In each panel, the vertical line represents the point where women and men have the same proportion. Data for Brazil and Suriname are for 2001; data for Honduras and Jamaica are for 2004. For panel b, *adults* refers to the population between 25 and 65 years of age. Countries are ranked according to the ratio of female to male average schooling years in descending order from left to right. Data refer to 2004–05 except for Chile (2003), Ecuador (2003), Haiti (2001), Jamaica (1999), Nicaragua (2001), Peru (2003), and Suriname (1999). Data for Argentina, Bolivia, Colombia, and Uruguay cover only urban areas.

the change in participation associated with changes in the amount of schooling—accounts for between 30 and 40 percent of the overall effect. Two notable exceptions are Panama and Uruguay, where changes in education explain more than 100 percent and about 60 percent, respectively, of the overall participation increase.

Declining fertility rates may be another important factor behind increasing participation rates. According to data from the Latin American and Caribbean Center for Demography (El Centro Latinoamericano y Caribeño de Demografía), fertility rates have declined quite rapidly. At the beginning of the 1970s, the total fertility rate[7] was above 5.0 children. By 2000, this rate had declined to 2.7, and by 2050, it is projected to drop to 1.9. Disentangling the effect of declining fertility on participation is not simple, however, because reverse causality is also at play: exogenous increases in participation reduce women's incentives to bear additional children (Goldin and Katz 2000).

In Latin America, female participation rates are higher among women who have children than among women who do not, which seems to support the need-driven hypothesis for increased female labor market entry. In the late 1990s, for the 14 countries analyzed here, the average participation rate of women in couple-headed households with children was 11 points higher than that of equivalent women without children (see table 2.3). In the case of single mothers, the difference escalates to 28 percentage points. However, although having children increases the probability of a woman's labor force participation, the amount of children seems to be negatively correlated with the probability of participation. For Latin America, the Inter-American Development Bank (IDB 1998) documents that, on average, women with five children participate about 7 percent less than women with one or two children.

Demand factors. The number and structure of jobs created are also likely to influence female participation patterns. The two most important factors examined here are the increasing shift of work toward the service sector and the shift toward low-pay and low-productivity jobs. Because women are largely overrepresented in these jobs, their expansion may have triggered an increasing demand for women, but in low-quality jobs.

Services account for a large proportion of total and new jobs for women. Female employment is highly concentrated in community, social, and personal services—more so than for males (figure 2.13). In Argentina, this sector employs 51 percent of women and only 19 percent of men (figure 2.13, panel a). In the rest of the countries—with the exception of Mexico—employment in this sector represents more than 40 percent of female employment but less than 20 percent of male employment. Another sector that employs a large number of women is the wholesale and retail trade, restaurants, and hotels sector, although for this sector the difference in employment shares for men and women is not as large as that for

Table 2.3 Urban Labor Force Participation, by Gender and Family Structure, Late 1990s

		Female participation rate (%)						*Male participation rate (%)*					
		Single-headed households			*Couple-headed households*			*Single-headed households*			*Couple-headed households*		
Country	*Year*	*With children*	*Without children*	*Difference*	*With children*	*Without children*	*Difference*	*With children*	*Without children*	*Difference*	*With children*	*Without children*	*Difference*
Argentina	1997	86	58	28	44	44	0	92	85	7	97	76	21
Bolivia	1999	94	59	35	59	53	6	97	70	27	97	77	20
Brazil	1995	70	43	27	43	33	10	80	76	4	89	68	21
Chile	1998	79	48	31	42	34	8	91	80	11	97	78	19
Colombia	1998	87	47	40	57	41	16	85	86	–1	96	75	21
Costa Rica	1995	75	47	28	36	29	7	96	77	19	97	79	18
Dominican Republic	1996	65	36	29	42	26	16	92	84	8	98	88	10
El Salvador	1997	61	53	8	60	44	16	95	85	10	96	80	16
Honduras	1998	78	58	20	50	33	17	87	90	–3	98	88	10
Mexico	1999	77	51	26	38	31	7	91	84	7	97	81	16
Nicaragua	1998	78	57	21	55	42	13	81	81	0	93	78	15
Paraguay	1999	76	52	24	55	47	8	88	84	4	96	84	12
Peru	1997	79	47	32	56	43	13	92	77	15	97	77	20
Venezuela, R.B. de	1996	83	46	37	47	34	13	93	88	5	97	82	15
Average				28			11			8			17

Source: World Bank Gender Database for Latin America and the Caribbean, based on tabulations of data from household surveys.

Figure 2.13 Distribution of Employment, by Sector and Gender

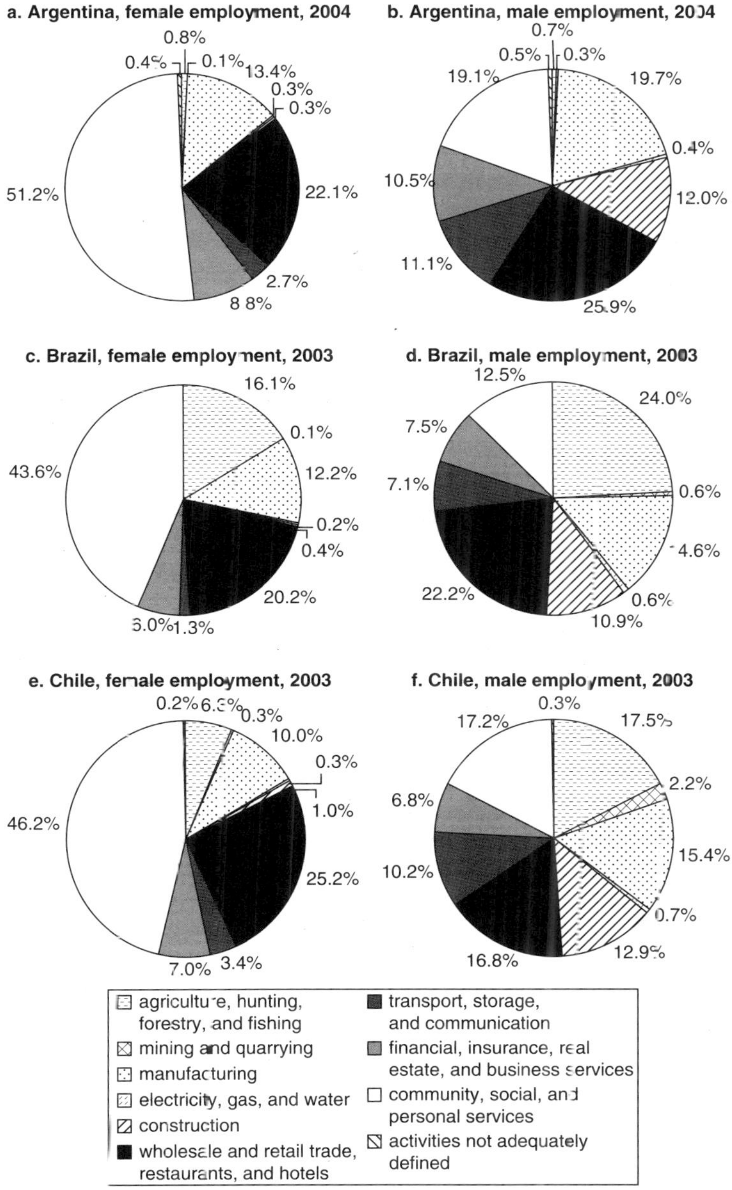

(continued)

Figure 2.13 Distribution of Employment, by Sector and Gender *(continued)*

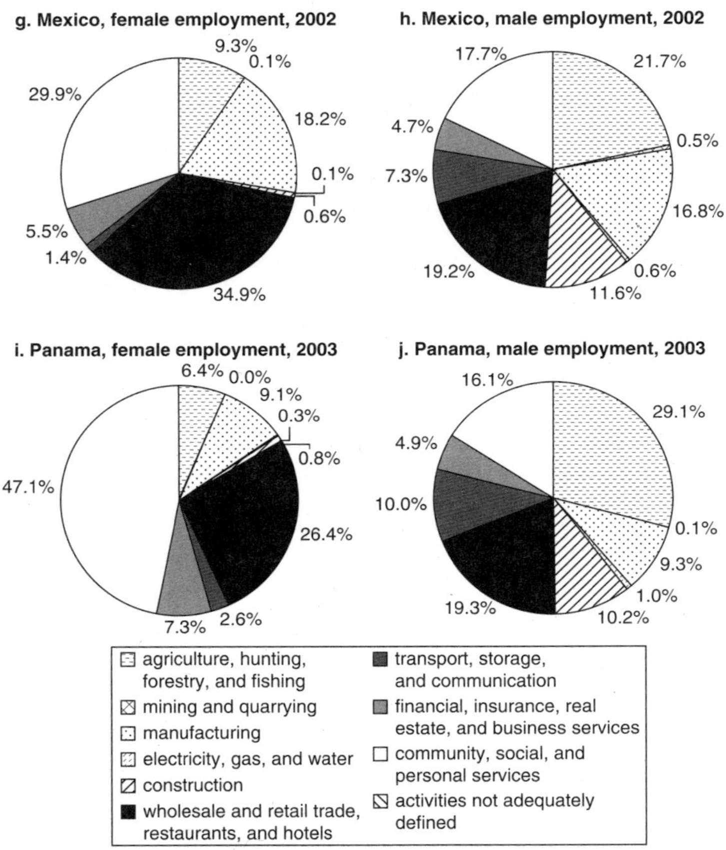

Source: Authors' calculations based on data from Galiani and others 2006.

Note: Data for Argentina cover urban areas only. The selection of periods for each country was dictated by the availability of the data and is as follows: Argentina (1990–2004), Brazil (1990–2003), Chile (1990–2003), Mexico (1992–2002), Panama (1987–2003).

community services. In contrast, women are much less represented than men in sectors such as manufacturing (with the exception of Mexico), agriculture, and construction.

The service sector has exhibited strong growth since the early 1990s, accounting for the largest majority of new jobs for women and men.

In Argentina, Chile, and Panama, more than 8 of every 10 jobs created opened in one of the service sectors. In Brazil and Mexico, manufacturing played an important role in job creation for women, but still more than 6 of every 10 jobs created were in services. In Chile, Mexico, and Panama, personal services and trade, restaurants, and hotels accounted for a larger proportion of new jobs for women than for men, while the reverse was the case in Argentina and Brazil (figure 2.14).

Nevertheless, the expansion of the traditionally feminine sectors accounts for less than 30 percent of the increase in the proportion of females in total employment. To assess how much of the female employment growth is accounted for by the expansion of sectors that traditionally employ large proportions of women, the growth of the percentage of women in total employment can be decomposed into three elements: (a) how much is accounted for by the expansion of female-intensive sectors, (b) how much is accounted for by an increase in the share of women within each sector, and (c) how much is given by a cross-term that reflects whether sectors that traditionally employ more women are growing faster than the average.

The results of this decomposition indicate that, quite surprisingly, the expansion of female-intensive sectors accounts for less than 30 percent of the overall feminization of the labor force, with a negative influence in Argentina and Brazil (table 2.4). Instead, the main effect is given by the increasing participation of women in all sectors of activity. Also interesting is that the cross-term is negative in all countries, indicating that the proportion of women has been increasing faster in those sectors that traditionally employed fewer women.

In sum, although in principle the expansion of the sectors that employ more women could have been the engine of growing female employment, in practice, this was not the case. Instead, women made important inroads in employment in all sectors of activity, exhibiting a faster growth in those sectors where traditionally they were less represented. The former suggests the growing participation of women in all sectors has more to do with the lifting of some constraints to female employment than to the expansion of employment in particular sectors that are women friendly but poorly paid.

Gender segregation is declining slowly. The preceding decomposition indicates that female participation in employment increased more in sectors where such participation was lower in the early 1990s. This trend reduced the degree of sector segregation of female employment. A useful measure of segregation is the Duncan index, which measures the degree by which women are overrepresented in certain sectors or occupations.[8] A computation of the Duncan index of sector segregation at the one-digit level of desegregation for the early 1990s and the mid 2000s confirms that female concentration across sectors is falling in all countries analyzed, with Chile and Panama showing the highest degree of concentration (table 2.5).

Figure 2.14 Distribution of Job Creation across Sectors: Five Countries

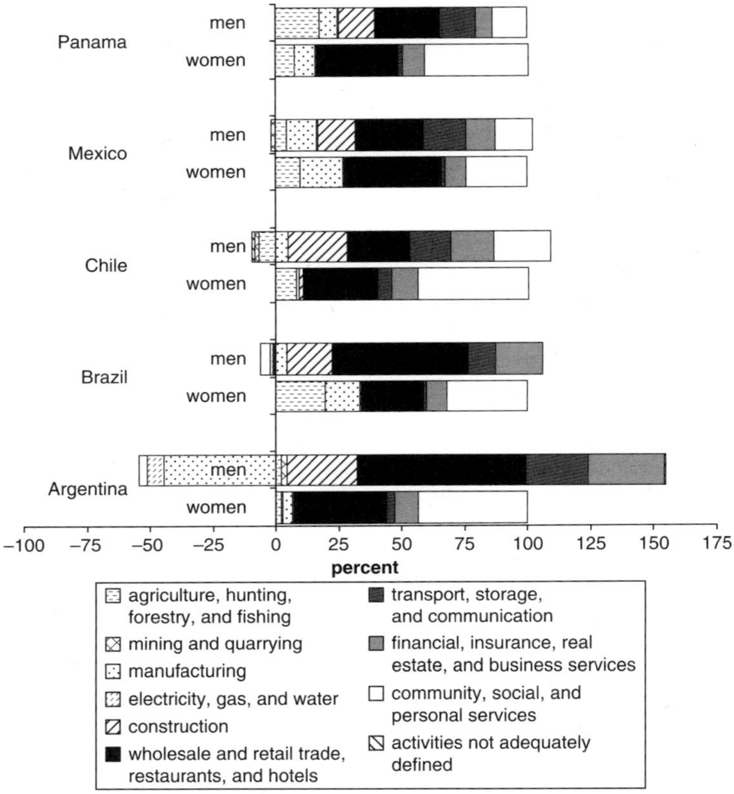

Source: Authors' calculations based on data from Galiani and others 2006.

Note: Data for Argentina cover urban areas only. The selection of periods for each country was dictated by the availability of the data and is as follows: Argentina (1990–2004), Brazil (1990–2003), Chile (1990–2003), Mexico (1992–2002), Panama (1987–2003).

Despite this progress, gender segregation is entrenched in the region. International comparisons suggest that occupational segregation is still very high in Latin America and the Caribbean, and according to various estimates, it could be the highest in the world (Blau and Ferber 1992). In addition, occupational segregation did not decline significantly during the 1990s for Costa Rica, Ecuador, and Uruguay (Deutsch and others 2005;

Table 2.4 Decomposition of Change in Share of Women in Employment, by Country

Country	Change in female employment share (%)	*Growth accounting* Share attributable to sector reallocation (% of total change)	Share attributable to change in female employment within sectors (% of total change)	Share attributable to relative growth of female-intensive sectors (% of total change)
Argentina	15.50	−0.77	16.75	−0.48
	(100)	(−5)	(108)	(−3)
Brazil	17.34	−0.38	19.40	−1.67
	(100)	(−2)	(112)	(−10)
Chile	15.60	5.05	10.75	−0.21
	(100)	(32)	(69)	(−1)
Mexico	26.35	3.59	22.88	−0.12
	(100)	(14)	(87)	(0)
Panama	12.37	4.10	9.37	−1.09
	(100)	(33)	(76)	(−9)

Source: Authors' calculations based on data from Galiani and others 2006.

Note: Data for Argentina cover urban areas only. The selection of periods for each country was dictated by the availability of the data and is as follows: Argentina (1990–2004), Brazil (1990–2003), Chile (1990–2003), Mexico (1992–2002), Panama (1987–2003).

Ferré and Rossi 2002), and in some countries (Argentina, Brazil, and Costa Rica), it increased (World Bank 2000). Occupational segregation is found to be much higher for women with lower levels of education (Deutsch and others 2005).

Gender wage differentials have been declining in most countries In 2000, women's monthly earnings in Latin America were on average 66 percent of men's (Abramo and Valenzuela 2005), up from 59 percent in 1990.[9] Such differences in pay correspond partly to differences in hours of work and partly to differences in hourly wages. A large number of studies have explored the evolution of gender wage differentials over the past 15 to 20 years in Latin America. These studies find that in most countries gender wage differentials have been declining. For example, World Bank (2000) reports that wage differentials decreased in Argentina and Brazil although they increased in Costa Rica between 1988 and 1997.

Table 2.5 Duncan Index of Sector Gender Segregation for Selected Countries, Early 1990s to Mid 2000s

	Duncan index	
Country	*Early 1990s*	*Mid 2000s*
Argentina	0.33	0.32
Brazil	0.36	0.31
Chile	0.40	0.38
Mexico	0.32	0.30
Panama	0.43	0.41
Average	0.37	0.34

Source: Authors' calculations based on data from Galiani and others 2006.

Note: Data for Argentina cover urban areas only. The selection of periods for each country was dictated by the availability of the data and is as follows: Argentina (1990–2004), Brazil (1990–2003), Chile (1990–2003), Mexico (1992–2002), Panama (1987–2003).

Duryea, Cox Edwards, and Ureta (2001) found that by the end of the 1990s wage ratios between women and men stood on average at about 85 percent.[10] They also found that in most countries the gap declined during the 1990s—particularly for older women (45–59 years of age)—with the only exceptions being Honduras and Peru.[11] In Costa Rica, wage gaps increased during the first half of the 1990s but later declined during the second half. Duryea, Cox Edwards, and Ureta (2001) also look at longer-term trends in female-to-male hourly earnings ratios for the overall population (ages 15–64) spanning the period from 1980 to 1999. These longer-term trends also confirm a secular decline in the wage gaps between males and females. León (2000) looks at the evolution of gender earnings differentials separately for salaried and self-employed workers in the period from 1988 to 1997.[12] He finds that for salaried employees, earnings differentials declined in all countries with the exception of Argentina, Colombia, and Mexico. Instead, gender pay differentials increased in many countries for self-employed workers.

Unconditional gender gaps do not control for differences in education, age, or other personal attributes between males and females. Moreover, the evolution of the unconditional gender gaps may be the reflection of secular gains in female educational attainment: as women become more educated relative to men, the unconditional wage gap declines. Another measure of the male-female gap is often computed to correct for these factors and assess whether women and men of equal observable characteristics earn similar wages. This measure, called the *conditional gap*, accounts for the gap that remains after differences in personal attributes are controlled for. Although many authors equate the magnitude of the conditional gap to gender discrimination, conditional differences must be interpreted with care; differences in characteristics that are often not observable in individual-level data sets—for example, occupational experience or tenure in a given job—and that often respond to choices made by women and determined outside the labor market explain a substantial share of the conditional wage gaps and do not necessarily relate to discrimination.

Duryea, Cox Edwards, and Ureta (2001) found that the conditional female wage penalty was closing at a rate of 1 percentage point per year in the 1990s. Arabsheibani, Galrão Carneiro, and Henley (2003) found similar results for Brazil, where the substantial decline of the wage gap (18 percentage points) is mostly explained by a decline in the conditional wage gap. Nevertheless, recent improvements in education and other endowments for women have also contributed to a reduction in male-female wage differentials.

Although under some indicators of job quality women outperformed men, in others that was not the case. Even though most new jobs went to women, no widespread evidence indicates that women took a disproportionate share of low-quality jobs, at least when measuring job quality using traditional informality measures. Thus, while as stated previously much discussion exists about how to rate the quality of jobs, new research suggests that many self-employed workers may be in this position by choice, whereas workers employed in micro firms receive lower wages than their counterparts employed in larger firms and would rather be employed in other jobs (Perry and others 2007). Under these measures, one could argue that in most countries women experienced an increase in job quality relative to men. Thus, in the majority of countries, the increase in women's share in total employment was accompanied by either a decline in their share in micro firm employment or an increase that was less than proportional to their increased participation in employment (figure 2.15). Instead, their participation in self-employment increased more than proportionally to their increased participation in employment.

Measures of social security coverage point in the opposite direction, however. Although measures of affiliation to social security through the job are available for only a few countries, they show that in four of seven, the participation of women in uncovered employment increased more than proportionally in relation to women's increased participation in employment, suggesting that, at least in those four countries, women took an increasing number of informal jobs (figure 2.15).

Even if the figures on self-employment and employment in micro firms are encouraging, other figures indicate that in most countries women are still more represented in informal employment than are men (figure 2.16).

In sum, this analysis has shown that under many indicators women have outperformed men in the labor market. Women had strong gains in

Figure 2.15 Average Annual Change in Female Share of Employment and Job Quality

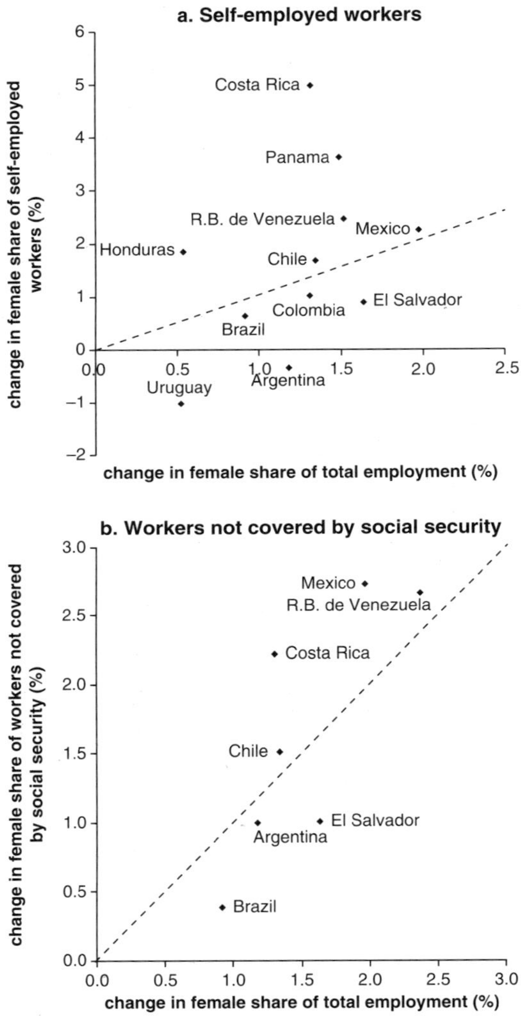

(continued)

Figure 2.15 Average Annual Change in Female Share of Employment and Job Quality *(continued)*

Sources: Sociómetro, Research Department, IDB; UNPD.

Note: For a detailed description of endpoint years used by country for this analysis, refer to annex table 2.A.1. Data for Argentina and Uruguay are urban.

both participation and employment rates, and such gains were mostly at the low end of the wage distribution, a group whose participation is challenged by the lack of affordable day care and limited opportunities in the job market. Wage differentials and data on the quality of jobs suggest that despite the rapid increase in employment, working conditions for women improved compared with those of men: wage gaps declined while at least some indicators of job quality suggest an improvement in the situation of women relative to men.

Interestingly, such strong gains cannot be fully explained either by improvements in education or by the strong expansion of the service sector. Instead, this analysis suggests the employment of women (a) increased at all education levels and in all sectors and (b) was higher in sectors that had lower starting female participation in employment. The former suggests that, to a large extent, rising female employment responded to improved opportunities for women relative to men. Other indications, however, are less clear-cut. Female work segregation continues to be high

Figure 2.16 Share of Adult Workers in Informal Jobs, by Country and Gender, Mid 2000s

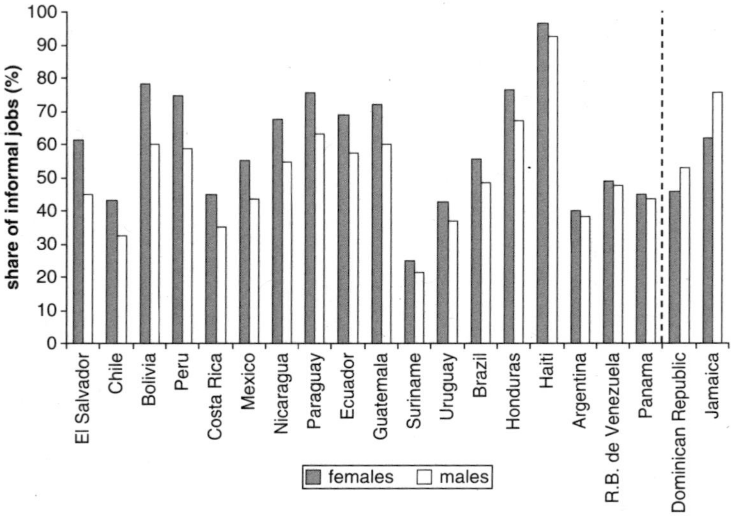

Source: SEDLAC.

Note: Countries are ranked according to the ratio of female to male share of informal workers in descending order. The vertical dashed line represents the point where women and men have the same proportion. See annex table 2.A.1 for the time period of each country.

and has declined slowly, female unemployment increased more rapidly than male unemployment, and the proportion of employed people not registered in social security increased faster for women than for men in some countries.

Youths and the Labor Market

Although the patterns of job creation have an important bearing on the welfare of all workers, they are particularly determinant for the youth labor market because newcomers are the most exposed to changing labor market conditions. Successful integration of youths in the labor market is key for the development of their career paths. It is also essential to reduce the incidence of important social problems to which youths are particularly vulnerable, such as violence and crime.

Declining Child and Youth Employment Rates and Increasing Employment Rates for Adults

Child labor remains a significant problem in a number in countries such as Bolivia, Brazil, Ecuador, Guatemala, Honduras, Nicaragua, and Paraguay, where more than 1 in 10 children are working (figure 2.17). An important development, however, is in the decline in the employment of children in most countries of the region since the early 1990s. Nonetheless, in five countries (Bolivia, the Dominican Republic, Honduras, Panama, and the República Bolivariana de Venezuela), the percentage of employed children increased.

The participation and employment rates of youths also declined in the majority of countries—especially in Brazil, Costa Rica, and Uruguay (figure 2.18, panel a). This decline coincided with an increase in employment of adults, fueled by an increase in participation of women. These figures suggest a reorganization of employment and participation within households, with lower participation of youths and higher participation of less educated women. In figure 2.18 and in the rest of this section, the youth category is defined as people 15 to 24 years of age. Separate examination of the relative performance of finer age categories, such as the evolution of employment and unemployment of youths ages 15 to 20 and 21 to 24, would be desirable. Unfortunately, however, such data were not readily available.

Increasing Rates of Schooling

The available data also indicate that these changes are driven by increases in schooling. Thus, the proportion of youths who were neither in the labor force nor in school also fell during the same period (figure 2.18, panel b). This increase in schooling may come not only as a response to the increasing demand for education, but also as the consequence of a perceived weak labor market. In any event, it is promoting a much-needed upgrading of the skills of the youth labor force.

Weak labor market conditions implied rising youth unemployment and a declining share of social security affiliation among youths. In most countries, the unemployment rates and the duration of unemployment of youths increased (see figure 2.19). Moreover, the proportion of young workers without social security or in informal jobs[13] increased in a number of countries (see figure 2.20). By the mid 2000s, the regional unweighted average for the youth unemployment rate was 20 percent, whereas for adults the same figure was 9 percent (figure 2.21, panel a). In addition, the average unweighted affiliation rate to social security among salaried youths was 36 percent (figure 2.21, panel b), compared with 56 percent for prime-age workers.

Figure 2.17 Level and Evolution of Child Labor in Latin America and the Caribbean

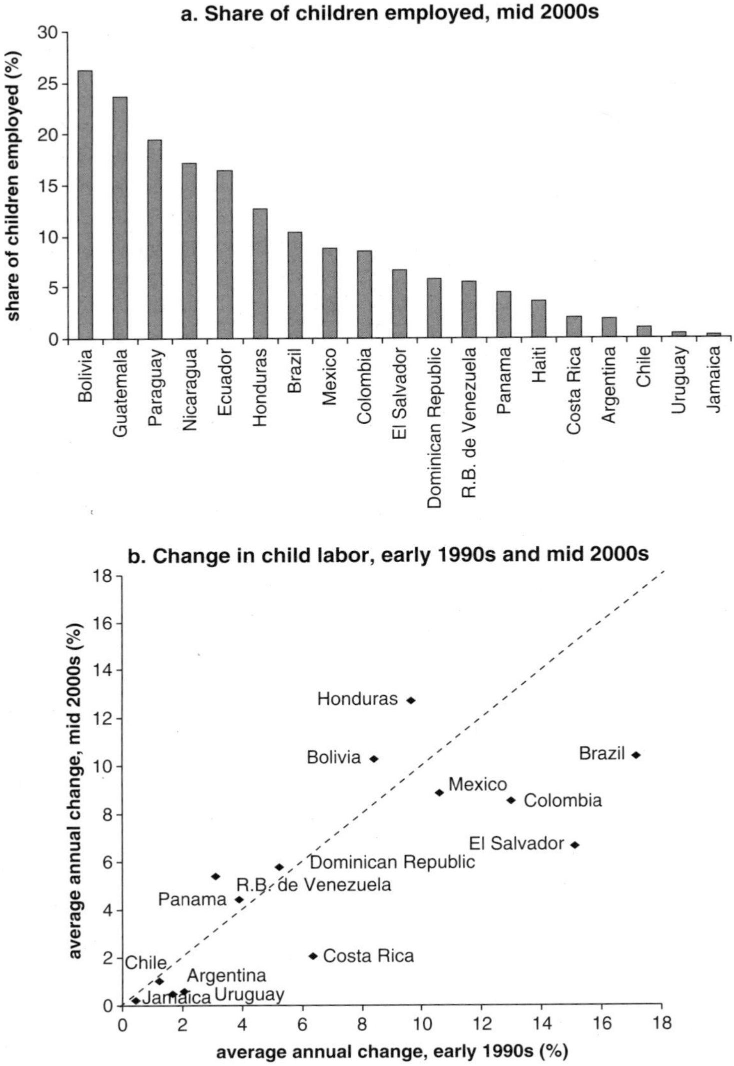

Source: SEDLAC.

Note: Children refers to the population 10 to 14 years of age. See annex table 2.A.1 for the time period of each country.

Figure 2.18 Participation and Idleness Rates for Youth, Early 1990s and Mid 2000s

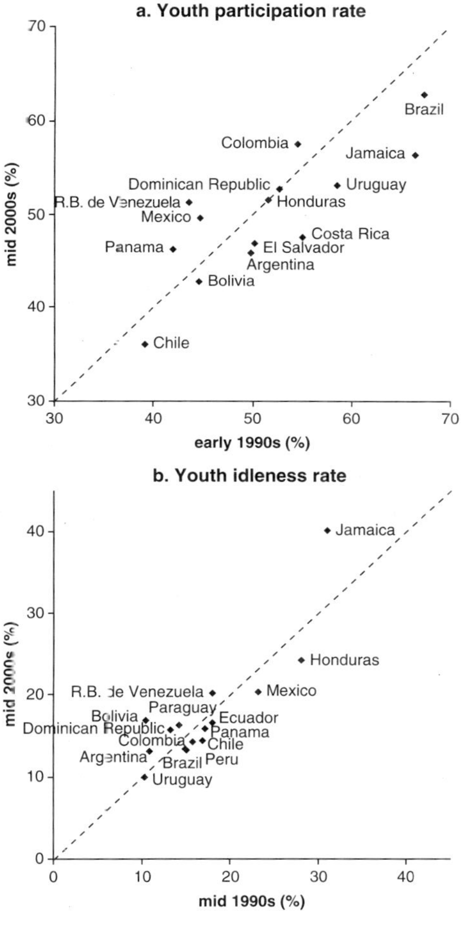

Sources: Participation rates are from SEDLAC, based on microdata from household surveys, except for data for Argentina and Colombia, which are from Sociómetro, Research Department, IDB. Idleness rates are from Fares, Montenegro, and Orazem (2006).

Note: Youth refers to the population 15 to 24 years of age. The share of idle youths refers to the share of the population 15 to 24 years of age that is neither in school nor in the labor force. See annex table 2.A.1 for the time period of each country.

Figure 2.19 Annual Percentage Change in Unemployment Rate and Unemployment Duration, by Age Group, Early 1990s to Mid 2000s

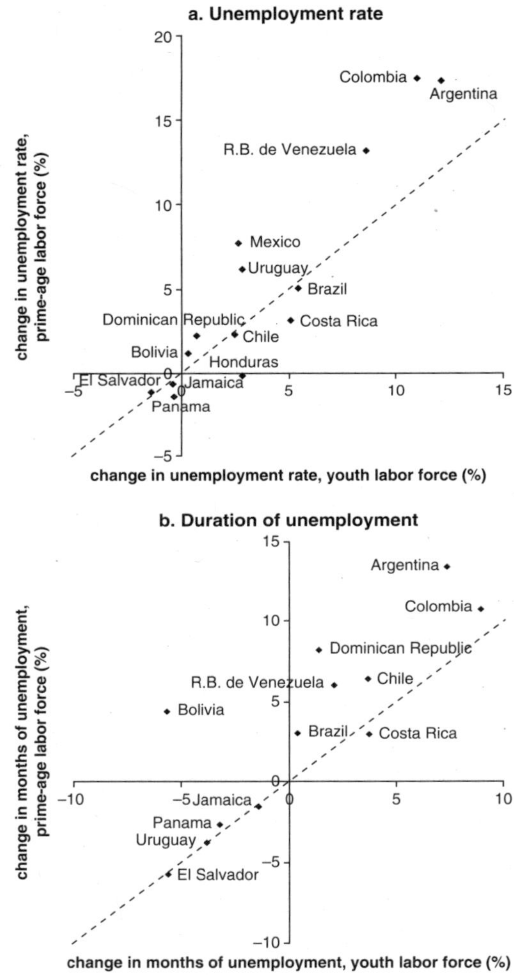

Source: SEDLAC.

Note: Youth refers to the population 15 to 24 years of age. *Prime age* refers to the population 25 to 64 years of age. See annex table 2.A.1 for the time period of each country.

Figure 2.20 Annual Percentage Change in the Share of Salaried Workers in Informal Jobs and Not Covered by Social Security, by Age Group, Early 1990s to Mid 2000s

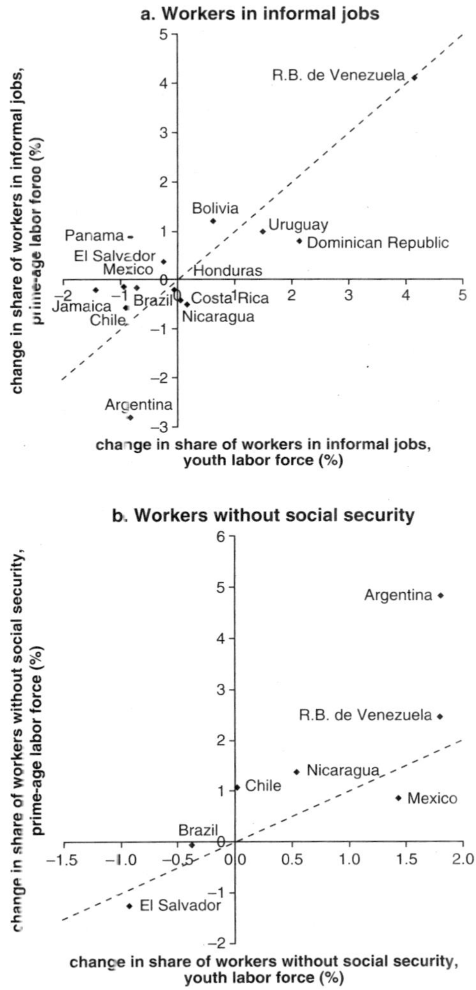

Source: SEDLAC.

Note: Informal employment refers to salaried workers in small firms, nonprofessional self-employed workers, and zero-income workers. *Youth* refers to the population 15 to 24 years of age. *Prime age* refers to the population 25 to 64 years of age. See annex table 2.A.1 for the time period of each country.

Figure 2.21 National Unemployment Rate and Share of Salaried Not Affiliated to Social Security, by Age Group, Mid 2000s

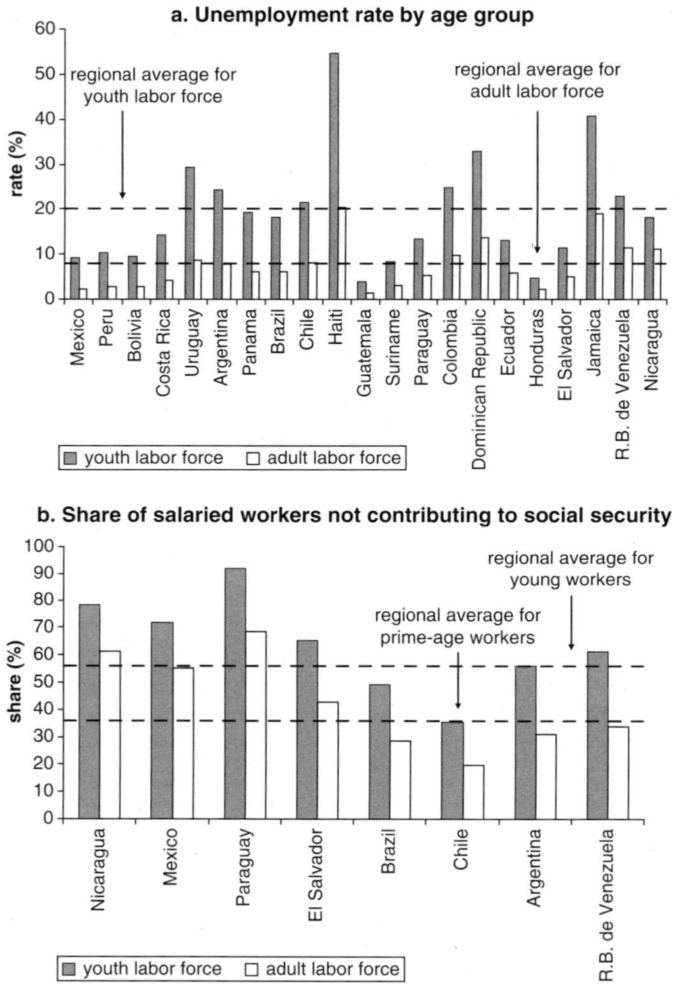

Source: SEDLAC.

Note: Youth refers to the population 15 to 24 years of age. *Adult* refers to the population 25 to 64 years of age. See annex table 2.A.1 for the time period of each country. In panel a, countries are ranked according to their youth-to-adult unemployment rate ratio in descending order. In panel b, countries are ranked according to their youth-to-adult informality rate ratio in descending order.

A comparison of the change in labor market conditions for youth and adult workers suggests a high correlation between changes in the market for adult workers and that for youths (figures 2.19 and 2.20). Such a comparison is relevant because it makes clear that the weak performance in youth employment and unemployment is not the result of problems that are specific to the youth market but rather relates to developments that affect all workers. Notwithstanding, high youth unemployment and informality rates constitute an important policy challenge. Low employment opportunities for youths are associated with a number of important social problems. In addition, the low contribution rates to social security for all workers, but particularly for youths, are important issues in most countries of the region because in countries with individual capitalization social security systems, such as those found in most Latin American and Caribbean countries, the contributions of workers at young ages have an inordinate weight in their final pension benefits (Berstein, Larrain, and Pino 2006), all of which may warrant interventions targeted to the youth market.

Small but Negative Effect of Sector Reallocation on the Demand for Young Workers

As discussed in the case of women, it is worth assessing whether changes in the composition of employment across sectors have played a role in affecting the demand for young workers. A shifting share decomposition allows distinguishing (a) how much of the decline in youth employment can be attributed to the reallocation of employment across sectors and (b) how much can be the result of declining youth employment within all sectors. The results, summarized in table 2.6, indicate that sector reallocation played a small but negative role in the demand for young workers. Depending on the country, between 4 and 9 percent of the total decline in youth employment was associated with the contraction of youth-intensive sectors. The exception to this pattern was Brazil, where the demand for youths was, if anything, slightly boosted by sector reallocation. A positive cross-term in the decomposition indicates that sectors that expanded more rapidly in terms of employment were also the sectors where the proportion of young workers expanded more rapidly. This result is not surprising because young workers are an important component of new hires.

In sum, the evidence indicates that supply and demand forces contributed to a decline in youth employment. Reduced labor market opportunities, particularly for the less skilled, and increasing returns to skill motivated many youths to postpone entry into the labor market and to expand schooling. Nevertheless, unemployment for youths increased, and on average it stands at about 20 percent of the youth labor force. Moreover, the quality of jobs held by youths appears to have deteriorated. Although such developments are driven by the same factors that drove increasing

Table 2.6 The Effect of Sector Reallocation on Youth Employment, Early 1990s to Mid 2000s

		Growth accounting		
Country	*Change in youth employment share (%)*	*Share attributable to sector reallocation (% of total change)*	*Share attributable to change in youth employment within sectors (% of total change)*	*Share attributable to relative growth of youth sectors (% of total change)*
Argentina	−18.51	−0.83	−19.51	1.83
	(100)	(4)	(105)	(−10)
Brazil	−22.54	0.51	−23.59	0.54
	(100)	(−2)	(105)	(−2)
Chile	−28.43	−2.52	−28.42	2.52
	(100)	(9)	(100)	(−9)
Mexico	−20.15	−1.29	−20.54	1.69
	(100)	(6)	(102)	(−8)
Panama	−23.51	−1.62	−22.37	0.47
	(100)	(7)	(95)	(−2)
Average	−22.63	−1.15	−22.89	1.41

Source: Authors' calculations based on household data from Galiani and others 2006.

Note: The selection of periods for each country was dictated by the availability of the data and is as follows: Argentina (1990–2004), Brazil (1990–2003), Chile (1990–2003), Mexico (1992–2002), Panama (1987–2003).

unemployment and informality among adult workers and although, in relative terms, youths did similarly and sometimes even better than their adult counterparts, high rates of unemployment and low rates of contribution to social security may warrant targeted interventions in the youth market.

Conclusions

This chapter has assessed the labor market performance of different groups of workers in the Latin American and Caribbean region. The findings suggest that, in a context of labor market slack and diminished employment opportunities, women fared surprisingly well—much better than their male counterparts. For their part, young workers responded to a deterioration of labor market conditions by reducing their participation in employment and seemingly postponing their entry in the labor market. The two trends combined suggest a reorganization of labor supply within households, with an increased participation of unskilled women and a reduced participation of youths. How women could improve their employment opportunities in such a weak labor market or what this finding implies for males is still unclear. However, the data strongly suggest that women's increased participation responds to improved (relative) job opportunities.

This chapter also confirms that, as pointed out by other authors, returns to education have kept up or, in some countries, even risen, despite an increasing supply of skilled labor. Unlike the findings in many OECD countries, particularly in continental Europe, no evidence suggests such a trend is accompanied by reduced employment rates of unskilled workers. As found in the United Kingdom and the United States, labor markets in Latin America and the Caribbean adjust more in terms of prices than quantities, suggesting high wage flexibility—probably as a result of the low incidence of collective bargaining and the high informality rates in the region.

These developments are worrisome because the rising price of skill is further increasing inequality in the region—already among the highest in the world. Educational policies need to address credit constraints and the low quality of education so that historically slow progress in education can be reversed.

Better work opportunities for women and higher schooling rates for youths should not lead to policy complacency. The discrimination and segregation problems faced by these groups—particularly women—although improving, are still pressing. Similarly, although youths fared better than adults, the deterioration of their situation in absolute terms is worrisome and may require special active labor policies to address their particular situation. A discussion of this topic is taken up in chapters 7 and 8.

Annex 2.A: Selection of Analysis Time Frame

Data limitations impede efforts to consider exactly the same periods across countries. In addition, given the short time-series component of the data used in this chapter, Hodrick-Prescott filters to smooth the effects of the business cycle could not be applied. For this reason, the end years were chosen so as to minimize the effect of the business cycle on trends. The main sources of data are two: the Socio-Economic Database for Latin America and the Caribbean (SEDLAC) and Sociómetro. SEDLAC is a joint project of the Center for the Study of Distribution, Labor, and Social

Table 2.A.1 Selection of End Years

	SEDLAC end years		*Sociómetro end years*	
Country	*Year 1*	*Year 2*	*Year 1*	*Year 2*
Argentina	1992	1998	1993	2000
Bolivia	1993	2002	1996	2002
Brazil	1992	2003	1992	2003
Chile	1990	2003	1990	2003
Colombia	1992	2000	1991	2003
Costa Rica	1990	2004	1990	2004
El Salvador	1991	2004	1996	2002
Honduras	1992	2005	1992	2003
Jamaica	1990	1999		
Mexico	1989	2002	1992	2004
Nicaragua	1993	2001	1993	2001
Panama	1995	2004	1995	2003
Paraguay	—	—	1995	2002
Peru	1997	2003	1991	2000
Uruguay	1992	2004	1992	2003
Venezuela, R.B. de	1992	2004	1991	2004

Source: Authors' compilation.
Note: — = not available.

Affairs (Centro de Estudios Distributivos, Laborales y Sociales) and the World Bank, whereas Sociómetro is the database of the Research Department of the Inter-American Development Bank. In both cases, the selection of end years is as shown in annex table 2.A.1.

Notes

1. The Heckscher-Ohlin and Stolper-Samuelson theorems of international trade predict that trade openness increases the price of the factor that is more abundant in a country. Under the hypothesis that Latin America is abundant in unskilled labor, these theorems would predict that trade openness leads to an increase in the price of unskilled labor and a decline in the returns to education.

2. Attanasio, Goldberg, and Pavcnik (2004) noted this trend for Colombia.

3. Cragg and Epelbaum (1996) noted that occupation-specific effects could explain most of the growing wage dispersion in Mexico.

4. Ferreira and Paes de Barros (1999) document a rapid decrease in male participation in Brazil during the 1990s and suggest that such trends are due to negative labor demand conditions that are forcing household heads, mostly men, to leave the labor force.

5. The countries covered in their study are Argentina, Brazil, Chile, Costa Rica, Uruguay, and the República Bolivariana de Venezuela.

6. They focus their analysis on a relatively homogenous group of urban women age 30 to 45.

7. The *total fertility rate* is the average number of children who would be born alive to a woman during her lifetime according to prevailing age-specific fertility rates.

8. This measure is given by $\sum_i 1/2|F_i - M_i|$, where F_i is the participation of women in the employment of a given sector or occupation and M_i is the participation of men. A value of 0 indicates no segregation, whereas 1 indicates maximum gender segregation.

9. The countries included in this average are Argentina, Brazil, Chile, Colombia, Costa Rica, Ecuador, El Salvador, Honduras, Mexico, Nicaragua, Panama, Paraguay, Peru, Uruguay, and the República Bolivariana de Venezuela.

10. The countries included in this study are Brazil, Colombia, Costa Rica, Honduras, Panama, Peru, Uruguay, and the República Bolivariana de Venezuela.

11. Ñopo (2006) finds that, in Peru, the wage gap declined during the early and mid 1990s but increased toward the end of the decade.

12. The countries studied by León (2000) are Argentina, Bolivia, Brazil, Colombia, Chile, Costa Rica, Mexico, Uruguay, and the República Bolivariana de Venezuela.

13. That is, the share of youth workers employed in small firms, self-employed in nonprofessional activities, or working in unpaid jobs.

References

Abramo, L., and M. E. Valenzuela. 2005. "Women's Labour Force Participation Rates in Latin America." *International Labour Review* 144 (4): 369–99.

Arabsheibani, G. R., F. Galrão Carneiro, and A. Henley. 2003. "Gender Wage Differentials in Brazil: Trends over a Turbulent Era." Policy Research Working Paper 3148, World Bank, Washington, DC.

Attanasio, O., P. Goldberg, and N. Pavcnik. 2004. "Trade Reforms and Wage Inequality in Colombia." NBER Working Paper 9830, National Bureau of Economic Research, Cambridge, MA.

Berstein, S., G. Larrain, and F. Pino. 2006. "Chilean Pension Reform: Coverage Facts and Policy Alternatives." *Economía* 6 (2): 227–79.

Blau, F. D., and M. A. Ferber. 1992. *The Economics of Women, Men, and Work*. Englewood Cliffs, NJ: Prentice-Hall.

Cragg, M. I., and M. Epelbaum. 1996. "Why Has Wage Dispersion Grown in Mexico? Is It the Incidence of Reforms or the Growing Demand for Skills?" *Journal of Development Economics* 51 (1): 99–116.

Cunningham, W. 1998. "Breadwinner versus Caregiver: Labor Force Participation and Sectoral Choice over the Mexican Business Cycle." World Bank, Washington, DC.

De Ferranti, D., G. E. Perry, I. S. Gill, J. L. Guasch, W. Maloney, C. Sánchez-Páramo, and N. Schady. 2003. *Closing the Gap in Education and Technology*. Washington, DC: World Bank.

Deutsch, R., A. Morrison, C. Piras, and H. Ñopo. 2005. "Working within Confines: Occupational Segregation by Sex for Three Latin American Countries." *ICFAI Journal of Applied Economics* 4 (3): 50–59.

Duryea, S., A. Cox Edwards, and M. Ureta. 2001. "Women in the Latin American Labor Market: The Remarkable 1990's." William Davidson Institute Working Paper 500, University of Michigan, Ann Arbor.

Fares, J., C. E. Montenegro, and P. F. Orazem. 2006. *How Are Youth Faring in the Labor Market? Evidence from around the World*. Background paper for *World Development Report 2007*, World Bank, Washington, DC.

Ferré, Z., and M. Rossi. 2002. "Segregación ocupacional de la mujer en el mercado de trabajo del Uruguay (1986–1997)." Documentos de Trabajo 0502, Department of Economics, Facultad de Ciencias Sociales, Universidad de la República, Montevideo.

Ferreira, F., and R. Paes de Barros. 1999. "The Slippery Slope: Explaining the Increase in Extreme Poverty in Urban Brazil, 1976–1996." Policy Research Working Paper 2210, World Bank, Washington, DC.

Galiani, S., F. Haimovich, C. Heuser, and H. Winkler. 2006. "Employment Reallocation in Latin America: Main Trends and Effects on Jobs, Wages, and Working Conditions." Background paper for this report, World Bank, Washington, DC.

Goldin, C., and L. F. Katz. 2000. "Career and Marriage in the Age of the Pill." *American Economic Review* 90 (2): 461–65.

IDB (Inter-American Development Bank). 1998. *Facing Up to Inequality in Latin America—1998/99 Report on Economic and Social Progress in Latin America*. Washington, DC: IDB.

———. 2003. *Good Jobs Wanted: Labor Markets in Latin America—2004 Report on Economic and Social Progress in Latin America*. Washington, DC: IDB.

León, F. 2000. "Mujeres y trabajo en las reformas estructurales latinoamericanas durante las decadas de 1980 y 1990." Mujer y Desarrollo 28, Economic Commission for Latin America and the Caribbean, United Nations, Santiago.

Ñopo, H. 2006. "The Gender Wage Gap in Chile 1992–2003 from a Matching Comparison Perspective." Research Department Working Paper 562, Inter-American Development Bank, Washington, DC.

Pavcnik, N., A. Blom, P. Goldberg, and N. Schady. 2003. "Trade Liberalization and Labor Market Adjustment in Brazil." Policy Research Working Paper 2982, World Bank, Washington, DC.

Perry, G., W. Maloney, O. Arias, P. Fajnzylber, A. Mason, and J. Saavedra-Chanduvi, eds. 2007. *Informality: Exit and Exclusion*. Washington, DC: World Bank.

Sánchez-Páramo, C., and N. Schady. 2002. "Off and Running? The Rising Demand for Skilled Workers in Latin America." Background paper for the regional report *Closing the Gap in Education and Technology in Latin America*, World Bank, Washington, DC.

Scarpetta, S., A. Bassanini, D. Pila, and P. Schreyer. 2000. "Economic Growth in the OECD Area: Recent Trends at the Aggregate and Sectoral Level." OECD Economics Department Working Paper 248, Organisation for Economic Co-operation and Development, Paris.

World Bank. 2000. "Labor Market Outcomes: Recent Trends and the Role of Gender in Three LAC Countries." Poverty Reduction and Economic Management Unit, World Bank, Washington, DC.

Part II

Structural Changes, Employment, and Productivity Growth: Main Patterns

Since the early 1990s, most countries in Latin America and the Caribbean have undertaken major macro and structural reforms, with sizable effects on the structure of the economy and its growth and job creation potentials. They have implemented major macrostabilization programs, aimed at curbing (hyper)inflation and restoring fiscal discipline. They have also undertaken major liberalization of trade and financial markets. Tariffs were reduced on average from 49 percent in the mid 1980s to 11 percent in 1999, and application of nontariff restrictions has decreased from 38 percent of imports in the mid 1980s to only 6 percent of imports by the mid 1990s (IDB 2003). The liberalization of the financial sector was also impressive, with significant reductions in the reserve ratios, elimination of controls over interest rates, opening of the sector to foreign investment, and privatization of public banks (IDB 2001). The countries in the region have also privatized many state-owned enterprises in key sectors of the economy. After the transition economies of Eastern Europe and the former Soviet Union, Latin American countries are those with the largest decline in the state's share of production since the mid 1980s (Chong and López-de-Silanes 2005), especially in the infrastructure sector. All of these major reforms took place in a rapidly changing global environment in which countries in the region have had greater access to foreign markets and technologies but were also more directly affected by competition from other emerging countries.

The scope and depth of macro and structural reforms, as well as the changes in the exposure to global competition, vary significantly across countries in the region. Nevertheless, in all of them these changes were expected to have major implications for both firms and workers in different sectors, with strong pressures to reallocate output and inputs across firms, sectors, and geographic locations. According to standard trade theories, for example, the reduction of restrictions on international trade should have implied a reallocation of resources toward the sectors with a comparative advantage—that is, the sectors intensive in the relatively abundant factor in each country. Within each sector, stronger competition imposed by cheap imported goods should have produced a selection process by which less productive firms would have been closed down while surviving firms would have had stronger incentives to improve their efficiency. The privatization of formerly state-owned enterprises should have been associated with job losses in the short run, given that these enterprises were generally overstaffed. Dismissed workers should have had to find employment in new activities or to adapt to perform their former jobs in new outsourcing firms that provide services to the privatized company. Financial liberalization[1] should have affected not only the financial sector itself but also other sectors. Such liberalization should have implied the elimination of some credit lines designed by governments to favor certain industries and activities and the simultaneous creation of new credit opportunities for other sectors.[2] Firms of different sizes should have been affected asymmetrically by the financial liberalization as well.

This second part of the book sheds light on the magnitude and characteristics of structural changes in the region from the sectoral (chapter 4) and the firm-level (chapter 5) perspectives. In particular, it looks at the effects of these structural changes for overall employment (quantity of jobs) and labor productivity (quality of jobs) and indicates a number of market- and policy-driven factors that may be responsible for the observed patterns. These factors are further analyzed in part III of the book, which focuses on policies.

The main findings of this part can be summarized as follows:

- The region has been characterized since the early 1990s by a sizable process of resource reallocation, even if somewhat lower than that observed in rapidly growing, dynamic emerging economies.
- The reallocation of resources—including labor—has not necessarily gone toward more productive uses in the region. Many countries have witnessed significant shifts in employment from relatively more productive activities in manufacturing to low-productivity activities in services. This fact helps explain the observed low productivity growth at the aggregate level and relatively strong patterns of employment. The manufacturing sector has lost ground not only in terms of employment—which is fairly common in many countries—but also in terms of output. Moreover, in some countries, including Argentina, Colombia, and Mexico, labor has moved from more to relatively less productive uses even within manufacturing.

- Evidence from firm-level data suggests a polarization between micro units and medium to large units, with a missing middle of small and medium-size firms. This finding matters to the extent that the missing small and medium-size businesses are those with the strong potential to create more jobs—and more productive jobs.
- With the exception of Argentina, there are no major barriers to entry in Latin American and Caribbean countries. In Brazil and Mexico, almost a quarter of all businesses are created or destroyed every year. What characterize countries of the region are barriers to survival in the market—only about one-third of all new firms are in business seven years later.
- Productivity increases have largely been driven by within-firm growth, a common phenomenon in most market economies, but this growth has often been achieved through downsizing rather than by investing and innovating. However, at least in high-tech industries, the entry of new firms has also contributed to increased productivity. For many new successful businesses, however, the difficulty in expanding also affects their ability to contest the market vis-à-vis well-established larger units. Indeed, contrary to the case in other countries, the entry and exit of firms do not seem to stimulate incumbents to improve their performance.
- The implications of these findings are that barriers to survival and to expansion are key factors in explaining overall productivity and job creation performance in the region. Even successful new firms have difficulty surviving and hiring more workers. New firms have harsh times in the early years of life in all market economies, but in Latin America and the Caribbean, even successful new businesses have difficulties expanding. This situation is probably due to lack of access to finance or to uncertainties about the institutional and market environment in which these firms operate.

Notes

1. Financial liberalization implied reduction of reserve ratios, elimination of controls over interest rates, opening of the sector to foreign investment, and privatization of public banks, among other characteristics. See IDB (2001) for details.

2. Some credit lines to small farmers and for dwellings were rapidly eliminated in many countries.

References

Chong, A., and F. López-de-Silanes. 2005. "The Truth about Privatization in Latin America." In *Privatization in Latin America: Myths and Reality*, ed. A. Chong and F. López-de-Silanes, 1–66. Palo Alto, CA: Stanford University Press.

IDB (Inter-American Development Bank). 2001. *Competitiveness: The Business of Growth—2001 Report on Economic and Social Progress in Latin America.* Washington, DC: IDB.

———. 2003. *Good Jobs Wanted: Labor Markets in Latin America—2004 Report on Economic and Social Progress in Latin America.* Washington, DC: IDB.

3

Role of Structural Changes for Employment and Productivity Growth

This chapter sheds light on the process of economic restructuring in Latin America and the Caribbean by assessing the magnitude and characteristics of the reallocation of output and labor across sectors in the countries of the region since 1990. How has the structural composition of the economy evolved over time in the countries of the region? Has a sizable reallocation of output and labor occurred across sectors in the region compared with the situation in comparator countries? Have sectors that displayed significant improvements in productivity also expanded in terms of employment? What was the role of reallocation of factors to more productive uses for overall productivity growth? These are some of the questions this chapter addresses. The next chapter goes into more details of the process of reallocation by drawing from microdata from enterprise and household surveys.

Structural Changes in the Region

How sizable were the structural changes since the early 1990s, and how did they affect output and job growth patterns? One commonly used method for assessing the magnitude of the processes of reallocation of output and inputs is based on the Lilien index. The index measures the degree of dispersion in the rate of growth across sectors.[1] The indicator reaches its lowest value of zero in the case of no reallocation across sectors. Figure 3.1 suggests that the magnitude of output and labor reallocation was sizable in all subregions of Latin America and the Caribbean (see annex 3.E for country details).[2] However, when compared with that of other developing and industrial countries, the size of reallocation was relatively low.

Figure 3.1 Reallocation of Employment and Output across Sectors: Lilien Index, Early 1990s to Early 2000s

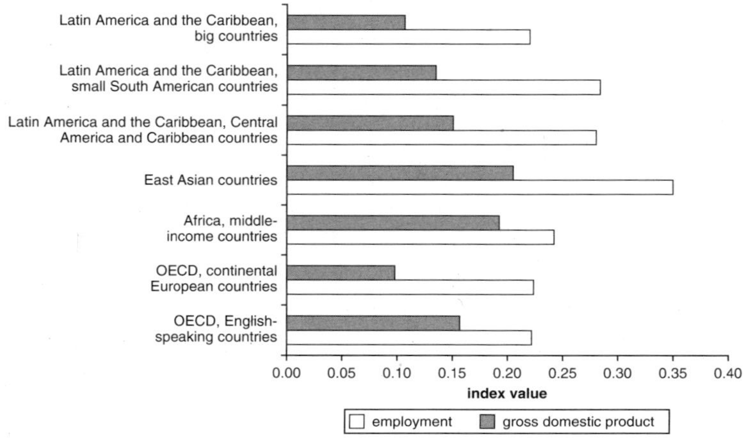

Source: Authors' calculations.

Note: Computed by authors from gross domestic product series by economic activity at one-digit level of disaggregation, at constant 1990 prices in U.S. dollars, from the United Nations Statistics Division (UNSD).

In particular, output reallocation in the region did not display the pace observed in some of the fast-growing countries in East Asia, such as the Republic of Korea or Malaysia.

A Shift in Output and Employment from Agriculture Activities—and Often from Manufacturing to Services

In past decades, structural shifts in outputs and inputs have been an important factor behind productivity growth in most countries, as resources moved from low-productivity agricultural activities to more productive manufacturing activities and, at higher stages of development, from manufacturing to services. However, more recently a stronger contribution to overall productivity seems to be coming from within-sector reallocation of resources from less to more productive firms (see OECD 2003).

How does the Latin American and Caribbean experience compare with these general trends? Several patterns are confirmed in most of the countries of the region (figures 3.2 and 3.3). In particular, the agricultural sector has lost ground in terms of output share, with a few exceptions, most notably in Ecuador, Nicaragua, and Paraguay, and also, although

Figure 3.2 Changes in the Structure of Economies, Sectoral GDP, 1990–2003

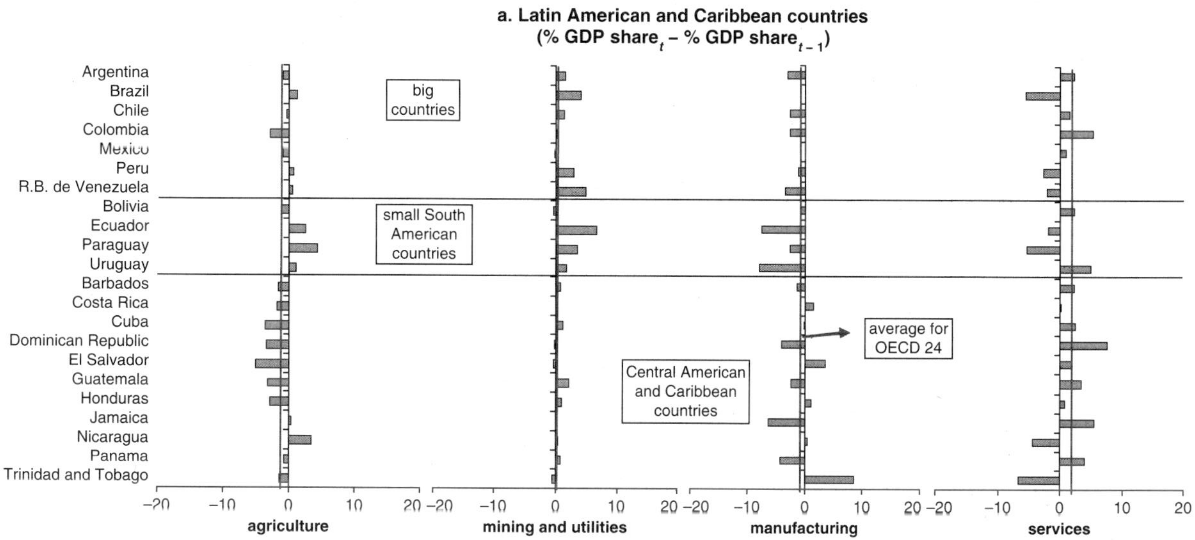

(continued)

Figure 3.2 Changes in the Structure of Economies, Sectoral GDP, 1990–2003 *(continued)*

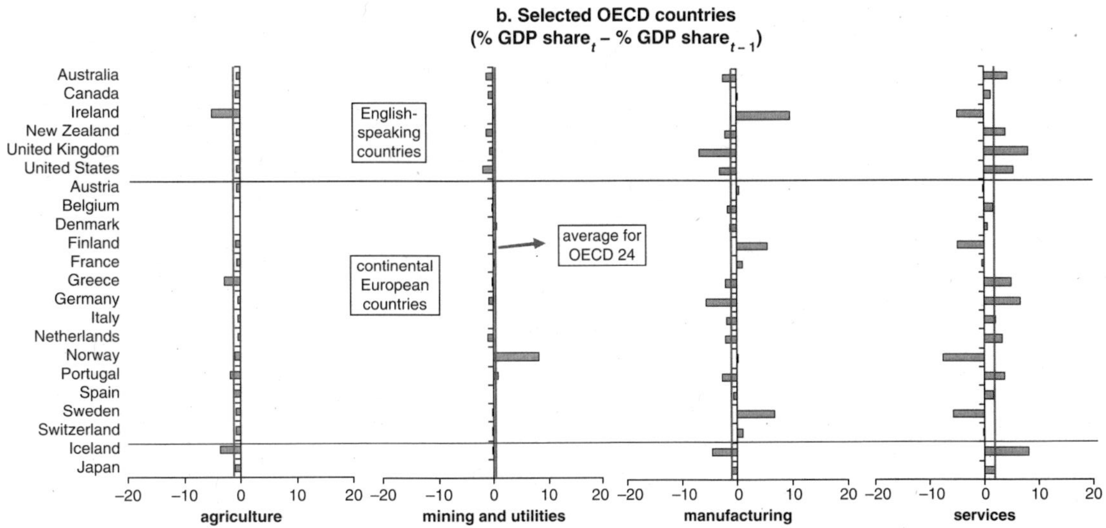

(continued)

Figure 3.2 Changes in the Structure of Economies, Sectoral GDP, 1990–2003 *(continued)*

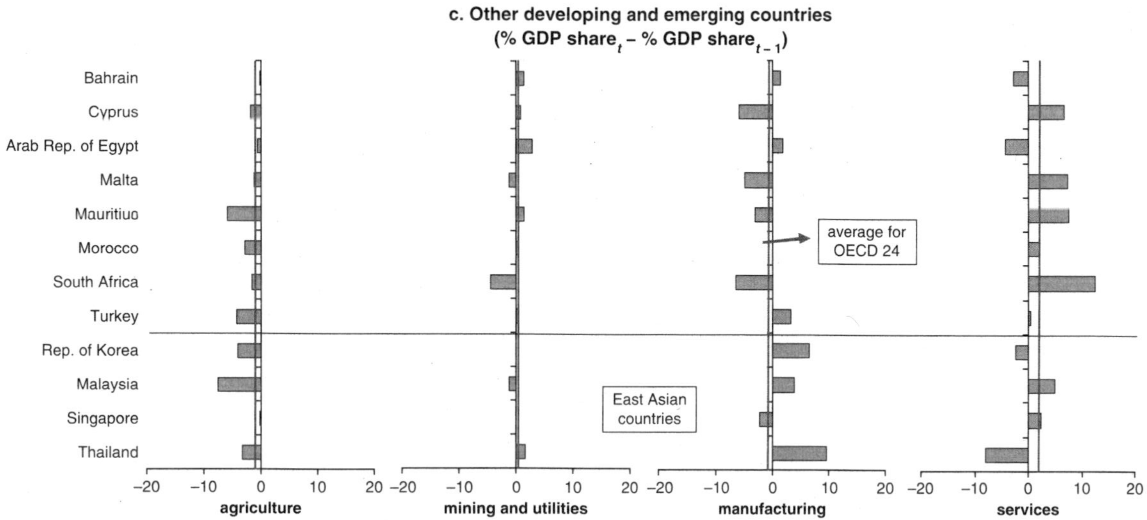

Source: UNSD.

Note. Table shows change in GDP by economic activity, at constant 1990 prices in U.S. dollars. *Agriculture* includes agriculture, hunting, forestry, and fishing. *Mining and utilities* includes mining and quarrying and electricity, gas, and water. *Services* includes construction; wholesale and retail trade, restaurants, and hotels; transport, storage, and communication; financial, insurance, real estate, and business services; and community, social, and personal services.

Figure 3.3 Changes within Services, 1990–2003

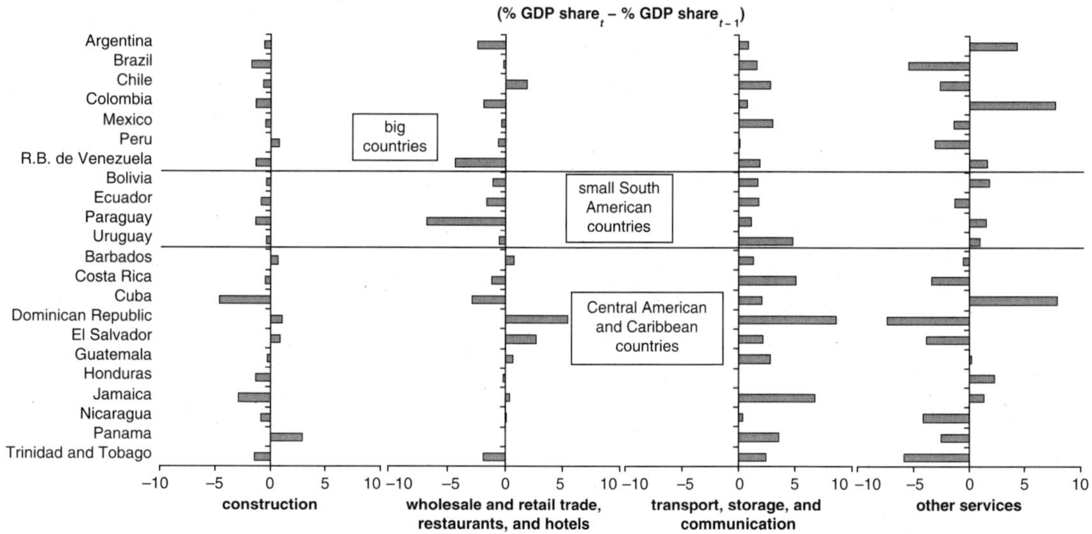

Source: UNSD.

Note: Table shows change in GDP by economic activity, at constant 1990 prices in U.S. dollars. *Other services* includes financial, insurance, real estate, and business services, as well as community, social, and personal services.

less prominently, in Brazil. This finding contrasts with the contraction of agriculture as a share of total gross domestic product (GDP) in all comparator countries considered. Instead, the share of output coming from the service sector has increased in many countries of the region, a pattern also observed in the rest of the economies presented in figure 3.2 (panels b and c). Most prominently, the share of mining and utilities has expanded, whereas manufacturing has contracted in most countries of the region. Although the shrinking share of manufacturing is consistent with the experience of many countries of the Organisation for Economic Co-operation and Development (OECD), it is at odds with a number of comparator emerging economies and high-growth OECD countries, such as Ireland or Finland, where manufacturing was a major driver of overall output growth and gained output shares. For example, in Argentina, Chile, Jamaica, Panama, and Uruguay, the share of manufacturing in total output shrank significantly.[3]

In other smaller economies and Mexico, manufacturing maintained or even increased its share in total output growth. For example, in Trinidad and Tobago, the manufacturing share in total GDP increased by 8 percentage points, an increase that is comparable with that observed in rapidly growing countries, such as Ireland, Korea, or Thailand. The surge in manufacturing in Mexico and other smaller economies has been supported by significant foreign direct investment (FDI) that was concentrated in both mature industries in some countries—for example, automobiles in Mexico and textiles in other Central American countries—and in clusters of high-tech activities. Costa Rica, for example, has been the Central American country that attracted the most high-tech FDI through the development of a dynamic cluster in electronics activities.[4]

The drivers of service sector expansion have some common patterns across the region's countries but also some peculiarities (figure 3.3). In most cases, the transport and communications industry expanded significantly, thanks to a privatization process that boosted productivity and the growing demand for telecommunications services. In countries such as Barbados and Jamaica, the development of services that use information and communication technologies was actively promoted by policy interventions aimed at export diversification and attracting FDI (De Ferranti and others 2002).[5] The other service sectors had varying performances across the board, with big contractions in wholesale and retail trade, restaurants, and hotels in Argentina, Paraguay, and the República Bolivariana de Venezuela as well as in financial and business services together with community, social, and personal services ("other services" in figure 3.3) in Brazil, the Dominican Republic, Nicaragua, and Trinidad and Tobago.

The changes in the output structure of the economy in the countries of the region are mirrored in the reallocation of labor (figure 3.4). However, cross-country patterns of labor reallocation are more homogeneous than

Figure 3.4 Changes in the Structure of the Economies: Sectoral Employment, Early 1990s to Early 2000s

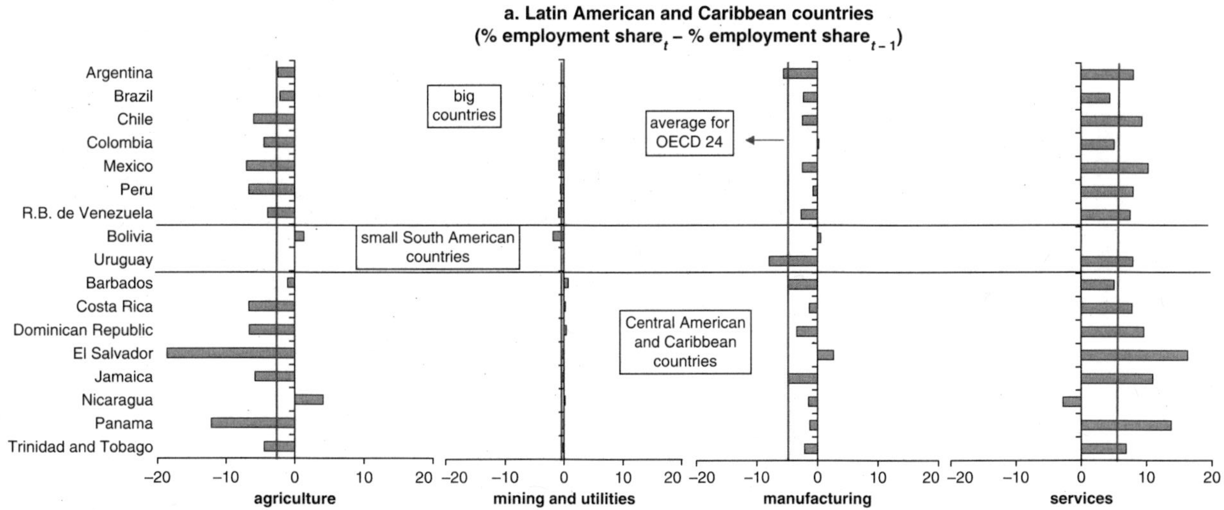

(continued)

Figure 3.4 Changes in the Structure of the Economies: Sectoral Employment, Early 1990s to Early 2000s *(continued)*

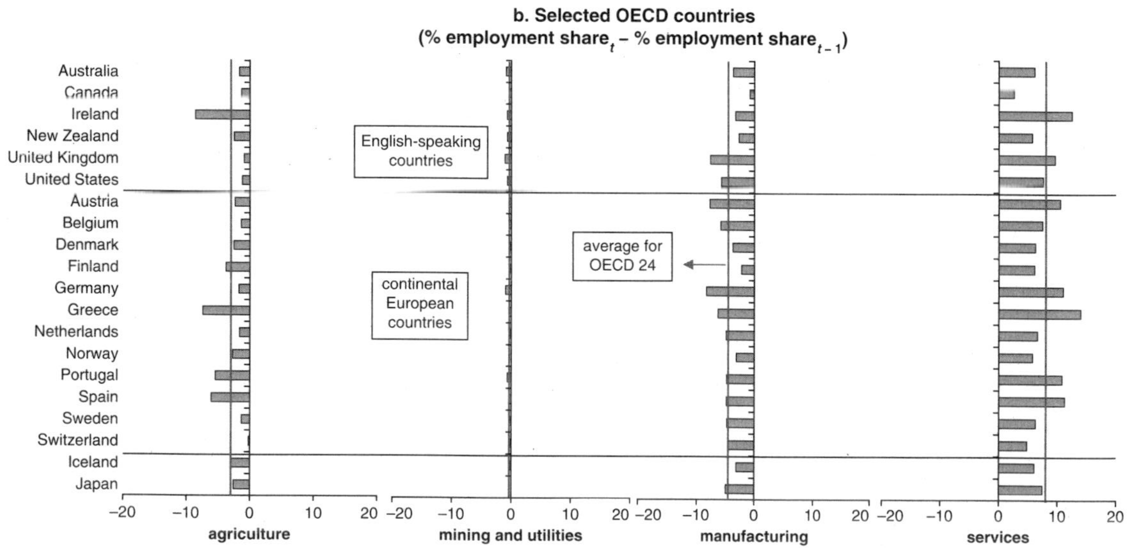

(continued)

Figure 3.4 Changes in the Structure of the Economies: Sectoral Employment, Early 1990s to Early 2000s *(continued)*

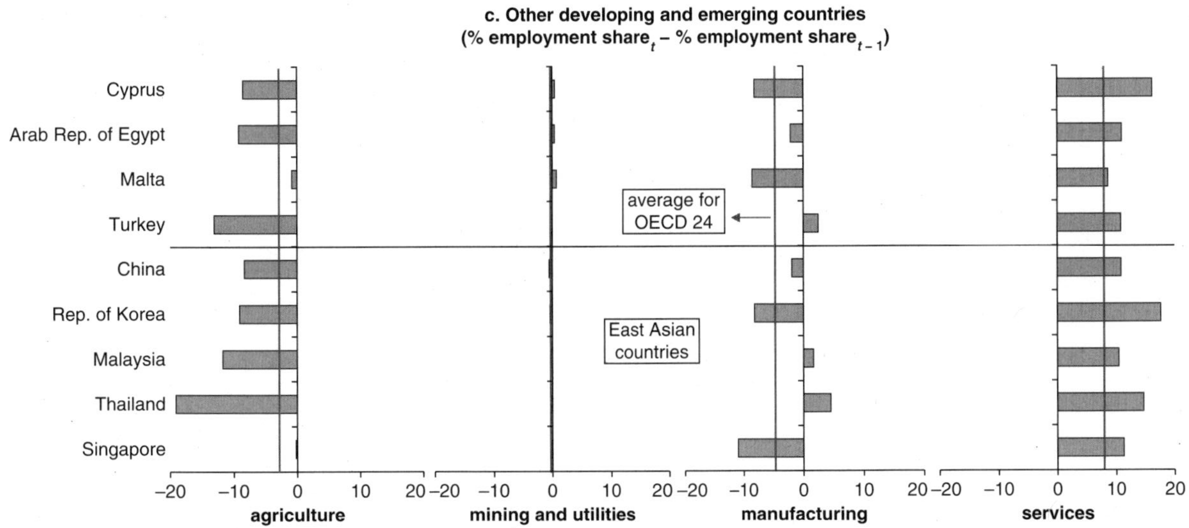

Sources: For countries of Latin America and the Caribbean, annex table 3.A.1; for all other countries, International Labour Office.

Note: Agriculture includes agriculture, hunting, forestry, and fishing. *Mining and utilities* includes mining and quarrying and electricity, gas, and water. *Services* includes construction; wholesale and retail trade, restaurants, and hotels; transport, storage, and communication; financial, insurance, real estate, and business services; and community, social, and personal services. Data correspond to the period from 1990 to 2003. Exceptions in panel a are as follows: Barbados (1993–2003); Bolivia (1989–2003); Trinidad and Tobago (1990–2004); Uruguay (1992–2003). Exceptions in panel b are as follows: Germany (1991–2003); Iceland (1991–2002); the Netherlands (1990–2002); Switzerland (1991–2003). Exceptions in panel c are as follows: China (1990–2002); Singapore (1989–2003).

those observed on the output side, suggesting large cross-country differences in the sectoral evolution of productivity. In particular, with only two exceptions, all countries experienced a decline in employment in agriculture[6] and in manufacturing, whereas the service sector experienced large increases. The only two exceptions to this general trend are El Salvador,[7] which saw a relative increase in employment in manufacturing, and Nicaragua, which had an increase in agricultural employment.[8] Similar patterns of reallocation of employment from agriculture and manufacturing to services are observed in OECD countries and most comparator countries. However, in some of the fast-growing countries of East Asia—for example, Malaysia and Thailand—manufacturing not only had a stronger contribution to output but also absorbed more employment.

Concentration of Job Creation in Low-Productivity Service Sectors

As shown in table 3.1, the service sectors all together accounted for 70 percent of the overall employment growth in the region over the past decade. Although all main service sector industries have expanded, the relatively low-productivity ones—for example, (a) wholesale and retail trade, restaurants, and hotels and (b) community, social, and personal services—were the most dynamic.

Retail and tourism have been particularly important for the generation of jobs in Brazil, the Dominican Republic, El Salvador, Mexico, Peru, and the República Bolivariana de Venezuela, where this sector was responsible for more than 35 percent of the employment growth. Tourism has been an important substitute for the declining sugar and banana industries in many Central American and Caribbean countries.

Community, social, and personal services represented the most significant source of employment growth in Argentina, Chile, and Colombia. The professional activities in health, education, and consulting were the most dynamic drivers of employment in the three countries. Although public employment increased in the early 1990s, the public sector has gradually lost its role as the employer of last resort. The privatization of state-run companies, which were generally overstaffed, as well as the stronger need to contain public expenditures as part of the macrostabilization programs, made the public administration more responsible in its hiring policy than in the previous decades (Chong and Saavedra 2003).

Sectoral Composition of the Region's Economies

Where do the countries of the region stand today in terms of their output and employment structure compared with OECD countries and other comparator economies? One way to assess the current structure of Latin American and Caribbean countries from an international perspective is to

Table 3.1 Sectoral Contribution to Employment Growth as a Percentage of Total Growth, Early 1990s to Early 2000s

		Sectoral contribution (%)							
Country	*Annual employment growth rate (%)*	*Agriculture*	*Mining and utilities*	*Manufacturing*	*Construction*	*Wholesale and retail; restaurants and hotels*	*Transport, storage, and communications*	*Financing, insurance, real estate, and business services*	*Community, social, and personal services*
Nicaragua	4.8	51	1	5	12	17	2	1	11
Costa Rica	4.4	4	2	14	6	34	9	16	15
Venezuela, R.B. de	4.1	1	–1	7	9	37	9	4	33
Panama	3.7	–7	0	7	15	33	12	10	30
El Salvador	3.6	–23	0	26	7	59	7	13	11
Dominican Republic	3.4	–2	2	6	14	38	12	1	29
Peru	3.0	12	–1	8	2	36	0	9	35
Mexico	2.8	5	–1	14	7	35	10	11	19

(continued)

Table 3.1 Sectoral Contribution to Employment Growth as a Percentage of Total Growth, Early 1990s to Early 2000s *(continued)*

		Sectoral contribution (%)							
Country	*Annual employment growth rate (%)*	*Agriculture*	*Mining and utilities*	*Manufacturing*	*Construction*	*Wholesale and retail; restaurants and hotels*	*Transport, storage, and communications*	*Financing, insurance, real estate, and business services*	*Community, social, and personal services*
Brazil	2.2	9	–1	9	8	40	6	14	15
Chile	2.0	–9	–2	6	13	25	14	21	32
Paraguay	1.9	19	1	13	4	29	5	1	28
Colombia	1.8	–13	–6	15	–15	9	11	–5	103
Argentina	0.8	–23	1	–61	–4	26	28	50	82

Sources: Regional statistical institutes. See annex table 3.A.1 for a complete description of sources.

Note: A growth rate preceded by a negative sign indicates a sector that has experienced a decline in employment. The periods covered by the data are as follows: Argentina (1991–2001); Brazil (1990–2003); Chile (1990–2003); Costa Rica (1990–2000); Dominican Republic (1991–2003); El Salvador (1992–2001); Mexico (1992–2002); Nicaragua (1990–2001); Panama (1990–2003); Peru (1989–2000); República Bolivariana de Venezuela (1990–2002). *Agriculture* includes agriculture, hunting, forestry, and fishing. *Mining and utilities* includes mining and quarrying, electricity, gas, and water, except in Peru, where the term refers to mining only. The contribution of each sector is computed as the employment growth times the employment share at the beginning of the period.

compare their GDP and employment distribution by sectors with those prevailing in market-oriented economies of similar income per capita. This exercise offers only an illustration of the potential gap in the structural composition and possible directions of further changes. Figures 3.5 through 3.7 present the evolution of the share of GDP in manufacturing since the 1980s and compares it with the market-based benchmark constructed from a large sample of developing, emerging, and industrial countries (see box 3.1 for details on the construction of the benchmarks).

Looking at the evolution of the share of manufacturing in total value added suggests that most countries in the region experienced a process of deindustrialization over the past two decades. Interestingly, the position with respect to the benchmark is not clearly related to the level of development. The process of deindustrialization seems to have taken place in a number of cases during recessions and major economic crises, but the lost shares in manufacturing were not regained during expansionary periods (figures 3.5 through 3.7). Among large countries of the region, deindustrialization has been particularly marked in Argentina, Brazil, and Colombia. However, from an international perspective, most of these countries are at—or near—the benchmark in terms of the share of output from manufacturing in the most recent years. The exception is Chile because of its high dependence on mineral extraction.

Among the Central American and Caribbean countries, a significant reduction has also occurred in the share of manufacturing in total GDP (figures 3.6 and 3.8). Even more dramatic, however, is the fall observed in some of the small countries of South America—in particular, Ecuador, Paraguay, and Uruguay—which have experienced a decline of more than 10 percentage points in the share of value added from manufacturing since the 1980s, going well below the market-based international benchmark.

Moving to the sectoral distribution of employment (see figure 3.9), one sees that a number of countries still have a share of employment in agriculture that is higher than in the industrial countries and in many comparator countries at similar levels of development. In particular, Guatemala, Honduras, Nicaragua, and Paraguay, which all have relatively low incomes within the region, depend on agriculture as an important generator of value added (and employment), with shares that exceed the OECD average by 15 percentage points.

Although mining and utilities are important generators of output in countries with substantial petroleum resources, such as Ecuador, Trinidad and Tobago, or the República Bolivariana de Venezuela, and although the extraction of copper is of huge importance to Chile's economy, these sectors account for a comparably small share of employment. These activities are intensive in natural resources and capital and make little use of labor input.

The share of employment in manufacturing is not only lower than that in the OECD countries but also lower than that in most comparator countries. The shares of services are generally less important in Latin America and the

Figure 3.5 Evolution of the Manufacturing Share of GDP in Latin America and the Caribbean: Big Countries

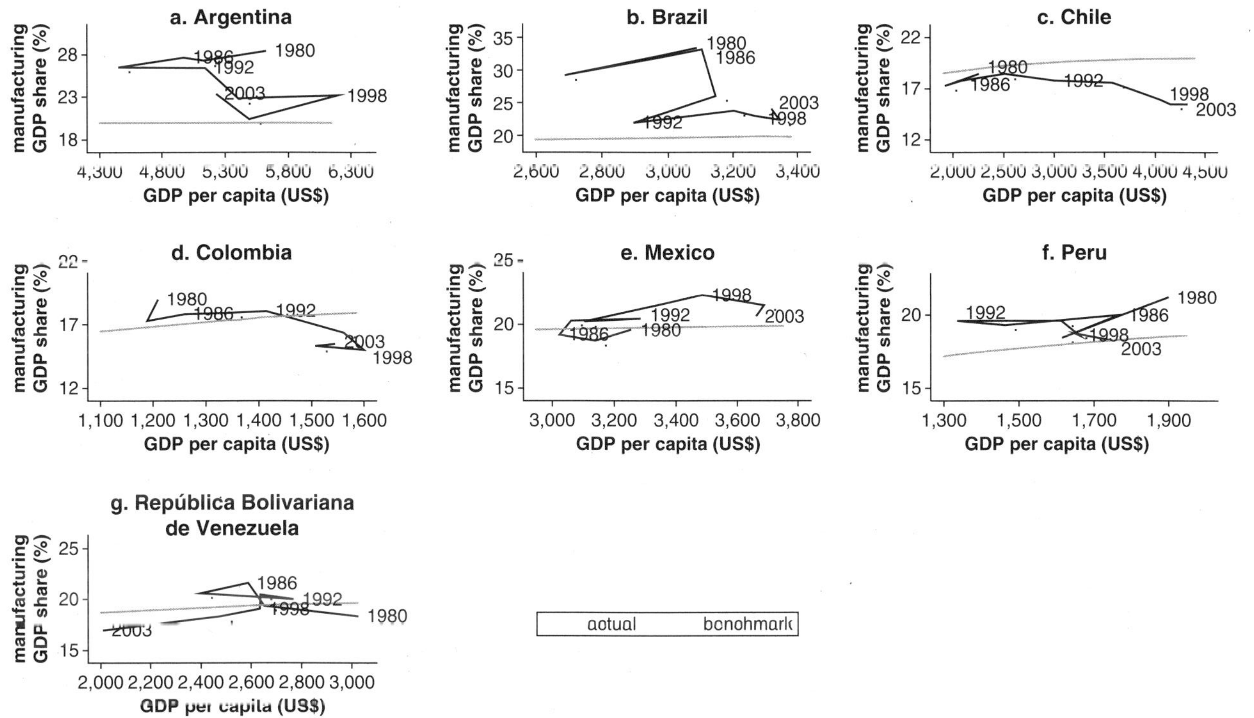

Source: Authors' calculations.

Figure 3.6 Evolution of the Manufacturing Share of GDP in Latin America and the Caribbean: Central America and the Caribbean

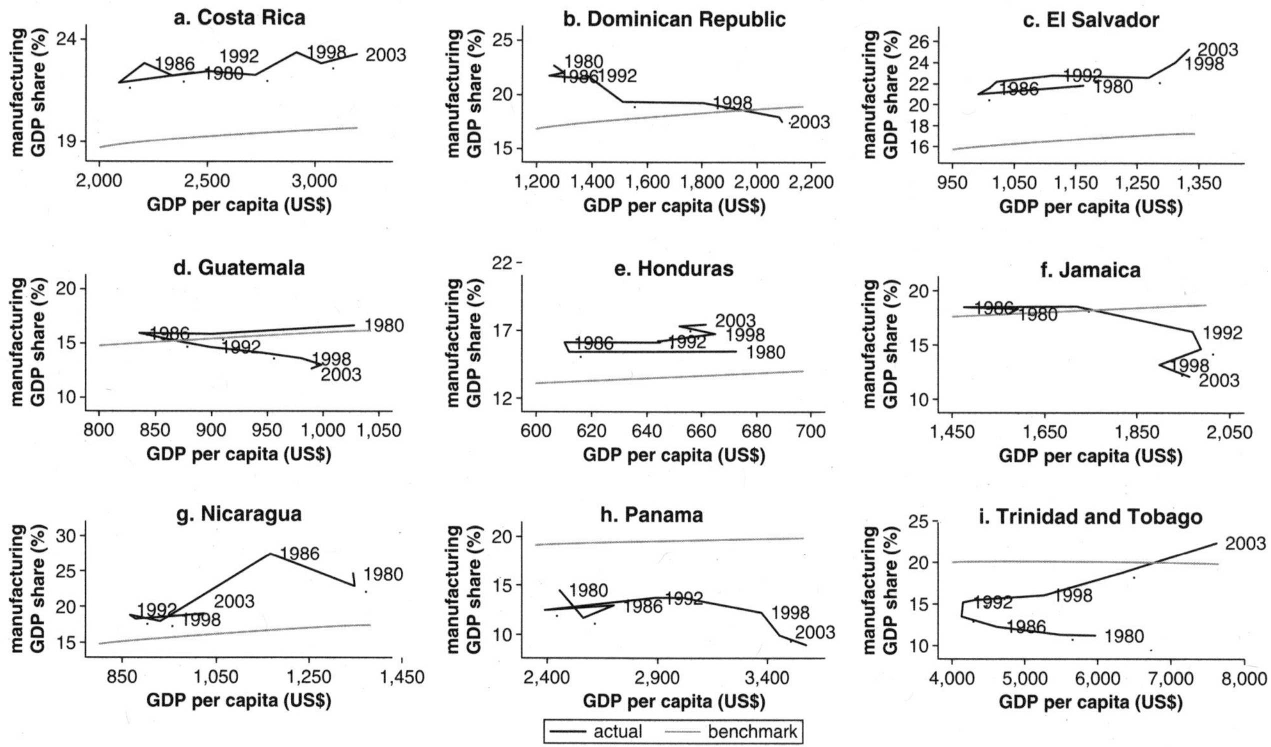

Source: Authors' calculations.

Figure 3.7 Evolution of the Manufacturing Share of GDP in Latin America and the Caribbean: Small South American Countries

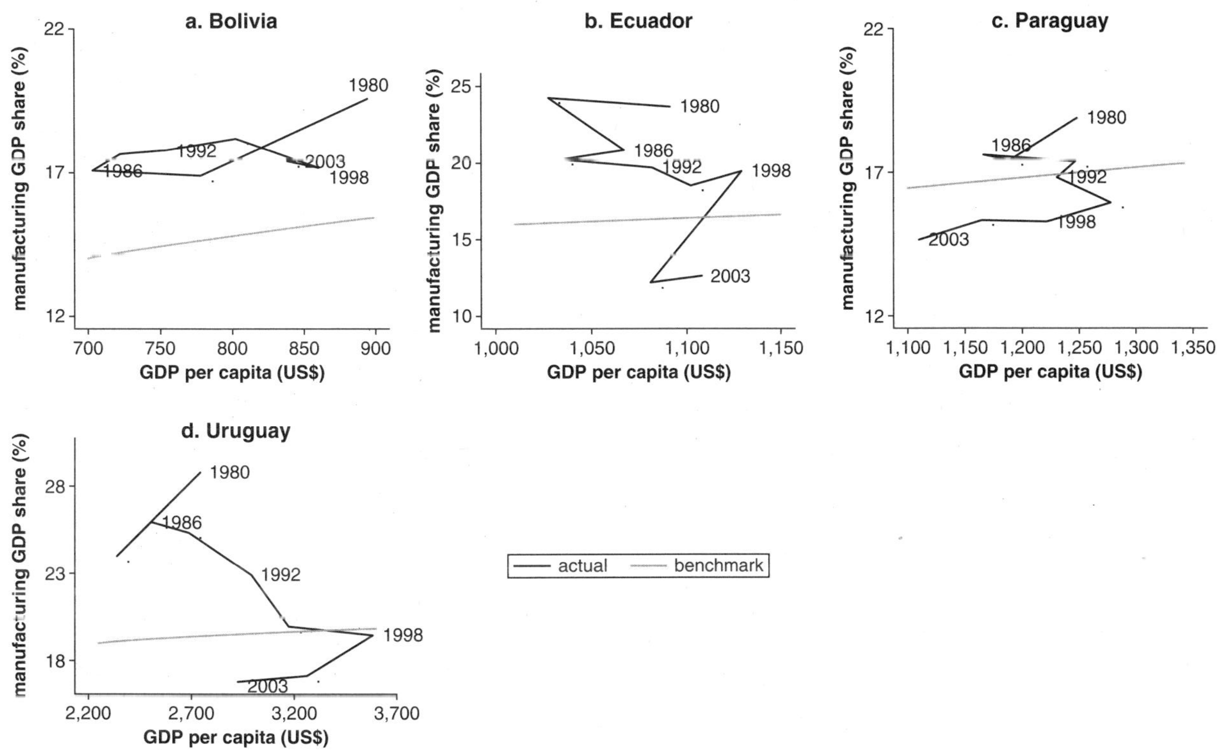

Source: Authors' calculations.

Box 3.1 Economic Development and the Employment Structure

The economic literature has identified a number of typical development patterns (Chenery and Taylor 1968; Rowthorn and Ramaswamy 1997). For example, the share of agriculture in GDP and employment tends to fall as economies grow richer, whereas the share of manufacturing in GDP and employment increases at low levels of income per capita and shows a decline at higher levels of income per capita, as employment shifts toward services. Therefore, the share of services and, in particular, market-oriented services rises with income per capita for a cross-section of 50 countries. For each sector, the share in employment is regressed on the log of GDP per capita and its square.

This chapter follows Raiser, Schaffer, and Schuchhardt (2003) and constructs a benchmark that is based on regression analyses of data for 65 developing, emerging, and industrial countries. The benchmark measures the typical share of manufacturing in countries at similar levels of GDP to those observed in Latin America and the Caribbean. Formerly centrally planned economies of Eastern Europe and the former Soviet Union, countries dominated by oil exports, very small countries, and those affected by severe conflicts in the period covered by the data are excluded from the construction. Following is the resulting list of countries used in the benchmark: Algeria, Australia, Austria, Bahrain, Bangladesh, Belgium, Botswana, Burkina Faso, Cameroon, Canada, Cape Verde, Côte d'Ivoire, Cyprus, Denmark, Djibouti, the Arab Republic of Egypt, Fiji, Finland, France, Gabon, Germany, Ghana, Greece, Guinea, Iceland, India, Indonesia, Ireland, Italy, Japan, Jordan, Kenya, the Republic of Korea, Lesotho, Madagascar, Malaysia, Mali, Malta, Mauritius, the Federated States of Micronesia, Morocco, Mozambique, the Netherlands, New Zealand, Nigeria, Norway, Pakistan, the Philippines, Portugal, Samoa, Senegal, Singapore, the Solomon Islands, South Africa, Spain, Swaziland, Sweden, Switzerland, Thailand, Tunisia, Turkey, the United Kingdom, the United States, Zambia, and Zimbabwe.

The benchmarking analysis is based on the share of GDP—not employment—to maximize time and country coverage. Data of sectoral GDP and GDP per capita, both expressed in 1990 U.S. dollars, are from the United Nations Statistics Office. The benchmarking regression consists of a fixed effect estimation of a panel of countries from 1970 to 2003 where the explained variable is the GDP share of each sector, which is regressed on the logarithm of per capita GDP, the square of the logarithm of per capita GDP, and country fixed and year effects. The results, displayed in box table 3.1.A, show significant coefficients for both variables in all sectors, suggesting a quadratic relation between the sector shares of GDP

(continued)

Box 3.1 Economic Development and the Employment Structure *(continued)*

and per capita GDP. The sign and magnitude of the estimated coefficients are robust to changes in the group of countries or periods considered.

Box Table 3.1.A Benchmarking Regression

	Dependent variable: GDP share			
	Manufacturing	*Agriculture*	*Market services*[a]	*Mining and utilities*
Log GDP per capita	0.2571 (0.0121)***	−0.41144 (0.0126)***	0.0990 (0.0133)***	−0.40381 (0.1643)***
(Log GDP per capita)^2	−0.0150 (0.0008)***	0.0235 (0.0008)***	−0.0057 (0.0008)***	0.0221 (0.0010)***
Constant	−0.8987 (0.0484)***	1.9276 (0.0500)***	−0.1167 (0.0528)**	1.8901 (0.0672)***

Source: Authors' calculations.

Note: Standard errors are in parentheses; * = significant at 10 percent; ** = significant at 5 percent; *** = significant at 1 percent.

a. Because of data limitations, market services include only construction; wholesale and retail trade, restaurants, and hotels; and transport, storage, and communications.

The regression was replicated to test whether Latin American and Caribbean economies have a different structure than that of comparator countries. The regression included the region's countries in the sample but also allowed the coefficients for the region to be different from those of the other countries. Formally, the regression is based on the following specification:

$$\begin{aligned} share\_manuf_{it} = {} & c + SA - CAC + d_t + gdp\_pc_{it} + SA * gdp\_pc_{it} \\ & + CAC * gdp\_pc_{it} + gdp\_pc\text{^}2_{it} + SA * gdp\_pc\text{^}2_{it} \\ & + CAC * gdp\_pc\text{^}2_{it} + \mu_{it} \end{aligned}$$

where SA is a dummy for South America, CAC stands for Central America and the Caribbean, and d_t denotes the year effect. See box table 3.1.B.

(continued)

Box 3.1 Economic Development and the Employment Structure *(continued)*

Box Table 3.1.B Additional Regression

	1970–89	*1990–2003*
South America	1.478 (3.01)***	–1.145 (1.22)
Central America and the Caribbean	–0.366 (0.50)	–0.073 (0.07)
Log GDP/pc	0.182 (11.88)***	0.079 (3.35)***
south*Log GDP/pc	–0.355 (2.63)***	0.36 (1.51)
cent*Log GDP/pc	0.144 (0.72)	0.074 (0.27)
(Log GDP/pc)^2	–0.011 (10.93)***	–0.002 (1.73)*
south*(Log GDP/pc)^2	0.022 (2.34)**	–0.027 (1.78)*
cent*(Log GDP/pc)^2	–0.013 (0.92)	–0.008 (0.44)
Constant	–0.584 (9.82)***	–0.301 (3.15)***
Observations	1,720	1,204

Source: Authors' calculations.

Note: Absolute value of *z* statistics is in parentheses; * = significant at 10 percent; ** = significant at 5 percent; *** = significant at 1 percent.

The results suggest a lower share of manufacturing GDP at relatively low levels of income in South America in the 1970 to 1989 period, which weakens in the most recent period. However, in the most recent period, the process of deindustrialization at higher levels of income tends to be more marked in South America.

Figure 3.8 Sectoral GDP Shares, 2003

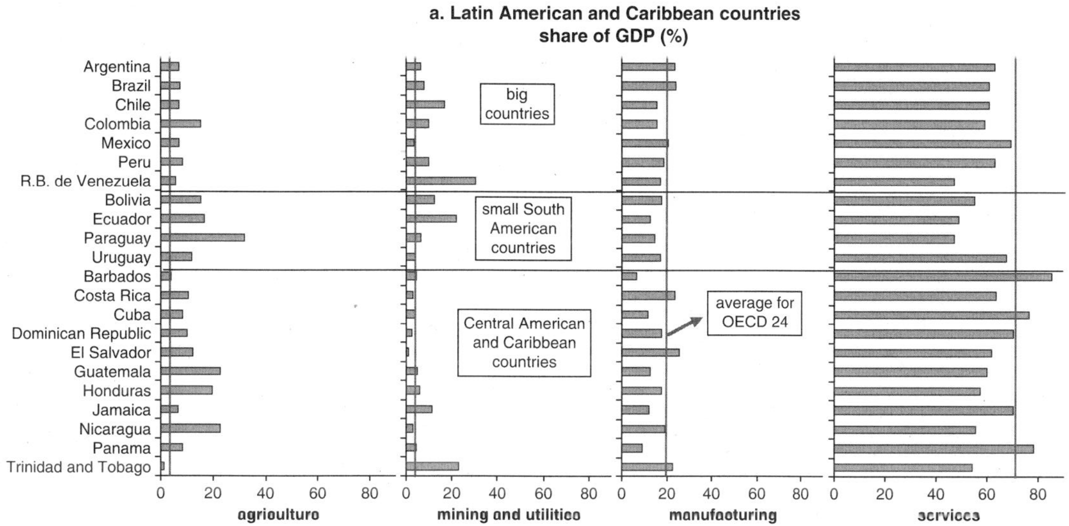

(continued)

Figure 3.8 Sectoral GDP Shares, 2003 *(continued)*

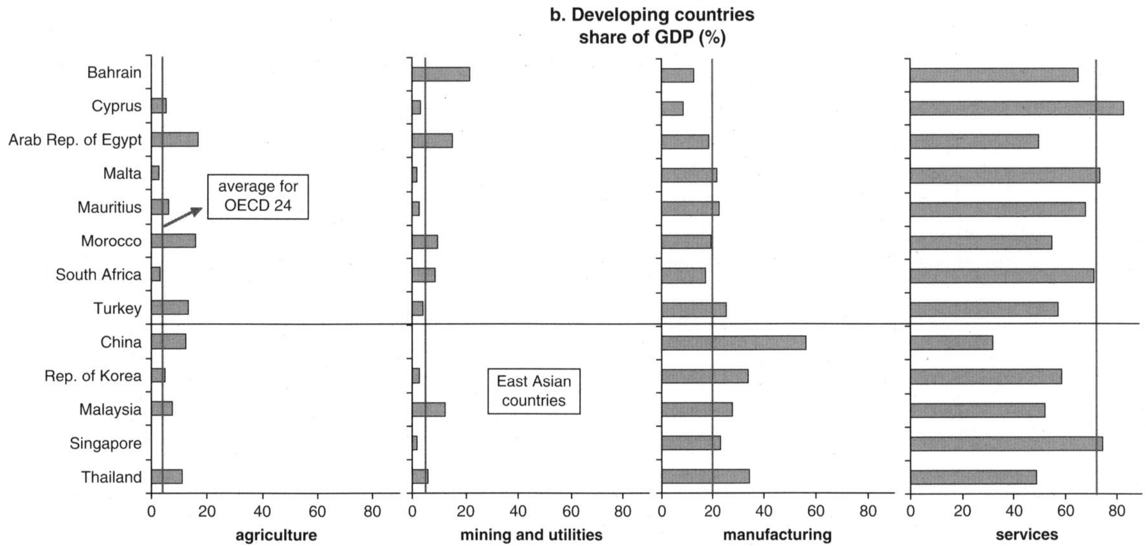

Source: UNSD.

Note: Table shows share of GDP by economic activity, at constant 1990 prices in U.S. dollars. *Agriculture* includes agriculture, hunting, forestry, and fishing. *Mining and utilities* includes mining and quarrying and electricity, gas, and water. *Services* includes construction; wholesale and retail trade, restaurants, and hotels; transport, storage, and communication; financial, insurance, real estate, and business services; and community, social, and personal services.

Figure 3.9 Sectoral Employment Shares, Early 2000s

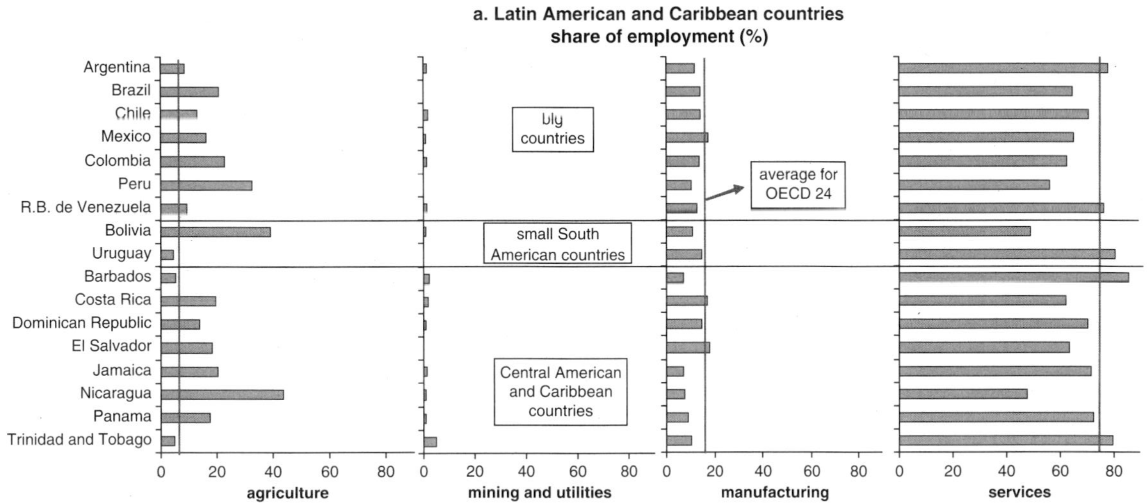

(continued)

Figure 3.9 Sectoral Employment Shares, Early 2000s *(continued)*

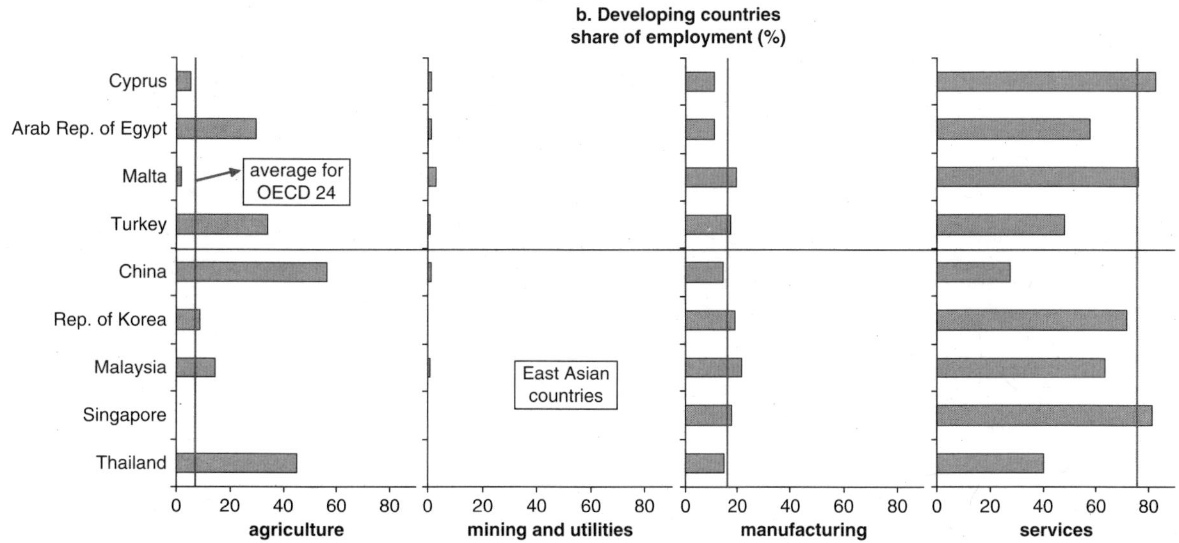

Sources: For panel a, national statistics offices; for panel b, International Labour Office. See annex table 3.A.1 for a list of individual country sources.

Note: Agriculture includes agriculture, hunting, forestry, and fishing. *Mining and utilities* includes mining and quarrying and electricity, gas, and water. *Services* includes construction; wholesale and retail trade, restaurants, and hotels; transport, storage, and communication; financial, insurance, real estate, and business services; and community, social, and personal services.

Caribbean than in the OECD but fairly similar to those of the comparator countries. Interestingly, the difference in the share of employment in services with respect to the OECD is smaller than that based on GDP, suggesting that the labor productivity in services is far smaller in the region than in the comparator countries.

All in all, the economic structure of the region's countries has gone through significant changes since the 1990s. Many countries have gone through a process of deindustrialization, often with significant increases in service sector activities. Although this process is common in most market economies as they progress along the income ladder, the magnitude and composition of the changes have specific characteristics in Latin America and the Caribbean. Compared with those of East Asia, the region's countries had a similar share of GDP in manufacturing in the 1970s. The share dropped to about 15 percent by 2003, while it rose to about 30 percent in East Asia. In many Latin American and Caribbean countries, the process of deindustrialization has been propelled by economic crises with large drops in output and manufacturing and has not picked up during the recovery period. Moreover, the composition of service sectors is skewed toward low-productivity activities that absorbed large shares of employment released by the manufacturing sector but often with low-productivity performance and thus lower contributions to overall output and wage growth.

Is deindustrialization and rapid increase in employment in low-productivity service sectors a source of concern? This question is a subject of intense debate in the region. Several theories have stressed the importance of manufacturing as an engine for development and modernization of the economy. In particular, the manufacturing sector plays an important role in the creation of backward and forward links, technological innovation, and other potential externalities that are not found in other sectors.[9] However, others have indicated that the deliberate choice of many countries of the region to promote manufacturing in the mid 20th century in a natural resource–rich region has led to the development of a sector with limited potential for long-term productivity growth at the expense of the traditional or potential sources of growth in the resource-intensive sectors (De Ferranti and others 2002; Martin and Mitra 2001). Indeed, natural resource–based activities can also have important spillover effects by promoting technological progress and productivity growth.[10] Moreover, developing dynamic natural resource–based activities is not incompatible with building new comparative advantages in manufacturing, as the experiences of a number of industrial countries suggest. For natural resource–based activities to be an engine of growth, however, complementary investment is needed in good institutions, human capital, and knowledge.[11] These complementary investments seem to have been lacking in many countries in Latin America and the Caribbean, thus limiting the role that natural resources could have played in driving growth and technological advances.

Sectoral Reallocation and Productivity

Productivity measurement at the sector level is constrained by the degree of detail and by measurement problems in particular in services. The following productivity analysis focuses on one-digit industry-level data.[12] Moreover, the sectoral decomposition of productivity does not take into account sectoral interactions attributable to the role that goods and services of some sectors play in the production process of other sectors and vice versa. Bearing these caveats in mind, table 3.2 presents the level of labor productivity (measured as simple GDP per worker) in the different sectors of the economy for countries of Latin America and the Caribbean as well as for a set of comparator countries.[13] Table 3.3 then presents the contributions of each sector to the aggregate productivity growth.

Effect of Shifts toward Low-Productivity Services on Productivity Growth

Tables 3.2 and 3.3 suggest that sectors with relatively low labor productivity levels have been the drivers of job creation, whereas some of the more dynamic sectors in terms of productivity have shed employment or contributed only minimally to job creation.[14] The construction and trade sectors tend to have only a fraction of the productivity of manufacturing, and the gap is larger than that generally observed in OECD or comparator countries. Although construction has had only a modest role in total job creation in the region, wholesale and retail trade accounted for 30 to 50 percent of total job creation (see table 3.1). The case of Brazil illustrates the trade-off between productivity contribution and employment contribution in the trade sector. Overall labor productivity was very modest in Brazil in the early 1990s to early 2000s (0.3 percent per year). The trade sector had a major negative contribution to productivity growth while, at the same time, it accounted for more than one-third of total employment growth. A similar story applies to El Salvador, Paraguay, Peru, and the República Bolivariana de Venezuela.

At the other end of the productivity distribution ladder, the transport and communication sector and the mining and utilities sector have high levels of productivity in most countries, but their share in total employment growth has been very modest. There are, however, a few exceptions, such as Mexico, where the transport, storage, and communication sector made a significant contribution to productivity and also created more employment.

The effects of shifts in sectoral shares on aggregate productivity growth can be calculated using different techniques. One approach, shown in equation 3.1, is based on the *shift-and-share analysis* that decomposes

Table 3.2 Labor Productivity by Sectors, Relative to Manufacturing, Early 2000s

Country	*Agriculture, hunting, forestry, fishing*	*Mining and utilities*	*Manufacturing*	*Construction*	*Wholesale, retail trade; restaurants and hotels*	*Transport, storage, and communication*	*Other services*	*Productivity in manufacturing*
Latin American and Caribbean countries								
Argentina	46	292	100	41	38	52	56	37,859
Brazil	23	n.a.	100	52	24	87	90	19,622
Chile	48	871	100	86	73	102	78	31,665
Colombia	61	781	100	63	38	121	106	14,679
Mexico	35	315	100	46	107	239	71	21,422
Peru	15	809	100	81	60	n.a.	49	17,867
Venezuela, R.B. de	37	1,877	100	45	37	59	42	31,590
Average	38	824	100	59	54	110	70	24,958
OECD and developing countries								
Cyprus	125	325	100	72	103	283	142	26,656
Egypt, Arab Rep. of	33	606	100	34	65	95	38	21,841
Malta	128	64	100	n.a.	70	121	108	39,199

(*continued*)

Table 3.2 Labor Productivity by Sectors, Relative to Manufacturing, Early 2000s *(continued)*

Country	*Agriculture, hunting, forestry, fishing*	*Mining and utilities*	*Manufacturing*	*Construction*	*Wholesale, retail trade; restaurants and hotels*	*Transport, storage, and communication*	*Other services*	*Productivity in manufacturing*
Turkey	27	307	100	59	81	195	57	31,965
Greece	44	271	100	93	89	156	114	36,220
Portugal	57	503	100	50	90	200	160	24,531
Spain	81	305	100	64	61	106	91	45,428
East Asia								
Korea, Rep. of	31	387	100	57	25	99	50	60,959
Malaysia	40	1,103	100	26	46	111	85	25,505
Singapore	27	264	100	71	62	103	67	58,849
Thailand	11	597	100	26	37	163	61	30,757
OECD 24								
Average	65	341	100	61	63	118	80	53,736

Sources: For employment in Latin America and the Caribbean, see annex table 3.A.1; for all other countries, International Labour Office. GDP data from the UNSD and Groningen Growth and Development Centre and the Conference Board, Total Economy Database, August 2005.

Note: Labor productivity is defined as the simple ratio of output over employment. The data of GDP by sector were constructed by taking the distribution of output among economic activities according to UNSD data and applying these distributions to the series of total GDP (in 1990 U.S. dollars), converted at Geary Khamis's purchasing power parities obtained from Groningen Growth and Development Centre and the Conference Board. All series were smoothed by application of a Hodrick-Prescott filter.

Table 3.3 Sectoral Contribution to Labor Productivity Growth as Percentage of Total Growth, Early 1990s to Early 2000s

		Sectoral contribution (%)						
Country	*Total labor productivity growth (%)*	*Agriculture*	*Mining and utilities*	*Manufacturing*	*Construction*	*Wholesale and retail; restaurants and hotels*	*Transport, storage, and communication*	*Other services*
Chile	4.4	12	26	15	4	14	12	17
		–9	–2	6	13	25	14	53
Dominican Republic	2.8	12	3	18	7	23	39	–3
		–2	2	6	14	38	12	30
Argentina	1.6	16	19	22	4	–4	1	42
		–23	1	–61	–4	26	28	132
Costa Rica	1.2	22	5	76	–4	–23	28	–3
		4	2	14	6	34	9	31
Panama	0.9	49	22	–8	–10	–38	56	29
		–7	0	7	15	33	12	40
Colombia	0.8	55	59	–8	–2	–22	5	13
		–13	–6	15	–15	9	11	97

(continued)

Table 3.3 Sectoral Contribution to Labor Productivity Growth as Percentage of Total Growth, Early 1990s to Early 2000s *(continued)*

		Sectoral contribution (%)						
Country	*Total labor productivity growth (%)*	*Agriculture*	*Mining and utilities*	*Manufacturing*	*Construction*	*Wholesale and retail; restaurants and hotels*	*Transport, storage, and communication*	*Other services*
El Salvador	0.6	115	7	52	–1	–119	40	6
		–23	0	26	7	59	7	24
Mexico	0.5	35	24	59	–7	13	85	–109
		5	–1	14	7	35	10	30
Brazil	0.3	10	0	90	–44	–279	52	217
		9	–1	9	8	40	6	29
Paraguay	0.2	315	168	–49	–37	–281	40	–55
		19	1	13	4	29	5	29
Peru	–0.1	–34	296	158	146	–311	0	–543
		12	–1	8	2	36	0	43

(continued)

Table 3.3 Sectoral Contribution to Labor Productivity Growth as Percentage of Total Growth, Early 1990s to Early 2000s *(continued)*

		Sectoral contribution (%)						
Country	*Total labor productivity growth (%)*	*Agriculture*	*Mining and utilities*	*Manufacturing*	*Construction*	*Wholesale and retail; restaurants and hotels*	*Transport, storage, and communication*	*Other services*
Nicaragua	–1.2	–83	4	22	–25	–13	7	–13
		51	1	5	12	17	2	12
Venezuela, R.B. de	–2.0	0	30	–9	–9	–58	–6	–48
		1	–1	7	9	37	9	37

Sources: For employment, see annex 3.A; for GDP, UNSD.

Note: A minus sign indicates the sector that has experienced a decline in labor productivity. The contribution of each sector was computed as the difference of the contribution of the GDP and the contribution of employment. The contribution of GDP and employment were computed as the growth rate of each sector times the share at the beginning. *Agriculture* includes agriculture, hunting, forestry, and fishing. *Mining and utilities* includes mining and quarrying, as well as electricity, gas, and water because of a source constraint. *Other services* includes financing, insurance, real estate, and business services and community, social, and personal services. The years covered are as follows: Argentina (1991–2001); Brazil (1990–2003); Chile (1990–2003); Colombia (1990–2003); Costa Rica (1990–2000); Dominican Republic (1991–2003); El Salvador (1992–2001); Mexico (1992–2002); Nicaragua (1990–2001); Panama (1990–2003); Paraguay (1990–2003); Peru (1989–2000); República Bolivariana de Venezuela (1990–2002). The rows shaded gray are the sectoral contribution to employment growth from table 3.1.

productivity for the economy as a whole as the sum of the productivity level of each sector weighted by the sectoral employment shares:

$$P_m = \frac{Y_m}{L_m} = \sum_{j=1}^{n} \frac{Y_j}{L_j} * \frac{L_j}{L_m} = \sum_{j=1}^{n} P_j * S_j, \tag{3.1}$$

where Y is output, L is employment by sector $(j = 1.....n)$ and the total economy (m), P is labor productivity (Y/L), and S is the sectoral employment share. In a discrete time perspective, the expression can be rewritten as follows:

$$\frac{P^t - P^0}{P^0} = \frac{\sum_{j=1}^{n}\left(P_j^t - P_j^0\right) * S_j^0}{\sum_{j=1}^{n} P_j^0 * S_j^0} + \frac{\sum_{j=1}^{n} P_j^0 * \left(S_j^t - S_j^0\right)}{\sum_{j=1}^{n} P_j^0 * S_j^0} + \frac{\sum_{j=1}^{n}\left(P_j^t - P_j^0\right) * \left(S_j^t - S_j^0\right)}{\sum_{j=1}^{n} P_j^0 * S_j^0} \tag{3.2}$$

for a current year t and a base year 0.[15]

The first term on the right-hand side is the *within-industry contribution* to overall productivity growth. The second term can be defined as the *net shift effect*—that is, the contribution coming from changes in the sectoral composition of employment. The third term is derived as a residual and represents the joint effect of changes in employment shares and sectoral productivity: it is positive if sectors with above-average productivity growth increase their share of total employment; it is negative if either expanding sectors have below-average productivity growth or sectors with high-productivity growth are also declining in their shares of total employment.[16]

The shift-and-share analysis sheds further light on the process of reallocation and its effect on productivity in the region (figure 3.10):[17]

- *Within effect.* Much of the overall productivity growth comes from within-sector productivity changes. This result is common for industrial countries, especially in recent years (see Bassanini and others 2000). But in previous decades, when structural changes were more marked, productivity was also largely driven by substantial shifts in employment from less productive to more productive industries.
- *Between effect.* The effect of reallocation of labor from less productive to more productive industries is positive in most countries, albeit generally small. This result is largely because employment has moved from low-productivity agricultural activities to manufacturing

Figure 3.10 Labor Productivity Growth Decomposition, Early 1990s to Early 2000s

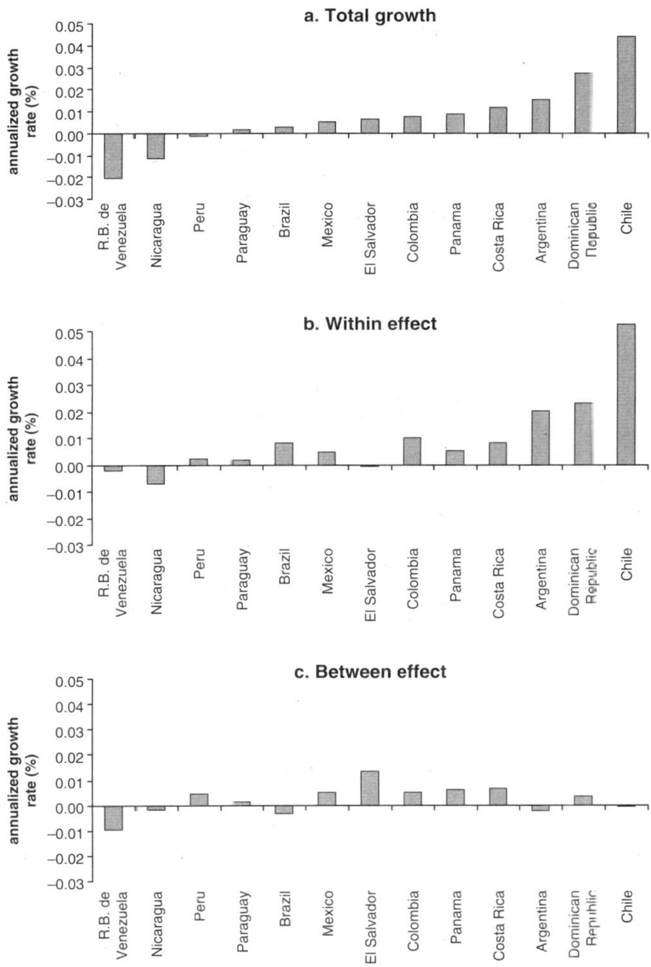

(continued)

and especially to service sectors with relatively higher productivity levels.

- *Cross-term.* A more worrisome element is that the cross-term of the decomposition is negative in all countries. In other words, those industries that contributed the most to aggregate labor productivity

Figure 3.10 Labor Productivity Growth Decomposition, Early 1990s to Early 2000s *(continued)*

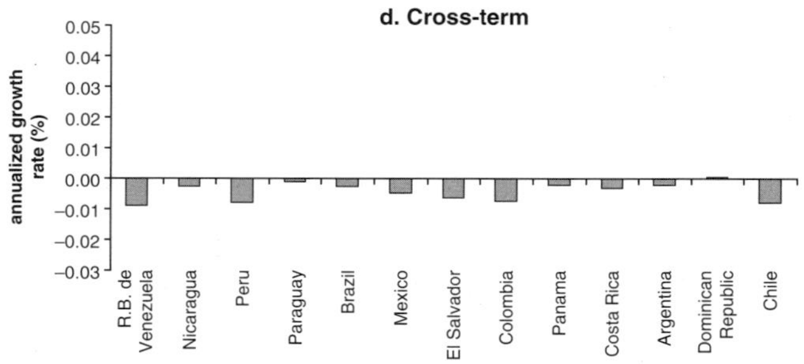

Sources: See annex table 3.A.1 for a complete list of sources.
Note: All series were smoothed by application of a Hodrick-Prescott filter.

growth were also shrinking in size, whereas those with below-average productivity growth gained—in relative terms—in employment shares. The República Bolivariana de Venezuela presents the most difficult case, because the negative productivity growth was associated with resource reallocation from more productive to less productive industries, while those industries growing more rapidly lost employment shares.

Scraping the Surface: What Drove the Deindustrialization Process?

When the productivity decomposition is replicated within manufacturing, labor reallocation is observed to often go from high- to low-productivity activities. The shift-and-share decomposition is applied to a subset of Latin American countries for which three-digit International Standard Industrial Classification (ISIC) data are available from the United Nations Industrial Development Organization (UNIDO). As in the case of the decomposition for the entire economy, the within effect tends to dominate the growth in productivity in the manufacturing sector of most countries (for example, Argentina, Chile, and Mexico) (figure 3.11).[18] But the between term is negative in four of the six countries, suggesting that some of the more productive industries have been downsizing while some of the less productive have gained employment shares. This finding is coupled with a nil or negative cross-term, suggesting that industries with rapidly growing productivity have not expanded.

Figure 3.11 Labor Productivity Growth Decomposition in Manufacturing, Early 1990s to Early 2000s

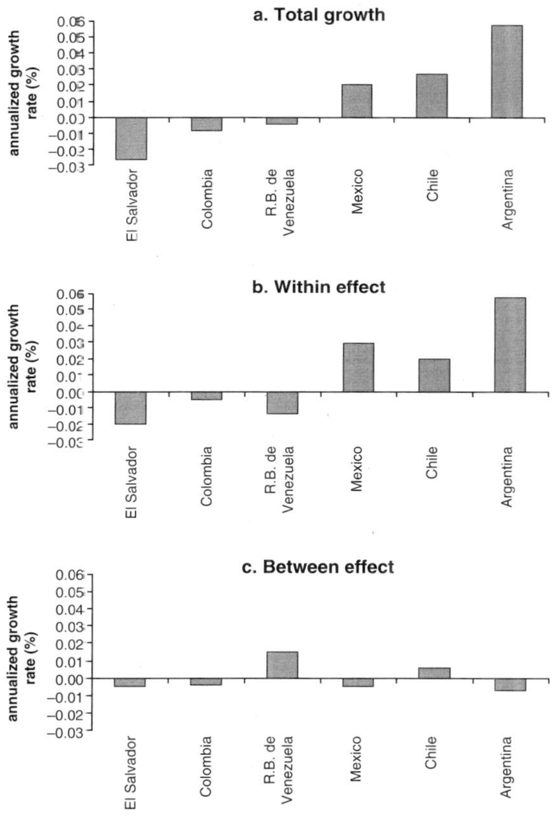

(continued)

Associated Losses in Comparative Advantages in Rapidly Growing Sectors

To assess why manufacturing is shrinking, particularly in high-productivity industries, this chapter uses a simple indicator of comparative advantages: the Balassa index (BI) (see Bartelsman and others 2004 for a similar application to the OECD countries). The BI is defined as the share of a product in a country's export basket relative to the product's share of world trade.

Figure 3.11 Labor Productivity Growth Decomposition in Manufacturing, Early 1990s to Early 2000s *(continued)*

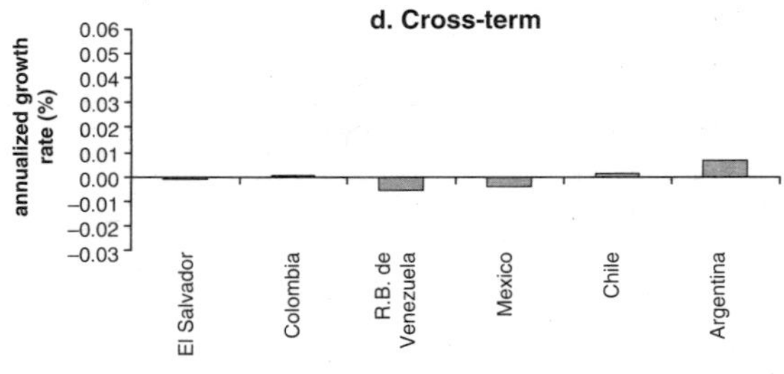

Sources: The shares of employment and output across sectors are obtained from the United Nations Industrial Development Organization (UNIDO) industrial database. They were then applied to the level of employment and output in manufacturing, the sources of which are listed in annex table 3.A.1.

Note: All series were smoothed by application of a Hodrick-Prescott filter. The periods covered are the following: Argentina (1990–99); Chile (1990–2000); Colombia (1990–2000); El Salvador (1992–98); Mexico (1990–2000); República Bolivariana de Venezuela (1990–97).

It is computed on the basis of the categories of products (at two digits) that occupied the top positions of world trade importance up to a share of 45 percent in each of the years considered (that is, 1970, 1980, 1990, and 2000).[19] The index captures the ability of a given country in redirecting its exports toward rapidly growing markets. By no means should Latin American and Caribbean countries have a comparative advantage in high-demand products, but the deterioration in the index may indicate their inability to invest resources in—or acquire skills and invest in needed infrastructure for the development of—those areas where world demand is increasing.

Since the 1980s, many countries in the region have reduced their ability to shift resources toward highly dynamic sectors of activity. Figure 3.12 suggests a sharp decline in the BI, especially in the large countries—in particular, Argentina, Chile, and the República Bolivariana de Venezuela—and in some of the smaller countries, such as Bolivia, Ecuador, and Paraguay. Mexico stands out among the large Latin American countries as the one with a significant improvement according to this index, largely because of the expansion of its exports in motor vehicles and electrical machinery and apparatus. Similarly, some of the countries in Central America have experienced a significant improvement in the BI. This change is largely due to the boom in exports of textiles and—to a lesser degree—of some electrical equipment, which have dominated the BI since the 1990s, replacing the former prevalence of vegetable and fruit exports.

Figure 3.12 Comparative Advantage in Products of High International Demand, 1970–2000

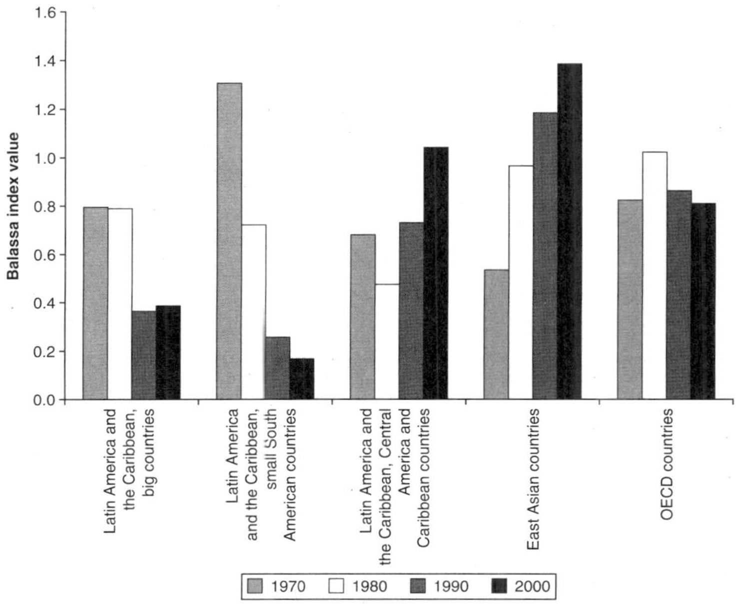

Source: Authors' calculations.

Shifts away from Capital-Intensive Industries

Associated with the loss in comparative advantages in dynamic industries is the downsizing of capital-intensive activities—those with the highest potential to generate high-productivity jobs—largely in favor of natural resource–intensive activities in which countries of the region maintained or increased their comparative advantages (figures 3.13 and 3.14). This finding contrasts with the experience of most comparator countries, where capital-intensive and labor-intensive industries have been gaining shares in employment and value added. Natural resource–intensive industries typically produce in automated plants, employing little unskilled labor and a few high-skill workers (Katz and Stumpo 2001). The exceptions within the region are Costa Rica, El Salvador, and Mexico, where the patterns of specialization have been leading toward the assembly industries of electronics, computers, automobiles, and textiles that are serving primarily the U.S. market. Most of these industries use relatively low technology, operate under the maquiladora regime, and make intensive use of low-skill labor.

Figure 3.13 Changes in the Structure of Employment in Manufacturing by Input Intensity's Technology, Early 1990s to Early 2000s

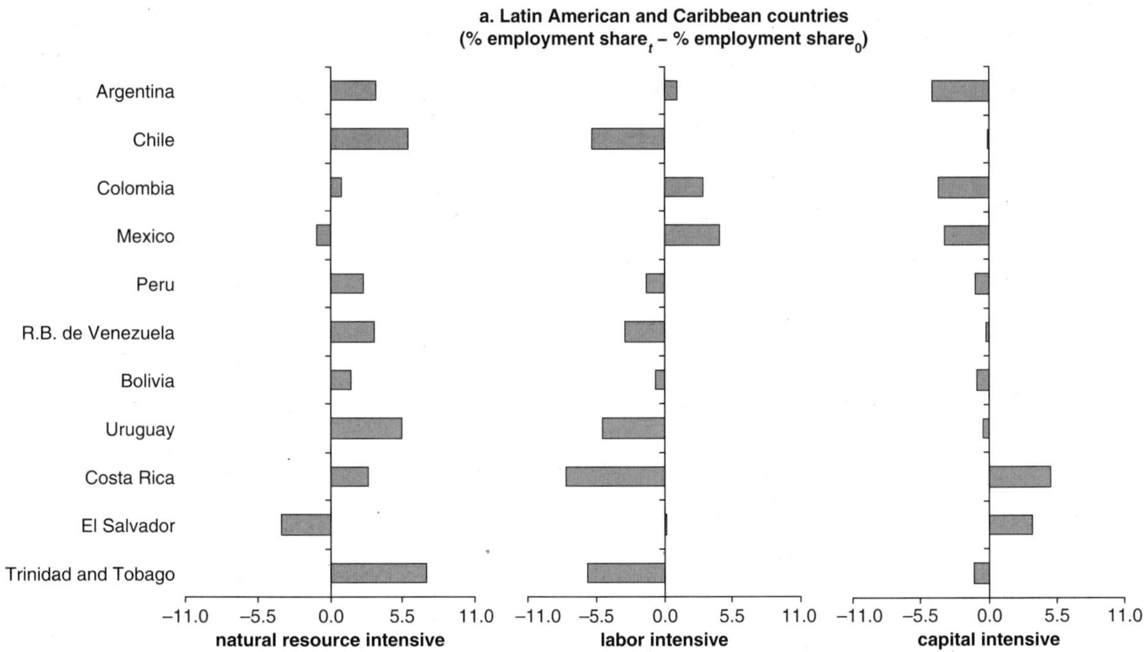

(continued)

Figure 3.13 Changes in the Structure of Employment in Manufacturing by Input Intensity's Technology, Early 1990s to Early 2000s *(continued)*

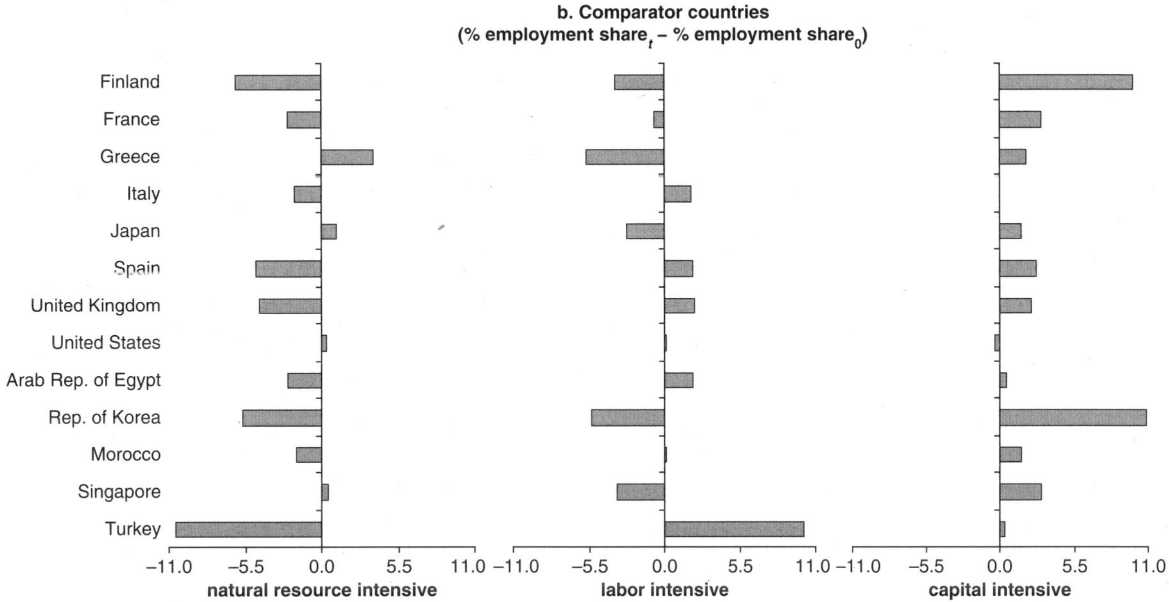

Source: UNIDO.

Note: See annex 3.G for the classification of industries according to input intensity's technology. For panel a, the periods covered by the data are as follows: Argentina (1990–99); Bolivia (1990–2000); Chile (1990–2000); Colombia (1990–2000); Costa Rica (1990–2000); El Salvador (1992–98); Mexico (1990–2000); Peru (1990–96); Trinidad and Tobago (1990–2000); Uruguay (1990–2000); República Bolivariana de Venezuela (1990–97). For panel b, the periods covered by the data are as follows: Arab Republic of Egypt (1990–96); Finland (1990–2000); France (1990–2000); Greece (1990–98); Italy (1990–98); Japan (1990–2000); Republic of Korea (1990–2000); Morocco (1992–2000); Singapore (1990–2000); Spain (1990–2000); Turkey (1990–2000); United Kingdom (1990–2000); United States (1990–2000).

Figure 3.14 Changes in the Structure of Manufacturing's Value Added by Input Intensity's Technology, Early 1990s to Early 2000s

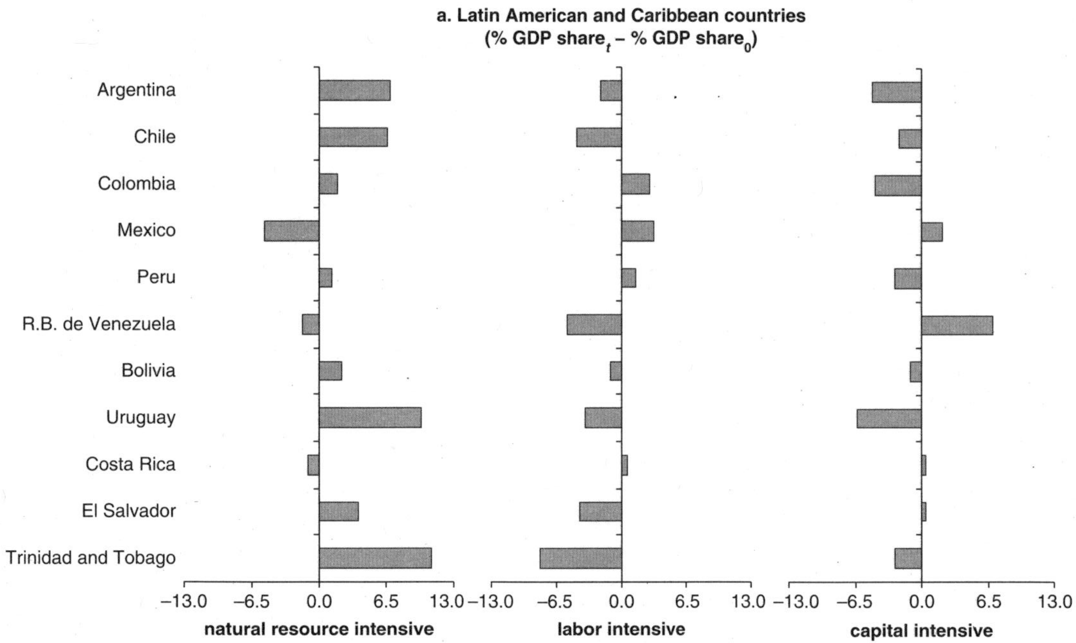

(continued)

Figure 3.14 Changes in the Structure of Manufacturing's Value Added by Input Intensity's Technology, Early 1990s to Early 2000s *(continued)*

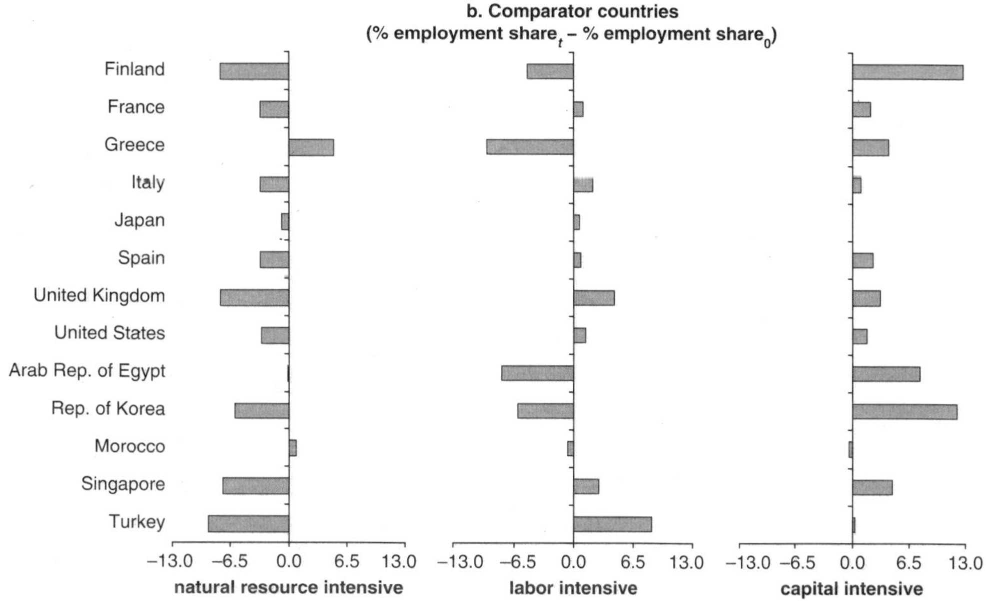

Source: UNIDO.

Note: See annex 3.G for the classification of industries according to input intensity's technology. For panel a, the periods covered by the data are as follows: Argentina (1990–99); Bolivia (1990–2000); Chile (1990–2000); Colombia (1990–2000); Costa Rica (1990–2000); El Salvador (1992–98); Mexico (1990–2000); Peru (1990–96); Trinidad and Tobago (1990–2000); Uruguay (1990–2000); República Bolivariana de Venezuela (1990–97). For panel b, the periods covered by the data are as follows: Arab Republic of Egypt (1990–96); Finland (1990–2000); France (1990–2000); Greece (1990–98); Italy (1990–98); Japan (1990–2000); Republic of Korea (1990–2000); Morocco (1992–2000); Singapore (1990–2000); Spain (1990–2000); Turkey (1990–2000); United Kingdom (1990–2000); United States (1990–2000).

All in all, productivity growth has been very low in most Latin American and Caribbean countries, not only because of poor performance in most sectors of the economy, but also because these countries have seen a process of deindustrialization in favor of low-productivity service sectors. Within manufacturing, these countries seem to have lost comparative advantages in rapidly growing activities and to have concentrated in natural resource–intensive sectors. The latter do not have great potential for creating many jobs. This general picture hides a significant heterogeneity across the countries in the region. In particular, Mexico and some of the Central American countries have been able to attract substantial FDI in assembly industries of electronics, computers, automobiles, and textiles. Although in these countries overall employment in manufacturing has held up better than in the other countries, the productivity and earnings of the jobs in the assembly industries have often been fairly low and have thus been unable to compensate for the many other jobs lost in more productive manufacturing industries.

Role of Policy in the Process of Reallocation

What has been the role of structural reforms in affecting the magnitude and characteristics of the reallocation of output and labor across sectors? All countries in the region have been exposed to major shocks that have affected relative prices, demand, and access to foreign markets and new technologies. At this point, whether the changes observed in the economic structure were a product of the reforms or a part of a continuous process of factor reallocation attributable to other forces must be determined.

One can distinguish three types of effects that these reforms could have produced on employment and productivity performances within each sector as well as on the reallocation of output and inputs across sectors. First, reforms could strengthen competition in each market and reduce or eliminate implicit or explicit subsidies to incumbent firms. This effect could generate greater churning of firms and employment across firms of the same sector, with not only a downsizing or exit of previously protected firms but also the creation or expansion of more productive businesses. Second, this greater competition in reformed sectors may have spillover effects on other sectors that use their goods and services. Third, trade reforms and exchange rate policy shifts may severely affect comparative advantages, implying a reallocation of output and inputs across manufacturing industries and between tradable and nontradable sectors.

Effect of Trade Reforms: Greater Churning and Selection within Sectors but Little Reallocation across Sectors

Ample evidence indicates that trade liberalization not only tends to promote productivity growth but also leads to a higher pace of resource reallocation, creating firms and jobs in expanding sectors as well as encouraging the exit of unviable firms and job destruction in declining sectors. Paus, Reinhardt, and Robinson (2003), for example, found that, other things being equal, trade liberalization, measured by export and import growth and an index of commercial reform, led to higher productivity growth in manufacturing in Latin American and Caribbean countries over the past decade.[20] In addition, they found that external factors, such as the rate of global productivity growth, measured by growth in U.S. industries, also had a significant effect in promoting industry-level productivity growth in the region, which could suggest a strong spillover effect from outward movements in the international technology frontier.

Trade liberalization has led to more churning within sectors but not necessarily to faster reallocation across them. Wacziarg and Wallack (2004), for example, did not find evidence of increasing reallocation of labor across sectors at the one-digit ISIC level in the aftermath of trade liberalization, but they did find evidence of a small increase in intersectoral reallocation within manufacturing at the three-digit level of disaggregation using a sample of 25 countries, of which 13 are from the region. The effect of changes in trade exposures seems to take place within the sectors affected and not necessarily to influence the net flows of employment. Levinsohn (1999) documented the large amount of churning in manufacturing in Chile during a period of tariff reduction that was not associated with changes in the aggregate level of employment in the sector. Haltiwanger and others (2004) found an increase in within-sector job reallocation in the aftermath of trade liberalization in the region, but also lower net employment growth.

Why did trade reforms not lead to greater reallocation across sectors, as predicted by standard trade theories? Theoretical models based on increasing return to scale and monopolistic competition offer a possible explanation: under those assumptions, trade liberalization tends to generate reallocation within industries with countries specializing in a lower number of varieties but expanding the output of each variety (Krugman 1979). For example, Álvarez and Braun (2006), considering a large sample of countries, found evidence of variation in employment and GDP shares caused by trade openness in industries with constant return to scale, whereas this effect vanished in the case of industries characterized by increasing returns to scale.[21]

Consistent with the idea of greater reallocation within sectors exposed to foreign competition is also the evidence that trade openness was associated with an expansion of the more productive firms together with the downsizing or death of less productive plants. In Argentina, for instance, trade liberalization has fostered a process of creative destruction within manufacturing, whereby inefficient incumbent firms were displaced by more efficient producers (Sánchez and Butler 2004). Pavcnik (2002) finds that market share reallocations contributed significantly to productivity growth following trade liberalization in Chile.[22] Moreover, self-selection into export markets by more productive plants is well documented by Clerides, Lach, and Tybout (1998) for Colombia and Mexico.[23] Underlying this process is the existence of substantial sunk costs to enter export markets, documented by Roberts and Tybout (1997) for Colombia and by Bernard and Bradford Jensen (1999a) for the United States. The improvements in productivity registered in agriculture can also be associated to the greater exposure to import competition in the countries of the region (De Ferranti and others 2002).

All in all, the empirical evidence for Latin America and the Caribbean suggests that trade liberalization has had only a limited effect in strengthening the allocation of resources to more productive uses. Although firms in tradable sectors have arguably been exposed to stronger competition, other factors characterizing the business environment (see part III) have possibly prevented these stronger competitive forces from fully displaying their effect in the market and ultimately leading to stronger productivity growth.

Effect of Exchange Rates on Employment and Job Flows

Other key drivers of changes in comparative advantages and employment allocation across sectors in Latin America and the Caribbean have been the shifts in exchange rate regimes. These shifts have significantly affected relative prices and comparative advantages (Baldi and Mulder 2004).[24] During the 1990s, many countries in the region adopted, de jure or de facto, fixed regimes varying from a currency board or plain dollarization to crawling pegs (Levy-Yeyati and Sturzenegger 2003). The larger portfolios' inflows during these periods of fixed exchange rate regimes often led to a real appreciation of the currencies and, consequently, a change in relative prices of tradables versus nontradables.

The resulting currency appreciation put extra pressure on firms concerning the productivity gains needed to remain competitive and deepened the process of cleansing of obsolete firms. That is how the fixed exchange regimes exacerbated the differential of productivity between tradable and nontradable sectors (Baldi and Mulder 2004) and, within each tradable sector, between more productive and less productive firms, leading the latter to shed significant employment.[25] This effect was associated with increases in job destruction in low-productivity firms in the most open industries and some increase in job creation in nontradable sectors—for example, Argentina (1991–2001), Brazil (1994–98), and Mexico (1990–95).

Significant Effect of Privatization on Employment and Sectoral Allocation of Resources

The privatization of state-owned enterprises also had significant effects on sectoral employment and reallocation. The process tackled long-standing problems of low productivity in public services and led not only to downsizing in a number of instances, but also to capital investment and services expansions (Galiani and others 2005; World Bank 2003b). In Chile and Colombia, firms increased their labor productivity by about 25 and 43 percent, respectively, on average after privatization (Fischer, Gutiérrez, and Serra

2005; Pombo and Ramírez 2005). The employment changes associated with the process of privatization varied substantially across sectors and countries. For example, sectors such as rail and ports have generally experienced larger downsizing than, for example, the telecommunications and water sectors. Some of the enterprises privatized in the transport sector were largely overstaffed, and the privatization generated mass layoffs (World Bank 2003b). The hiring behavior of firms in the postprivatization period helps change this raw image of job losses. A significant number of the dismissed employees were rehired by the same firm or could get a job with very similar duties in a supplier of the original firm. On average, enterprises in the region rehired 53 percent of the workers, and 20 percent of the workers were rehired to the same job as previously held (Chong and López-de-Silanes 2005).

All in all, the countries of Latin America and the Caribbean have experienced significant reforms that have changed comparative advantages and competitive pressure in individual sectors. Although trade liberalization per se cannot be singled out as the main factor behind the observed changes in sectoral composition of employment and productivity, it contributed to stronger competition and selection of firms. More important, appreciation of the exchange rates in the 1990s in many countries negatively affected some tradable sectors and contributed to job losses in the most exposed activities. Finally, privatization was a major force behind structural changes in former state-owned enterprises. Although privatization often led to major improvements in productivity of the firms concerned, the employment effects have been more mixed and were largely driven not only by the extent of overstaffing before privatization but also by the patterns of demand for the goods and services produced by the privatized firms. In any event, given the relatively limited share of total employment and value added of the privatized firms, the effect of privatization has been rather limited from an aggregate perspective (IDB 2003).

Conclusions

This chapter has shed light on the process of output and employment reallocation in Latin America and the Caribbean since the 1990s and its effect on productivity and employment growth. The main emerging results can be summarized as follows:

- Most countries in the region have been exposed to major structural changes and demand shocks since the early 1990s. These changes have been coupled with major changes in the global economy that have affected significantly the competitive position of the countries in the different market segments.
- These structural and global changes have led to a sizable process of reallocation of output and labor across sectors and, within each of

them, across firms and locations. Although this reallocation process has been large in absolute terms and, no doubt, has had profound economic and social implications, it has been somewhat smaller than that observed in many other developing and emerging economies, especially those that have experienced strong and sustained economic growth in recent decades.

- More important, structural changes in the region have not necessarily implied shifting resources toward more productive uses. For example, many countries have experienced shifts in employment—and in some cases output—away from relatively more productive manufacturing activities toward service sector activities. Evidence indicates that this process of deindustrialization was propelled by economic crises: large drops in output in the manufacturing sector took place largely during economic crises, but they were not regained during the subsequent recovery periods.
- Shifting resources toward service sectors is a common phenomenon in most market economies as they progress along the income ladder. However, in Latin America and the Caribbean, the magnitude and composition of the changes have specific characteristics that contribute to explain the low-quality job creation observed in many countries. Indeed, the main service sector activities that absorbed large shares of employment released by the manufacturing sector often had low productivity performance and thus lower contributions to overall output and wage growth.
- These general patterns hide significant differences across countries. In some cases, such as Brazil, Ecuador, Nicaragua, and Paraguay, the introduction of new crops with high international demand led to the expansion of the agricultural sector. Similarly, in countries such as Brazil, Chile, and the República Bolivariana de Venezuela, strong demand for mineral products contributed to relatively strong economic growth, even if not necessarily the creation of many productive jobs, given the very high capital intensity of the mineral industry. Only a few countries, such as Costa Rica, El Salvador, and Mexico, have managed to acquire specialization in the assembly industries of electronics, textiles, and automobiles.
- Even within manufacturing, there is little evidence of productivity-enhancing reallocation, with resources shifting toward more productive industries. Most of the overall manufacturing productivity growth has been achieved by within-industry improvements, and many of the industries experiencing strong productivity growth have done so by downsizing rather than by investing and expanding.

Although the *tertiarization* of the economy is common to most emerging and industrial economies, the fact that most activities have been created in the low-productivity segments of the service sector clearly indicates a limit in the ability of the countries of the region to generate high-productivity jobs. Likewise, although strong global demand and clear comparative advantages have boosted natural resource activities in agriculture and mining, their contribution to job creation has been limited. The next chapter looks in more depth at the process of resource reallocation, productivity, and job creation and at the factors potentially limiting job creation in highly productive segments of the economy. The chapters in part III assess challenges and constraints posed by policy and institutional factors and provide suggestions for overcoming them.

Annex 3.A: Employment and GDP by Sector Data Sources

Employment Data

In an effort to maintain coherence with the data used in chapter 1 of this book and to allow comparisons at different points in time across countries, data on employment by sector have been obtained by applying the observed distribution of employment by economic activities from censuses and household survey data (see annex table 3.A.1 for sources) to the smoothed series of total employment in levels that are used in chapter 1.

GDP Data

GDP data were obtained from the United Nations Statistics Division and are available at http://unstats.un.org/unsd/snaama/selectionbasicFast.asp. GDP is considered by economic activity, at constant 1990 prices, in U.S. dollars. Because of data constraints, the following one-digit industries were considered:

- ISIC 1: Agriculture, hunting, forestry, and fishing
- ISIC 2 and ISIC 4: Mining and quarrying and electricity, gas, and water
- ISIC 3: Manufacturing
- ISIC 5: Construction
- ISIC 6: Wholesale and retail trade and restaurants and hotels
- ISIC 7: Transport, storage, and communication
- ISIC 8 and ISIC 9: Financial, insurance, real estate, and business services and community, social, and personal services.

Annex 3.B: Differences among Labor Productivity Computations

There is considerable variability among the measures of labor productivity in Latin America and the Caribbean computed by different authors for similar periods of time. For example, in the case of the manufacturing sector in

Table 3.A.1 Sources of Employment by Sector Data

Country	*Years*	*Sources*	*Age (years)*
Argentina	1991 and 2001	National Census of Population and Housing (Censo Nacional de Población y Vivienda), National Institute of Statistics and Censuses (Instituto Nacional de Estadística y Censos)	14 and more
Barbados	1990 and 2004	Continuous Labour Force Sample Survey	15 and more
Brazil	1990 and 2002	National Research for Sample Households (Pesquisa Nacional por Amostra de Domicilios), Brazilian Institute of Geography and Statistics (Instituto Brasileiro de Geografia e Estatística) *Statistical Yearbook of Brazil* (*Anuário Estatístico do Brasil*), Brazilian Institute of Geography and Statistics	10 and more
Chile	1990 and 2003	National Survey for Socioeconomic Characterization (Encuesta de Caracterización Socioeconómica Nacional), National Institute of Statistics (Instituto Nacional de Estadísticas)	15 and more
Colombia	1993 and 2000	1993 Census (Censo 1993), National Administrative Department of Statistics (Departamento Administrativo Nacional de Estadística) Encuesta Nacional de Hogares, Total Nacional por Regiones (National Household Survey, National Total for Regions), National Administrative Department of Statistics Expanded data with estimated projections on the basis of the results of the 1993 Census, National Administrative Department of Statistics	12 and more
Costa Rica	1990 and 2000	Statistics of Employment (Estadísticas de Empleo), National Institute of Statistics and Censuses (Instituto Nacional de Estadística y Censos) Census of the Population 2000 (Censo de Población 2000)	12 and more
Dominican Republic	1991 and 2003	Department of National Accounts and Economic Statistics (Departamento de Cuentas Nacionales y Estadísticas Económicas), Central Bank of the Dominican Republic (Banco Central de la República Dominicana)	10 and more

(continued)

Table 3.A.1 Sources of Employment by Sector Data *(continued)*

Country	*Years*	*Sources*	*Age (years)*
El Salvador	1992 and 2001	Labor force survey, General Directorate of Statistics and Censuses (Dirección General de Estadísticas y Censos)	10 and more
Mexico	1990 and 2004	Eleventh General Census of Population and Housing, 1990 (XI Censo General de Población y Vivienda, 1990), National Institute of Statistics, Geography, and Informatics (Instituto Nacional de Estatística Geográfica e Informática) National Survey of Employment, 2004 (Encuesta Nacional de Empleo, 2004), National Institute of Statistics, Geography, and Informatics	12 and more
Nicaragua	1990 and 2001	Central Bank of Nicaragua (Banco Central de Nicaragua) National Institute of Statistics and Censuses (Instituto Nacional de Estadísticas y Censos) Ministry of Labor (Ministerio del Trabajo)	10 and more
Panama	1990 and 2003	Continuous Household Survey (Encuesta Continua de Hogares), Directorate of Statistics and Census (Dirección de Estadística y Censo)	15 and more
Paraguay	1991 and 2004	Departamento de Cuentas Nacionales y Mercado Interno (Department of National Accounts and the Domestic Market), Central Bank of Paraguay (Banco Central del Paraguay)	—
Peru	1989 and 2000	*Peru: Statistical Compendium 1990–1991* (*Perú: Compendio Estadístico 1990–1991*), National Institute of Statistics and Informatics (Instituto Nacional de Estadísticas e Informática) Program of Labor Statistics and Studies (Programa de Estadísticas y Estudios Laborales), National Institute of Statistics and Informatics and Ministry of Work and Employment Promotion (Ministerio de Trabajo y Promoción del Empleo)	15 and more
Venezuela, R.B. de	1990 and 2001	National Institute of Statistics (Instituto Nacional de Estadística) System for Information about the Labor Markets 2000 (Sistema de Información sobre Mercados Laborales 2000) International Labour Office	15 and more

Source: Authors' compilation.
Note: — = not available.

Brazil, Bonelli (2002) reports annual increases of labor productivity between 7 percent and 8 percent over the 1990s. These figures are considerably larger than those computed by the Central Bank and the Ministry of Planning of Brazil (around 1.1 percent) or those estimated by the World Bank (around 1.9 percent, according to Loayza 2001). This annex provides a brief explanation of the possible sources of these differences, using Mexico as an example.

The most common source of variation across estimates of labor productivity comes from different estimates of employment. The countries collect different kinds of information on employment through population and economic censuses, household surveys, employment surveys, industrial surveys, and national accounts. These sources generally have different coverage, and some of them are used as input for the computation of other sources. For example, certain parameters extracted from the censuses and information from the surveys are typically used to compute series of employment and output for the national account methodology.

Annex 3.C: Sensitivity Analysis of Labor Productivity Growth

Annex table 3.C.1 provides a sensitivity analysis of the estimated overall labor productivity growth using three different data sources:

- Source A: employment data gathered for this study (see chapter 1)
- Source B: data on employment and real GDP converted at purchasing power parity from the Groningen Growth and Development Centre and the Conference Board's Total Economy Database, August 2005
- Source C: data on real GDP from the United Nations Statistics Division.

The table shows the productivity growth computations for the raw data and for the series smoothed by application of a Hodrick-Prescott filter.

Annex 3.D: Data on GDP and Employment Shares, by Sector

Annex tables 3.D.1 and 3.D.2 show GDP and employment shares, respectively, by sector. In these tables, the agriculture sector comprises agriculture, hunting, forestry, and fishing. The mining and utilities sector includes mining and quarrying as well as electricity, gas, and water. The services sector covers construction; wholesale and retail trade, restaurants, and hotels; transport, storage, and communication; financial, insurance, real estate, and business services; and community, social, and personal services.

Table 3.C.1 Overall Labor Productivity Growth Rate: Sensitivity Analysis
Annualized percentage rate

		Source B: GDP Source A: employment		*Source C: GDP Source A: employment*		*Source B: GDP Source B: employment*	
Country	*Period*	*Raw data*	*Smooth data*	*Raw data*	*Smooth data*	*Raw data*	*Smooth data*
Argentina	1991–2001	2.16	1.41	2.62	1.57	1.37	0.76
Brazil	1990–2002	0.37	0.20	0.48	0.26	0.82	0.50
Chile	1990–2003	4.29	3.88	4.86	4.38	3.57	3.31
Colombia	1993–2000	0.57	0.70	0.73	0.76	0.16	0.38
Costa Rica	1990–2000	—	—	1.60	1.17	—	—
Dominican Republic	1991–2003	—	—	3.79	2.76	—	—
El Salvador	1992–2001	—	—	0.45	0.64	—	—
Mexico	1991–2004	0.28	0.52	0.30	0.52	0.30	0.51
Nicaragua	1990–2001	—	—	–0.46	–1.16	—	—
Panama	1990–2003	—	—	1.07	0.89	—	—
Paraguay	1991–2004	—	—	–0.20	0.18	—	—
Peru	1989–2000	0.52	–0.09	0.49	–0.11	0.52	–0.09
Venezuela, R.B. de	1990–2001	–1.05	–1.88	–1.32	–2.03	–0.68	–1.50

Source: Authors' calculations.
Note: — = not available.

Table 3.D.1 GDP Share by Sector, 1970–2003

	GDP (US$ at constant 1990 prices)															
	Agriculture				*Mining and utilities*				*Manufacturing*				*Services*			
Country	*1970*	*1980*	*1990*	*2003*	*1970*	*1980*	*1990*	*2003*	*1970*	*1980*	*1990*	*2003*	*1970*	*1980*	*1990*	*2003*
Latin America and the Caribbean																
Argentina	6.6	6.3	8.0	7.2	2.5	3.4	4.7	6.4	31.4	28.4	26.5	23.4	59.4	61.9	60.7	63.0
Barbados	8.6	7.6	5.4	3.7	1.1	2.9	3.7	4.6	7.3	9.6	8.0	6.5	83.0	79.9	82.9	85.1
Bolivia	14.6	14.0	16.4	15.4	14.6	12.9	12.7	12.4	19.1	19.6	18.2	17.4	51.7	53.5	52.7	54.9
Brazil	8.7	6.3	6.0	7.3	3.1	3.3	3.7	8.0	29.6	33.4	24.1	24.1	58.6	57.0	66.2	60.6
Chile	5.5	5.2	7.1	6.8	14.8	15.1	15.4	16.8	21.6	18.4	18.0	15.4	58.0	61.2	59.5	61.0
Colombia	21.5	19.2	18.3	15.4	6.5	6.0	9.8	10.0	18.2	19.0	18.1	15.5	53.8	55.9	53.8	59.1
Costa Rica	15.1	11.2	12.1	10.4	1.7	2.1	2.8	3.0	19.0	22.4	22.0	23.3	64.3	64.3	63.2	63.4
Cuba	23.2	17.7	12.1	8.5	3.4	2.9	2.6	3.9	18.2	15.8	11.6	11.5	55.3	63.7	73.7	76.2
Dominican Republic	23.3	16.5	13.3	9.9	1.7	3.4	2.7	2.5	22.6	22.7	21.6	17.5	52.4	57.4	62.4	70.1
Ecuador	—	11.4	13.9	16.5	—	10.3	15.2	22.0	—	23.7	20.1	12.6	—	54.7	50.8	48.9
El Salvador	19.0	18.6	17.1	12.0	1.0	1.3	1.5	1.2	22.4	21.8	21.8	25.3	57.6	58.3	59.6	61.5
Guatemala	27.3	24.8	25.9	22.6	1.3	2.2	2.7	5.0	15.8	16.7	15.1	12.7	55.6	56.3	56.3	59.8
Honduras	29.0	21.8	22.4	19.5	3.9	3.7	4.9	5.9	14.6	15.5	16.3	17.4	52.5	59.1	56.3	57.2
Jamaica	5.8	7.3	6.0	6.4	9.2	11.7	11.1	11.5	19.3	17.8	18.4	12.1	65.7	63.2	64.5	70.1

(continued)

Table 3.D.1 GDP Share by Sector, 1970–2003 *(continued)*

	GDP (US$ at constant 1990 prices)															
	Agriculture				*Mining and utilities*				*Manufacturing*				*Services*			
Country	*1970*	*1980*	*1990*	*2003*	*1970*	*1980*	*1990*	*2003*	*1970*	*1980*	*1990*	*2003*	*1970*	*1980*	*1990*	*2003*
Mexico	11.1	8.3	7.8	6.8	3.3	3.6	3.7	3.7	17.9	19.5	20.6	20.6	67.7	68.5	68.0	69.0
Nicaragua	12.4	12.7	19.1	22.6	3.1	4.3	2.7	3.2	19.1	24.6	18.4	18.9	65.3	58.3	59.7	55.3
Panama	12.1	7.9	9.0	8.3	1.9	2.5	3.5	4.4	17.7	14.5	13.3	9.0	68.3	75.1	74.2	78.2
Paraguay	30.8	25.4	27.8	32.1	0.0	1.5	2.8	6.5	19.8	18.9	17.3	14.7	49.5	54.2	52.1	46.8
Peru	8.8	5.6	7.7	8.4	5.6	8.3	7.1	10.2	22.8	21.2	19.5	18.3	62.7	64.9	65.7	63.1
Trinidad and Tobago	3.1	1.5	2.6	1.1	26.4	23.4	23.1	22.6	16.9	11.2	13.8	22.4	53.5	63.9	60.5	53.9
Uruguay	13.8	10.9	10.7	11.8	1.2	1.5	2.3	4.1	28.0	28.8	24.8	16.8	57.1	58.8	62.2	67.3
Venezuela, R.B. de	4.4	4.7	5.4	5.8	42.7	24.0	25.1	30.1	13.8	18.3	20.4	17.0	39.1	52.9	49.1	47.1
Developing countries																
Bahrain	1.1	0.7	0.8	0.7	54.5	50.2	20.1	21.5	8.6	5.5	11.0	12.6	35.9	43.6	68.1	65.2
Cyprus	17.0	9.9	6.9	5.1	3.0	2.2	2.3	3.2	13.8	17.0	14.3	8.6	66.2	70.9	76.5	83.2
China	46.8	33.8	27.0	12.2	—	—	—	—	27.1	38.2	37.0	56.2	26.1	27.9	36.0	31.7

(continued)

Table 3.D.1 GDP Share by Sector, 1970–2003 *(continued)*

	GDP (US$ at constant 1990 prices)															
	Agriculture				*Mining and utilities*				*Manufacturing*				*Services*			
Country	*1970*	*1980*	*1990*	*2003*	*1970*	*1980*	*1990*	*2003*	*1970*	*1980*	*1990*	*2003*	*1970*	*1980*	*1990*	*2003*
Egypt, Arab Rep. of	26.7	21.6	17.2	16.7	12.9	10.4	12.0	15.0	15.6	13.8	16.9	18.7	44.7	54.2	53.9	49.6
Ghana	53.6	57.2	52.7	47.9	9.1	5.4	6.9	7.7	14.2	11.2	10.4	9.8	23.1	26.1	30.0	34.6
Korea, Rep. of	18.8	9.7	8.9	4.8	2.4	3.2	3.0	2.9	19.1	25.7	27.3	33.8	59.7	61.4	60.8	58.4
Malaysia	23.7	19.2	15.0	7.4	18.7	14.2	13.8	12.5	13.8	18.1	23.8	27.8	43.7	48.5	47.3	52.2
Malta	8.3	4.0	3.8	2.5	2.8	1.9	3.2	2.0	23.1	31.4	26.5	21.7	65.9	62.7	66.5	73.8
Mauritius	19.8	14.9	12.1	6.1	1.3	1.6	1.6	2.9	17.8	18.6	25.9	22.9	61.1	65.0	60.5	68.1
Morocco	27.4	19.0	18.6	15.9	10.6	10.5	9.1	9.6	18.3	18.8	19.4	19.4	43.6	51.8	52.9	55.1
Mozambique	64.5	64.5	64.5	51.8	2.7	2.7	2.7	6.5	14.4	14.4	14.4	19.9	18.4	18.4	18.4	21.8
Nigeria	49.6	26.8	32.4	23.0	28.8	43.7	33.9	56.4	2.8	6.3	6.5	3.9	18.8	23.2	27.2	16.6
Senegal	26.5	22.5	19.9	14.2	2.5	2.9	2.5	3.7	12.1	12.0	13.1	11.8	58.9	62.6	64.5	70.3
Singapore	2.2	1.0	0.3	0.1	2.0	2.0	1.9	1.9	23.4	27.1	25.5	23.3	72.4	69.9	72.3	74.7
South Africa	2.9	3.2	4.6	2.9	15.6	10.7	13.2	8.7	15.8	19.4	23.6	17.3	65.7	66.7	58.6	71.1
Thailand	27.7	21.3	14.4	11.2	1.9	2.7	4.2	5.9	15.0	20.5	24.9	34.4	55.5	55.6	56.6	48.5
Turkey	32.3	24.8	17.6	13.4	2.4	3.1	3.6	3.9	15.4	17.4	22.2	25.5	49.9	54.7	56.6	57.1

(continued)

Table 3.D.1 GDP Share by Sector, 1970–2003 *(continued)*

	GDP (US$ at constant 1990 prices)															
	Agriculture				*Mining and utilities*				*Manufacturing*				*Services*			
Country	*1970*	*1980*	*1990*	*2003*	*1970*	*1980*	*1990*	*2003*	*1970*	*1980*	*1990*	*2003*	*1970*	*1980*	*1990*	*2003*
Zambia	9.6	8.1	12.4	14.2	44.0	39.9	22.6	4.6	15.0	15.3	22.2	24.5	31.4	36.7	42.8	56.6
Zimbabwe	16.5	15.6	16.1	17.4	10.4	7.7	7.0	6.3	18.9	22.2	22.3	15.9	54.2	54.5	54.6	60.4
Selected OECD countries																
Australia	4.4	3.6	3.8	3.3	7.7	7.2	8.8	7.5	17.5	16.6	13.6	11.2	70.4	72.5	73.7	78.1
Austria	5.0	4.1	3.8	3.2	4.2	4.2	3.5	3.8	22.1	21.7	21.5	21.9	68.7	70.0	71.2	71.1
Belgium	2.6	2.0	1.9	1.9	2.8	4.1	4.1	4.0	20.6	20.5	21.8	20.2	74.1	73.4	72.2	73.9
Canada	4.0	2.9	2.9	2.1	9.2	8.4	7.6	6.7	18.0	17.5	16.9	17.2	68.7	71.2	72.6	74.1
Denmark	3.2	3.6	4.2	4.2	2.3	2.4	3.1	3.7	18.4	18.7	17.3	16.0	76.0	75.3	75.4	76.1
Finland	9.4	10.4	6.3	5.4	2.1	2.2	2.4	2.7	20.6	21.8	22.4	28.0	67.8	65.6	68.8	63.9
France	5.6	4.1	3.8	3.1	2.7	3.3	2.1	2.2	16.8	20.1	18.0	18.9	74.9	72.5	76.1	75.7
Germany	1.9	1.7	1.7	1.3	3.9	3.5	3.3	2.4	33.8	30.3	28.2	22.7	60.3	64.5	66.8	73.6
Greece	17.0	13.7	10.2	7.4	3.3	3.9	3.6	3.5	14.2	16.7	15.5	13.5	65.4	65.8	70.6	75.6
Iceland	14.1	15.1	11.5	7.9	3.6	4.6	4.1	3.9	13.2	16.7	15.6	11.1	69.1	63.6	68.8	77.0
Ireland	16.5	11.4	9.2	4.1	2.7	2.6	1.8	2.2	25.8	25.1	28.2	37.8	55.1	60.9	60.8	55.9
Italy	6.0	4.6	3.4	3.1	3.8	2.8	2.6	2.6	23.7	25.0	23.5	21.6	66.5	67.6	70.5	72.7

(continued)

Table 3.D.1 GDP Share by Sector, 1970–2003 *(continued)*

	GDP (US$ at constant 1990 prices)															
	Agriculture				*Mining and utilities*				*Manufacturing*				*Services*			
Country	*1970*	*1980*	*1990*	*2003*	*1970*	*1980*	*1990*	*2003*	*1970*	*1980*	*1990*	*2003*	*1970*	*1980*	*1990*	*2003*
Japan	4.7	3.2	2.4	1.3	3.1	3.3	2.7	2.8	23.0	24.0	25.9	24.9	69.2	69.4	69.0	71.0
Netherlands	3.0	3.6	4.4	4.0	2.9	6.4	5.1	4.2	22.3	18.0	18.9	16.8	71.8	72.0	71.6	75.1
New Zealand	6.2	6.8	6.7	6.0	4.8	4.8	4.7	3.4	19.6	19.4	18.0	16.0	69.4	69.0	70.6	74.5
Norway	5.1	3.9	3.4	2.5	8.3	13.2	16.8	25.0	20.1	16.1	12.5	12.8	66.5	66.8	67.4	59.8
Portugal	14.6	11.0	8.0	6.3	3.5	3.5	3.6	4.4	20.0	19.7	20.2	17.5	61.9	65.8	68.1	71.9
Spain	7.7	7.2	6.6	5.4	3.3	3.6	3.3	3.4	21.3	23.1	21.3	20.7	67.7	66.1	68.7	70.5
Sweden	4.2	3.2	3.3	2.5	3.8	3.5	3.4	3.2	22.4	20.6	20.4	27.1	69.7	72.7	72.9	67.2
Switzerland	4.0	3.5	2.8	2.0	3.0	3.6	3.1	2.9	23.5	23.6	20.2	21.3	69.4	69.3	74.0	73.8
United Kingdom	2.9	2.1	1.8	0.9	4.6	9.1	4.9	4.2	31.7	25.5	22.4	15.7	60.8	63.2	70.9	79.2
United States	2.1	1.6	1.9	1.4	5.6	5.1	4.8	3.0	21.6	19.8	18.2	15.0	70.8	73.5	75.0	80.6

Source: United Nations Statistics Division.
Note: — = not available.

Table 3.D.2 Employment Share by Sector, Early 1990s to Early 2000s

	Agriculture		*Mining and utilities*		*Manufacturing*		*Services*	
Country	*Early 1990s*	*Early 2000s*	*Early 1990s*	*Early 2000s*	*Early 1990s*	*Early 2000s*	*Early 1990s*	*Early 2000s*
Latin America and the Caribbean								
Argentina	11.1	8.7	1.2	1.2	17.4	11.9	70.2	78.2
Barbados	6.2	5.1	1.5	2.3	11.6	6.9	80.7	85.8
Bolivia	37.9	39.3	2.8	1.0	10.3	10.8	49.0	49.0
Brazil	22.8	20.7	0.0	0.0	16.5	14.3	60.6	65.0
Chile	19.0	13.0	2.8	1.9	16.5	14.1	61.7	71.0
Colombia	27.2	22.7	2.0	1.1	13.2	13.5	57.6	62.7
Costa Rica	26.1	19.4	1.4	1.6	18.1	16.8	54.4	62.1
Dominican Republic	20.4	13.7	0.7	1.1	18.1	14.7	60.8	70.4
El Salvador	36.8	18.2	0.7	0.3	15.1	17.8	47.4	63.6
Grenada	18.0	14.3	2.0	1.7	8.0	7.7	72.0	76.3
Jamaica	26.2	20.4	1.4	1.1	11.9	7.0	60.5	71.5
Mexico	23.5	16.5	1.8	1.0	19.9	17.4	54.8	65.1
Nicaragua	39.3	43.4	0.7	0.9	9.2	7.7	50.7	47.9
Panama	29.7	17.5	1.3	0.9	10.2	8.9	58.8	72.6

(continued)

Table 3.D.2 Employment Share by Sector, Early 1990s to Early 2000s *(continued)*

	Agriculture		*Mining and utilities*		*Manufacturing*		*Services*	
Country	*Early 1990s*	*Early 2000s*	*Early 1990s*	*Early 2000s*	*Early 1990s*	*Early 2000s*	*Early 1990s*	*Early 2000s*
Peru	39.2	32.5	1.2	0.6	11.1	10.4	48.5	56.5
Trinidad and Tobago	9.5	5.1	4.9	4.7	12.6	10.5	72.9	79.8
Uruguay	4.5	4.5	0.1	0.1	22.6	14.6	72.8	80.7
Venezuela, R.B. de	13.4	9.5	2.0	1.1	15.5	12.9	69.0	76.5
Developing countries								
China	64.9	56.6	2.0	1.5	16.4	14.5	16.7	27.5
Cyprus	13.7	5.2	0.8	1.3	19.1	11.0	66.3	82.6
Egypt, Arab Rep. of	39.1	29.9	1.0	1.4	13.0	10.9	46.8	57.8
Korea, Rep. of	17.9	8.8	0.8	0.4	27.1	19.0	54.1	71.8
Malaysia	26.0	14.3	1.2	0.9	19.9	21.6	52.8	63.3
Malta	2.5	1.7	2.1	2.8	27.9	19.4	67.4	76.0
Singapore	0.5	0.2	0.6	0.5	29.0	17.9	70.0	81.3
Thailand	64.0	44.9	0.5	0.4	10.2	14.7	25.3	40.0
Turkey	46.9	33.9	1.1	0.9	14.8	17.3	37.1	47.9

(continued)

Table 3.D.2 Employment Share by Sector, Early 1990s to Early 2000s *(continued)*

	Agriculture		*Mining and utilities*		*Manufacturing*		*Services*	
Country	*Early 1990s*	*Early 2000s*	*Early 1990s*	*Early 2000s*	*Early 1990s*	*Early 2000s*	*Early 1990s*	*Early 2000s*
Selected OECD countries								
Australia	5.6	3.9	2.5	1.6	15.0	11.4	76.9	83.0
Austria	7.9	5.6	1.5	1.1	27.1	19.3	63.5	74.0
Belgium	3.1	1.8	1.3	0.9	23.3	17.5	72.3	79.8
Canada	4.1	2.8	2.4	2.0	15.4	14.6	78.1	80.7
Denmark	5.5	3.0	0.8	0.7	20.1	16.4	73.6	79.8
Finland	8.8	5.1	1.3	1.1	20.8	18.7	69.1	75.2
Germany	4.2	2.5	2.1	1.1	31.1	22.8	62.6	73.6
Greece	23.9	16.5	1.6	1.2	19.4	13.1	55.1	69.1
Iceland	10.2	7.2	1.2	1.2	17.2	14.2	71.4	77.4
Ireland	15.1	6.5	1.8	1.1	19.3	16.1	63.8	76.3
Japan	7.3	4.7	0.6	0.6	24.2	19.3	68.0	75.4
Netherlands	4.6	3.0	0.8	0.6	18.8	14.0	75.8	82.4
New Zealand	10.6	8.2	1.3	0.6	17.1	14.5	70.9	76.7
Norway	6.4	3.7	2.2	2.2	15.3	12.3	76.1	81.9

(continued)

Table 3.D.2 Employment Share by Sector, Early 1990s to Early 2000s *(continued)*

	Agriculture		*Mining and utilities*		*Manufacturing*		*Services*	
Country	*Early 1990s*	*Early 2000s*	*Early 1990s*	*Early 2000s*	*Early 1990s*	*Early 2000s*	*Early 1990s*	*Early 2000s*
Portugal	17.9	12.5	1.7	1.0	24.6	19.9	55.8	66.6
Spain	11.8	5.7	1.4	0.9	22.3	17.5	64.5	75.8
Sweden	3.4	2.1	1.0	0.8	21.0	16.3	74.5	80.8
Switzerland	4.3	4.1	0.8	0.7	20.7	16.2	74.2	79.1
United Kingdom	2.1	1.3	2.1	1.0	22.4	14.8	73.3	83.0
United States	2.9	1.7	1.9	1.2	18.0	12.3	77.2	84.8

Sources: See annex 1.A; ILO for the rest of the countries.

Note: For Latin American and Caribbean countries: Bahamas (1991–2003); Barbados (1993–2003); Bolivia (1989–2003); Grenada (1991–98); Trinidad and Tobago (1990–2004); Uruguay (1992–2003); see annex 1.A for all other Latin American and Caribbean countries. For developing countries: China (1990–2002); Singapore (1989–2003); for all other developing countries, 1990–2003. For OECD countries, Germany (1991–2003); Iceland (1991–2002); Netherlands (1990–2002); Switzerland (1991–2003); for all other OECD countries, 1990–2003.

Annex 3.E: Lilien Index

The Lilien index measures the degree of dispersion in the rate of growth across sectors. Figures 3.E.1, 3.E.2, and 3.E.3 show the results for Latin American and Caribbean countries, OECD countries, and developing countries, respectively.

Annex 3.F: Balassa Index

The Balassa index is defined as the share of a product in a country's export basket relative to the product's share of world trade. It is computed on the basis of the two-digit Standard International Trade Classification (SITC) categories that occupy the top positions of world trade importance up to a share of 45 percent in each of the years considered (that is, 1970, 1980, 1990, and 2000). The source of data is the National Bureau of Economic Research's United Nations Trade Data, 1962–2000. This database was constructed by Robert Feenstra and Robert Lipsey. The list of categories considered is shown in annex table 3.F.1. Petroleum, petroleum products, and related materials were excluded. Annex figure 3.F.1 shows comparative advantages of Latin American and Caribbean countries, as indicated by the index.

Annex 3.G: Classification of Sectors by Input Intensity

Annex table 3.G.1 shows industry classifications according to the input intensity of the production function.

Annex 3.H: Classification of Sectors by Productivity

This classification was performed using the average of the sectoral labor productivity of the Group of Seven (G7) countries over the 1990s. Sectors were defined as *low productivity* if their level of productivity was lower than or equal to 33 percent of the distribution across sectors. They were classified as *medium productivity* if their level of productivity was between 33 and 66 percent. If their level of productivity was higher than or equal to 66 percent, they were classified as *high productivity*. The source of data for the classification was UNIDO. Classifications at the three-digit and two-digit levels are shown in annex tables 3.H.1 and 3.H.2, respectively.

A Spearman rank correlation is presented in annex table 3.H.3 to assess how the sectoral productivity ranking of the G7 countries fits with that of the countries of Latin America and the Caribbean. As can be observed, the correlations are very high in all cases.

Figure 3.E.1 Lilien Index Results for Latin American and Caribbean Countries

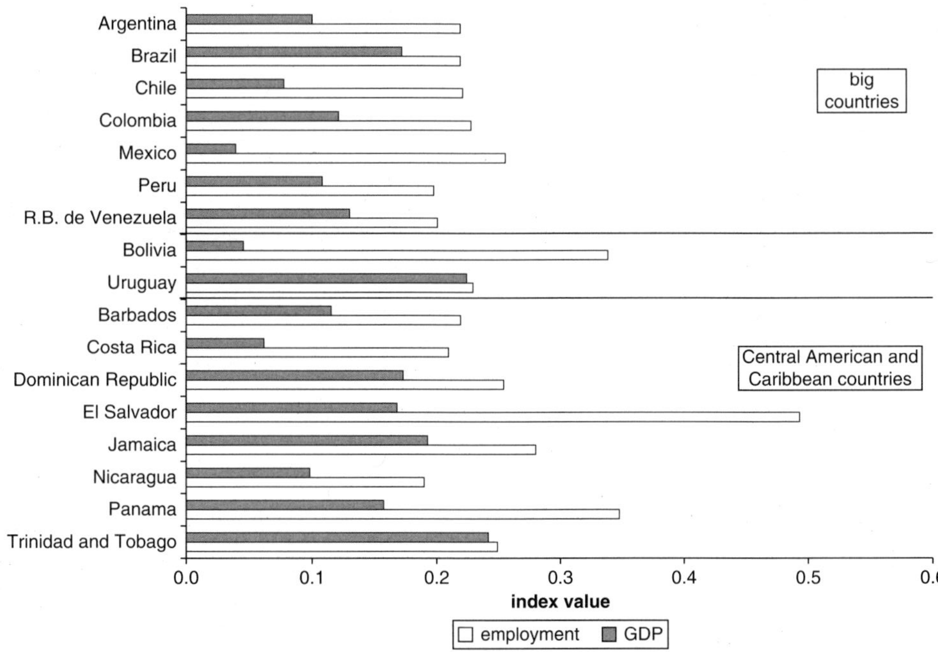

Sources: For employment, see annex 3.A; for GDP, UNSD.

Figure 3.E.2 Lilien Index Results for Selected OECD Countries

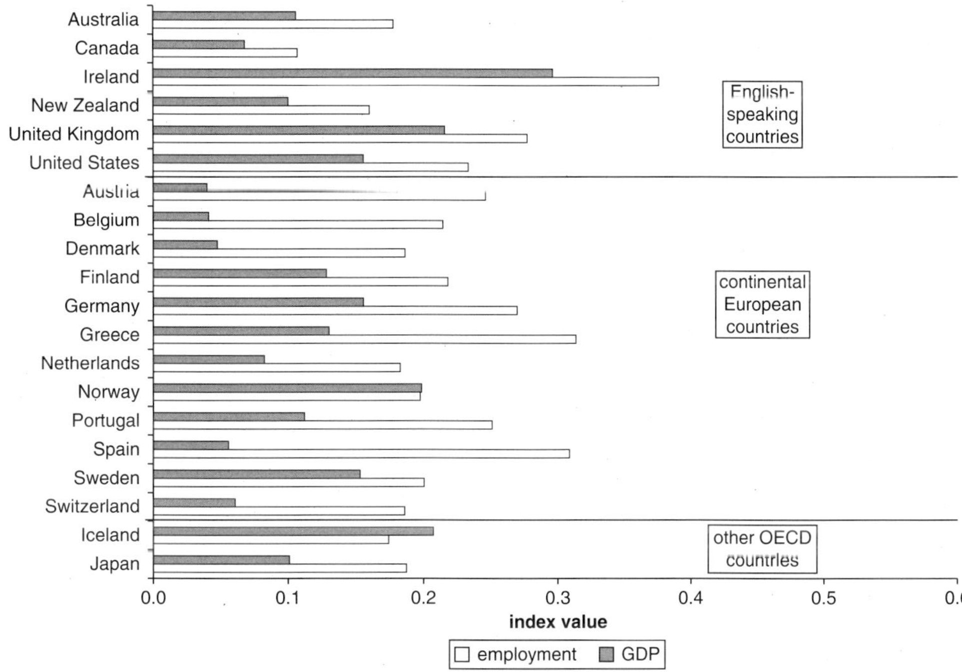

Sources: For employment, International Labour Office; for GDP, UNSD.

Figure 3.E.3 Lilien Index Results for Developing Countries

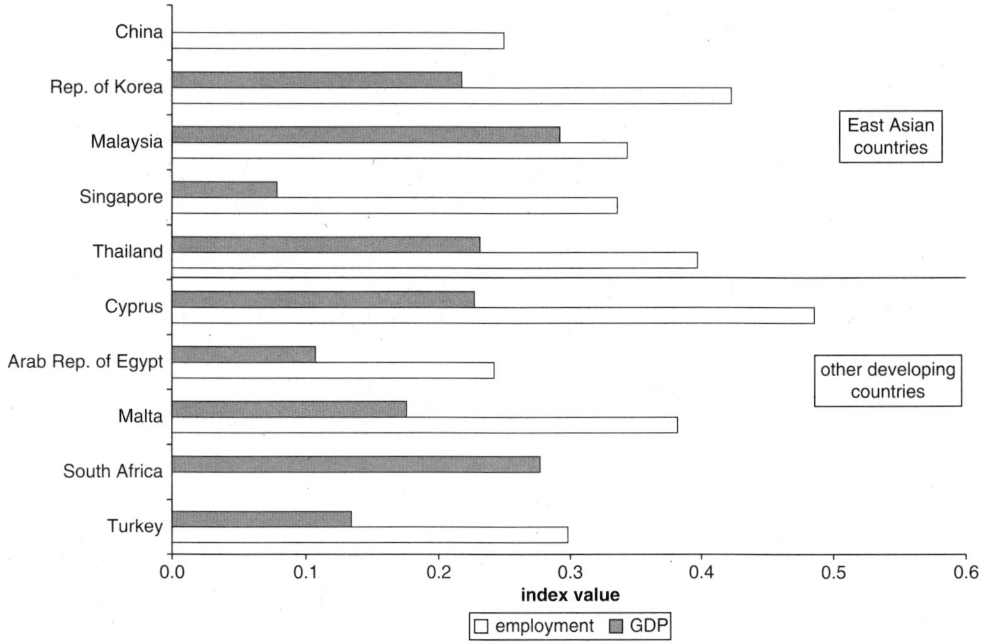

Sources: For employment, International Labour Office; for GDP, UNSD.

Table 3.F.1 Top Sectors by World Trade Importance

SITC Revision 3	Ranking	Description
1970		
78	2	Road vehicles
67	3	Iron and steel
72	4	Machinery specialized for particular industries
65	5	Textile yarn, fabrics, and made-up articles
68	6	Nonferrous metals
74	7	General industrial machinery and equipment not elsewhere specified and machine parts
77	8	Electrical machinery, apparatus, and appliances not elsewhere specified and electrical parts thereof
28	9	Metalliferrous ores and metal scrap
04	10	Cereals and cereal preparations
05	11	Vegetables and fruit
79	12	Tobacco and tobacco manufactures
1980		
78	2	Road vehicles
67	3	Iron and steel
77	4	Electrical machinery, apparatus, and appliances not elsewhere specified and electrical parts thereof
72	5	Machinery specialized for particular industries

(continued)

Table 3.F.1 Top Sectors by World Trade Importance *(continued)*

SITC Revision 3	*Ranking*	*Description*
74	6	General industrial machinery and equipment not elsewhere specified and machine parts
65	7	Textile yarn, fabrics, and made-up articles
68	8	Nonferrous metals
66	9	Nonmetallic mineral manufactures
04	10	Cereals and cereal preparations
84	11	Articles of apparel and clothing accessories
69	12	Manufactures of metals
89	13	Miscellaneous manufactured articles
79	14	Tobacco and tobacco manufactures
51	15	Organic chemicals
76	16	Telecommunications and sound-recording and sound-reproducing apparatus and equipment
28	17	Metalliferrous ores and metal scrap
34	18	Gas, natural and manufactured
1990		
78	2	Road vehicles
77	3	Electrical machinery, apparatus, and appliances not elsewhere specified and electrical parts thereof
89	4	Miscellaneous manufactured articles

(continued)

Table 3.F.1 Top Sectors by World Trade Importance *(continued)*

SITC Revision 3	*Ranking*	*Description*
75	5	Office machines and automatic data-processing machines
74	6	General industrial machinery and equipment not elsewhere specified and machine parts
72	7	Machinery specialized for particular industries
84	8	Articles of apparel and clothing accessories
67	9	Iron and steel
65	10	Textile yarn, fabrics, and made-up articles
76	11	Telecommunications and sound-recording and sound-reproducing apparatus and equipment
79	12	Tobacco and tobacco manufactures
2000		
77	1	Electrical machinery, apparatus, and appliances not elsewhere specified and electrical parts thereof
78	3	Road vehicles
75	4	Office machines and automatic data-processing machines
76	5	Telecommunications and sound-recording and sound-reproducing apparatus and equipment
89	6	Miscellaneous manufactured articles
74	7	General industrial machinery and equipment not elsewhere specified and machine parts
84	8	Articles of apparel and clothing accessories
71	9	Power-generating machinery and equipment
72	10	Machinery specialized for particular industries

Figure 3.F.1 Comparative Advantage of Products of High International Demand

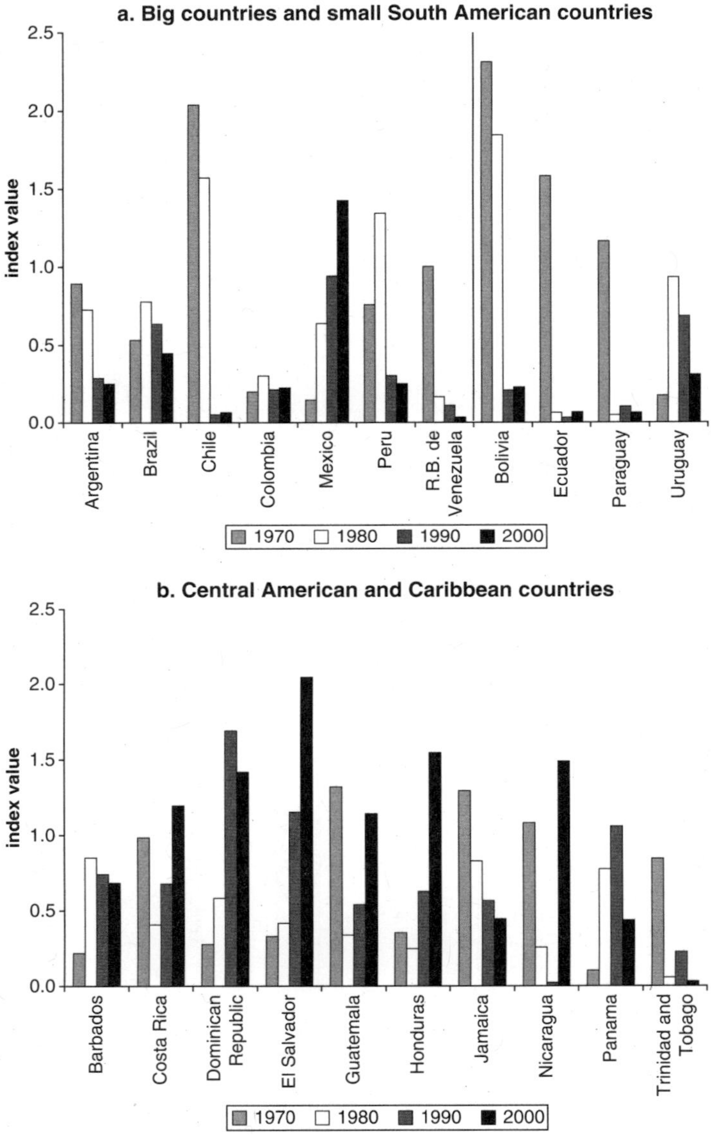

Source: Authors' calculations.

Table 3.G.1 Industry Classification by Input Intensity of the Production Function

ISIC Revision 2	*Industry*	*Input intensity*
311	Food products	Natural resources
313	Beverages	Natural resources
314	Tobacco	Natural resources
331	Wood products, except furniture	Natural resources
341	Paper and products	Natural resources
351	Industrial chemicals	Natural resources
354	Miscellaneous petroleum and coal products	Natural resources
355	Rubber products	Natural resources
362	Glass and products	Natural resources
369	Other nonmetallic mineral products	Natural resources
371	Iron and steel	Natural resources
372	Nonferrous metals	Natural resources
321	Textiles	Labor intensive
322	Wearing apparel, except footwear	Labor intensive
323	Leather products	Labor intensive
324	Footwear, except rubber or plastic	Labor intensive
332	Furniture, except metal	Labor intensive
342	Printing and publishing	Labor intensive
352	Other chemicals	Labor intensive
356	Plastic products	Labor intensive
361	Pottery, china, and earthenware	Labor intensive
390	Other manufactured products	Labor intensive
381	Fabricated metal products	Capital intensive
382	Machinery, except electrical	Capital intensive
383	Electric machinery	Capital intensive
384	Transport equipment	Capital intensive
385	Professional and scientific equipment	Capital intensive
353	Petroleum refineries	Capital intensive

Sources: Program of Analysis of Industrial Dynamics (Programa de Análisis de la Dinámica Industrial), Economic Commission for Latin America and the Caribbean; Katz and Stumpo 2001.

Note: Petroleum refineries were excluded from the analysis, as well as the cooper production for Chile. Capital-intensive sectors are also known as *engineering-intensive sectors*.

Table 3.H.1 Classification of Sectors by Productivity: Three Digits of ISIC Revision 2

ISIC	*Industry*	*Classification*
322	Wearing apparel, except footwear	Low productivity
324	Footwear, except rubber or plastic	Low productivity
321	Textiles	Low productivity
332	Furniture, except metal	Low productivity
323	Leather products	Low productivity
361	Pottery, china, and earthenware	Low productivity
331	Wood products, except furniture	Low productivity
390	Other manufactured products	Low productivity
381	Fabricated metal products	Low productivity
356	Plastic products	Medium productivity
355	Rubber products	Medium productivity
385	Professional and scientific equipment	Medium productivity
382	Machinery, except electrical	Medium productivity
342	Printing and publishing	Medium productivity
311	Food products	Medium productivity
383	Electric machinery	Medium productivity
362	Glass and products	Medium productivity
372	Nonferrous metals	Medium productivity
341	Paper and products	Medium productivity
384	Transport equipment	High productivity
369	Other nonmetallic mineral products	High productivity
371	Iron and steel	High productivity
352	Other chemicals	High productivity
313	Beverages	High productivity
354	Miscellaneous petroleum and coal products	High productivity
351	Industrial chemicals	High productivity
353	Petroleum refineries	High productivity
314	Tobacco	High productivity

Source: UNIDO.

Table 3.H.2 Classification of Sectors by Productivity: Two Digits of ISIC Revision 2

ISIC	*Industry*	*Classification*
32	Textile, wearing apparel, and leather industry	Low productivity
33	Manufacture of wood and wood products, including furniture	Low productivity
39	Other manufacturing industries	Low productivity
36	Manufacture of nonmetallic mineral products, except products of petroleum and coal	Medium productivity
38	Manufacture of fabricated metal products, machinery, and equipment	Medium productivity
34	Manufacture of paper and paper products, printing, and publishing	Medium productivity
37	Basic metal industries	High productivity
35	Manufacture of chemicals and chemical, petroleum, coal, rubber, and plastic products	High productivity
31	Manufacture of food, beverages, and tobacco	High productivity

Source: UNIDO.

Table 3.H.3 Testing the Classification for Latin America and the Caribbean: Spearman Rank Correlation

Country	*United States*	*Average of G7*
Argentina	0.6902**	0.8090**
Chile	0.8181**	0.9146**
Colombia	0.8835**	0.9069**
Mexico	0.8070**	0.9091**
El Salvador	0.7935**	0.7470**
Venezuela	0.8455**	0.8566**

Source: Authors' calculations.

Note: ** = rejected at the 1 percent level. Test of Ho: variable1 and variable2 are independent.

Notes

1. The Lilien index (Lilien 1982) measures the dispersion in the growth rate across industries and is defined as follows:

$$\sigma_t = \left[\sum_s \frac{x_{st}}{X_t} (\Delta \ln x_{st} - \Delta \ln X_t)^2 \right]^{1/2}, \qquad (3.3)$$

where s indexes the sectors and t is the time.

2. It should be stressed at the outset that analysis of output and productivity growth in the countries of the region is an arduous task given the widespread informality and concentration in certain activities. See annex 3.A for more details.

3. However, it is noteworthy that the manufacturing sector recovered substantially in Argentina and Uruguay after the devaluation in 2002. The GDP share of manufacturing grew from 24.6 percent in 2002 to 26.9 percent in 2004 in Argentina and from 16.9 percent to 18.6 percent in Uruguay during the same period.

4. In the Southern Cone, most FDI was directed to natural resource sectors and nontradable infrastructure services. FDI in manufacturing was oriented to the local market rather than to the creation of export platforms. Thus, the main receptor industries of FDI were automobiles, food, soft drinks and other beverages, and chemicals. In contrast, in Mexico and Central America, FDI pursued an efficiency-improving strategy with a view to entering third markets, particularly the United States. See ECLAC (2005) and OECD (2004).

5. Governments are enhancing the skills of the population by adapting the curricula of secondary schools and transforming university programs. The telecommunications infrastructure was improved as well, offering broadband Internet at a low cost with a special tariff for the enterprises that provide informational services.

6. In Chile, the agriculture sector has undergone a large transformation since 1990, thanks to the incorporation of new technologies. De Ferranti and others (2002) describe how this change was implemented in the fruit industry. These new technologies implied the automation of many activities and a net reduction in employment of 9 percent. More generally, Stallings and Peres (2000) study nine Latin American and Caribbean countries and report an increase in the proportion of land dedicated to livestock and forest plantation, activities that typically require few workers.

7. See Global Policy Network (2005) for the experience of El Salvador.

8. Nicaragua experienced a large expansion of land under cultivation after the civil war and the incorporation of nontraditional farming based on labor-intensive technologies (World Bank 2003a).

9. The experience of a number of the rapidly growing Asian countries suggests a major role played by manufacturing industries in promoting productivity enhancements and output growth (Radelet and Sachs 1997). More generally, Johnson, Ostry, and Subramanian (2006) examined 80 episodes of sustained growth (more than 2 percent for at least eight years) identified by Hausmann, Pritchett, and Rodrik (2005) and found that in nearly all these cases the share of manufacturing in total exports demonstrated rapid increases. Jones and Olken (2005) found that up-breaks in output growth were very often associated with increases in manufacturing employment, while down-breaks witnessed declines in manufacturing employment. See also Rodrik (2006), who pointed out the large decline in the share of GDP in manufacturing as one of the factors behind the low growth performance in Latin America and the Caribbean.

10. The traditional idea that natural resources are a curse for growth (for example, Prebisch 1959) rests on the hypothesis that natural resources draw away resources from other economic sectors with higher potential for productivity growth. However, many natural resource–rich countries (for example, Australia, Finland, Sweden, and the United States) have used this natural endowment as a key driver for growth and as a source of technological progress. Sachs and Warner (2005), using cross-section regressions, have found a robust negative correlation between economic growth and the share of natural resource exports in total GDP. However, other studies have questioned these results. Manzano and Rigobon (2001), as well as Lederman and Maloney (2002), did not find empirical support to the idea that natural resource abundance has a robust effect on growth performance.

11. For example, Bravo-Ortega and De Gregorio (2003) used a panel of developing and developed countries over the period from 1970 to 1990 and found that the estimated negative effect of natural resources on GDP growth is more than offset by the positive effect of the interaction between human capital and natural resources.

12. A more detailed analysis is discussed in the next chapter for a subset of countries.

13. The selection of countries was motivated by the availability of data on GDP converted at purchasing power parities with a homogenous methodology, thus making the levels of productivity comparable.

14. This general picture of low productivity in the trade sector hides significant cross-country differences. In some countries, such as Argentina, Brazil, and Chile, the wholesale and retail sector went through a major transformation because of the large inflows of FDI in hypermarkets that reshaped the retail market and its practices (OECD 2004).

15. The decomposition was done at the one-digit level of International Standard Industrial Classification (ISIC) rev. 2. Because of a data constraint, categories 8 and 9 had to be used as a single category.

16. This decomposition has several limitations. First, it focuses on labor productivity and not on multifactor productivity. Second, it assumes that marginal productivity of factor inputs moving in or out of an industry is the same as average productivity. Finally, if output growth is positively related to productivity growth (that is, dynamic increasing returns, or the Verdoorn effect), the effect of structural change may be underestimated, because part of the shift to rapid-growth sectors will be counted in the within effect.

17. Bassanini and others (2000) made this decomposition for the nonfarm business of the OECD countries and found that the bulk of the productivity improvements is given by the within effect in all the countries.

18. In the República Bolivariana de Venezuela, the negative *within* term is almost offset by a positive *between* term. This finding implies that the negative growth in labor productivity, within each sector, is compensated by better allocation of resources across industries.

19. Petroleum, petroleum products, and related materials were excluded in the four years. See annex 3.F for more details.

20. Their study is based on data on manufacturing activity in Latin America from the Economic Commission for Latin America and Caribbean. They investigate the relationship between trade opening and productivity growth at the three-digit ISIC level for seven Latin American countries during 1970 to 1998.

21. The effect of tariff reduction on agricultural employment has not been so largely documented. However, IDB (2003) stresses that it would be a mistake to think that trade openness was the major cause of the decline in employment in agriculture, given that the sector was exposed to other significant factors, such as the

incorporation of new technologies, reduction of cultivated land, and displacement of livestock and forest plantation to crops (Stallings and Peres 2000).

22. Aw, Chung, and Roberts (2000) also found that exposure to trade forces the exit of the least efficient producers in Korea and Taiwan, China. Likewise, Bernard and Bradford Jensen (1999b) found that intraindustry reallocations to higher-productivity exporters can explain up to 20 percent of productivity growth in U.S. manufacturing.

23. Similar results are also found by Bernard and Bradford Jensen (1999a) for the United States and by Aw, Chung, and Roberts (2000) for Taiwan, China.

24. Given the prices of a country's trading partners, international price equalization occurs either through the nominal exchange rate or the domestic price of tradables. Under a flexible regime, the nominal exchange rate ensures international price equalization. However, with a fixed regime, the adjustment is through the domestic price of tradable goods (Baldi and Mulder 2004).

25. Gourinchas (1998) also provides evidence of the strong effect of exchange rate movements on job flows. He finds that job creation and destruction commove positively following a real exchange shock. Appreciation tends to be associated with additional turbulence, whereas depreciation tends to reduce job fluctuations. Klein, Schuh, and Triest (2003) found strong effects of real exchange rate on job flows in the United States.

References

Álvarez, R., and M. Braun. 2006. "Trade Liberalization, Price Distortions, and Resource Reallocation." Working Paper 374, Central Bank of Chile, Santiago.

Aw, B. Y, S. Chung, and M. J. Roberts. 2000. "Productivity and Turnover in the Export Market: Micro-level Evidence from the Republic of Korea and Taiwan (China)." *World Bank Economic Review* 14 (1): 65–90.

Baldi, A.-L., and N. Mulder. 2004. "The Impact of Exchange Rate Regimes on Real Exchange Rates in South America, 1990–2002." OECD Economics Department Working Paper 396, Organisation for Economic Co-operation and Development, Paris.

Bartelsman, E. J., A. Bassanini, J. Haltiwanger, R. S. Jarmin, and T. Schank. 2004. "The Spread of ICT and Productivity Growth: Is Europe S. Scarpetta, Lagging Behind in the New Economy?" In *The ICT Revolution: Productivity Gains and the Digital Divide*, ed. D. Cohen, P. Garibaldi, and S. Scarpetta. Oxford, U.K.: Oxford University Press.

Bassanini, A., D. Pilat, S. Scarpetta, and P. Schreyer. 2000. "Economic Growth in the OECD Area: Recent Trends at the Aggregate and Sectoral Level." Economics Department Working Paper 248, Organisation for Economic Co-operation and Development, Paris.

Bernard, A. B., and J. Bradford Jensen. 1999a. "Exceptional Exporter Performance: Cause, Effect, or Both?" *Journal of International Economics* 47 (1): 1–25.

———. 1999b. "Exporting and Productivity." NBER Working Paper 7135, National Bureau of Economic Research, Cambridge, MA.

Bonelli, R. 2002. "Labor Productivity in Brazil during the 1990s." Discussion Paper 906, Institute of Applied Economic Research, Rio de Janeiro.

Bravo-Ortega, C., and J. De Gregorio. 2003. "The Relative Richness of the Poor? Natural Resources, Human Capital, and Economic Growth." Policy Research Working Paper 3484, World Bank, Washington, DC.

Chenery, H. B., and L. Taylor. 1968. "Development Patterns: Among Countries and over Time." Review of Economics and Statistics 50 (4): 391–416.

Chong, A., and F. López-de-Silanes. 2005. "The Truth about Privatization in Latin America." In *Privatization in Latin America: Myths and Reality*, ed. A. Chong and F. López-de-Silanes, 1–66. Palo Alto, CA: Stanford University Press.

Chong, A., and J. Saavedra. 2003. "Explaining Increases in 'Legal Informality' during the Nineties in Latin America: The Case of Peru." Inter-American Development Bank, Washington, DC.

Clerides, S., S. Lach, and J. R. Tybout. 1998. "Is Learning by Exporting Important? Micro-Dynamic Evidence from Colombia, Mexico, and Morocco." *Quarterly Journal of Economics* 113 (3): 903–47.

De Ferranti, D., G. E. Perry, D. Lederman, and W. Maloney. 2002. *From Natural Resources to the Knowledge Economy: Trade and Job Quality*, Washington, DC: World Bank.

ECLAC (Economic Commission for Latin America and the Caribbean). 2005. *Foreign Direct Investment in Latin America and the Caribbean, 2004*. Santiago: United Nations.

Fischer, R., R. Gutiérrez, and P. Serra. 2005. "The Effects of Privatization on Firms: The Chilean Case." In *Privatization in Latin America: Myths and Reality*, ed. A. Chong and F. López-de-Silanes, 197–274. Palo Alto, CA: Stanford University Press.

Galiani, S., P. Gertler, E. Schargrodsky, and F. Sturzenegger. 2005. "The Benefits and Costs of Privatization in Argentina: A Microeconomic Analysis." In *Privatization in Latin America: Myths and Reality*, ed. A. Chong and F. López-de-Silanes, 67–116. Palo Alto, CA: Stanford University Press.

Global Policy Network. 2005. "Desempeño económico y del mercado de trabajo de El Salvador 2004/2005." Fundación Nacional para el Desarrollo, Área Macroeconomía y Desarrollo, San Salvador.

Gourinchas, P.-O. 1998. "Exchange Rates and Jobs: What Do We Learn from Job Flows?" NBER Working Paper 6864, National Bureau of Economic Research, Cambridge, MA.

Haltiwanger, J., A. Kugler, M. Kugler, A. Micco, and C. Pagés. 2004. "Effects of Tariffs and Real Exchange Rates on Job Reallocation: Evidence from Latin America." *Journal of Policy Reform* 7 (4): 191–208.

Hausmann, R., L. Pritchett, and D. Rodrik. 2005. "Growth Accelerations." *Journal of Economic Growth* 10 (4): 303–29.

IDB (Inter-American Development Bank). 2003. *Good Jobs Wanted: Labor Markets in Latin America—2004 Report on Economic and Social Progress in Latin America*. Washington, DC: IDB.

Johnson, S., J. Ostry, and A. Subramanian. 2006. "Levers for Growth: Policy Lessons from Earlier Bouts of Growth in Developing Countries." *Finance and Development* 43 (1): 28–31.

Jones, B. F., and B. A. Olken. 2005. "The Anatomy of Start-Stop Growth." NBER Working Paper 11528, National Bureau of Economic Research, Cambridge, MA.

Katz, J., and G. Stumpo. 2001. "Regímenes sectoriales, productividad y competitividad internacional." *Revista de la CEPAL* 75 (December): 137–59.

Klein, M., S. Schuh, and R. K. Triest. 2003. "Job Creation, Job Destruction, and the Real Exchange Rate." *Journal of International Economics* 59 (2): 239–65.

Krugman, P. R. 1979. "Increasing Returns, Monopolistic Competition, and International Trade." *Journal of International Economics* 9 (4): 469–79.

Lederman, D., and W. Maloney. 2002. "Trade Structure and Growth." Policy Research Working Paper 3025, World Bank, Washington, DC.

Levinsohn, J. 1999. "Employment Responses to International Liberalization in Chile." *Journal of International Economics* 47 (2): 321–44.

Levy-Yeyati, E., and F. Sturzenegger. 2003. "To Float or to Fix: Evidence on the Impact of Exchange Rate Regimes on Growth." *American Economic Review* 93 (4): 1173–93.

Lilien, D. 1982. "Sectoral Shifts and Cyclical Unemployment." *Journal of Political Economy* 90 (4): 777–93.

Loayza, N. 2001. "Growth in Brazil." World Bank, Washington, DC.

Manzano, O., and R. Rigobon. 2001. "Resource Curse or Debt Overhang." NBER Working Paper 8390, National Bureau of Economic Research, Cambridge, MA.

Martin, W., and D. Mitra. 2001. "Productivity Growth and Convergence in Agriculture versus Manufacturing." *Economic Development and Cultural Change* 49 (2): 402–22.

OECD (Organisation for Economic Co-operation and Development). 2003. *The Sources of Growth in OECD Countries*. Paris: OECD.

———. 2004. *Trade and Competitiveness in Argentina, Brazil, and Chile: Not as Easy as A-B-C*. Paris: OECD.

Paus, E., N. Reinhardt, and M. Robinson. 2003. "Trade Liberalization and Productivity Growth in Latin American Manufacturing, 1970–98." *Journal of Policy Reform* 6 (1): 1–15.

Pavcnik, N. 2002. "Trade Liberalization, Exit, and Productivity Improvements: Evidence from Chilean Plants." *Review of Economics Studies* 69 (1): 245–76.

Pombo, C., and M. Ramírez. 2005. "Privatization in Colombia: A Plant Performance Analysis." In *Privatization in Latin America: Myths and Reality*, ed. A. Chong and F. López-de-Silanes, 275–348. Palo Alto, CA: Stanford University Press.

Prebisch, R. 1959. "Commercial Policy in the Underdeveloped Countries." *American Economic Review* 49 (2): 251–73.

Radelet, S., and J. Sachs. 1997. "Asia's Reemergence." *Foreign Affairs* 76 (6): 44–59.

Raiser, M., M. Schaffer, and J. Schuchhardt. 2003. "Benchmarking Structural Change in Transition." Working Paper 79, European Bank for Reconstruction and Development, London.

Roberts, M. J., and J. R. Tybout. 1997. "The Decision to Export in Colombia: An Empirical Model of Entry with Sunk Costs." *American Economic Review* 97 (4): 545–64.

Rodrik, D. 2006. "Industrial Development: Stylized Facts and Policies." John F. Kennedy School of Government, Harvard University, Cambridge, MA.

Rowthorn, R. E., and R. Ramaswamy. 1997. "Deindustrialization: Causes and Implications." Working Paper 97/42, International Monetary Fund, Washington, DC.

Sachs, J., and A. Warner. 2005. "Natural Resource Abundance and Economic Growth." NBER Working Paper 5398, National Bureau of Economic Research, Cambridge, MA.

Sánchez, G., and I. Butler. 2004. "Market Institutions, Labor Market Dynamics, and Productivity in Argentina during the 1990s." *Policy Reform* 7 (4): 249–78.

Stallings, B., and W. Peres. 2000. *Growth, Employment, and Equity: The Impact of the Economic Reforms in Latin America and the Caribbean*. Washington, DC: Brookings Institution Press.

Wacziarg, R., and J. S. Wallack. 2004. "Trade Liberalization and Intersectoral Labor Movements." *Journal of International Economics* 64 (2): 411–39.

World Bank. 2003a. "Nicaragua Poverty Assessment: Raising Welfare and Reducing Vulnerability." Report 26128-NI, World Bank, Washington, DC.

———. 2003b. *Regional Research Project: An Analysis of Court Users and Uses in Two Latin American Countries*. Washington, DC: World Bank.

4

Creative Destruction, Productivity, and Job Creation

Chapter 3 has clearly indicated that the countries of Latin America and the Caribbean have experienced a large reallocation of labor across the main sectors of the economy. However, the magnitude of the reallocation process is somewhat smaller than that observed in dynamic emerging economies and, more important, does not seem to lead to shifts from less productive to more productive uses. As well documented in a growing microliterature (see, for example, Bartelsman and Doms 2000; Bartelsman, Haltiwanger, and Scarpetta 2004), macro and industry-level analysis may hide much of the heterogeneity in firm characteristics and behavior and thus offer only a partial picture of the drivers of growth and job creation, especially in countries that have experienced major structural changes, such as those in Latin America and the Caribbean.

The pace and depth of enterprise restructuring and the reallocation of resources across firms have been affected by improvements in corporate governance (for example, changing managers) brought by privatization of previously state-owned enterprises and stronger competition in product markets attributable to regulatory reforms and greater exposure to foreign competition. The investment climate in which firms operate has also changed, often substantially, with the liberalization of conditions for entry, price liberalization, and macroeconomic stabilization. All these factors have taken different forms in the region, with different implications for output, productivity, and employment growth.

How successful are the countries of the region in reallocating resources to more productive uses? Are large differences observed between industries in the manufacturing sector and those in the service sector? How important is firm entry and exit for productivity and job creation and destruction? Which firms contribute most to job creation? Does policy have a role in influencing the pace and nature of the process of labor reallocation? This chapter addresses these questions using a harmonized firm-level database that includes information for five Latin American countries: Argentina, Brazil, Chile, Colombia, and Mexico. It should be stressed at the outset that the data used for these countries are from enterprise surveys and social security records. As such, they do not include firms that are not registered to the business register or to the social security administration. As stressed in the previous chapters, informality looms large in Latin America and the Caribbean, and many small and even medium-size businesses operate in the informal sector. In this respect, this chapter's analysis looks at the potentially more productive and possibly larger firms—those that can afford the costs of formality or, because of their size and activity, cannot escape administrative controls. Nevertheless, assessing how formal firms behave in comparison to their counterparts in other countries is of great importance. After all, the creation of more jobs—and more productive jobs—depends to a large extent on the expansion of formal businesses.

What Is the Role of Firm Restructuring and the Entry and Exit of Firms in Job Creation?

The analysis of employment shifts across macrosectors can hide the potentially greater dynamism taking place within each sector because new firms enter the market and displace obsolete units and existing firms are continuously adapting to changing market and technological conditions. In this context, the magnitude and characteristics of job flows (job creation and destruction) should first be assessed and then linked to productivity and output growth.

High Rates of Job Creation and Destruction in Latin American Countries

Table 4.1 presents job creation and job destruction rates in the sample of Latin American countries for which firm-level data are available: Argentina, Brazil, Chile, Colombia, and Mexico. It suggests that job reallocation (the sum of job creation and destruction) is very high in most of the countries, reaching more than 20 to 25 percent of the total workforce on average in the past decade (see box 4.1 for details on the firm-level data). In other words, on average, almost a quarter of all jobs are created or destroyed every year.[1] Job creation and job destruction rates in the region tend to exceed those in most industrial countries. Major differences also exist within the region. Argentina seems to be characterized by a fairly low degree of job reallocation, whereas Brazil and Mexico are at the top of the country ranking in terms of labor reallocation.

Table 4.1 Job Creation and Destruction of Entering, Exiting, and Continuer Firms, 1990–Early 2000s

Country	*Job creation: firm entry (%)*	*Job creation: continuing firms (%)*	*Job destruction: firm exit (%)*	*Job destruction: continuing firms (%)*	*Total turnover (%)*
Business sector, firms with 1 or more employees					
France	3.3	15.5	4.0	14.5	37.4
Mexico	**5.7**	**11.7**	**3.7**	**7.7**	**28.8**
Netherlands	5.5	10.8	5.5	5.2	26.9
Finland	5.0	8.7	4.0	8.7	26.4
Hungary	5.3	8.5	4.0	8.5	26.2
Romania	5.6	5.6	2.6	12.3	26.1
Argentina	**4.0**	**8.8**	**4.5**	**6.1**	**23.4**
Italy	3.9	8.2	4.4	6.3	22.8
Slovenia	4.3	6.0	4.0	7.5	21.7
United States	3.7	7.8	3.4	5.9	20.8
Manufacturing sector, firms with 1 or more employees					
Brazil	**4.7**	**11.4**	**4.5**	**8.5**	**29.0**
France	5.1	8.6	5.1	9.3	28.2
Mexico	**4.1**	**11.7**	**3.1**	**7.9**	**26.9**
Hungary	4.8	8.0	4.0	7.0	23.8
United Kingdom	5.2	6.8	5.8	6.1	23.8
Latvia	4.6	9.6	1.7	7.4	23.3
Netherlands	3.6	8.1	4.9	5.6	22.3
Finland	3.9	7.3	3.3	7.5	22.0
Romania	4.1	4.0	1.5	11.9	21.5
Italy	2.9	7.0	3.9	6.8	20.6
Estonia	3.9	7.3	3.5	5.9	20.6
Portugal	4.2	5.8	3.7	6.7	20.5
Argentina	**2.3**	**6.4**	**4.1**	**6.6**	**19.4**
Slovenia	3.5	4.1	4.1	7.1	18.8
United States	1.6	6.7	1.5	6.4	16.1

(continued)

Table 4.1 Job Creation and Destruction of Entering, Exiting, and Continuer Firms, 1990–Early 2000s *(continued)*

Country	*Job creation: firm entry (%)*	*Job creation: continuing firms (%)*	*Job destruction: firm exit (%)*	*Job destruction: continuing firms (%)*	*Total turnover (%)*
Manufacturing sector, firms with 20 or more employees					
France	4.3	11.4	4.2	9.7	29.6
Brazil	**3.1**	**11.0**	**3.4**	**7.4**	**24.9**
United Kingdom	3.9	7.3	5.5	7.8	24.4
Mexico	**2.8**	**11.9**	**2.0**	**6.4**	**23.1**
Chile	**3.7**	**7.5**	**4.7**	**6.4**	**22.4**
Hungary	4.0	7.7	3.8	6.3	21.8
Latvia	2.8	9.8	1.1	7.8	21.4
Romania	3.7	3.5	1.3	11.5	20.1
Colombia	**2.2**	**8.1**	**2.7**	**6.7**	**19.6**
Finland	3.6	6.4	2.9	6.6	19.6
Estonia	3.3	6.6	3.4	5.2	18.5
Netherlands	3.7	6.1	4.0	4.5	18.3
Italy	1.8	7.3	2.4	6.9	18.3
Slovenia	3.2	3.6	4.0	6.9	17.7
Argentina	**1.3**	**6.3**	**2.7**	**6.1**	**16.5**
Portugal	2.3	5.5	3.1	5.5	16.4
United States	1.2	6.4	1.1	5.8	14.5

Source: Authors' calculations.

Note: Sample countries for the region are in **bold**. Totals may differ because of rounding.

The Strong Role Played by the Entry and Exit of Firms

In most Latin American and Caribbean countries, a significant share of the overall job turnover is due to the creation and destruction of firms, generally about 20 to 30 percent of total job creation and destruction. Interestingly, however, with the sole exception of Mexico, entry plays a smaller role in total job creation than exits do for job destruction (figure 4.1). Entry accounts for less than 30 percent of total job creation, whereas exits generally account for 30 to 35 percent of total job destruction. This pattern is often not the case in Organisation for Economic Co-operation and Development (OECD) countries and especially in the transition economies of Eastern Europe.[2] In the latter, in particular, a much larger proportion of job creation comes from the entry of new firms, whereas job destruction is dominated by the restructuring of large privatized firms.

Increase in Firm Dynamics and the Associated Job Creation and Destruction

In both Chile and Colombia, for which longer time-series data are available, a significant increase has taken place in the pace of firm creation and firm destruction, with a stronger effect on job turnover (figure 4.2). The rate of firm entry is generally greater than that of firm exit, largely because new firms are much smaller than those they replace, as will be discussed later. More interestingly, the structural reforms of the 1990s have led to some increase in the pace of firm churning and, especially in the case of Chile, a stronger role played by the firm churning process in overall job creation and destruction. Although reforms had already started in Chile in

Box 4.1 A Consistent International Firm-Level Database

Available data at the firm level are usually compiled for fiscal and other purposes. Unlike macroeconomic data, there are few internationally agreed definitions and sources, although harmonization has improved over the years. The data used in this chapter are based on a harmonized firm-level database for 24 transition and emerging economies of the Organisation for Economic Co-operation and Development (OECD). The data set used in the study was collected in various stages. Most recently, the firm-level project organized by the World Bank collected indicators for 14 countries (in Eastern Europe, Estonia, Hungary, Latvia, Romania, and Slovenia; in Latin America, Argentina, Brazil, Chile, Colombia, Mexico, and the República Bolivariana de Venezuela; and in Asia, Indonesia, the Republic of Korea, and Taiwan, China). An earlier OECD study collected indicators based on information on firms from Canada, Denmark, Germany, Finland, France, Italy, the Netherlands, Portugal, the United Kingdom, and the United States (see Bartelsman, Haltiwanger, and Scarpetta forthcoming for details). The main source of the data and the period covered for the countries that are included in the sample are presented in the accompanying table. The República Bolivariana de Venezuela was not included in this chapter because of problems with the data on productivity.

(continued)

Box 4.1 A Consistent International Firm-Level Database *(continued)*

Data Sources and Periods

	Firm demographics and survival			*Labor productivity*			
Country	*Source*	*Period*	*Threshold*	*Source*	*Period*	*Threshold*	*Sectors*
Argentina	Register, based on Integrated System of Pensions	1995–2002	Employment ≥ 1	Annual industrial survey, National Institute of Statistics and Censuses (Instituto Nacional de Estadística y Censos)	1990–95 to 1996–2001	Employment ≥ 9 and US$2 million	Firm demographics: all; productivity: manufacturing
Brazil	Census	1996–2001		Annual industrial survey	1997–2001	Employment ≥30 plus sample of firms with 10–29 employees	Manufacturing
Chile	Annual industrial survey (Encuesta Nacional Industrial Anual)	1979–99	Employment ≥ 10	Annual industrial survey (Encuesta Nacional Industrial Anual)	1980–85 to 1994–99	Employment ≥ 10	Manufacturing
Colombia	Annual manufacturing survey (Encuesta Anual Manufacturera)	1982–98	Employment ≥ 10	Annual manufacturing survey (Encuesta Anual Manufacturera)	1982–86 to 1994–98	Employment ≥ 10	Manufacturing
Mexico	Social security	1985–2001	Employment ≥ 1				All

Source: Bartelsman, Haltiwanger, and Scarpetta 2004.

(continued)

Box 4.1 A Consistent International Firm-Level Database *(continued)*

Definition of Key Concepts

The *entry* rate is defined as the number of new firms divided by the total number of incumbent and entrant firms in a given year; the *exit rate* is defined as the number of firms exiting the market in a given year divided by the population of origin (that is, the incumbents in the previous year).

Labor productivity growth is defined as the difference between the rate of growth of output and the rate of growth of employment[a] and, whenever possible, controls for material inputs.

The *job creation rate* equals employment gains summed over all plants that expand in a given year, divided by the average employment in the period. The *job destruction rate* equals employment losses summed over all plants that contract in a given year, divided by the average employment in the period. The *job reallocation rate* is the sum of all plant-level employment gains and losses that occur in a given year.

The precise formulation of the job flows indicators is as follows:

Job creation rate: $POS_{isct} = \dfrac{\text{number of jobs created}_{isct}}{0.5\left(E_{isct} + E_{isc,t-1}\right)}$

Job destruction rate: $NEG_{isct} = \dfrac{\text{number of jobs destroyed}_{isct}}{0.5\left(E_{isct} + E_{isc,t-1}\right)}$

Job creation rate (entry): $POS_{isct} = \dfrac{\text{number of jobs created by entry}_{isct}}{0.5\left(E_{isct} + E_{isc,t-1}\right)}$

Job destruction rate (exit): $NEG_{isct} = \dfrac{\text{number of jobs destroyed by exit}_{isct}}{0.5\left(E_{isct} + E_{isc,t-1}\right)}$

Net employment growth: $NET_{isc} = POS_{isc} - NEG_{isc}$

Job reallocation rate: $SUM_{isc} = POS_{isc} + NEG_{isc}$,

where i represents industry, s represents size class, c represents country, and t represents time. The averages of POS and NEG are taken, and then NET and SUM are calculated.

(continued)

Box 4.1 A Consistent International Firm-Level Database *(continued)*

Comparability Issues

Two prominent aspects of the data have to be borne in mind when one is comparing firm-level data across countries:

- *Unit of observation.* The data used in this study refer to firms rather than establishments. Firm-based data are likely to more closely represent entities that are responsible for key aspects of decision making than are plant-level data. Nevertheless, business registers may define firms at different points in ownership structures; for example, some registers consider firms that are effectively controlled by a parent firm as separate units, whereas others record only the parent company.
- *Size threshold.* Although some registers include even single-person businesses, others omit firms smaller than a certain size, usually in terms of the number of employees but sometimes in terms of other measures, such as sales. Data used in this study exclude single-person businesses.

Source: Bartelsman, Haltiwanger, and Scarpetta 2004.
a. Available data do not allow controlling for changes in hours worked, nor do they distinguish between part- and full-time employment.

the 1980s, the evidence provided in figure 4.2 suggests an increase in labor mobility with the subsequent reforms of the 1990s.

The Key Role of Firm Creation and Destruction in Productivity Growth

One interesting result emerging from chapter 3 is that productivity growth was largely driven by performance within each industry rather than by reallocation of resources across industries. Moreover, this result applied to both a decomposition based on one-digit International Standard Industrial Classification (ISIC) industries in manufacturing and services and one based on two-digit ISIC manufacturing industries. To shed more light on this result, this chapter analyzes firm-level data to assess how the restructuring of existing firms and the process of creative destruction—that is, the entry of new firms that displace old and obsolete units—contribute to productivity growth.

Figure 4.1 Role of Firm Dynamics for Job Flows: Manufacturing Sector: 1990–Early 2000s

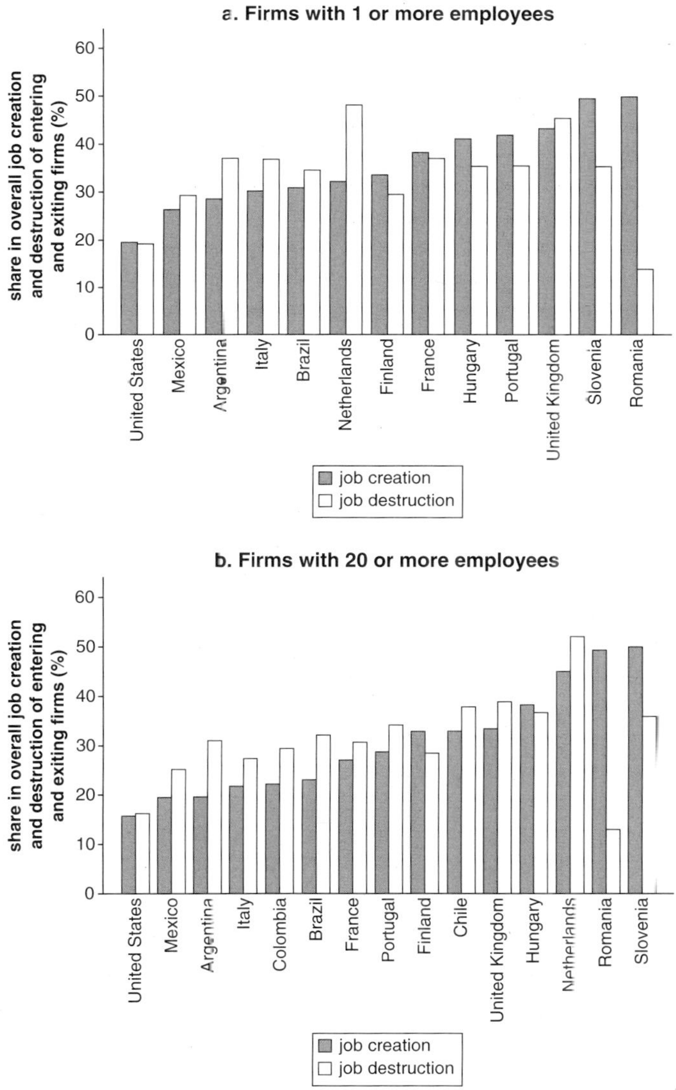

Source: Authors' calculations.

Aggregate productivity can be decomposed in a number of ways into (a) a within-firm component and (b) other components attributable to the reallocation of resources across firms. The approach used in this section distinguishes five different components of productivity growth: (a) *within* component, accounting for productivity increases within firms; (b) *between* component, reflecting reallocation of resources between firms; (c) *covariance*

Figure 4.2 Firm and Job Turnover over Time in Chile and Colombia: Manufacturing Sector

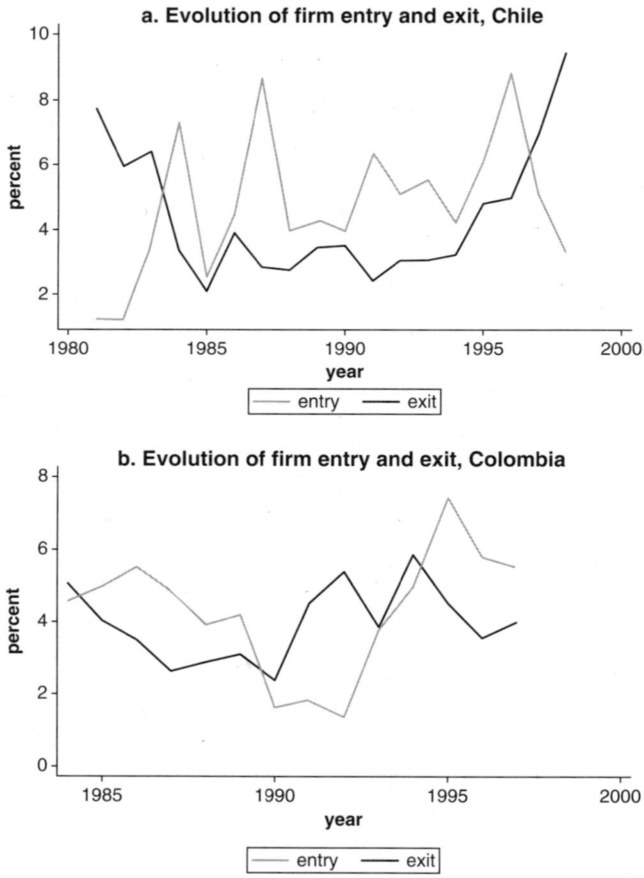

(continued)

Figure 4.2 Firm and Job Turnover over Time in Chile and Colombia: Manufacturing Sector *(continued)*

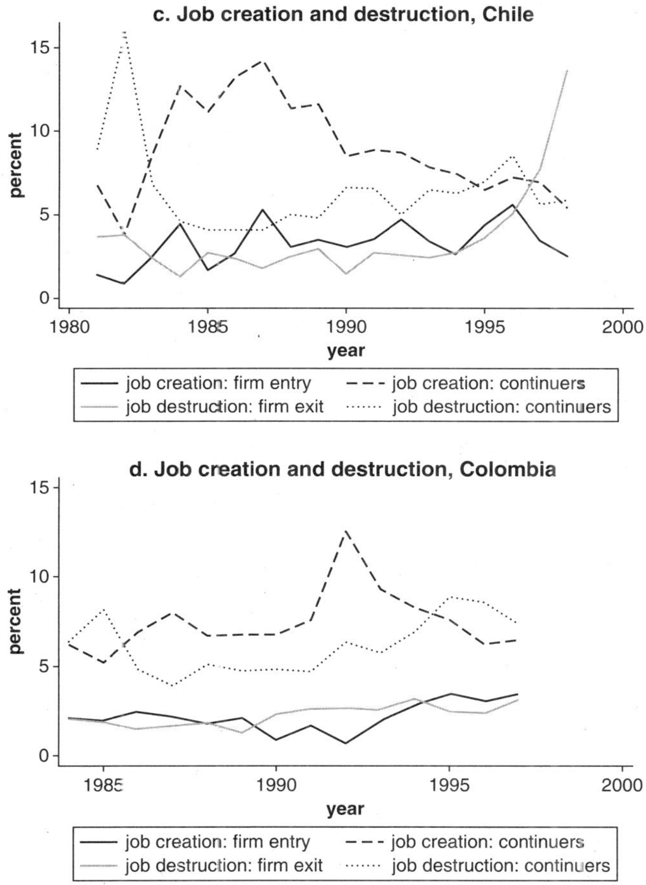

Source: Authors' calculations.
Note: Figure covers firms with 20 or more employees.

or *cross-term*, which combines changes in market shares and changes in productivity (it is positive if enterprises with growing productivity also experience an increase in market share); and components attributable to (d) *entry* and (e) *exit* of firms (see box 4.2 for further details).

Firm-level data for a sample of Latin American and Caribbean countries confirm the evidence discussed in chapter 3—namely, that a continuous

Box 4.2 Decomposition of Productivity Growth Using Firm-Level Data

One approach used to decompose productivity growth is from Foster, Haltiwanger, and Krizan (2006). It uses base year market shares as weights for each term of the decomposition:

$$\Delta P_t = \sum_{Continuers} \theta_{it-k} \Delta p_{it} + \sum_{Continuers} \Delta\theta_{it}(p_{it-k} - P_{t-k}) + \sum_{Continuers} \Delta\theta_{it} \Delta p_{it} + \sum_{Entries} \theta_{it}(p_{it} - P_{t-k}) - \sum_{Exits} \theta_{it-k}(p_{it-k} - P_{t-k}),$$

where Δ means changes over the k – years' interval between the first year ($\tilde{t}\ k$) and the last year (t); θ_{it} is the share of firm i in the given industry at time t (it could be expressed in terms of output or employment); p_i is the productivity of firm i; and P is the aggregate (that is, weighted average) productivity level of the industry. The first term is the *within* component; the second is the *between* component; the third component is the *covariance* or *cross-term* that combines changes in market shares and changes in productivity (it is positive if enterprises with growing productivity also experience an increase in market share); the fourth and fifth terms are the *entry* and *exit* components, respectively.

One of the main limitations of the Foster, Haltiwanger, and Krizan decomposition of productivity growth is that it is highly dependent on the time horizon of the analysis. In particular, in sectors with a high pace of learning by doing and experimentation by new firms as well as selection effects, the reallocation terms (entry and exit as well as the between effects) may be underestimated over short horizons. In addition, over relatively short horizons, measurement errors or transitory shocks may contribute to systematic variations in the reallocation terms. See Bartelsman, Haltiwanger, and Scarpetta (forthcoming) for more details.

process of retooling of existing businesses has a dominant role in overall labor productivity growth. Interestingly, firms with higher-than-average productivity levels tend to gain market shares—the between terms—in all countries of the sample, but also the cross-term, which captures the contribution to total productivity growth of the shift of resources toward firms with higher-than-average productivity growth, is negative. In other words, firms experiencing an increase in productivity were also losing employment shares: that is, their productivity growth was associated with restructuring and downsizing rather than expansion (figure 4.3).

Figure 4.3 Labor Productivity Growth Decomposition: Manufacturing, Five-Year Differencing

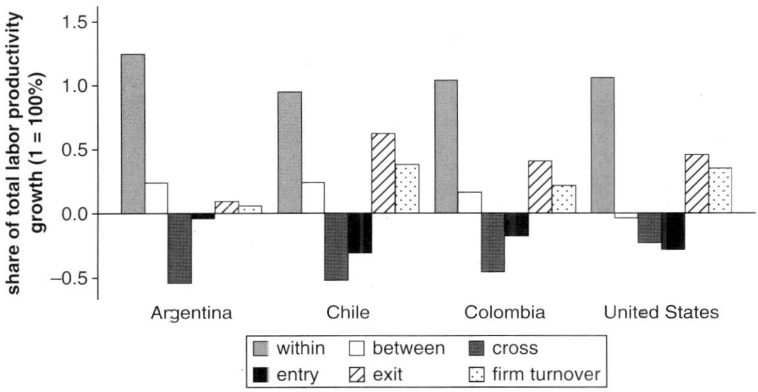

Source: Bartelsman, Haltiwanger, and Scarpetta 2009.

Note: Data are for real gross output for the following periods: Argentina (1995–2001); Chile (1985–99); Colombia (1987–98); United States (1992, 1997). Within = within-firm productivity growth; between = productivity growth attributable to reallocation of labor across existing firms; entry = productivity growth attributable to entry of new firms; exit = productivity growth attributable to exit of firms.

The firm turnover effect (or net effect of entry plus exit) is positive in all the countries, accounting for between 10 percent (Argentina) to almost 40 percent of total productivity growth (Chile). In particular, clear evidence shows that the exit of obsolete firms released resources that could be used more effectively by new or existing firms. Nevertheless, lack of experience and small size often make new firms less productive than the average incumbent.

Effect of New Technologies

Dividing manufacturing industries into a low-technology group and a medium- and high-technology group suggests important differences in the sources of productivity growth (figure 4.4). *Defensive restructuring*—that is, promoting productivity by downsizing—is largely concentrated in low-technology industries where the contribution of new firms to productivity growth is also negative. Similar to that for the United States, the cross-term of the decomposition is, in fact, largely negative. By contrast, new firms are on average as productive—if not more so—than the average

Figure 4.4 Foster, Haltiwanger, and Krizan Decomposition, Five-Year Differencing

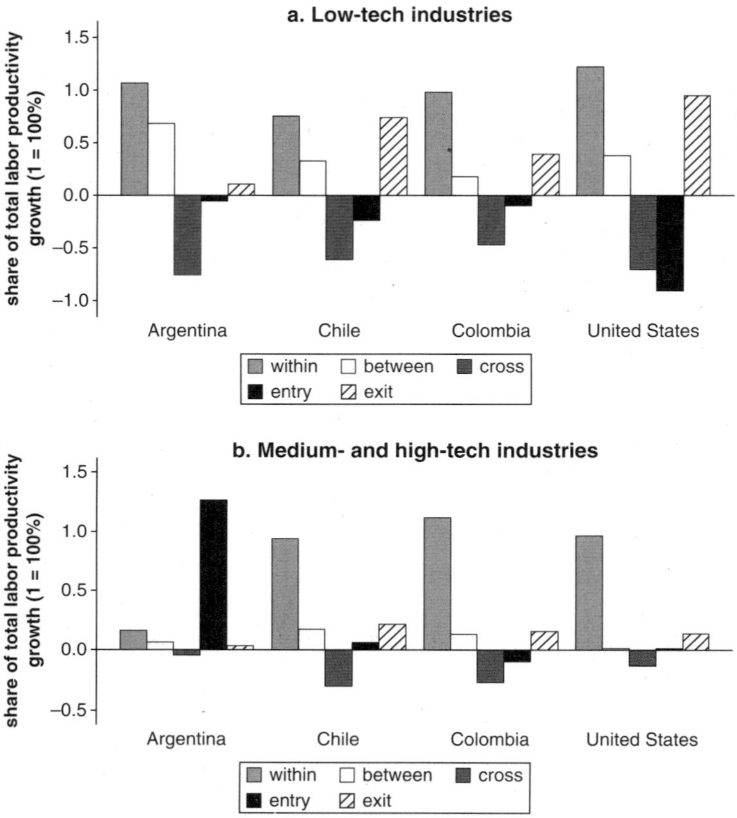

Source: Bartelsman, Haltiwanger, and Scarpetta 2009.

Note: Data are for real gross output for the following periods: Argentina (1995–2001); Chile (1985–99); Colombia (1987–98); United States (1992, 1997). Within = within-firm productivity growth; between = productivity growth attributable to reallocation of labor across existing firms; entry = productivity growth attributable to entry of new firms; exit = productivity growth attributable to exit of firms.

incumbents in medium- and high-technology industries. Argentina is the extreme case in which most of productivity growth comes from the entry of very productive units. More generally, the idea of a stronger contribution from new firms to productivity in high-tech industries is consistent with the idea that new firms play an essential role in areas where there are greater opportunities for adopting newer and better technologies. In contrast, the exit of less productive firms plays a more important role for overall productivity growth in low-technology sectors.

Ability to Allocate Resources to the Most Productive Uses

So far, this chapter has examined the role that firm creative destruction plays in productivity growth. This role is natural in this context because the creative destruction process is inherently dynamic. It is also interesting to look at how efficiently resources are allocated in a sector or a country at a given point in time. Dynamics can be examined here to the extent that the nature of the efficiency of the cross-sectional allocation of businesses can vary over time The approach used to address this question is based on the comparison between the observed level of aggregate labor productivity, which is a weighted average of firm-level labor productivity, and the unweighted average. The larger the gap between these two measures, the better the country is at allocating resources to the most productive uses, because more productive firms have larger market shares (see box 4.3).

Figure 4.5 shows the difference between the employment-weighted (logarithm of) labor productivity and the unweighted average (logarithm of) labor productivity. The difference measures the extent by which aggregate manufacturing labor productivity is higher than the average labor productivity of firms in manufacturing. By this measure, the three Latin American countries for which data are available have very different degrees of allocative efficiency. Argentina, with a much lower degree of firm creation and destruction, is also characterized by low efficiency in allocating resources. By contrast, in both Chile and Colombia, about 40 percent of the overall labor productivity level is driven by allocative efficiency.[3] As a reference, allocative efficiency explains only about 20 to 30 percent of total labor productivity in a number of European Union countries,[4] including France, Germany, the Netherlands, and the United Kingdom, but it accounts for almost 60 percent of total labor productivity in the United States[5] and in the dynamic economies of East Asia.

How should this apparently high degree of allocative efficiency in Chile and Colombia compared to that in other countries be interpreted? And how should it be squared with the overall fairly grim productivity growth in manufacturing, particularly in Colombia (see chapter 3)? An adverse business climate may affect both selection of firms in the market and reallocation of resources among firms in the market. The decomposition presented in this section looks only at the efficiency of resource allocation among existing formal firms. However, distortions in the business environment (see part III) may also prevent potentially very productive businesses from entering the market altogether and lead to a relatively greater homogeneity of incumbents, even if at a relatively low level of efficiency and productivity. These considerations suggest some caution in interpreting the Olley-Pakes decomposition; it should be looked at together with the dynamic decomposition of productivity growth

Box 4.3 The Olley-Pakes Method of Assessing Allocative Efficiency

This approach is based on a simple cross-sectional decomposition of productivity growth developed by Olley and Pakes (1996). They note that the level of productivity for a sector at a point in time can be decomposed as follows:

$$P_t = (1/N_t)\sum_i P_{it} + \sum_i \Delta\theta_{it}\Delta P_{it},$$

where N is the number of businesses in the sector and Δ is the operator that represents the cross-sectional deviation of the firm-level measure from the industry's simple average. The simple interpretation of this decomposition is that aggregate productivity can be decomposed into two terms involving the unweighted average of firm-level productivity plus a cross-term that reflects the cross-sectional efficiency of the allocation of activity. The cross-term captures allocative efficiency because it reflects the extent to which firms with high productivity have a greater market share.

Measurement problems make comparisons of the levels of either of these measures across sectors or countries very problematic, but taking the difference between these two measures reflects a form of a difference-in-difference approach. Beyond measurement advantages, this approach also has the related virtue that theoretical predictions are more straightforward. Distortions to market structure and institutions unambiguously imply that the difference between weighted and unweighted productivity (or equivalently the cross-term) should be smaller. However, this decomposition does not take into account selection effect on both the entry and the exit sides; the measurement of allocative efficiency focuses only on the businesses in operation, even if distortions (either market driven or policy driven) may affect the selection of businesses in the market and the potential allocation of resources.

that highlights the contribution of entry and exit to overall productivity (see Bartelsman, Haltiwanger, and Scarpetta forthcoming). Moreover, how the degree of allocative efficiency evolves in Latin American and Caribbean countries over time during the process of structural reforms is of interest.

Figure 4.6 presents the evolution of the indicator of allocative efficiency over time in three Latin American countries and two comparator countries. It suggests some significant improvements in Argentina during the 1990s, but from a very low starting level: allocative efficiency accounted for only about 12 percent of total labor productivity in the 1980s. In both

Figure 4.5 Allocative Efficiency: Olley-Pakes Decomposition Cross-Terms

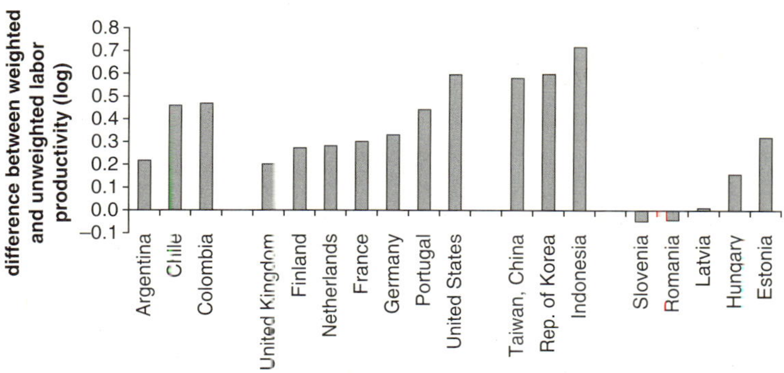

Source: Bartelsman, Haltiwanger, and Scarpetta 2009.
Note: Weighted averages of industry-level Olley-Pakes cross-terms.

Figure 4.6 Evolution of Allocative Efficiency in Latin American and Comparator Countries: Manufacturing Sector

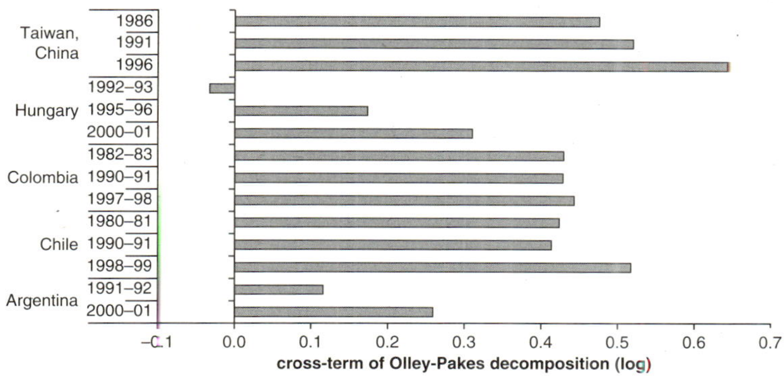

Source: Bartelsman, Haltiwanger, and Scarpetta 2009.

Colombia and Chile, however, allocative efficiency was much higher in the 1980s, but it hardly improved in Colombia, at least partly explaining why productivity growth in the Colombian manufacturing sector has been so meager. In contrast, allocative productivity improved significantly in Chile over the 1990s, contributing to its higher productivity growth in manufacturing.[6] Figure 4.6 also shows the impressive changes in allocative efficiency in Hungary during the transition from central planning to a market economy and in Taiwan, China, since 1986.

Effect of Firm Dynamics on Market Contestability and Productivity of Incumbents

Greater competitive pressures may induce incumbents to perform more efficiently. The previous analysis focuses on the direct contribution of the reallocation process to productivity growth (either with the dynamic or the cross-sectional decomposition). These decompositions lead one to think of the reallocation contributions and the within-firm contributions as being alternative explanations of productivity growth. The reallocation contributions are often interpreted in the literature as reflecting the creative destruction processes, while the within-firm contributions are interpreted as reflecting more traditional sources of productivity growth (the average firm becomes more productive with advancing technology). However, rather than being alternatives, these effects (within versus reallocation) may be closely related. That is, the pace of the creative destruction process might be interpreted as a measure of the contestability or competitiveness of markets. As such, greater competitive pressures may induce incumbents to perform more efficiently.

Figure 4.7 exploits not only the cross-country variation but also the variation across industries to increase the number of observations (and

Figure 4.7 Incumbent Productivity Growth versus Net Entry Contribution

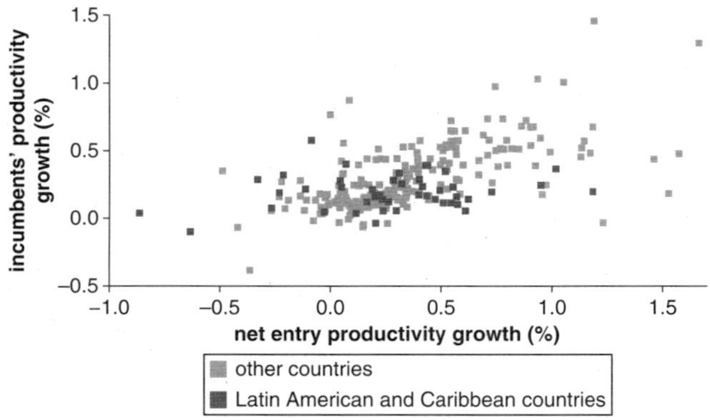

Source: Bartelsman, Haltiwanger, and Scarpetta 2004.
Note: Correlation = 0.58 (significant at 1% level).

because, in principle, the preceding arguments should apply across sectors as well as countries). In particular, it examines the relationship between the contribution of net entry in a country or sector (using time averages from the country-sector-year data) and the productivity growth from incumbents (the within term in the dynamic decomposition). Interestingly, a strong positive and statistically significant correlation is found between the net entry contribution and the productivity growth of incumbents. The data in figure 4.7 derive from the full set of countries available for this study, with the data points for the sectors in Latin American countries highlighted. Interestingly, the relationship in the Latin American countries is much weaker than that of the entire sample of countries. Indeed, although for the other countries the correlation is statistically significant at the 1 percent level, it is not statistically significant for the Latin American countries in this sample.

This finding suggests that there is a weak relationship between the creative destruction (reallocative) and within-firm sources of productivity growth in the region. In other words, contrary to the evidence for other countries, firm dynamics do not seem to affect productivity growth of incumbent firms through the contestability effect. The relationship between the firm turnover rate and the productivity growth of incumbents is also examined to further test this hypothesis. The data for the region and the other countries are shown in figure 4.8, where turnover is measured as the average annual rate of entry plus exit. Again a weak correlation is found.

Figure 4.8 Incumbent Productivity Growth versus Firm Turnover Rate

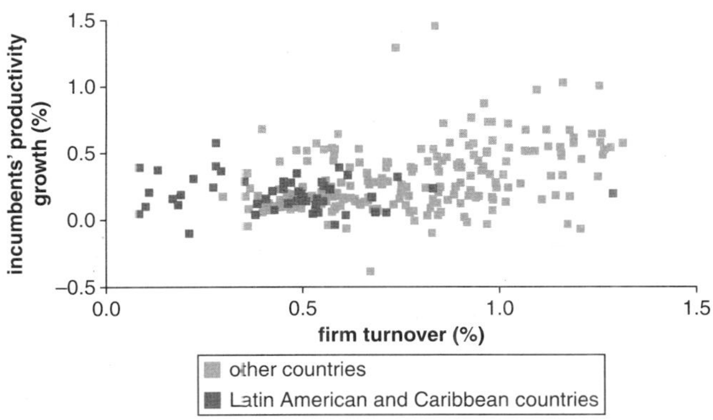

Source: Bartelsman, Haltiwanger, and Scarpetta 2004.
Note: Correlation = 0.58 (significant at 1% level).

Across industries characterized by rather different entry rates, productivity growth of incumbents has been very similar despite the potentially greater contestability pressure.

In sum, the analysis of the sources of productivity growth reveals that a lot of the observed aggregate growth comes from efficiency improvements in existing firms. Exiting firms contribute to free resources for more productive uses, particularly in low-technology sectors, while the entry of new firms plays a significant role in high- and medium-technology sectors, where new firms are better equipped to harness new technologies than many of the incumbent businesses. The analysis of data for Argentina, Chile, and Colombia also reveals different degrees of allocative efficiency across firms and different evolutions over time in the context of structural reforms. In particular, Colombia showed no improvement in allocative efficiency and low productivity growth in manufacturing, while some improvement in allocative efficiency was recorded in Chile and Argentina during the 1990s, although not as impressive as the improvement experienced in other emerging economies. A possible explanation is that an adverse investment climate simply prevents some potentially highly productive firms from entering the market altogether and promotes productivity performance of some well-established businesses by protecting their market shares. In this context, many of the firms with rapid productivity growth have done so by shedding labor rather than by investing and expanding. Also important, contrary to the evidence in many other countries, the entry and exit of firms does not seem to affect incumbents' performance. The next section explores in more detail the characteristics of those firms that enter and exit the market.

Firms' Characteristics and the Process of Firm Entry, Postentry Growth, and Exit

Size Distribution of Formal Firms

Firm size distribution provides information regarding the process of creative destruction and the way in which the economy responds to shocks. Furthermore, the size distribution may provide evidence of bottlenecks brought about by the regulatory environment. For example, one would expect high start-up costs to harm small entrants more than larger ones (see part III). However, if firms' access to credit is high and other regulations only become binding at a larger scale, then one would expect more entry of smaller firms. Of course, patterns of specialization may also contribute to the overall size distribution, and specialization may be more related to comparative advantage or to path dependence.

Figure 4.9 provides evidence on the distribution of employment by firm size. It suggests that the share of medium-size firms (20–99 employees)

Figure 4.9 Distribution of Employment by Firm Size

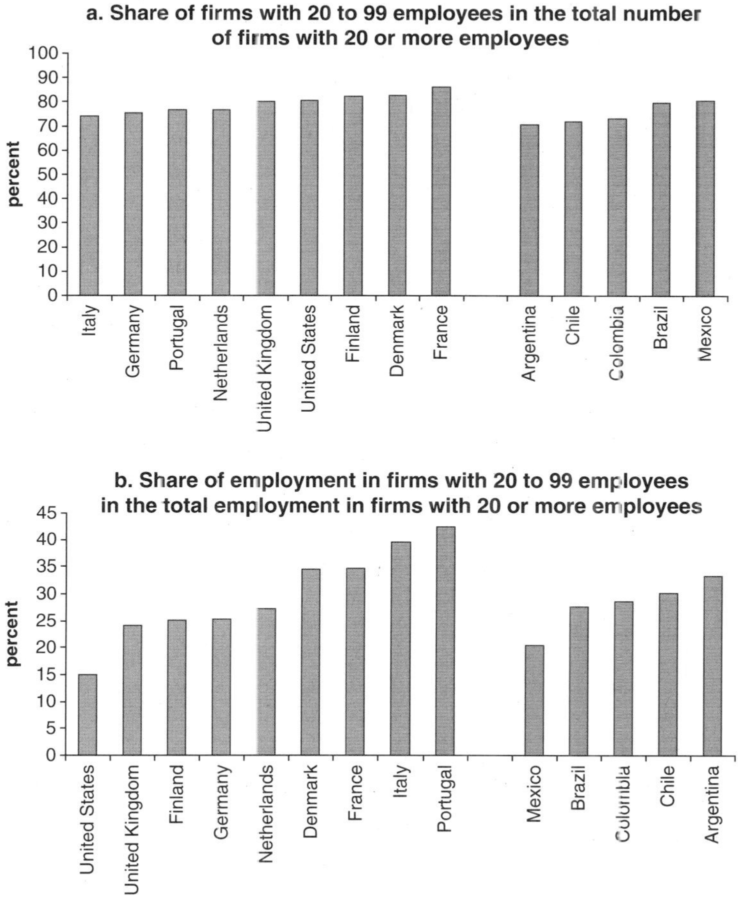

Source: Authors' calculations.

Note: Data for Germany do not include the territory of the former German Democratic Republic.

in Latin American and Caribbean countries is lower than, or in some cases close to, that of other countries. If one, however, takes into account that many micro and small firms in the region are informal and thus not recorded in the official data reported in the figure, one may be tempted to conclude that medium-size firms are significantly lacking. Of course, the size distribution of firms depends on the sectoral composition of the economy and also on the overall stage of development of the different countries. The first factor can be controlled for by running simple fixed effect regressions that control for sectoral effects, while the latter issue can be addressed by comparing countries in the region with other emerging economies. On average, the five Latin American countries for which data are available (Argentina, Brazil, Chile, Colombia, and Mexico) have a share of medium-size firms that is 5.2 percentage points smaller than the OECD average and 2 to 3 percentage points smaller than the average in East Asian or transition economies.[7]

To explain differences in firm size across countries, one can perform a more disaggregated analysis based on a shift-and-share decomposition. A shift-and-share decomposition allows the role of sectoral specialization to be assessed in comparison to within-sector differences. The idea behind this technique is to determine how much of the overall deviation of average size from a given benchmark (in this case, the cross-country average) is due to country specialization in sectors with different underlying technological and size characteristics and how much to the fact that average size within sectors tends to differ from that of the benchmark.

The shift-and-share decomposition shows that differences in firms' sizes are explained mainly by within-sector differences in the region. The shift-and-share decomposition (table 4.2) shows that the within-sector component is much larger (in absolute terms) than the sectoral composition component in Latin American and Caribbean and many other countries. In Argentina, the average firm size is about 25 percent smaller than for the comparator countries, and in Brazil it is about 15 percent. The bulk of this difference is within industries; that is, average firm size in the region is smaller in each of the industries, on average. The overall results suggest that both the size structure and the sectoral composition should be controlled for when one analyzes firm dynamics and its effects on aggregate performance.

Gross and Net Firm Flows

The next step in the analysis is to consider the magnitude and characteristics of firm entry and exit. As stressed earlier, firm dynamics have been an important driver of job creation and an engine for productivity growth. But how many firms enter and exit the market in Latin American and Caribbean countries? How many of them fail, and how many expand? What are the characteristics of new businesses compared with those of incumbents?

Confirming one of the key regularities found in the previous literature, figure 4.10 points to a high degree of turbulence in all countries (that is, many firms enter and exit most markets every year). However, Latin American and Caribbean countries occupy different positions in the country distribution by the size of firm turnover. Thus, Mexico (for the total economy) and Brazil, Chile, and Colombia (only for manufacturing) are

Table 4.2 Cross-Country Shift-and-Share Analysis of Firm Size

Country	*Sectoral decomposition*	*Average size of firms*	*Interaction between sectoral composition and size*	*Total*
Latin America				
Argentina	0.06	−0.28	−0.02	−0.25
Brazil	−0.01	−0.11	−0.03	−0.15
Mexico	0.09	0.00	−0.09	0.00
Comparator countries				
Denmark	0.03	−0.11	−0.02	−0.10
France	0.02	−0.09	−0.02	−0.09
Italy	−0.02	−0.38	−0.02	−0.42
Netherlands	0.05	−0.30	−0.06	−0.31
Finland	0.00	−0.12	−0.03	−0.16
Germany	0.22	0.01	−0.10	0.13
Portugal	−0.10	−0.05	0.04	−0.11
United Kingdom	0.01	−0.01	−0.07	−0.06
United States	0.02	0.88	−0.17	0.73
Estonia	−0.05	0.19	0.02	0.16
Hungary	0.02	0.27	−0.03	0.27
Latvia	−0.07	−0.42	0.08	−0.41
Romania	0.14	2.39	−0.84	1.69
Slovenia	0.04	0.63	−0.12	0.54
Taiwan, China	0.05	−0.29	−0.06	−0.30

Source: Bartelsman, Haltiwanger, and Scarpetta 2004, firm-level database.

Note: Data for Germany do not include the territory of the former German Democratic Republic. *Total* column represents the percentage deviation of average size from the cross-country average. The other columns decompose the total into subcomponents.

at the high end or intermediate position in terms of entry and exit rates, with only the transition economies of Eastern Europe having high firm dynamism. In Mexico, more than 20 percent of all businesses are created and destroyed every year. Even among firms with at least 20 employees, about 10 percent of firms enter and exit in Brazil and Mexico. By contrast, in Argentina, less than 20 percent of all businesses are created or destroyed every year, and the percentage drops to less than 6 percent in the case of firms with at least 20 employees.

What explains the firm churning in the region? Firm turnover rates vary significantly across sectors because of idiosyncratic demand and technological shocks. They also vary across size classes because small firms tend

Figure 4.10 Entry and Exit of Firms, 1990–Early 2000s

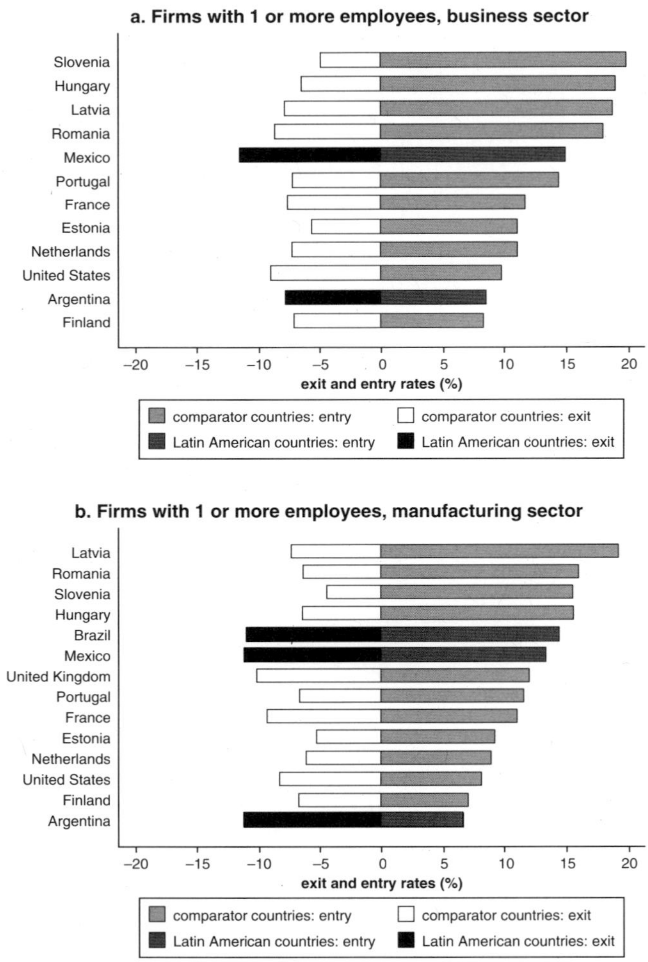

(continued)

Figure 4.10 Entry and Exit of Firms, 1990–Early 2000s *(continued)*

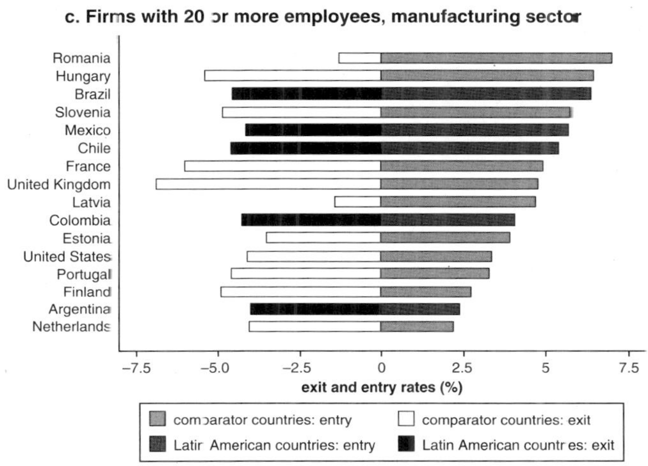

Source: Bartelsman, Haltiwanger, and Scarpetta 2009.

to be more volatile than larger ones.[8] Moreover, during the period covered by this chapter's firm-level data, Latin American countries have been exposed to major fluctuations in business cycles and severe economic crisis (for example, the Tequila crisis of 1994–95). All of these factors are likely to have influenced greatly the observed firm turnover rates. To control for these factors, figures 4.11 and 4.12 present the firm turnover rates in the sample of countries as deviations from the U.S. rates in panel a and the same rates controlling for a set of factors in panel b (see box 4.4 for the methodology). In particular, all estimates control for industry and size fixed effects. Moreover, differences in turnover rates are also presented controlling for gross domestic product (GDP) volatility. The countries are ordered according to the level of firm turnover obtained controlling for the industry, size, and volatility effects. The results suggest that composition significantly affects firm turnover rates; in general, less cross-country variation occurs when controlling for these differences. Argentina would have had higher turnover if it had an industry and size structure similar to that of the United States. By contrast, a concentration in small firms and high mobility sectors strongly influences the observed high firm turnover rates in Mexico and, to a lesser extent, Brazil. In all Latin American and Caribbean countries, high volatility affected the observed firm turnover rates, but the effect of controlling for those differences is not very large, with the sole exception of Argentina.

Figure 4.11 Turnover in Firms with One or More Employees: Manufacturing Sector

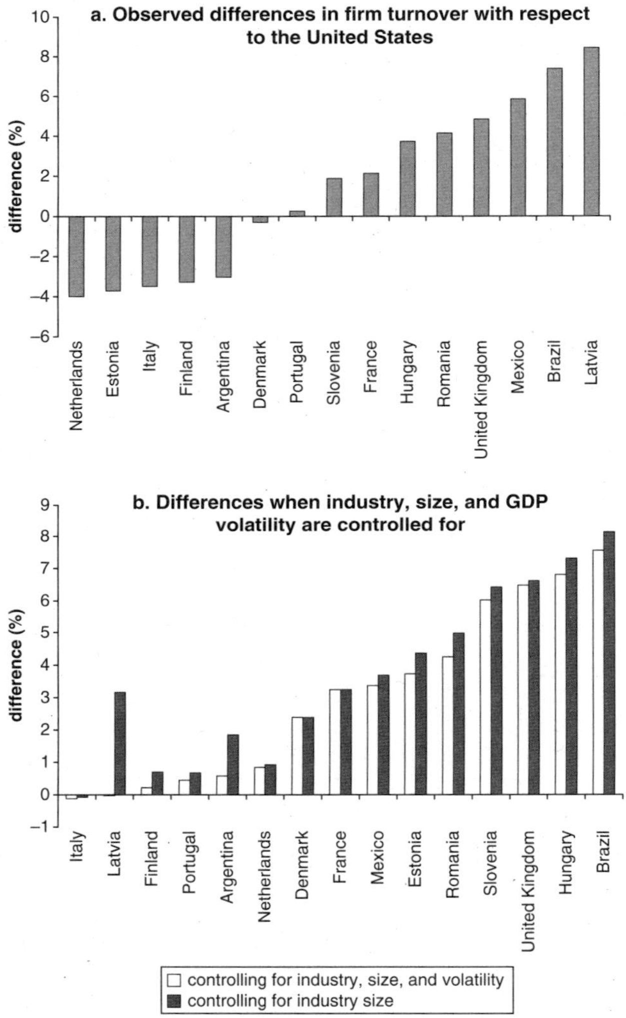

Source: Authors' calculations.

Figure 4.12 Turnover in Firms with 20 or More Employees: Manufacturing Sector

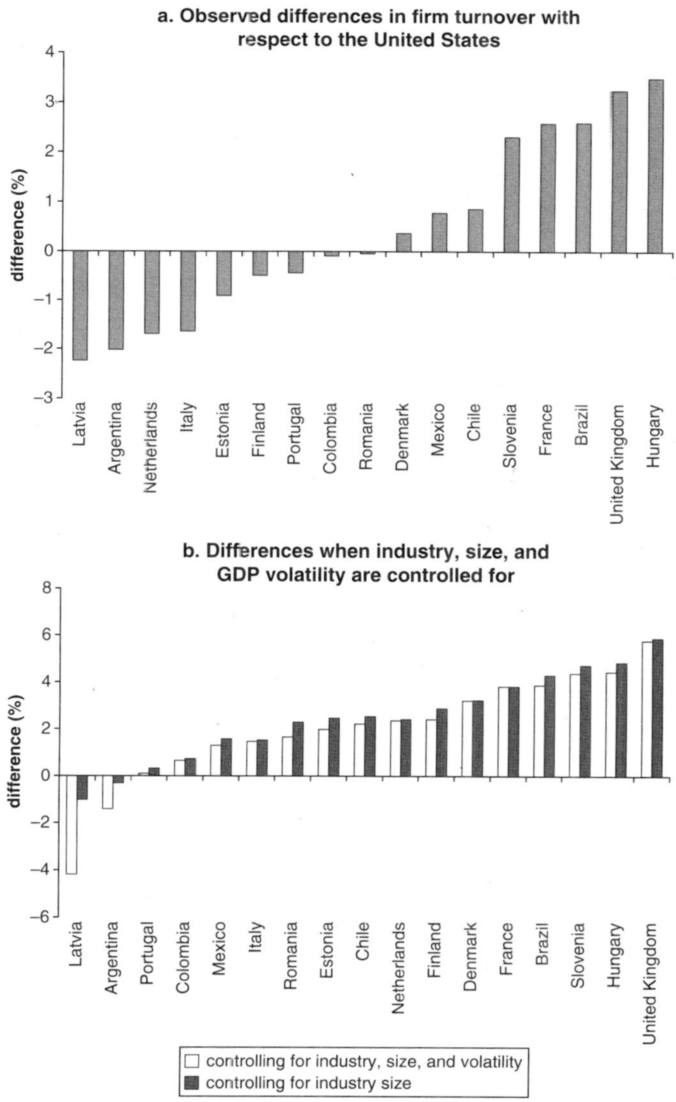

Source: Authors' calculations.

Box 4.4 Accounting for Differences in Industry and Size Composition in the Analysis of Firm Turnover

Cross-country differences in firm turnover can be affected by differences in the size and industry composition of firms. As discussed in this chapter, small firms tend to be characterized by a higher degree of volatility, and certain sectors tend to be more volatile than others because of frequency and magnitude of demand and technological shocks. Moreover, Latin American and Caribbean countries have been characterized over the period covered by the data by large swings in economic activities and marked by major crises.

To control for all these factors, this chapter uses a simple fixed effect regression in which the country fixed effects are identified after controlling for size, industry effects, and effects of volatility on firm turnover.

The proposed regression is as follows:

$$J_{tcis} = Const + C + I + S + t + Volatility\ index + u,$$

where J is the entry rate or firm turnover, C is the country dummy, I is the industry dummy, S is the firm size dummy, and t is the time dummy.

The measure for volatility used in the regressions is the following volatility index:

$$\frac{(y - y^*)^2}{y^*},$$

where y is the country GDP and y^* is the trend GDP.

Concentration of dynamism in low-tech activities. Figure 4.13 shows the entry and exit rates in high- and low-tech industries in the business sector relative to the entry and exit rates in medium-technology industries. Values above 100 among high- and low-technology industries would imply a stronger dynamism in sectors with high- and low-technology content than in intermediate sectors. The analysis is conducted for the entire business sector and focuses on Argentina, Brazil, and Mexico for Latin America. Although in many industrial countries firm dynamics—and especially the entry of new firms—are stronger in high-tech industries than in medium-tech industries, this is not the case in Latin America, where the high-tech sector is characterized by a lower degree of dynamism than the medium-tech sector and especially the low-tech sector.

Small size of entering firms. As is common in most countries, entry and exit of firms in the region occurs predominantly among smaller firms

Figure 4.13 Entry and Exit of Firms: Business Sector, 1990–Early 2000s

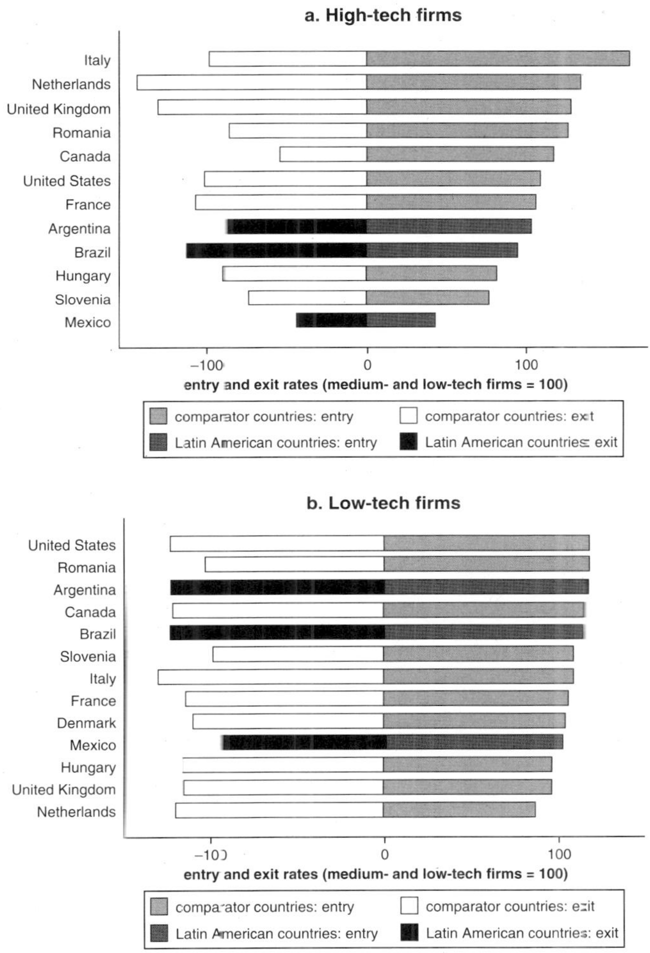

Source: Bartelsman, Haltiwanger and Scarpetta 2009, firm-level database.
Note: Data are for firms with one or more employees.

(see figure 4.14). Again, Brazil and Mexico and to some extent Colombia stand out with firms of a very low size at entry compared with the average incumbents. As discussed earlier, these countries also have relatively high entry and exit rates compared with those of industrial and other comparator countries. This evidence suggests that entry of small firms in the region is relatively easy, while large-scale entry is likely to be more difficult. Moreover, it is interesting to note that the average size of exiters is smaller than that of the average incumbents—and rather similar to that of entrants. Indeed, most of the exiting firms are relatively new businesses that fail before reaching the optimal efficiency scale.

Entries and exits as part of the same creative destruction process. Comparing entry and exit rates across sectors is an interesting way to test two competing theories. One hypothesis is that entry and exit rates at the sectoral level are mostly driven by sectoral shocks. Sectors with positive profit shocks will have high entry, and sectors with negative profit shocks will have high exit. If sectoral profit shocks are the predominant source of variation, then the cross-sectional correlation between entry and exit rates should be negative. Alternatively, entry and exit rates at the sectoral level might be driven by the within-sector creative destruction process. A sector with a high dispersion of idiosyncratic shocks or low barriers to entry and exit will exhibit both high entry and high exit rates. If the creative destruction process is the predominant factor driving entry and exit, then the cross-sectional correlation of entry and exit should be positive. In most industrial countries, entry and exit rates are generally positively correlated across industries (see Baldwin and Gorecki 1991; Geroski 1991), and the correlations are particularly strong when the entry and exit rates are weighted by employment. Table 4.3 presents the correlations between the average entry and exit rates for available Latin American countries and selected comparators during the 1990s. Argentina and Colombia are the only two countries where the instantaneous entry-exit correlation is weak without weighting by employment. However, the correlation becomes statistically significant when data are indeed weighted and when correlations are calculated on the basis of the average over the decade.[9] Table 4.3 confirms that entries and exits are largely part of a creative destruction process in which entry and exit consists of within-sector reallocation reflecting idiosyncratic differences across firms within sectors.[10] Apparently, clear compositional changes have not taken place across sectors over the decade in the region, with some industries having high exit and others high entry.

Postentry Performance of Firms

Understanding postentry performance is essential to shedding light on the market selection process that separates successful entrant firms from

Figure 4.14 Size of Entering and Exiting Firms Relative to Incumbents: Manufacturing Sector, 1990–Early 2000s

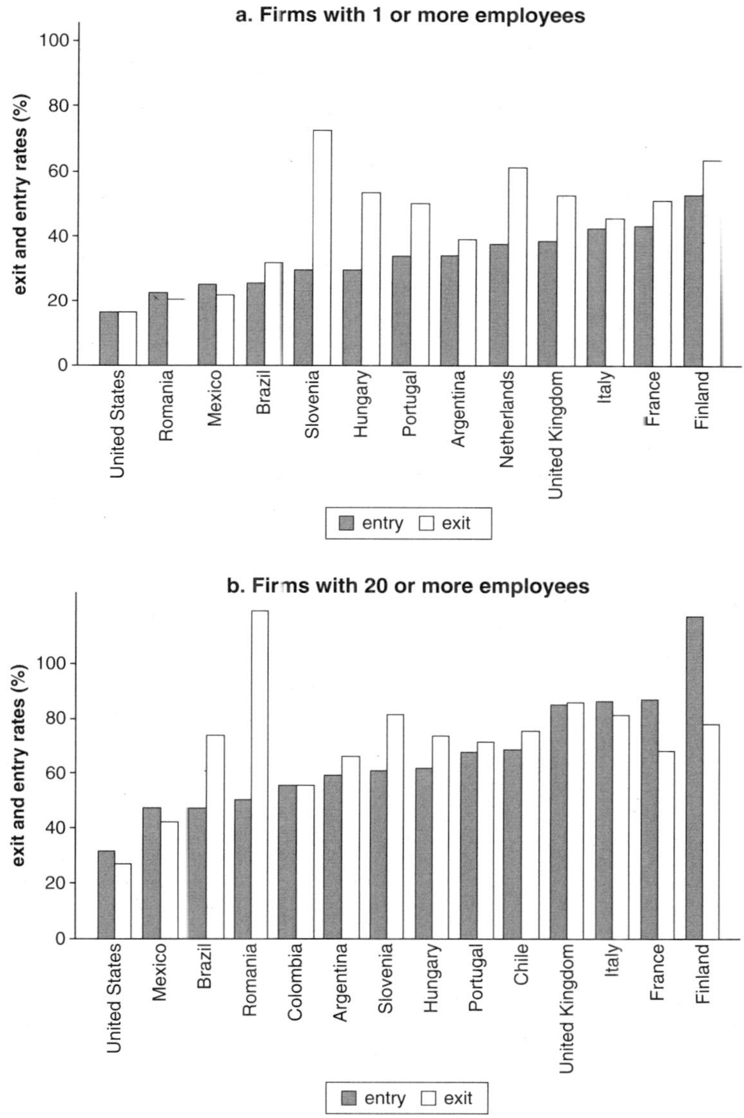

Source: Bartelsman, Haltiwanger, and Scarpetta 2009, firm-level database.

Table 4.3 Correlation between Entry and Exit Rates, 1990s

	Year industry*				*Industry (average over the period)*			
	Number of firms	*Entry-exit correlation*	*Number of firms*	*Entry-exit correlation (weighted)*	*Number of firms*	*Entry-exit correlation*	*Number of firms*	*Entry-exit correlation (weighted)*
Denmark	85	0.3731*	85	0.6687*	17	0.5681*	17	0.8739*
Finland	175	0.2717*	175	0.4084*	23	0.6002*	23	0.2521
Germany	130	0.6880*	130	0.6242*	13	0.7510*	13	0.7702*
France	131	−0.2449*	132	−0.1025	22	−0.5250*	22	−0.2986
Italy	125	0.0976	125	0.7999*	25	0.1011	25	0.6894*
Netherlands	72	0.3131*	175	0.0061	25	0.6702*	24	0.2981
Portugal	143	−0.1239	143	0.5671*	25	0.3526	25	0.0331
United Kingdom	105	0.2845*	105	0.6412*	15	0.4709	15	0.7389*
Canada	168	0.5782*	168	0.7683*	21	0.8252*	21	0.9301*
United States	125	0.7028*	125	0.8106*	25	0.8310*	25	0.9443*
Argentina	**100**	**0.0582**	**100**	**0.4971***	**25**	**0.3973***	**25**	**0.7432***
Brazil	**37**	**0.3472***	**38**	**0.5068***	**19**	**0.395**	**19**	**0.7880***
Chile	**128**	**0.6323***	**128**	**0.5504***	**18**	**0.0947**	**18**	**0.3741**
Colombia	**129**	**0.0319**	**129**	**0.1595**	**18**	**0.4385**	**18**	**0.5527***

(continued)

Table 4.3 Correlation between Entry and Exit Rates, 1990s *(continued)*

	Year industry*				*Industry (average over the period)*			
	Number of firms	*Entry-exit correlation*	*Number of firms*	*Entry-exit correlation (weighted)*	*Number of firms*	*Entry-exit correlation*	*Number of firms*	*Entry-exit correlation (weighted)*
Mexico	**220**	**0.1882***	**220**	**0.5441***	**20**	**0.7756***	**20**	**0.9159***
Indonesia	49	0.1988	49	0.0136	17	0.2248	17	0.0895
Taiwan, China	16	–0.5291*	16	0.1599	16	–0.5291*	16	0.1599
Estonia	59	0.4977*	59	0.2874*	24	0.3344	24	0.4621*
Hungary	145	0.2445*	145	0.5651*	25	0.1917	25	0.7793*
Latvia	98	–0.0609	98	0.1511	24	0.294	24	0.1772
Romania	119	0.0826	119	0.1209	21	0.6098*	21	0.4066
Slovenia	178	–0.05	178	0.7680*	25	–0.1602	25	0.4373*

Source: Authors' calculations.

Note: * = significant at the 10 percent level. Correlations are based on a maximum of 25 industries in the business sector. Sample countries for the region are in **bold**. Data for Germany do not include the territory of the former German Democratic Republic.

those that stagnate and eventually exit and, ultimately, to assessing the role of firm churning for net job creation. The similar magnitudes of entry and exit rates and the high cross-sectoral correlation between entry and exit rates indicate that firm dynamics (the entry and exit of firms) are not necessarily associated with changes in the size of the population of firms or in the number of products in the market, but rather with continuous changes in the characteristics of firms in each market. In this context, what happens to firms subsequent to their entry seems at least as important as the entry process itself.

Harsh market selection for new businesses in the region. Figure 4.15 presents nonparametric (graphic) estimates of survivor rates for firms that entered the market in the late 1980s and 1990s. The survivor rate specifies the proportion of firms from a cohort of entrants that are still in business at a given age. In the figure, the survival rates are averaged over different entry cohorts and do not take into account differences in the industry composition across countries. Firms in Argentina, Colombia, and especially Mexico have very low survival rates in the total business sector or in manufacturing (Colombia). In Mexico, 25 percent of entrant firms are no longer in the market after two years, and about 70 percent are no longer in business after seven years. Failure rates among young businesses are high in all market economies, but in industrial countries, about 50 to 60 percent of new firms are still in business after seven years.[11]

The next step is to see whether the relatively low survival rates are associated with the sector structure—that is, whether the high failure rates in the region simply reflect a specialization in industries with high firm turnover and high attrition rates. Table 4.4 shows the four-year survival rate by industry, calculated as the average of the comparator countries. The first column of the table presents the cross-country average survival rate for each industry, the second column reports the deviations from this average for industrial countries, and the other columns present the deviations for Latin American and comparator countries individually. The main point that emerges from the table is that the survival rates in Latin American countries are lower than the average in comparator countries for almost all industries. Chile and to some extent Colombia show some low-tech industries and a few high-tech industries with higher-than-average survival.

High expansion rates in Mexico but very low expansion rates in Argentina. Each cohort of new firms tends to increase in the initial years because failures are highly concentrated among its smallest units and because of the significant growth of survivors. These facts are best presented by looking at the employment-weighted survival rates (figure 4.16) as well as the gains in average firm size among surviving firms (figure 4.17). The time profile of the survival function expressed in terms of employment is shifted upward and is flatter compared with the survival function of firms, because of the exit of predominantly smaller units. This finding is

Figure 4.15 Firm Survival at Different Lifetimes, 1990s

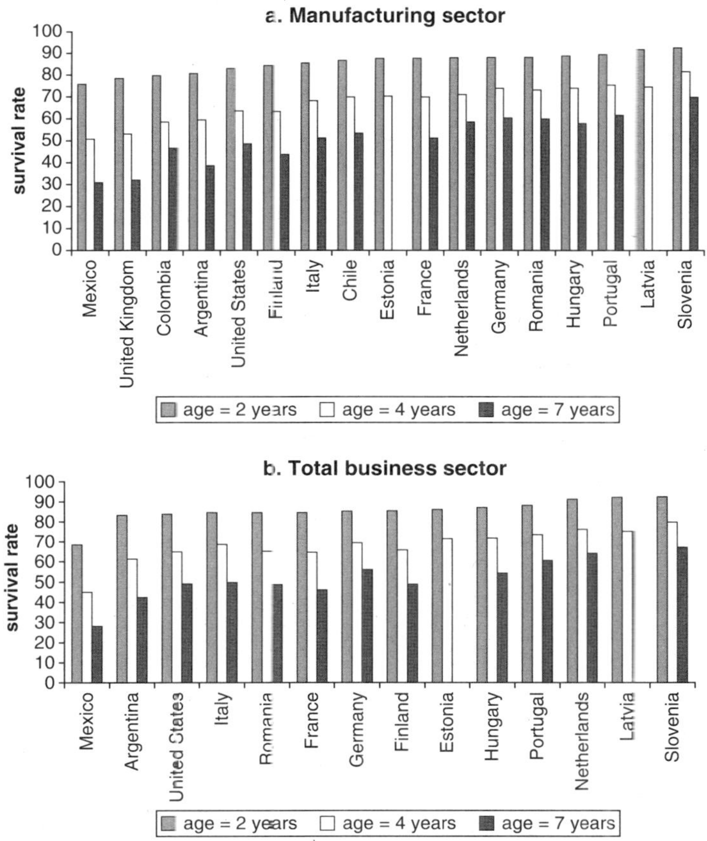

Source: Bartelsman, Haltiwanger, and Scarpetta 2009, firm-level database.

Note: Data for Germany do not include the territory of the former German Democratic Republic.

particularly notable in some of the Latin American countries. In Mexico, the very large market selection of new firms is reduced dramatically if firm size is taken into account. In other words, selection is strong in Mexico, but surviving firms add so much employment that after seven years more workers are employed by surviving firms than by the corresponding cohort of firms at entry. Indeed, the 25 percent of firms that survive to the seventh year of activity more than double in size.

Table 4.4 Survival Rate at Four Years, Relative to Cross-Country Sectoral Average

Sectors	*Cross-country average*	*OECD*	*Argentina*	*Chile*	*Colombia*	*Mexico*	*Romania*	*Slovenia*
Total manufacturing	0.67	1.00	*0.89*	1.04	*0.87*	*0.76*	**1.09**	**1.22**
Food products, beverages, and tobacco	0.68	**1.04**	*0.86*	**1.03**	0.95	*0.80*	–	**1.15**
Textiles, textile products, leather, and footwear	0.61	0.93	0.91	**1.08**	*0.87*	*0.80*	–	**1.20**
Wood and products of wood and cork	0.62	**1.07**	*0.83*	**1.13**	*0.77*	*0.69*	–	**1.26**
Pulp, paper, paper products, printing, and publishing	0.70	0.97	0.93	1.09	**1.02**	*0.77*	**1.06**	**1.23**
Coke, refined petroleum products, and nuclear fuel	0.70	**1.09**	*0.83*	0.93	**1.11**	0.92	**1.37**	**1.37**
Chemicals and chemical products	0.68	**1.03**	1.02	1.00	1.00	*0.86*	**1.09**	**0.95**
Rubber and plastic products	0.74	0.97	0.94	**1.02**	0.90	*0.81*	**1.05**	**1.20**
Other nonmetallic mineral products	0.67	**1.04**	*0.89*	0.98	*0.83*	*0.74*	**1.09**	**1.22**
Basic metals	0.70	0.98	0.90	**1.13**	0.92	*0.78*	**1.03**	**1.32**

(continued)

Table 4.4 Survival Rate at Four Years, Relative to Cross-Country Sectoral Average *(continued)*

Sectors	*Cross-country average*	OECD	*Argentina*	*Chile*	*Colombia*	*Mexico*	*Romania*	*Slovenia*
Fabricated metal products, except machinery and equipment	0.68	1.02	*0.85*	1.00	*0.82*	*0.70*	**1.09**	**1.27**
Machinery and equipment not elsewhere classified	0.72	**1.02**	*0.86*	0.97	*0.75*	–	**1.03**	**1.20**
Office, accounting, and computing machinery	0.77	0.80	*0.60*	1.42	1.42	–	**1.02**	**1.22**
Electrical machinery and apparatus not elsewhere classified	0.78	0.88	0.93	**1.14**	0.98	–	**1.10**	**1.13**
Radio, television, and communication equipment	0.77	0.85	*0.86*	**1.06**	**1.04**	–	**1.07**	**1.22**
Medical, precision, and optical instruments	0.80	0.92	0.99	1.04	*0.81*	–	**1.01**	**1.12**
Motor vehicles, trailers, and semitrailers	0.71	0.98	0.95	0.96	*0.83*	*0.81*	**1.14**	**1.16**
Other transport equipment	0.66	0.97	*0.83*	0.88	*0.88*	*0.76*	**1.21**	**1.06**
Manufacturing not elsewhere classified, recycling	0.65	**1.04**	*0.89*	**1.07**	*0.78*	*0.70*	**1.11**	**1.17**

Source: Authors' calculations.

Note: — = not available. The figures in **bold** are above unity (that is, higher-than-average survival rate); those in *italic* are below 90 percent of the cross-country average.

Figure 4.16 Employment-Based Survival Rates at Different Lifetimes: Total Employment, 1990s

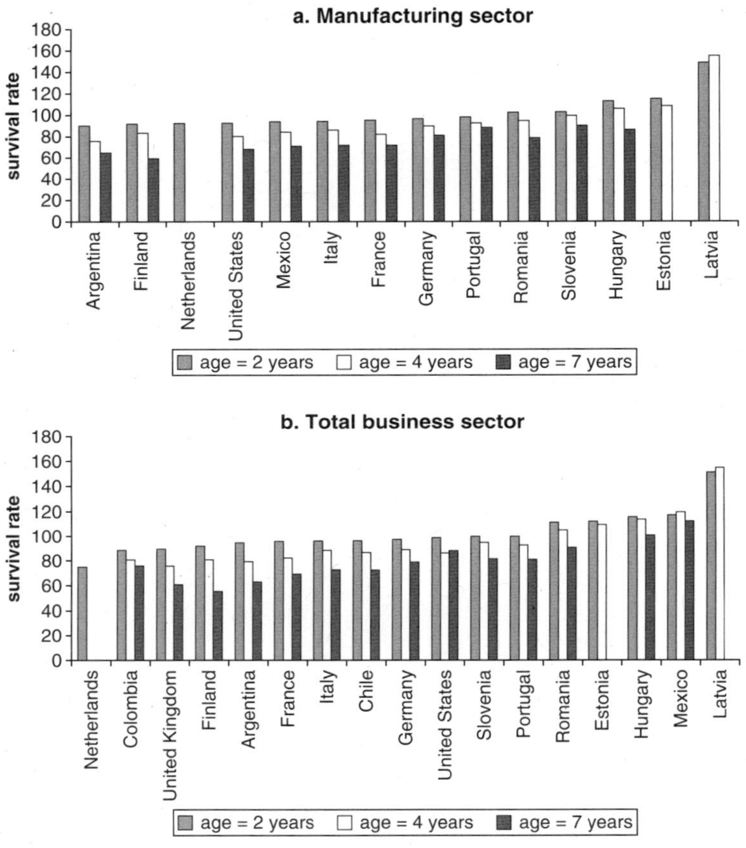

Source: Authors' calculations.

Note: Data for Germany do not include the territory of the former German Democratic Republic.

Table 4.5 shows the evolution in average firm size of survivors as they age for the different industries. As in table 4.4, the first column presents the cross-country average postentry growth at age four years; the other columns present the country deviations from this average. The table confirms a widespread strong growth of successful new business in all manufacturing industries in Mexico, in some of the medium-high-tech industries in Argentina, and in only a few industries in Chile and Colombia.

Figure 4.17 Average Firm Size Relative to Entry, by Age

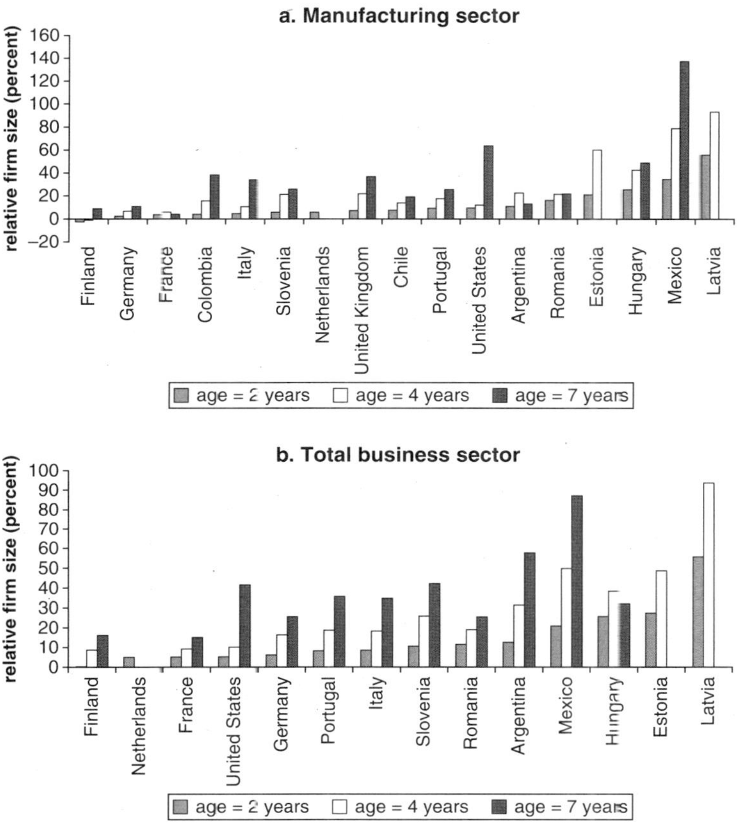

Source: Bartelsman, Haltiwanger, and Scarpetta 2009, firm-level database.
Note: Data for Germany do not include the territory of the former German Democratic Republic.

All in all, the evidence presented in this subsection suggests different characteristics of firms in the business sector and manufacturing across the countries of the region and with respect to industrial and emerging economies. A common pattern in Latin America and the Caribbean is the relatively small share of intermediate-size firms—20 to 100 employees—with many firms being either very small or relatively large. However, although Brazil and especially Mexico show high firm dynamics, with 20 to 25 percent of firms being created or destroyed every year, Argentina

Table 4.5 Postentry Employment Growth at Four Years, Relative to Cross-Country Sectoral Average

Sectors	*Cross-country average*	*Argentina*	*Chile*	*Colombia*	*Mexico*	*Estonia*	*Hungary*	*Latvia*	*Romania*	*Slovenia*
Food products, beverages, and tobacco	1.47	**1.03**	0.87	0.84	**1.10**	**1.93**	0.79	**2.09**	–	0.72
Textiles, textile products, leather, and footwear	1.87	0.62	0.73	0.72	**1.12**	**1.80**	0.74	0.52	–	0.57
Wood and products of wood and cork	1.30	0.90	0.82	0.92	**1.12**	**1.11**	**1.10**	**2.08**	–	0.75
Pulp, paper, paper products, printing, and publishing	1.16	**1.26**	**1.03**	1.09	**1.51**	**2.32**	**1.08**	**1.61**	0.90	0.89
Coke, refined petroleum products, and nuclear fuel	1.49	**1.56**	0.44	1.47	**1.22**	–	0.63	–	0.68	0.76
Chemicals and chemical products	1.51	**1.32**	0.65	0.82	**1.16**	0.64	0.67	0.72	**1.14**	0.82
Pharmaceuticals	1.64	**1.19**	1.00	0.88	1.00	–	0.71	0.61	**1.36**	**1.16**
Chemicals excluding pharmaceuticals	1.49	**1.45**	0.62	0.80	**1.19**	0.64	0.66	0.74	**1.12**	0.82
Rubber and plastic products	1.89	0.82	0.74	0.72	**1.21**	–	0.70	0.50	1.00	0.59

(continued)

Table 4.5 Postentry Employment Growth at Four Years, Relative to Cross-Country Sectoral Average *(continued)*

Sectors	*Cross-country average*	*Argentina*	*Chile*	*Colombia*	*Mexico*	*Estonia*	*Hungary*	*Latvia*	*Romania*	*Slovenia*
Other nonmetallic mineral products	1.42	0.81	0.83	0.80	**1.15**	0.64	0.75	**1.13**	0.94	0.75
Basic metals	1.28	0.88	0.90	0.81	**1.53**	–	**1.12**	**8.17**	0.74	0.47
Fabricated metal products, except machinery and equipment	1.46	0.90	0.97	0.84	**1.13**	**1.67**	**1.02**	**1.28**	0.67	0.68
Machinery and equipment not elsewhere classified	0.56	**2.33**	**2.02**	2.45	–	6.66	**2.50**	**3.97**	0.46	**1.80**
Office, accounting and computing machinery	3.61	0.46	–	0.25	–	–	**1.35**	0.18	0.57	0.53
Electrical machinery and apparatus not elsewhere classified	1.56	0.81	0.91	0.73	–	–	**1.38**	0.58	0.86	0.74
Radio, television, and communication equipment	1.95	0.74	1.09	0.59	–	–	**1.38**	0.45	0.29	0.88
Medical, precision, and optical instruments	1.15	**1.13**	**1.22**	0.80	–	0.39	0.85	**1.80**	**1.34**	**1.14**

(continued)

Table 4.5 Postentry Employment Growth at Four Years, Relative to Cross-Country Sectoral Average *(continued)*

Sectors	*Cross-country average*	*Argentina*	*Chile*	*Colombia*	*Mexico*	*Estonia*	*Hungary*	*Latvia*	*Romania*	*Slovenia*
Motor vehicles, trailers, and semitrailers	2.15	0.36	0.56	0.54	**1.39**	–	0.91	–	0.57	0.36
Other transport equipment	0.90	0.99	0.56	0.68	**1.60**	**2.04**	**1.59**	**2.84**	0.91	0.90
Railroad equipment and transport equipment not elsewhere classified	1.03	**1.77**	0.76	–	**1.26**	–	**1.30**	–	**1.10**	0.75
Aircraft and spacecraft	0.59	**1.37**	0.67	–	**4.82**	–	**5.40**	**1.71**	**1.28**	**3.63**
Manufacturing not elsewhere classified, recycling	1.65	0.96	0.77	0.74	**1.18**	**1.14**	0.82	**1.78**	0.78	0.69

Source: Authors' calculations.

Note: — = not available. The figures in **bold** are above unity (that is, higher-than-average survival rate).

shows one of the lowest levels of firm dynamics in the sample of countries. Market selection is harsh in all countries of the region, but particularly in Argentina and Mexico (in Argentina despite the low number of entrants), where only about 25 to 30 percent of new businesses are in operation after seven years. In other words, while in Argentina entry and postentry constraints seem to be severe, in Mexico entry of small firms seems easy, but market selection very strong, and only a few productive firms manage to survive and expand rapidly. All of this evidence suggests very different conditions affecting firms in the countries of the region. These conditions need to be assessed against objective and subjective indicators of the investment climate. The report turns to this evaluation in chapter 5.

Summing Up: The Need for Entry Conditions and Incentives to Create Jobs

This chapter has provided further details on the process of job creation and productivity growth in Latin America and the Caribbean. Consistent with the evidence discussed in the previous chapter, most countries of the region—with the clear exception of Argentina—display a sizable process of reallocation of resources through the entry and exit of firms as well as through reallocation of labor among incumbent firms. The entry of new firms and especially the exit of obsolete firms enhance productivity in all countries of the region, but overwhelming evidence indicates that most of the rapidly growing productivity businesses are doing so by downsizing rather than by investing more and expanding.

The other salient feature of firms in the region is the polarization between micro units and medium to large units, with a missing middle of small and medium-size firms of 20 to 49 or 50 to 99 employees. This picture emerges from the analysis of registered firms, but if the many informal businesses were also included, the distribution of firms would look even more skewed toward micro units. Does such a polarization of firms toward micro units and large firms matter? It does to the extent that the missing small and medium-size businesses are those with the strongest potential to create more jobs.

This chapter also suggests that—with the exception of Argentina—no major barriers exist to entry in Latin American and Caribbean countries. In Brazil and Mexico, almost a quarter of all businesses are created or destroyed every year. Rather than barriers to entry, what seem to characterize the countries of the region are barriers to survival in the market: only about one-third of all new firms are in business seven years after entry, a smaller proportion than that observed in most other countries. High failure rates are not necessarily a problem if they are associated with market experimentation, whereby new firms enter with new products and production processes, test the market, and expand if successful or exit if not. But high failure rates are present in the region even in mature and low-tech industries, where the scope for experimentation is more limited. This finding, together with the fact that even successful firms have difficulty expanding in some countries, such as Argentina, Colombia, and Chile, suggests potential barriers to survival and especially to the expansion of successful businesses.

The chapter also reveals that the reallocation of resources is efficiency enhancing in the region: although productivity increases have largely been driven by within-firm forces, resulting in defensive restructuring, the exit of obsolete firms and, at least in high-tech industries, the entry of new firms have contributed to boost productivity growth. Contrary to the case in other developed and developing countries, however, the entry and exit of firms does not seem to stimulate incumbents to improve their performance. In part, this result is because most of the exiting firms are relatively new ventures that do not manage to survive in what appears to be a very difficult business environment.

The implications of these findings are that barriers to survival and to expansion are key factors in explaining overall productivity and job creation performance in the region. Even successful new firms have difficulty surviving and hiring more workers. These issues will be taken up in part III of the book, which assesses how the business environment in the countries of the region influences firms' behavior and hiring decisions.

Notes

1. This measure of job turnover may underestimate overall worker mobility, because it considers job creation and destruction only across firms and not labor movements within the firm, nor does it include movement in and out of unemployment or in and out of the labor force.

2. For the sample of transition countries included in the analysis, the entry of firms contributed on average 38 percent to the total job creation rate (ranging from 25 percent in Latvia to 50 percent in Romania). This finding suggests that the entry of firms indeed played an exceptionally important role in job creation in transition countries. In contrast, at 28 percent, the average share of firm exits in job destruction was below the OECD group's average of about 35 percent.

3. Because productivity is measured in logs, this finding implies that within the average Colombian or Chilean manufacturing sector, productivity would be 40 log points smaller if labor were allocated randomly across firms.

4. The European Union countries enjoy on average a 25 percent productivity boost from rational allocation of resources but have not seen much change on balance over time.

5. In comparing these findings to the existing literature, it is worth noting that Olley and Pakes (1996) found a positive cross-term using total factor productivity as the measure of productivity in the U.S. telecommunications industry and that the cross-term increased substantially following deregulation of the industry.

6. Using total factor productivity instead of labor productivity, Eslava and others (2004) found that the Olley-Pakes cross-term rose substantially within three-digit ISIC Colombian industries in the 1990s.

7. These differences are statistically significant at the 1 percent level.

8. For a review of these factors, see Bartelsman, Haltiwanger, and Scarpetta (2004, 2009).

9. Perhaps not surprisingly, entry and exit rates are loosely or even negatively correlated in some of the transition economies where traditional manufacturing sectors are losing ground while new service sectors are expanding, as well as in some emerging economies (Colombia), where, again, rapid structural changes have occurred in the period covered by the data.

10. Dunne, Roberts, and Samuelson (1988) suggest that entry and exit rates are correlated with a lag in the United States. However, even then the entry rate in a given five-year period is positively correlated with exit rates in the following five years. For an extensive discussion on this issue, see Caves (1998). Caves also signals that the correlation between entry and exit reverts to negative in the early and late phases of a product's life cycle.

11. For Estonia and Latvia, survival data do not allow following firms for more than five to six years.

References

Baldwin, J. R., and P. K. Gorecki. 1991. "Entry, Exit, and Productivity Growth." In *Entry and Market Contestability: An International Comparison*, ed. P. A. Geroski and J. Schwalbach, 244–56. Oxford, U.K.: Blackwell.

Bartelsman, E. J., and M. Doms. 2000. "Understanding Productivity: Lessons from Longitudinal Microdata." *Journal of Economic Literature* 38 (3): 569–95.

Bartelsman, E. J., J. Haltiwanger, and S. Scarpetta. 2004. "Microeconomic Evidence of Creative Destruction in Industrial and Developing Countries." IZA Discussion Paper 1374, Institute for the Study of Labor, Bonn, Germany.

———. 2009. "Measuring and Analyzing Cross-Country Differences in Firm Dynamics." In *Producer Dynamics: New Evidence from Micro Data*, ed. T. Dunne, J. B. Jensen, and M. J. Roberts. Chicago: University of Chicago Press.

Caves, R. E. 1998. "Industrial Organization and New Findings on the Turnover and Mobility of Firms." *Journal of Economic Literature* 36 (4): 1947–82.

Dunne, T., M. Roberts, and L. Samuelson. 1988. "Patterns of Firm Entry and Exit in U.S. Manufacturing Industries." *Rand Journal of Economics* 19 (4): 495–515.

Eslava, M., J. Haltiwanger, A. Kugler, and M. Kugler. 2004. "The Effects of Structural Reforms on Productivity and Profitability Enhancing Reallocation: Evidence from Colombia." *Journal of Development Economics* 75 (2): 333–71.

Foster, L., J. Haltiwanger, and C. J. Krizan. 2006. "Market Selection, Reallocation, and Restructuring in the U.S. Retail Trade Sector in the 1990s." *Review of Economics and Statistics* 88 (4): 748–58.

Geroski, P. 1991. *Market Dynamics and Entry*. Oxford, U.K.: Basil Blackwell.

Olley, G. S., and A. Pakes. 1996. "The Dynamics of Productivity in the Telecommunications Equipment Industry." *Econometrica* 64 (6): 1263–97.

Part III

Policies to Foster the Creation of Good Jobs and Help Workers through Labor Market Transitions

The previous chapters have painted a relatively disappointing picture of the labor market performance in most countries of Latin America and the Caribbean. In some, growth has not led to much job creation, while in others, the employment creation that has accompanied economic growth has been concentrated in low-productivity jobs.

The required policy interventions to address these issues go well beyond the labor market. Looking at labor market performance from the demand side, chapter 5 seeks to identify the main constraints that firms face in doing business. The chapter shows that, despite strong improvements in the past decades, several elements of the investment climate are still less favorable in Latin America and the Caribbean than in many rapidly growing developing and emerging economies. One element that is lacking is macroeconomic stability, which is crucial to foster economic activity. Beyond macroeconomic instability, the main obstacles to doing business can be grouped in two sets: (a) government effectiveness and the rule of law and (b) cost of and access to finance, tax rates, and administration.

Although labor market regulations are ranked as being relatively less important, this fact mostly attests to the particularly difficult business environment that firms face. Indeed, the evidence, based on analysis both at firm and country levels, suggests that labor regulations matter for aggregate labor market performance, especially in terms of employment creation. The three chapters that compose the rest of part III therefore focus on ways to improve labor market policies in the region and attempt to identify the main areas of intervention.

Chapter 6 reviews employment protection legislation and income-support schemes for the unemployed in the region. After showing that protecting jobs impairs employment and productivity performance, the chapter moves on to argue that labor market policy needs to evolve from the logic of *protecting jobs* to that of *protecting workers*. To do so, policy needs to promote change from the current mechanisms, which are based on employment protection legislation, toward income-support mechanisms for the unemployed. The latter can provide adequate protection against the risk of unemployment while creating fewer distortions in economic activity. In the context of most of the countries of the region (except Peru), the main areas of intervention lie in shifting from high firing costs, which protect only a small share of workers at a high expense, to designing income-support programs (which need not be publicly funded—that is, individual savings accounts could be used) that can improve individuals' ability to cope with economic and social risks. In particular, to face up to the challenge of protecting informal workers as well as formal workers, governments need to develop integrated welfare states that extend coverage to all workers, for example, by funding programs from general revenues or developing appropriate alternatives for workers who do not participate in contribution-based systems.

Chapter 7 argues that the region has the potential to scale up active labor market policies to complement income-support schemes and provide the means, incentives, and motivation for workers to exit unemployment and improve their productivity in their next job. In particular, it suggests that job intermediation services can be a good and relatively cheap way of helping to match workers with adequate jobs and that efforts should be made to expand such services. Likewise, while acknowledging that training programs cannot replace formal education, the chapter suggests that they can help to reduce skill shortages under certain circumstances. Finally, it concludes that employment subsidy programs can create employment for certain vulnerable groups or partially make up for the inefficiencies created by other policies, although at the cost of substitution effects and high fiscal outlays.

Finally, chapter 8 looks at policies to improve the quality of jobs to ensure that the labor market produces equitable and efficient outcomes. Governments may intervene in different ways: (a) imposing standards in workplace practices; (b) promoting risk pooling to diversify sickness, disability, and old-age risks across a large number of workers; (c) promoting collective bargaining; (d) setting minimum wages to limit the risk of poverty for the working poor; and (e) fostering skill upgrading through on-the-job training.

Although advances in mandatory benefits tend to be viewed as advances in workers' welfare, excessive and burdensome regulations also lead to poor job creation, particularly in higher-paying firms (see chapter 5). For this reason, governments need to walk the fine line between legislating better work conditions and assessing whether such conditions are appropriate given the level of development and labor productivity of a country. This situation particularly applies when enforcement capabilities are weak and inappropriate regulations lead firms or workers to opt out of such higher standards and to work under informal or substandard conditions.

5

The Business Environment

Policy Challenges for Promoting Investment and Job Creation

The modest growth performance of many Latin American and Caribbean countries and the associated inefficient dynamism—that is, high firm and job turnover but limited effect on efficient allocation and productivity growth—point to potential problems in the investment climate.[1] These problems seem to affect not only the entry of new productive firms but also the expansion of successful ones and the creation of rewarding jobs. Moreover, many firms seem to be engaged in defensive restructuring, whereby they improve their efficiency by downsizing rather than investing.

The entry and postentry growth of firms depends on the costs of starting a business and also on the future expected benefits and costs of operating and expanding the business. Similarly, firm restructuring and growth depend on the rate of return to investment, which, in turn, is influenced by competitive pressures in the product market, access to new technologies, and internal governance.

Most countries in the region have engaged in structural reforms since the early 1990s that have arguably improved their investment climate. These reforms have included, with different pace and intensity across countries, macrostabilization measures, trade and financial market reforms, and privatization of many state-owned enterprises. However, many components of the investment climate in the region are still less favorable than in many developing and emerging economies with which the Latin American and Caribbean countries are competing in the globalized economy.

The assessment of the stance of the investment climate in the region is performed using two complementary instruments: (a) an in-depth review of regulatory indicators derived from laws and regulations and (b) the analysis of firm-level data drawn from surveys of enterprises. Objective measures of the investment climate, which rely on observation of the law, help in assessing the regulatory burden and constraints to growth imposed on formal firms (World Bank 2003, 2004a, 2005b, 2006a), but because the effect of a given set of rules and regulations also depends on the capacity of the country to enforce them, one must go beyond the review of formal regulations. Accounting for the enforcement of regulations is important in any analysis of the investment climate, but it is likely to be a more pressing issue in countries that have a large informal economy, like many of the Latin American and Caribbean countries. A way around this issue is to use surveys of entrepreneurs and various stakeholders. These special surveys, known as World Bank Enterprise Surveys, were conducted between 2000 and 2005.[2] They collect direct information on how the real actors in the market perceive the regulatory environment in which they operate and rank the constraints affecting their future decisions on investment and hiring. Box 5.1 describes the methodology used.

Box 5.1 Identifying the Firms That Suffer Most from Weak Investment Climate: Multivariate Analysis of Firm-Level Data

This chapter draws from two in-depth econometric analyses of the investment climate. Both analyses are based on the Enterprise Surveys that have been conducted by the World Bank in recent years. The sample of firms in each survey is stratified by size, sector, and location. Each survey, therefore, oversamples large firms compared to their share in the number of firms, but not in terms of their contribution to gross domestic product. The unit of analysis is the "establishment" in the manufacturing and service sectors. The surveys are generally thought to capture formal firms, given that most of them are registered with local authorities, although such firms may be in only partial compliance with labor and tax authorities. In some countries, including Brazil and Guatemala, the World Bank has also conducted surveys specifically directed at informal firms.

The data include variables that define the firm's characteristics, such as size, age, ownership, exports, and industry. A set of 18 variables defines the investment climate faced by the firm as perceived by its manager. The firms were asked whether a series of investment climate constraints were an obstacle to the operation and growth of their business. A rating of 0 denoted no obstacle; 1, a minor obstacle; 2, a moderate obstacle; 3, a major obstacle; and 4, a very severe obstacle. The investment climate constraints included a broad range of components related to infrastructure, regulations, economic policies, and legal institutions that influence firms' performance and decisions. The data also provide objective information

(continued)

Box 5.1 Identifying the Firms That Suffer Most from Weak Investment Climate: Multivariate Analysis of Firm-Level Data *(continued)*

on investment climate constraints, such as the number of days the firm did not have access to electricity or water, whether bribes are paid, and the number of weeks required to fill a skilled vacancy.

The first study (carried out for this book) analyzes the data that relate to the region only and documents the main (subjective) constraints of firms in the region (see annex 5.A for the results from estimation of the base model). The Latin American and Caribbean sample contains 11 countries (Bolivia, Brazil, Chile, Costa Rica, Ecuador, El Salvador, Guatemala, Guyana, Honduras, Nicaragua, and Peru). The sample sizes vary between 163 firms in Guyana and more than 1,600 for Brazil. The sample comprises 42 percent small firms (20 employees or less), 38 percent medium-size firms (21–100 employees), and 20 percent large firms (more than 100 employees). It includes fairly new firms: 51 percent of the firms have been operating 15 years or fewer; only about 6 percent have been in operation for more than 50 years.

The constructed dependent variables (one for each constraint) consist of binary variables equal to 1 if the firms reported the constraint to be a major or very severe obstacle and 0 otherwise. A probit model is used to estimate the relationship between these dependent variables and a set of explanatory variables. The basic model includes the following variables: age group, size group, exporter, foreign ownership, public ownership, innovative firm, industry dummies, proportion of other constraints cited as major or very severe obstacles by the firm, and country dummies. In complementary specifications, the industry variable is replaced by classification of industries into low-, medium-, and high-productivity industries and into dynamic and less dynamic industries.

The second study (Aterido, Hallward-Dreimeier, and Pagés 2007) uses all the years and countries available in the database and looks at the link between investment climate and firms' employment decisions. The database includes 54,321 firms from 83 emerging countries in six different regions surveyed since 2000. Within the region, the data contain information on Argentina, Bolivia, Brazil, Chile, Colombia, Costa Rica, the Dominican Republic, Ecuador, El Salvador, Guatemala, Guyana, Honduras, Jamaica, Mexico, Nicaragua, Panama, Paraguay, Peru, and Uruguay.

The analysis examines the degree to which firms report that their business is affected by investment climate constraints and identifies patterns in their responses. In addition, the study measures the effect of the elements of the investment climate (except the legal system) on employment growth. To this end, employment growth at the individual firm level is regressed against a number of variables to control for firm size, age of the firm,

(continued)

Box 5.1 Identifying the Firms That Suffer Most from Weak Investment Climate: Multivariate Analysis of Firm-Level Data *(continued)*

whether the firm is an exporter, type of ownership (public versus private or foreign versus local), whether the firm is located in the capital city, and industry.[a] Regressions also control for unobservable country, year, and industry factors by adding country, year, and industry fixed effects. Size of the firm, a key variable in this study, is divided across micro firms (fewer than 10 employees) and small (10–49 employees), medium (50–199 employees), large (200–499 employees), and very large (more than 500 employees) firms, although in some of the regressions the two last categories are lumped together. Importantly, size is defined according to the *initial* number of employees one, two, or three years before the year of the survey, depending on the country. Finally, the authors added a set of controls to account for such differences across surveys and for the fact that employment growth is also computed one, two, or three years apart across different surveys and firms. The main variable of interest, employment growth, is measured as the change in the enterprise's permanent employment during the period $t - x$ to t (x being the last available year), divided by the firm's simple average of permanent workers during the same period. The employment growth measure is symmetric around zero and bounded by values –2 and +2.

In this study, the authors give priority to objective rather than subjective indicators of business climate conditions because of the observation that subjective indicators are strongly correlated with performance. Nonetheless, any estimated relation between employment growth and objective measures of business climate conditions reported by individual firms could be driven by reverse causality. The authors therefore address this endogeneity problem by replacing individually reported measures of business climate by the average of those values within country, firm size, city (capital or not), and industry cells.

Sources: Aterido, Hallward-Dreimeier, and Pagés 2007; authors' calculations.

a. These regressions are based on a sample of countries around the world, including a number of Latin American and Caribbean countries. They are not specific to the region and do not identify the region's idiosyncrasies.

This chapter investigates the elements of the investment climate that are most important for the prospect of job creation and productivity growth in the region. It identifies the major constraints along three main axes: (a) risks of doing business, (b) costs and barriers affecting the decision to invest and adopt new technologies, and (c) competition in the product market that hinders an efficient allocation of resources and hampers the entry of new firms and the exit of otherwise unviable firms. The chapter looks, in particular, at whether firms of different characteristics (size, age, dynamism, and so on) face specific constraints.

Role of the Investment Climate in Explaining Labor Market Performance in the Region

The relatively low level and quality of private investment in Latin America and the Caribbean indicates that the investment climate is an issue in the region. The review of the investment climate in the region and its effect on the creation of productive jobs begins by looking at the aggregate level of investment. On average, as a proportion of gross domestic product (GDP), investment by the private sector, where job creation and productivity growth should come from, tends to be lower than in Eastern Europe and Central Asia and much lower than in the dynamic emerging economies of East Asia (figure 5.1). The investment rate has improved in many countries of the region since 1990, but it actually declined in some of the smaller countries of South America. It varies widely within the region from below 10 percent in Bolivia and Uruguay to over 20 percent in Jamaica and Nicaragua.

Figure 5.1 Gross Fixed Capital Formation as a Percentage of GDP: Private Sector

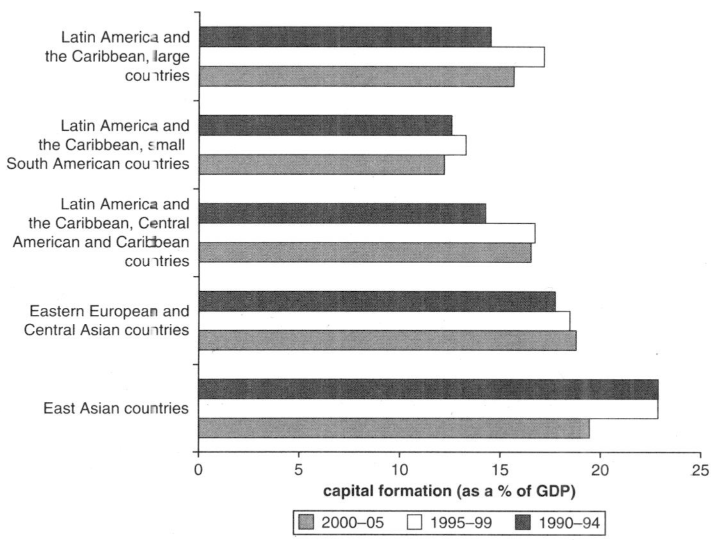

Source: World Bank 2006b.

Figure 5.2 Investment in High-Productivity Sectors Relative to Low-Productivity Sectors

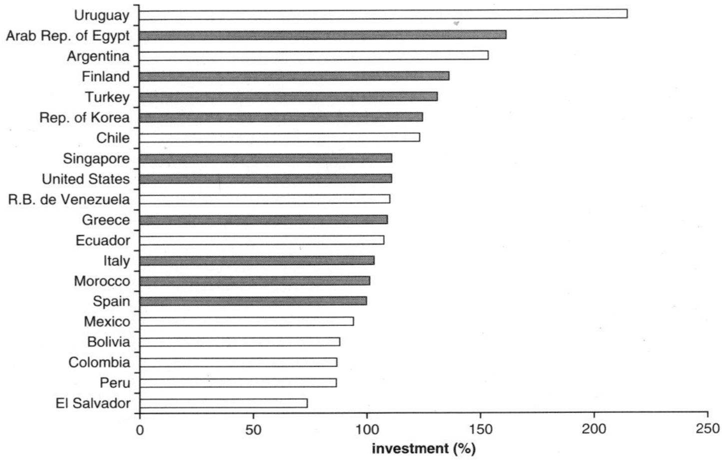

Source: United Nations Industrial Development Organization (UNIDO).

Note: The exercise was done with the ratio of gross fixed capital formation to value added. The figure displays an average of the following years: Argentina: 1993; Bolivia: 1993–94, 1996–98; Chile: 1993–98; Colombia: 1993–98; Ecuador: 1993–98; Arab Republic of Egypt: 1993–95; El Salvador: 1993–98; Finland: 1993–96; Greece: 1993–98; Italy: 1993–98; Republic of Korea: 1993–98; Mexico: 1994–98; Morocco: 1993–98; Peru: 1994–96; Singapore: 1993–98; Spain: 1993–98; Turkey: 1993–98; United States: 1993–95, 1997–98; Uruguay: 1993–97; República Bolivariana de Venezuela: 1993–97.

If one then distinguishes between total investment and business sector investment, several countries—in particular the small South American countries—are seen to have declined in private investment since 1990. Moreover, if one looks at the sectors that have played a major role in driving overall business sector investment, in many countries investment is disproportionately taking place in low-productivity sectors (figure 5.2). Thus, at a first inspection, there seems to be a lack of investment by the business sector in many countries of the region and, in particular, a lack of investment in potentially more productive and innovative sectors.

Main Obstacles Faced by Firms in the Region

Different aspects of the business climate have a bearing on output and employment growth through their influence on real or perceived risks, costs of production, and distortions to competition. Why is investment so low in the region, especially in the most productive sectors? Many different aspects of the business climate have a bearing on firms' investment. For the purpose of this study, grouping these factors according to the three main channels by which they affect employment is useful:

- *Risks.* The business environment may affect the risks (real or perceived) of investing in a given country or sector. Although a certain level of risk is intrinsically associated with firms' investment decisions, undue risks may bias firms' investment decisions away from riskier but more innovative and productive activities, thereby affecting the productivity and the quality of jobs created.
- *Costs.* Similarly, investment climate aspects affecting the costs of producing and distributing goods influence the range of activities that are profitable in a country. Moreover, in the context of countries with insufficient enforcement, business environment–induced costs can distort the firm size and sector composition of employment because certain types of firms or sectors may be able to avoid such costs. For example, firms potentially facing large costs may choose to remain small so that they can remain invisible to the authorities.
- *Competition.* Finally, the business climate may affect the quantity and quality of employment creation by affecting the rules of competition in the product market (for example, regulations on firms' entry and exit or tariffs protecting domestically produced goods from foreign competition).

On average, Latin American firms complain most about macroinstability, cost of financing, corruption, and rule of law issues.

How important are the various elements of the investment climate that affect risks, costs, and competition in the market? The World Bank's Enterprise Surveys ask individual firms to rank a number of different aspects of the business environment in terms of how much of an obstacle they are for firm growth. The results, at first glance, indicate that issues associated with corruption and the rule of law are among the most important constraints in the region. (Corruption is ranked first, while anticompetitive and informal practices of competitors are ranked third, and crime, theft, and disorder are in sixth place.) Risks are generally perceived as seriously hurting business performance and investment decisions. In fact, among the main obstacles to employment growth are the risks involved in production associated with an *unstable macroeconomic situation* (second place) and the *instability of economic and regulatory policies* (fourth place). Importantly, in an international context, macroeconomic and policy risks are more of an obstacle in Latin America and the Caribbean than in any other region of the world. Among factors that affect the cost of production, the cost of and lack of access to financing (seventh place) and tax rates (fifth place) play the most important roles (figure 5.3).

Interestingly, factors directly related to the labor market—that is, labor market regulations and shortages of skills—were perceived in the region as less important in relative terms. This finding suggests, prima facie, that policies affecting labor demand may have a stronger effect on job creation than those aimed at improving the mobility and quality of the labor force. Although the latter are obviously very important to ensure a healthy labor market performance, many constraints to job creation lie outside the realm of labor policies.

Figure 5.3 Ranking the Investment Climate Constraints in the Region

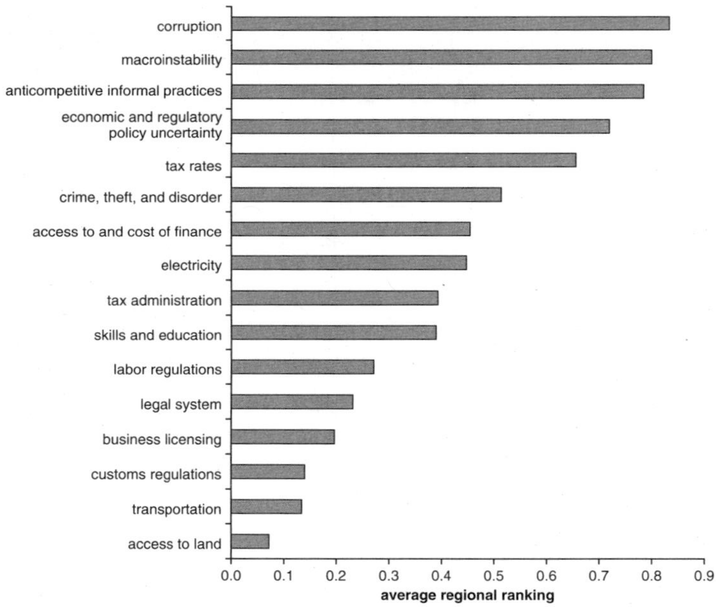

Source: World Bank Enterprise Surveys.

Note: This figure is based on an index that ranks obstacles of each country, standardized to take values between 0 (smallest obstacle) and 1 (greatest obstacle). Data are for the following years and countries: 2003: Brazil, Ecuador, El Salvador, Guatemala, Honduras, and Nicaragua; 2004: Chile and Guyana; 2005: Costa Rica; 2006: Argentina, Bolivia, Colombia, Mexico, Panama, Paraguay, Peru, and Uruguay.

Risk: The Main Constraint in Most Countries

Its history and institutions make Latin America and the Caribbean one of the regions where firms are the most vulnerable to risks. In particular, firms face economic instability, regulatory uncertainty, corruption, crime, and anticompetitive or informal practices (figure 5.4). Although the countries of the region have come a long way in terms of democratization and government accountability, they are still behind countries with similar economic development in terms of implementing and enforcing public policy in a reliable legal environment.

Surveys of employers in the region reveal that risks are among the most important constraints. Of regional firms, 47 percent and 44 percent,

Figure 5.4 Risks as the Most Important Constraints within the Region and with Respect to Other Regions

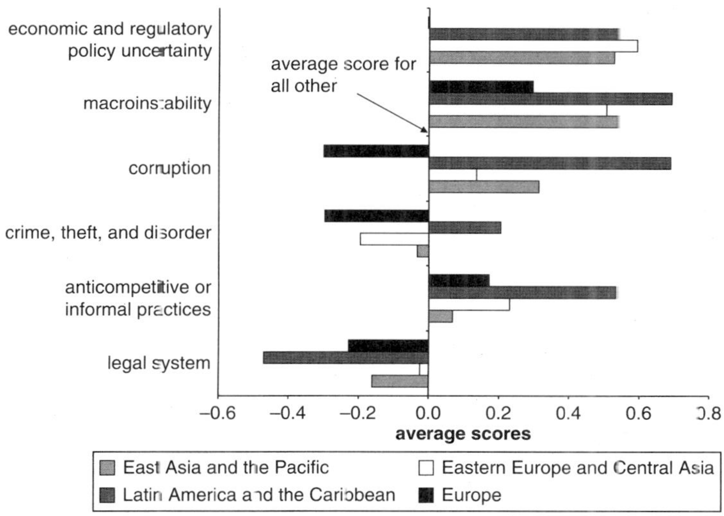

Source: World Bank Enterprise Surveys.

Note: Data are for the following years and countries: 2003: Brazil, Ecuador, El Salvador, Guatemala, Honduras, and Nicaragua; 2004: Chile and Guyana; 2005: Costa Rica; 2006: Argentina, Bolivia, Colombia, Mexico, Panama, Paraguay, Peru, and Uruguay. For a more meaningful comparison across countries and regions, perceptions are standardized as the deviation of the score (*DC*) from the average score of all other constraints. For each firm *i* and constraint j:$DC_{ij} = C_{ij} - (\Sigma_{k \neq j} C_{ik}/K - 1)$, with *K* the total number of constraints and *C* the score, taking values 0 (no obstacle) to 4 (very severe obstacle). These scores are then averaged by country and then by region.

respectively, see (a) macroeconomic instability and (b) economic and regulatory uncertainty as major or very severe obstacles. Volatile economic conditions as well as recurrent changes in macroeconomic and other economic policies are associated with uncertainty. In a context of major macro and structural reforms, such as those experienced by the region since 1990 (with sizable effects on the structure of the economy), such concerns are not surprising. Uncertainty is reinforced when the government lacks effectiveness in implementing economic policies, as several countries of the region have experienced.

The region lags others in terms of rule of law and government effectiveness. The predictability and consistency of the interpretation of policies, as well as the efficiency of governments to deliver services, are an important element in firms' investment decisions. The region appears to fare particularly badly in these dimensions according to surveys of employers. In particular, the region features the lowest proportions of firms satisfied with their government in those two aspects (figures 5.5 and 5.6). Interestingly, whereas the larger countries of the region fare relatively well compared with the rest of the region in terms of predictability, they fare worse, on

Figure 5.5 Low Predictability of Regulations

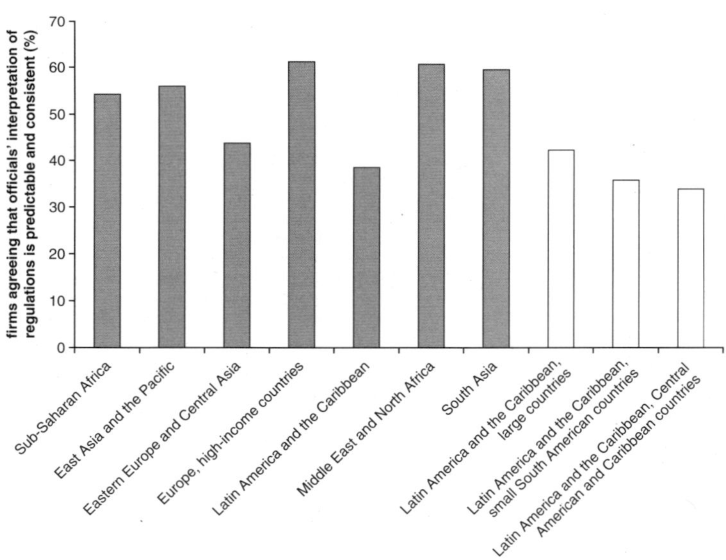

Source: World Bank Enterprise Surveys.

Figure 5.6 Lack of Government Efficiency

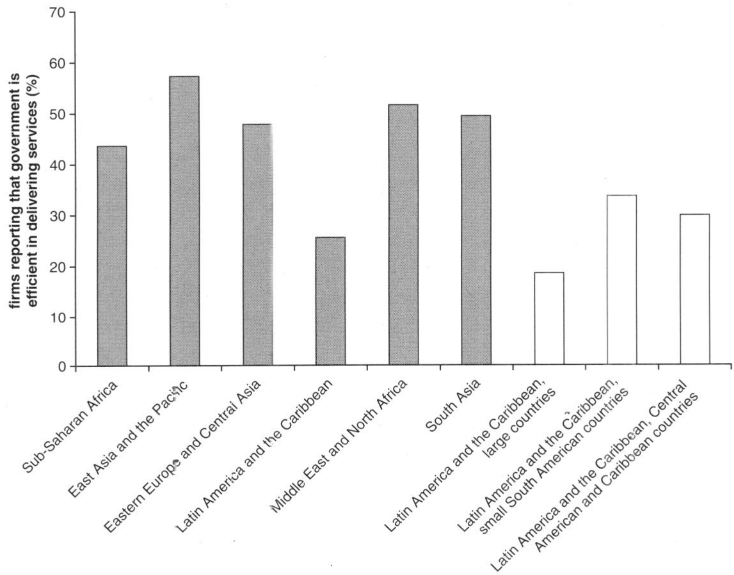

Source: World Bank Enterprise Surveys.

average, in terms of government efficiency. These results may be due to a genuine lack of effectiveness (for example, because of the greater size of the countries), but they also may indicate greater expectations of firms in those countries.

Additional evidence coming from governance indicators developed by the World Bank provides a more optimistic view of the situation on the region and suggests that it is on a positive path toward better governance.[3] These indicators show that rule of law and government effectiveness are in fact the weak points of the region. Compared with other regions, Latin America and the Caribbean is doing well in other aspects of governance, such as voice and accountability, regulatory quality, and political stability (table 5.1). Moreover, the region has already improved its rule of law and government effectiveness since the mid 1990s. The indicators of governance, which have been collected for 13 years now, indeed suggest that some improvements occurred in most aspects of governance (except regulatory quality, and voice and accountability, which were already high compared with the findings in other developing regions) over the period 1996 to 2004 (figure 5.7).

Table 5.1 Rank of Governance Indexes, Controlling for GDP Per Capita

Region or group	*Voice and accountability*	*Government effectiveness*	*Regulatory quality*	*Rule of law*	*Control of corruption*	*Political stability*
Sub-Saharan Africa	6	6	7	6	6	5
East Asia and the Pacific	5	1	3	3	5	1
Eastern Europe and Central Asia	4	7	5	7	7	3
Industrial countries	2	3	4	4	1	4
Latin America and the Caribbean	1	4	1	5	3	2
Middle East and North Africa	7	5	6	2	4	6
South Asia	3	2	2	1	2	7

Source: Kaufmann, Kraay, and Mastruzzi 2005.
Note: Table shows average of index values over the period 1996 to 2004.

Figure 5.7 Some Improvements in Governance

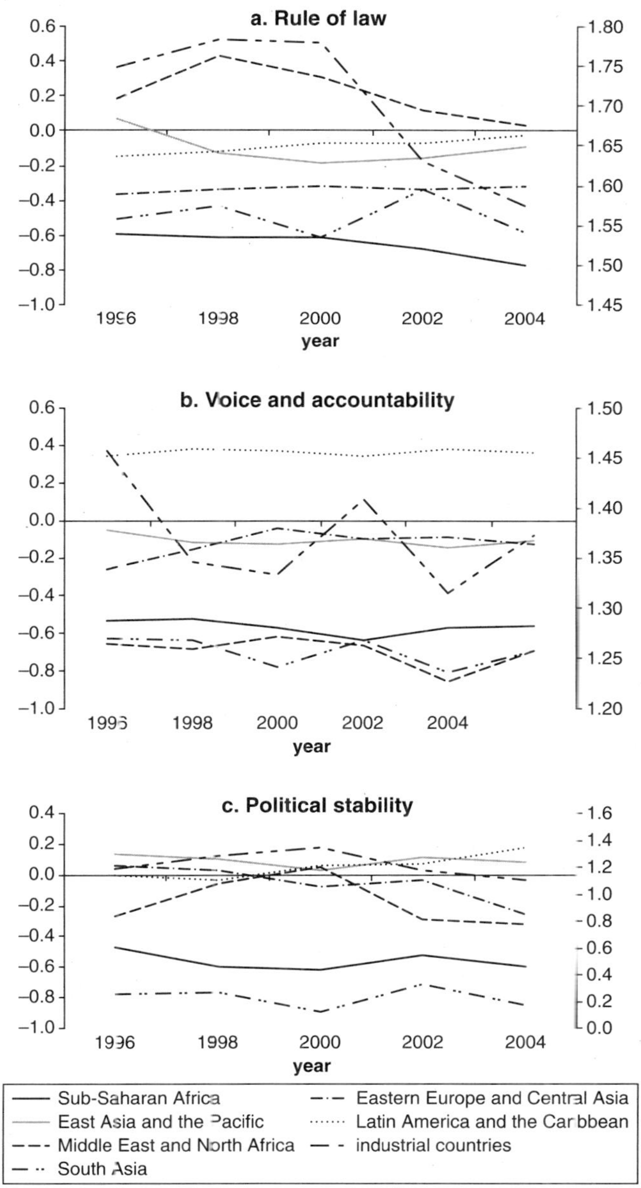

(continued)

Figure 5.7 Some Improvements in Governance *(continued)*

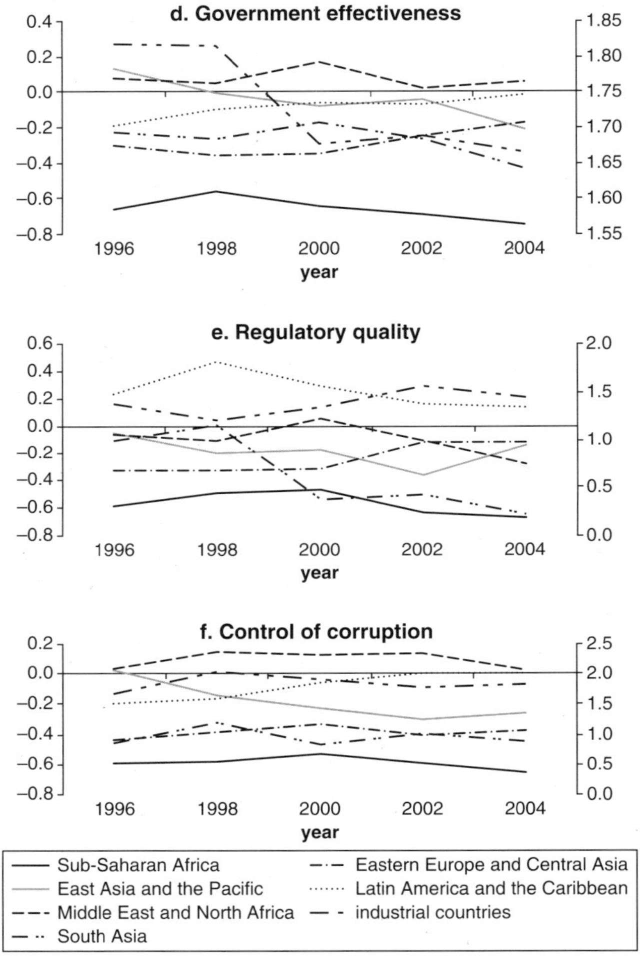

Source: Kaufmann, Kraay, and Mastruzzi 2005.

Note: The right axis refers to industrial countries; the left axis refers to all other regions.

Law enforcement authorities are not trusted to guarantee property and other rights. This lack of trust extends to the judicial system. Employers in the region are on average less confident in their judicial system's ability to enforce contractual and property rights disputes than in other regions (figure 5.8). Within the region, larger countries seem to have levels of

Figure 5.8 Low Trust in the Judicial System

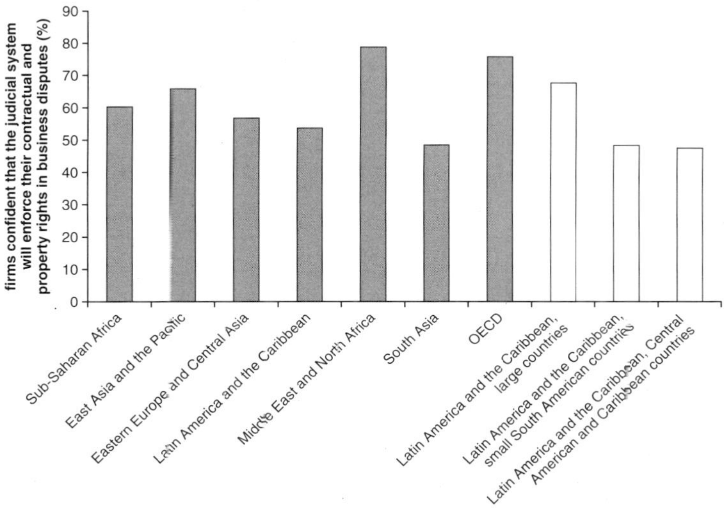

Source: World Bank Enterprise Surveys.

Note: In the case of the Latin American and Caribbean subgroups, large countries are Brazil, Chile, and Peru; small South American countries are Ecuador and Guyana; and Central American and Caribbean countries are Costa Rica, El Salvador, Guatemala, Honduras, and Nicaragua.

confidence similar to European countries when compared with the two other regional subgroups, but differences cut across this grouping. For example, over 70 percent of firms are confident in the judicial system's ability to enforce contractual and property rights disputes in Chile and Costa Rica compared with less than 30 percent in Ecuador and Guatemala. World ranking from the World Economic Forum's *Global Competitiveness Report* (Porter, Schwab, and López-Claros 2006) is consistent with these findings; out of 125 countries, Nicaragua, Paraguay, and the República Bolivariana de Venezuela are the ones where the judiciary is most influenced by the government, citizens, or firms. Barbados, Costa Rica, and Uruguay are well placed, respectively, at 16th, 33rd, and 37th.

Weak rule of law negatively affects employment growth. A significant example of how weak rule of law and weak enforcement of regulations can affect firms' development is the role of property rights in overall investment and investment patterns (as summarized in Claessens and Laeven 2003). In particular, the strength of a country's intellectual property rights is found to affect its innovative capacity, as measured by the degree of international patenting (Furman, Porter, and Stern 2002). New firm-level analysis that includes the results of this strand of literature aims at finding out how firms' employment decisions are affected. More secure property rights are found to allow the expansion of employment in industries dependent on intangible assets[4] in a sample that includes several countries of the region (Micco and Pagés 2006; see also chapter 6).

Costs: Concerns about Lack of Rule of Law, Financing, and Taxes

The costs of producing and distributing goods influence the range of activities that may be profitable. Moreover, in the context of the region, where low enforcement of regulations is pervasive, costs can lead to distorted firm and sectoral composition because certain types of firms or sectors may be able to escape regulations, lowering their costs of doing business. Three types of costs emerge as dominant in Latin America and the Caribbean: the relative lack of rule of law and a high regulatory burden translate into significant costs for firms, and financing costs are also an issue in most countries.

The regulatory environment and corruption make the region one of the costliest in the world. The lack of rule of law that has been identified previously translates into tangible costs for the day-to-day operation of businesses in the region. For example, payments to officials to "get things done" are among the highest in the world (figure 5.9). Whereas such payments are not an issue in the larger countries of the region, they are a significant issue in the other subregions. Indicators of the business cost of corruption, which are based on firms' answers to whether corruption imposes costs or has other negative effects on their firms, show that countries of the region tend to rank among countries with higher costs (López-Claros, Porter, and Schwab 2005; Porter, Schwab, and López-Claros 2006; Porter and others 2004).[5] The 2006 ranking suggests that this is especially the case of Paraguay (100th of 125), the República Bolivariana de Venezuela (104th), and Ecuador (109th). Chile (21st), Barbados (23rd), and Uruguay (29th), in contrast, are the countries with the lowest associated costs in the region. They rank behind many high-income countries of the Organisation for Economic Co-operation and Development (OECD) but above several European countries, such as Greece and Italy. Chile and Barbados rank above Belgium and Spain (Porter, Schwab, and López-Claros 2006).[6]

A high regulatory burden also translates into costs in terms of staff time. In particular, surveys of employers reveal that a lot of time is lost dealing with regulations and their associated procedures: the time spent by senior management dealing with regulations is higher in Latin America and the Caribbean—especially in Central America—than in other regions (figure 5.10). In addition, Latin America and the Caribbean is the region where resolving payment disputes takes the longest and requires the most procedures, although in terms of cost it is in the middle (figure 5.11). This

Figure 5.9 High Informal Payments

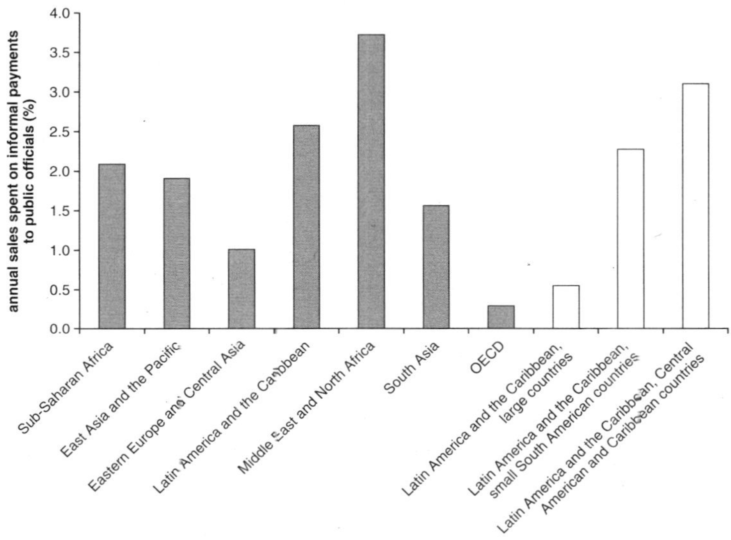

Source: World Bank Enterprise Surveys.

Note: In the case of the Latin American and Caribbean subgroups, large countries are Brazil and Chile; small South American countries are Ecuador and Guyana; and Central American and Caribbean countries are Costa Rica, El Salvador, Guatemala, Honduras, and Nicaragua.

unfavorable overall picture hides strong differences across countries. The number of procedures to settle payment disputes varies from 20 or fewer in Brazil and Jamaica to 45 or more in Panama and Paraguay, the number of days varies from fewer than 200 in Nicaragua to more than 550 in the Dominican Republic, Guatemala, and Uruguay.

Corruption and Inconsistent Business Regulations as an Impediment on Job Growth

Results obtained from the Enterprise Surveys strongly suggest that corruption and a high regulatory burden slow down the creation of jobs in the private sector (Aterido, Hallward-Dreimeier, and Pagés 2007; annex table 5.B.1). If one controls for firm characteristics and country, year, and sector dummies, one finds that fewer jobs are created, especially in larger firms, when (a) the incidence of bribes, (b) the amount of those bribes as a percentage of sales, (c) the number of firms that report that government

Figure 5.10 Time Spent Dealing with Regulations

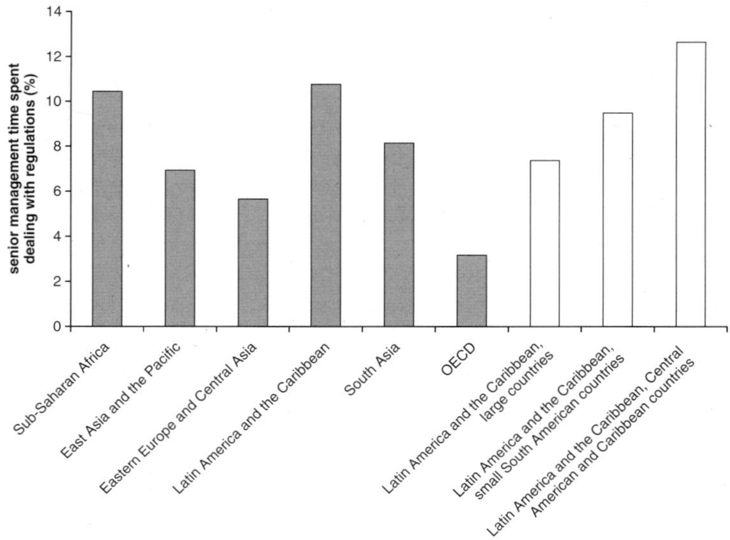

Source: World Bank Enterprise Surveys.

Note: In the case of the Latin American and Caribbean subgroups, large countries are Brazil and Chile; small South American countries are Ecuador and Guyana; and Central American and Caribbean countries are Costa Rica, El Salvador, Guatemala, Honduras, and Nicaragua.

officials expect unofficial payments in exchange for services, or (d) the value of those gifts as a percentage of the value of a contract is high.

Consistent enforcement is found to help the growth of all firms, with particular benefits to small firms (annex table 5.B.1, row 11). Results suggest that not all interactions with officials are detrimental. Some interactions with officials indicate firms are accessing needed services. Moreover, there can be a public good component in increased enforcement of labor regulations or regulations in general. Yet there are limits: Aterido, Hallward-Dreimeier, and Pagés (2007) show that the benefits are offset as the overall time managers spend with officials increases. They also find that employment costs are associated with pure red tape and bureaucratic delays. These findings are seen more clearly in the costs of delays in clearing customs (annex table 5.B.1, rows 9–10).

Even when one controls for characteristics of firms and sectors, the region appears to suffer from a huge burden of corruption. Table 5.2 indicates that, on average, other regions report a lower incidence of bribes and

Figure 5.11 Barriers to Resolving Payment Disputes

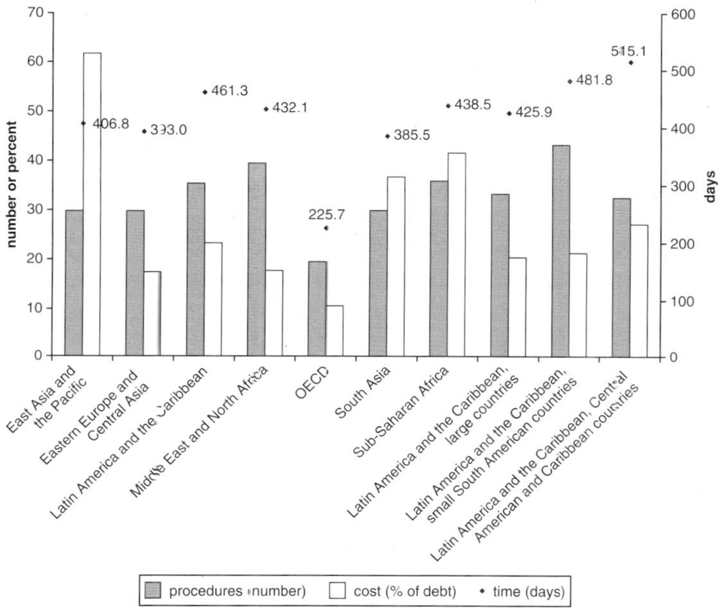

Source: World Bank Doing Business database.

lower bribes as a percentage of sales or total value of contracts than does Latin America and the Caribbean.

The cost of financing is also perceived as an important constraint. Two main investment climate issues are the cost of financing and, to a lesser degree, the difficulty of accessing it. Lack of financing directly affects firms' employment decisions: investments in capital goods cannot be made, leading to lesser use of other factors of production—in particular, labor. Even in firms that do not use capital intensively, lack of credit may restrict working capital and negatively affect employment decisions (IDB 2003). More generally, more developed domestic financial markets may help firms accommodate external demand shocks (Beck, Lundberg, and Majnoni 2006) and reduce exposure to capital flows volatility (Caballero and Krishnamurthy 2001). They therefore are associated with improved long-term growth and productivity.

One in two firms of the region reports the cost of financing as a major or very severe obstacle to doing business. The cost of financing is among the top three complaints in Brazil, Costa Rica, Guyana, Honduras, and Nicaragua.

Table 5.2 Measures of Corruption across Different Regions of the World, Controlling for Firm and Sector Characteristics

Region	*Firm reports bribes to get things done*	*Bribes as percentage of sales*	*Percentage value of government contract in gifts*
Africa	0.018*	0.528***	–0.157
	(0.010)	(0.142)	(0.154)
East Asia and the Pacific	0.055***	–0.317**	–2.150***
	(0.012)	(0.130)	(0.205)
Eastern Europe and Central Asia	–0.117***	–1.262***	–1.928***
	(0.009)	(0.106)	(0.106)
European high-income countries	–0.213***	–2.082***	–2.294***
	(0.011)	(0.122)	(0.120)
Middle East and North Africa	–0.023**	2.174***	–1.526***
	(0.010)	(0.198)	(0.118)

Source: Based on the sample of countries used by Aterido, Hallward-Dreimeier, and Pagés (2007); see box 5.1.

Note: * = significant at the 10 percent level; ** = significant at the 5 percent level; *** = significant at the 1 percent level. Standard errors are in parentheses. Table shows the results from regressing each investment climate variable at the firm level against firm characteristics, sector and year dummies, and regional dummies. The omitted region is Latin America and the Caribbean. All values are relative to the Latin American and Caribbean region. A positive number indicates higher values than in Latin America and the Caribbean; a negative number indicates a lower average than in Latin America and the Caribbean.

The direct costs of financing clearly show that the region is at a disadvantage. According to the World Economic Forum's *Global Competitiveness Report* (Porter, Schwab, and López-Claros 2006), countries of the region, at an average of 11 percentage points, have a significantly higher interest rate spread (the difference between typical lending rate and deposit rate) than comparator countries (at an average of 5.3 percentage points).[7]

Access to financing is another dimension in which firms could be constrained, but this issue does not appear to be specific to the region. Objective indicators from the World Bank's Doing Business database show that the region performs relatively well compared with other developing regions in terms of dissemination of credit information and slightly less well in terms of the degree to which legal rights facilitate credit (figure 5.12), but all developing regions perform much worse than the OECD countries.

Similar results are found from the Enterprise Surveys (see table 5.3), which indicate that firms in Latin America and the Caribbean have higher access to overdraft accounts as well as external credit to finance sales,

Figure 5.12 Dissemination of Credit Information

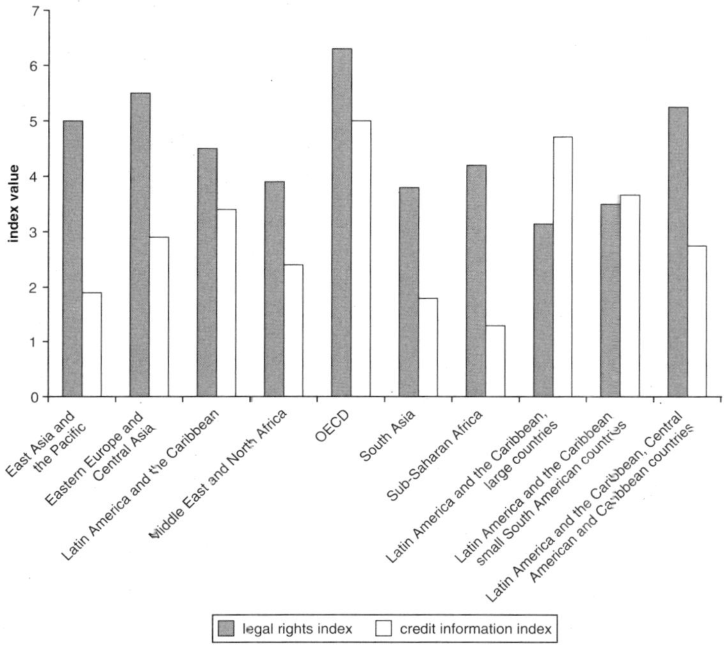

Source: World Bank Doing Business database.

working capital, and investments than other regions, with the exception of the high-income countries in Western Europe.

The literature on the link between financing and firms' performance has outlined the importance of well-developed financial markets. In particular, firms that depend more on external finance are found to develop faster in countries with better-developed financial markets (Rajan and Zingales 1998). Along the same lines, another study using comparable firm-level data for 16 countries found that financial development—private credit to GDP and stock market capitalization—plays a strong role in fostering the entry of new firms and the postentry growth of successful new businesses, especially in those industries that depend more on external financing (Aghion, Fally, and Scarpetta 2007; see box 5.2). Likewise, in new industry-level microanalysis for a sample of countries, including some from the region, capital market development is found to allow the expansion of employment in sectors with a higher dependency from external

Table 5.3 Measures of Access to Finance across Different Regions of the World

Region	*Firm has overdraft account*	*Share of sales on credit*	*Share of working capital financed externally*	*Share of investments financed externally*
Africa	−0.122***	−10.944***	−12.172***	−4.159***
	(0.008)	(0.614)	(0.473)	(0.736)
East Asia and the Pacific	−0.419***	−20.230***	−5.947***	−7.329***
	(0.009)	(0.667)	(0.646)	(0.895)
Eastern Europe and Central Asia	−0.166***	−9.626***	−11.052***	−7.905***
	(0.013)	(0.553)	(0.415)	(0.596)
European high-income countries	0.000	6.705***	−2.990***	9.168***
	(0.000)	(0.861)	(0.647)	(0.965)
Middle East and North Africa	−0.266***	−10.919***	−16.869***	−17.504***
	(0.008)	(0.663)	(0.437)	(0.706)

Source: Based on the sample of countries used by Aterido, Hallward-Dreimeier, and Pagés (2007); see box 5.1.

Note: *** = significant at the 1 percent level. Standard errors are in parentheses. Table shows the results from regressing each access to finance variable at the firm level against firm characteristics, sector and year dummies, and regional dummies. The omitted region is Latin America and the Caribbean.

funds (Micco and Pagés 2006; see also chapter 6). Evidence from the Enterprise Surveys also indicates that the availability of capital increases employment growth (Aterido, Hallward-Dreimeier, and Pagés 2007) and that such effects vary by firm size, age, ownership structure, and exporting behavior of firms (see the next section).

Taxes may be excessive in some countries compared to international standards. The importance of the tax burden imposed on firms is a function of efficiency and equity considerations as well as the capacity of the government to collect revenues. In particular, governments in developing countries may collect a larger share of their revenues from firms than those in developed countries because of narrow tax bases and weak tax administration (World Bank 2004e). A narrow tax base, caused by the large informal economy, is likely to be the biggest challenge to Latin American and Caribbean governments. The effect of high taxes on firms' employment decisions can be significant. Taxes that make capital cheaper to use than labor may discourage labor demand (IDB 2003). Evidence for Colombia shows that such taxation lowers the demand for low-skill workers while

Box 5.2 Credit Constraints for Entry and Postentry Growth of Firms

Aghion, Fally, and Scarpetta (2007) use a harmonized firm-level database (see also chapter 3 for a discussion on these data) to assess the role of financial development on firm entry, size at entry, and postentry performance of new firms. Their sample comprises 16 industrial, transition, and Latin American and Caribbean countries.[a] They implement a difference-in-difference approach to test whether industries with greater dependence on external financing or greater potential for growth—as measured by the relative GDP growth of the sector in the United States—experience greater firm dynamism in countries with more developed financial markets. Because entry and postentry growth of new firms are likely to depend on a host of other factors, in the empirical analysis they also consider start-up regulations and employment protection legislation, which, by raising entry costs or labor adjustment costs, may discourage entry and postentry growth.

A first finding of the empirical analysis is that finance matters most for the entry of small firms, especially in sectors that are more dependent on external finance or that have larger growth opportunities. This finding should not come as a big surprise: small firms face the largest financial constraints, as discussed in several papers (for example, Bernanke and Gertler 1990; World Bank 2004e; this chapter). The findings also imply that finance helps improve the selection process by allowing small firms to compete on a more equal footing with large firms. More finance permits small firms to take advantage of growth opportunities, especially in growing sectors where large firms would predominate otherwise. Higher entry, in turn, can be shown to be growth enhancing, because entrants can force inefficient incumbents to exit or force efficient ones to innovate (see Aghion, Fally, and Scarpetta 2007; Bartelsman, Haltiwanger, and Scarpetta 2004).

A second finding is that financial development improves postentry growth of successful new firms. Of course, one might argue that higher postentry growth mainly reflects a better selection at entry and the improved access to credit for smaller entrants. However, the positive effect of financial development on postentry growth holds when one controls for the size of entrants.

These results are robust to the inclusions of other regulations that may also affect entry and postentry growth. Although some evidence indicates that stringent employment protection legislation affects the entry of firms in more volatile sectors, the effect of this legislation on postentry growth is not clear-cut. Similarly, start-up costs are found to discourage entry of firms, but their inclusion does not affect the results concerning financial development.

(continued)

Box 5.2 Credit Constraints for Entry and Postentry Growth of Firms *(continued)*

The results provide support for the view that financial development may be a key factor in promoting the expansion and job creation of successful new business. They also point to the importance of both banking and securities markets in providing support to new and expanding small businesses. Small businesses are found to be of particular relevance. Indeed, several studies have stressed that in bank-based systems, the links between lenders and small borrowers tend to be weaker and potentially less effective, especially in the case of innovative start-ups.[b] Although the development of stock markets depends on the level of development of the country, several studies have highlighted the significant role of legal systems (civil versus common law) as well as other factors that are more amenable to policy interventions, such as accounting standards and regulations (Demirgüç-Kunt and Levine 2001).

Source: Aghion, Fally, and Scarpetta 2007.

a. The countries included in the analysis are Argentina, Chile, Colombia, Denmark, Finland, France, Germany, Hungary, Italy, Mexico, the Netherlands, Portugal, Romania, Slovenia, the United Kingdom, and the United States.

b. Stein (2003), for example, has argued that the difficulty in lending effectively to small borrowers is in the nature of being a bank. The tendency for banks to be large increases the distance between the owners and the loan officers who deal with small borrowers. Moreover, to minimize risks, large banks tend to restrict the discretion of loan officers (for example, by making rules based on easily measured characteristics of the borrower). Such restrictions, Stein argues, while covering the bank, may make the lending to small firms more difficult and less effective. A recent survey conducted by the OECD also finds no strong evidence of a "financing gap" for small and medium-size enterprises, but lack of appropriate financing is a hindrance to the expansion of the *innovative* small and medium-size enterprises—that is, firms in technology sectors, with new business models and high growth prospects. Traditional bank finance may be of little relevance for these firms because they have untried business models and high risk (see OECD 2006).

increasing the demand for high-skill workers who complement capital (Cárdenas and Gutiérrez 1997).

Although in all countries, inside and outside the region, firms have a natural tendency to complain about taxes, in several countries of the region—particularly the larger countries—the tax burden on firms may be excessive. According to employer surveys, tax rates are a major obstacle for a significant proportion of firms in most countries of the region.[8] In some countries, such as Brazil, taxes are among firms' main concerns. The total amount of taxes payable by businesses is slightly higher in Latin American and Caribbean countries than in OECD countries (World Bank 2006a). Interestingly, larger countries are very different from other countries in the region; they tend to have much higher total tax rates (figure 5.13). This finding is not unexpected because larger countries tend to provide more public services and, in particular, more social protection than others in the region. However, compared with OECD countries (even restricting the comparison to civil law countries), total tax rates are higher in the larger countries of the Latin American and Caribbean region.

Evidence from the employer surveys indicates that firms that report taxes as a major or very severe obstacle are also more likely to report a lower percentage of sales being declared for tax purposes. This finding holds throughout the world, but in the region, it translates into a particularly low average proportion of sales being declared (figure 5.14).

Figure 5.13 Total Tax Rate

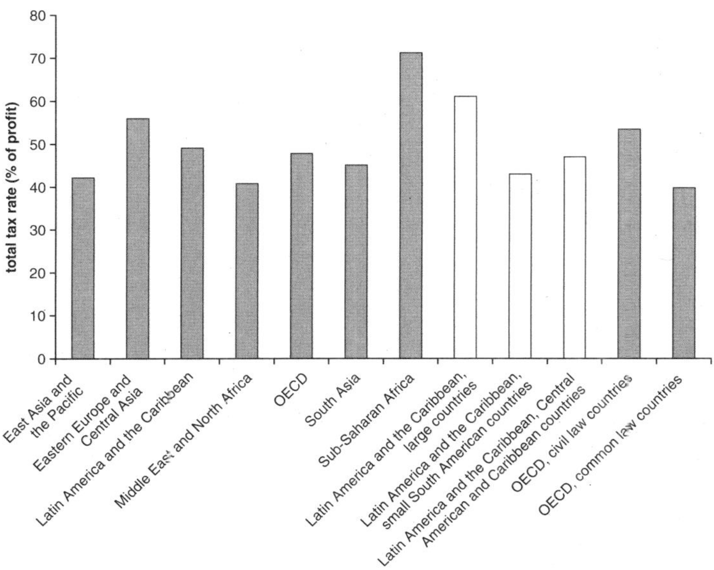

Source: World Bank Doing Business database.

Figure 5.14 Average Proportion of Sales Declared for Tax Purposes

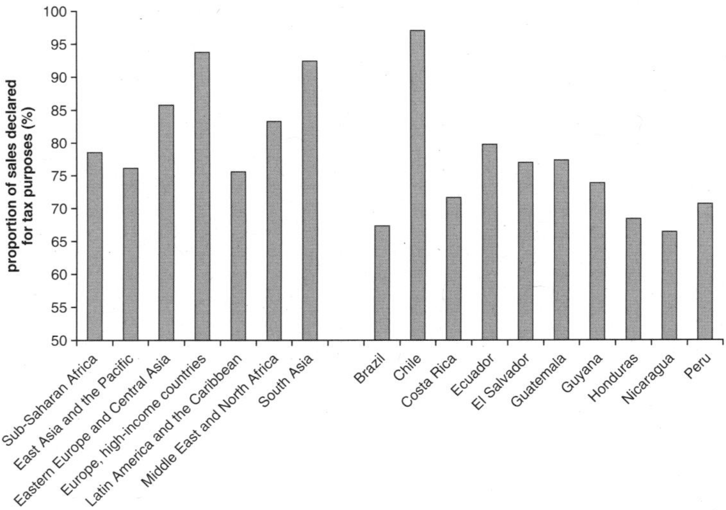

Source: World Bank Enterprise Surveys.

Barriers to Competition

Fostering competition in the product market is a healthy process that gives firms incentives to innovate, to improve productivity, and to share the rents from productivity gains with consumers and workers (World Bank 2004e). Governments have a role to play in this process because they influence the level of competition through the regulations they impose on firms' entry and exit in the domestic and global markets, as well as through the way they deal with anticompetitive practices in their countries.

Competitive pressure has increased dramatically in the countries of the region as they have opened up to foreign trade and fostered competition among domestic firms. However, in addition to the costs and risks of doing business, which tend to disproportionately affect new entrants, specific barriers to competition exist in the form of large start-up costs. Moreover, the lack of rule of law that has been identified may give way to anticompetitive practices from firms and more generally a climate where private sector governance may be lacking.

The region has already made progress in the area of trade regulations. Consistent with policies of trade liberalization, the region has loosened its regulations on imports and exports. For example, on average, Latin America and the Caribbean tends to fare well compared with other regions in terms of regulations and costs pertaining to trading abroad: export and import procedures are comparatively less constraining. The region is the third best, behind OECD industrial countries and East Asia and the Pacific (see figure 5.15 for exports; results are similar for imports). In this context, employer surveys reveal that customs regulations are among the least problematic issues of firms (figure 5.3). It is worth noting again that vast country differences exist. For example, the costs to export vary from about US$500 per container in Chile and Honduras to US$3,600 in Guyana (see also IDB 2003). Trade reforms in the region were associated with greater churning of labor within sectors and improvements in productivity of the exposed sectors (see chapter 1).

Starting a business is expensive. Evidence shows that individual countries within the region have excessively costly start-up regulations compared with the region's average and that the region as a whole is among the costliest of the world. Start-up costs are an obvious indicator of the

Figure 5.15 Complexity of Procedures to Export Goods

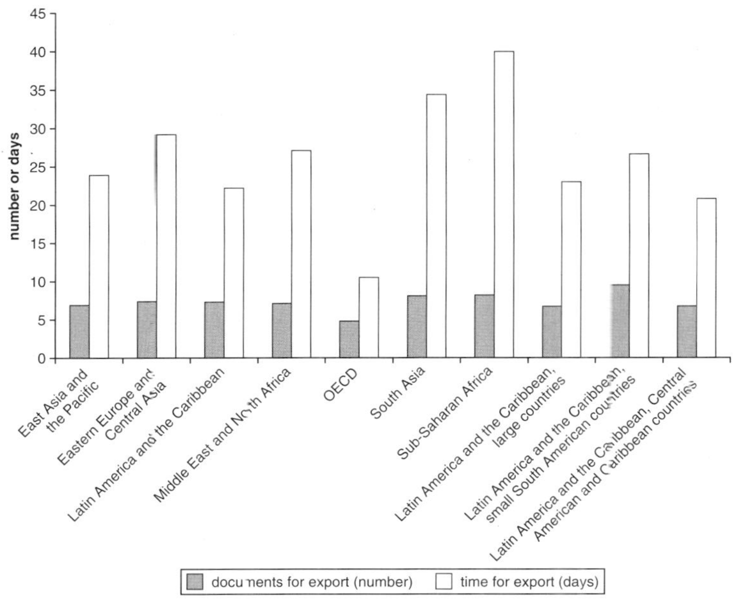

Source: World Bank Doing Business database.

difficulty of setting up a new business. Regulatory indicators show that start-up costs tend to be high compared with those in other regions. In terms of number of procedures and number of days involved, Latin America and the Caribbean on average is close to the experience of Sub-Saharan Africa; the two regions have the longest and most complicated systems (figure 5.16). Latin America and the Caribbean has among the highest monetary start-up costs, behind Sub-Saharan Africa and Middle East and North Africa. However, within Latin America and the Caribbean, a lot of variation exists. The number of procedures varies from 6 in Jamaica, Nicaragua, and St. Lucia to 17 in Brazil and Paraguay; the number of days varies from 8 in Jamaica to more than 100 in Brazil, Suriname, and the República Bolivariana de Venezuela. These differences in regulations translate into a different ranking in terms of cost as percentage of gross national income per capita: poorer countries, such as Bolivia, El Salvador, Guyana, Haiti, Nicaragua, Paraguay, and Suriname, have the highest costs, whereas richer countries, such as Argentina, Brazil, Chile, and Jamaica, have the lowest costs.

Figure 5.16 Starting a Business Is Relatively Expensive

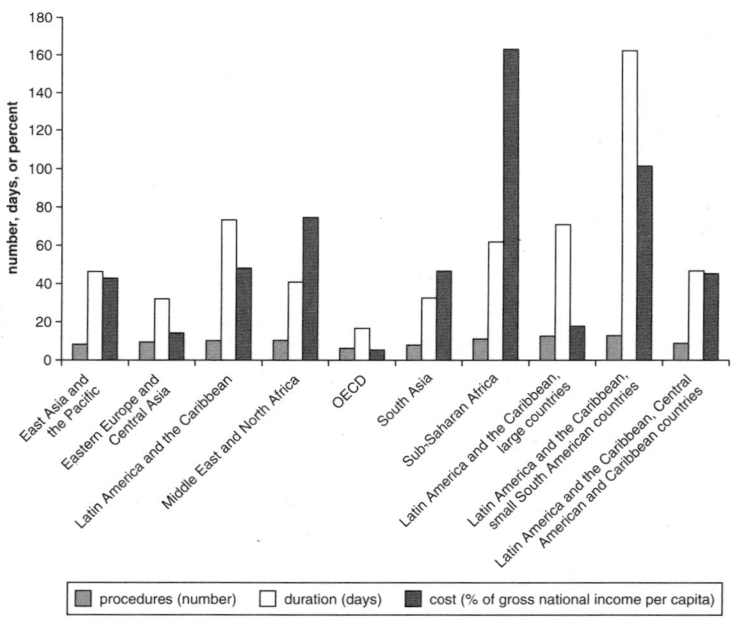

Source: World Bank Doing Business database.

Confirming these "objective" indicators, results from opinion surveys such as the 2004–05 *Global Competitiveness Report*[9] (Porter and others 2004) suggest that countries of the region tend to be ranked among those where the administrative burden for start-ups is difficult and time consuming. This finding was particularly notable in Argentina, Bolivia, Brazil, Ecuador, Honduras, Mexico, Peru, and the República Bolivariana de Venezuela. Other countries (for example, Colombia, Costa Rica, the Dominican Republic, El Salvador, Guatemala, Panama, and Paraguay), although placed among the countries with the most administrative burden, were within the range of some continental European countries, such as France, Greece, Italy, or Spain.

In the context of Latin America and the Caribbean, where law enforcement tends to be lacking, high start-up costs may be linked to the large informal sector: informal sector firms may have disincentives to join the formal sector because of the cumbersome and numerous procedures for becoming formal. Consistent with this idea, employer surveys reveal that across all countries of the world, the complexity of starting up a business is positively and significantly linked with informality.[10]

What Investment Climate Constraints Characterize "Jobless Growth" Countries?

The grouping of countries as "jobless growth" and "growthless jobs" that has been used in this book is not easily linked with specific investment climate constraints. Group averages do not reveal what elements of the investment climate explain the different outcomes experienced by countries in the two groups. This result suggests that there is no simple relationship between the investment climate and aggregate labor market outcomes. The combination of constraints that brings a particular outcome (for example, jobless growth) is specific to each country of the region.

However, multivariate regressions reveal three noteworthy results (figure 5.17). First, labor market regulations are more constraining for firms in countries that perform less well in terms of employment growth. Firms in jobless growth countries are more likely to report labor regulations as a major obstacle than are firms in growthless jobs countries or countries with positive employment and productivity growth. Second, firms in countries with relatively worse economic performance are more likely to report being constrained in terms of access and cost of financing. Firms in both jobless growth and growthless jobs countries are more likely to report access and cost of financing as a major obstacle than are countries with positive employment and productivity growth. Third, firms in jobless growth countries complain less than the two other groups of countries about corruption, the legal system, informal practices, and the instability of economic and regulatory policies. The

Figure 5.17 Economic Performance and Investment Climate Constraints

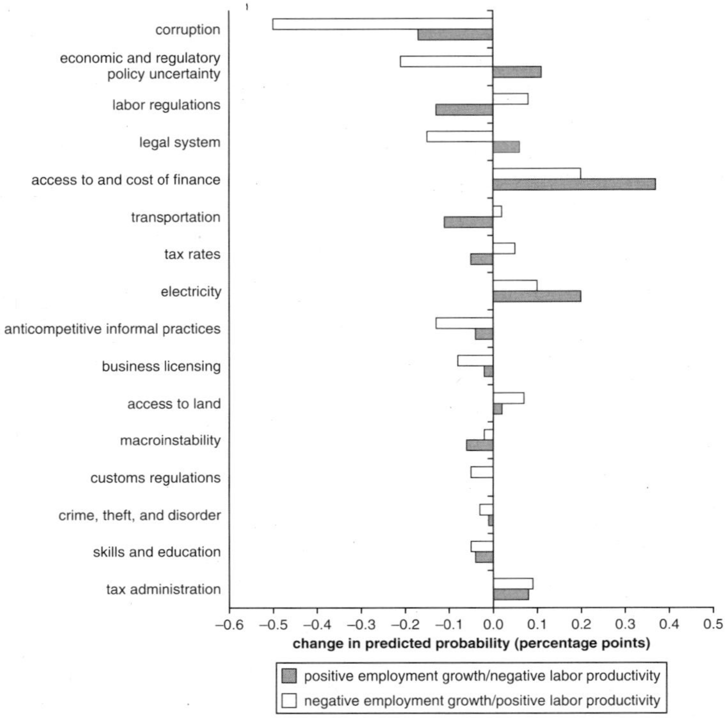

Source: Authors' calculations.

Note: Based on regression analysis controlling for age, public or private ownership, domestic or foreign ownership, size, country, industry, and average perception for all other constraints. The numbers are marginal effects of a dummy variable that groups countries in four categories, with base category countries with positive employment and productivity growth. They represent the difference in the predicted probability of reporting an element of the investment climate to be a major or very severe constraint for firms in countries belonging to a group compared with the base group. Although the third category (countries with negative employment and productivity growth) is controlled for, no inference is made for this group because it contains only Paraguay.

last result suggests that lack of employment growth is not especially associated with such constraints.

This section has helped identify the main areas of the investment climate that are a concern to firms in the region in their decision to invest and create more jobs; therefore, it may help explain the labor market performance of the region's countries. The next sections investigate the effect of investment climate conditions on different types of firms. In particular, they look at the effect of investment climate conditions on firms that are a potential source of good jobs (medium-size firms and firms in productive sectors).

Strong Constraints to Firm Expansion Curbing the Potential for Job Creation

Part II of this book has shown that small firms may have specific difficulties in expanding in the region. Moreover, the reallocation of resources has not necessarily been productivity enhancing. This section investigates the role of the investment climate in this phenomenon. The idea is that these findings are partly attributable to the distortionary effects that government policies have on the reallocation of resources and that these distortions may vary across types of firms (Hsieh and Klenow 2007; Restuccia and Rogerson 2008).

When looking across firm size, one clearly sees that the business environment constrains small and large firms differently (figure 5.18). Small firms tend to complain more about lack of access to, and cost of, financing; about economic and regulatory instability; and about corruption, crime, and anticompetitive informal practices. Instead, large firms report higher obstacles in the legal system, regulatory issues (such as customs and labor), and skill shortages.

Business Regulations

Uneven enforcement of regulations creates comparative advantages for micro and small firms and disincentives for expansion. Across the world, enforcement of regulations is lower among small firms, but particularly in Latin America and the Caribbean, where in comparative terms, government inspections concentrate more on larger firms than in other regions (figure 5.19). Similarly, management spends more time dealing with government regulations in larger firms than in smaller firms, but the difference between micro and small and medium-size firms is larger in Latin America and the Caribbean (figure 5.19), suggesting strong disincentives for micro firms to expand into small and medium-size firms.

As mentioned previously, although some regulations are helpful, excessive regulations are detrimental—particularly for the growth of larger firms. In fact, the results found by Aterido, Hallward-Dreimeier, and Pagés (2007) suggest that a large differential in regulatory enforcement between small and large firms may be detrimental to employment growth for both; it restricts access to public goods and services for micro and small enterprises and creates excessive regulatory burden for larger firms. The results also show that a consistent and predictable regulatory environment is associated with higher employment growth in small, medium-size, and large firms.

Figure 5.18 Perceptions about Investment Climate Obstacles: Medium-Size and Large Firms Relative to Small Firms

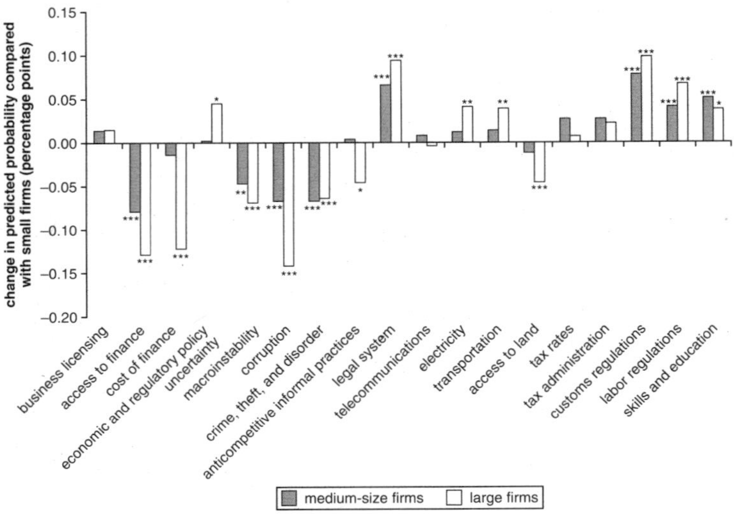

Source: World Bank Enterprise Surveys; authors' calculations (see box 5.1).

Note: Based on regression analysis controlling for age, public or private ownership, domestic or foreign ownership, size, country, industry, and average perception for all other constraints. The numbers are marginal effects of a dummy variable that groups firms by size. They represent the difference in the predicted probability of reporting an element of the investment climate to be a major or very severe constraint for firms belonging to a group compared with the base group (small firms). * Indicates the difference between formal and informal firms, significant at 10 percent. ** Indicates the difference between formal and informal firms, significant at 5 percent. *** Indicates the difference between formal and informal firms, significant at 1 percent.

Corruption

The empirical evidence suggests that corruption provides an advantage for the growth of micro firms and a disincentive for the expansion of small, medium, and large firms (Aterido, Hallward-Dreimeier, and Pagés 2007; annex table 5.B.1, rows 12–15).[11] The results mentioned in the previous section indicate that the effects of a given level of corruption on employment growth are larger in large firms. However, across the world, larger firms tend to complain more about corruption (in terms of both existence and value of bribes as a percentage of sales or government contracts) than do smaller firms, and more so in Latin America and the Caribbean than

Figure 5.19 Law Enforcement by Firm Size Relative to Micro Firms

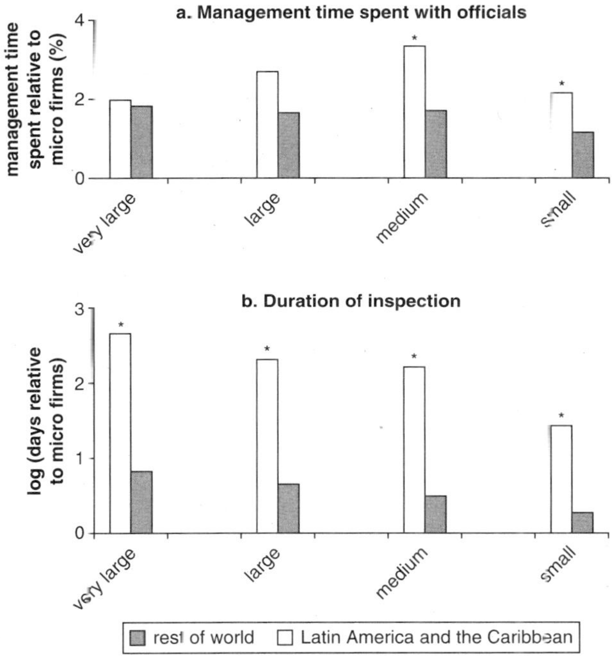

Source: Adapted from Aterido, Hallward-Dreimeier, and Pagés (2007) to include Latin American and Caribbean differences from the rest of the world.

Note: Figure is based on a regression of regulatory variables at the firm level on firm characteristics, country and sector dummies, and a Latin American and Caribbean region dummy interacted with firm characteristics. The figure reports the coefficients of firm size variables as well as the coefficients of the interactions of the Latin American and Caribbean dummies with the firm size variables. An asterisk indicates statistically significant differences between Latin America and the rest of the world.

in the rest of the world (figure 5.20). This tendency suggests that corruption may be a strong disincentive to firm growth for all firms.

High Cost and Restricted Access to Financing

Consistent with previous surveys of employers (IDB 2004), the Enterprise Surveys reveal that more smaller firms report being constrained by access and cost of financing across the developing world than do larger firms—and

Figure 5.20 Reports on Corruption and Value of Bribes, by Firm Size

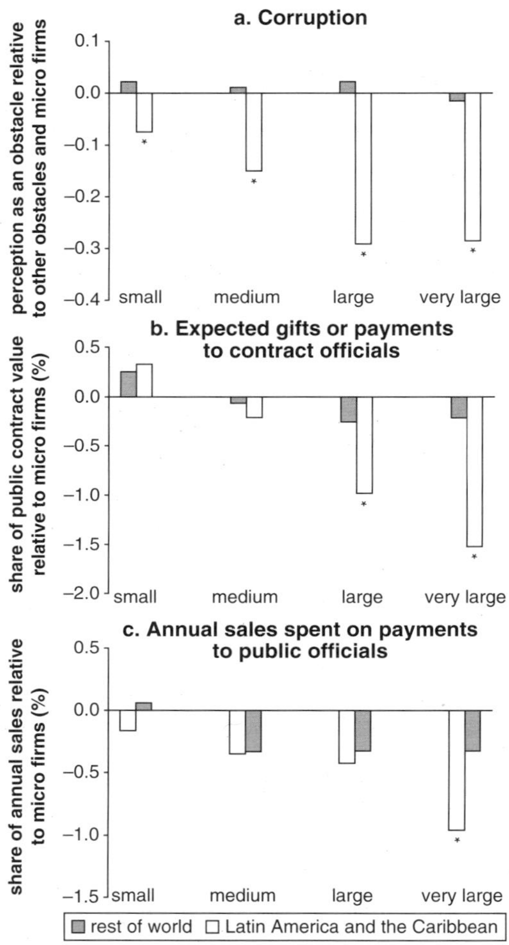

Source: Adapted from Aterido, Hallward-Dreimeier, and Pagés (2007) to include Latin American and Caribbean differences from the rest of the world.

Note: Figure is based on a regression of regulatory variables at the firm level on firm characteristics, country and sector dummies, and a Latin American and Caribbean region dummy interacted with firm characteristics. The figure reports the coefficients of firm size variables as well as the coefficients of the interactions of the Latin American and Caribbean dummies with the firm size variables. An asterisk indicates statistically significant differences between Latin America and the rest of the world.

particularly in Latin America and the Caribbean. Interestingly, however, objective indicators of access to credit do not suggest such differences (figure 5.21).

As stated in the previous section, evidence is mounting that poor access to financing dramatically limits the growth prospects of small and medium firms (Aghion, Fally, and Scarpetta 2007; Beck, Lundberg, and Majnoni 2006). This result suggests that financing is an important factor behind the observation that smaller firms' expansion appears particularly constrained in Latin America and the Caribbean, at least when the region is compared with industrial economies (see chapter 3). In particular, recent evidence indicates that even though better-performing firms may self-select into participating in formal institutions (including formal credit), doing so further improves their performance. In addition, better access to credit is associated with a greater probability that firms survive (Aghion, Fally, and Scarpetta 2007; Fajnzylber, Maloney, and Montes Rojas 2006).

Results reported by Aterido, Hallward-Dreimeier, and Pagés (2007) and annex table 5.B.1 (rows 1–4) indicate that higher financial development—measured by a higher availability of sales credit, a higher availability of overdraft facilities, or a higher share of working capital or investments financed externally—favors employment growth in all firms. In addition, this positive effect is found to be larger in smaller enterprises.

Effect of Business Climate Constraints on Employment Growth of Foreign-Owned and Exporting Firms

Foreign firms are an important source of investment. They are generally able to boost productivity growth because they come with an already developed know-how of their business area and often with external resources. A climate of worsened risk may lower their incentive to invest in the region. Similarly, firms that export are likely to be more productive and dynamic than others, given that they have to compete in the world market. The findings suggest that foreign firms are not more concerned about risks in the region than they are elsewhere in the world. In fact, domestic firms are more negatively affected by policy uncertainty than firms in the rest of the world. Furthermore, nonexporting firms in the region complain relatively more about rule of law, crime, and policy uncertainty.

The data also indicate that, other things being constant, foreign-owned firms tend to report lower incidence—and a lower value—of paid bribes than do domestically owned firms. Not surprisingly, therefore, higher levels of corruption tend to limit the expansion of domestically owned companies relative to foreign-owned ones.

Finally, financial constraints are less binding for foreign-owned and exporting firms. The expansion of credit and, in general, the development

Figure 5.21 Cost of and Access to Finance, by Firm Size

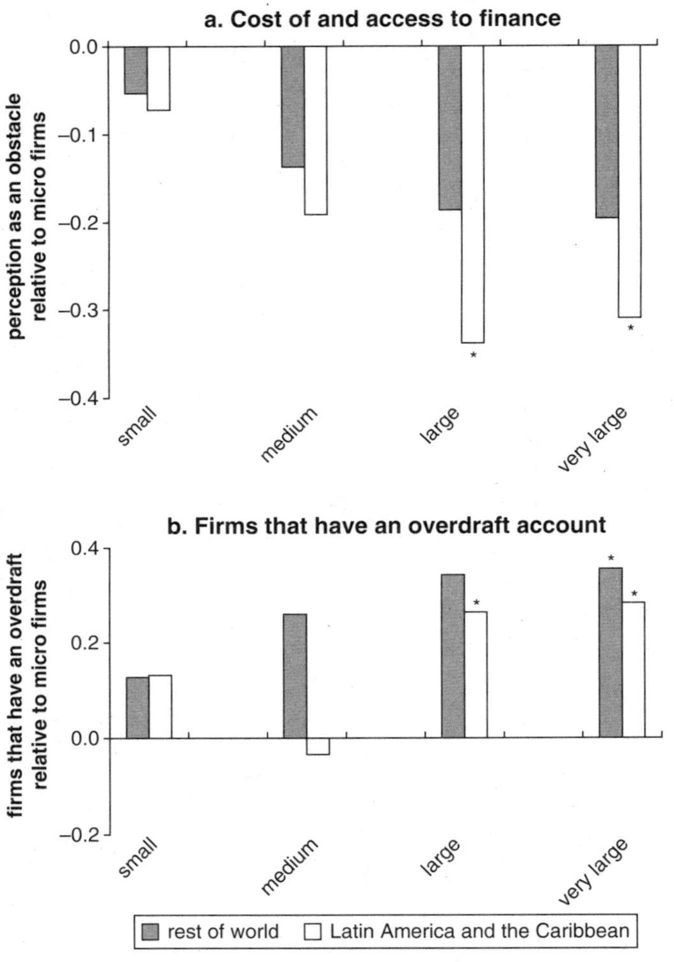

Source: Adapted from Aterido, Hallward-Dreimeier, and Pagés (2007) to include Latin American and Caribbean differences from the rest of the world.

Note: Figure is based on a regression of regulatory variables at the firm level on firm characteristics, country and sector dummies, and a Latin American and Caribbean region dummy interacted with firm characteristics. The figure reports the coefficients of firm size variables as well as the coefficients of the interactions of the Latin American and Caribbean dummies with the firm size variables. An asterisk indicates statistically significant differences between Latin America and the rest of the world.

of financial markets would therefore favor to a larger extent the growth of domestically owned and nonexporting firms.

Constraints on Informal Firms Compared with Constraints on Formal Ones

Comparisons of informal and formal micro firms reveal that informal firms also complain about the investment climate. Among the different elements of the investment climate, some, such as regulations, may be avoided by informal firms, whereas others, such as macroeconomic uncertainty or access to land, may be relevant to them. Informal firms were interviewed in Brazil and Guatemala, and these interviews bring some interesting insights, although they do not permit the results to be generalized. In a large and relatively rich country such as Brazil, informal firms are very similar to small formal firms. Interestingly, the main difference that can be identified is that they complain less about corruption (see box 5.3). This finding may reflect their ability to avoid corruption by remaining informal. In Guatemala, a comparatively smaller and poorer country, several more significant differences exist between formal and informal firms in addition to their perceptions on corruption. In particular, whereas formal firms complain more of elements such as electricity (as in Brazil), economic and regulatory uncertainty, macroinstability, and anticompetitive informal practices, informal firms report having greater issues with elements such as access to land, access to and cost of financing, and crime. These results suggest that whereas informal firms are able to diminish their exposure to government-imposed constraints, they face significant obstacles that are linked to their informal status.

Costs as the Main Obstacles for Firms in Productive Sectors

The lack of productivity-enhancing reallocation of labor in the region may be because the investment climate imposes limitations on the activities of firms that are a potential source of employment and, more generally, economic growth. Such firms include those that belong to productive or dynamic sectors, those that have innovated in the recent past (upgraded or created a new product line), those that compete on the international market, and those that are foreign owned.

No strong evidence exists that excessive risks affect disproportionately firms categorized as being in more dynamic and productive sectors (figures 5.22 and 5.23).[12] Notably, all industries seem to be affected in similar ways by economic and regulatory uncertainty and macroinstability.

Firms in more productive or dynamic sectors face limitations in terms of the available infrastructure (through constraints in transportation)

Box 5.3 Informal Firms Are Less Constrained by the Investment Climate

Brazil

Although one could expect that few informal firms report being constrained by the investment climate, employer surveys reveal that they are constrained. As could be expected, the worst constraint is cost of and access to financing. Informal firms are also concerned by macroinstability and economic and regulatory uncertainty. On average, they tend to complain slightly less than formal firms about most types of investment climate constraints except anticompetitive and informal practices, but when age, total employment, and sales performance are controlled for and when informal firms are compared with formal firms of similar sizes, the difference is significant only for electricity, macroinstability, and corruption. Most of the difference between formal and informal firms can be explained by the fact that informal firms tend to be very small (box figure 5.3.A).

Box figure 5.3.A Brazil: Share of Small Firms That Report Various Elements as Major Constraints

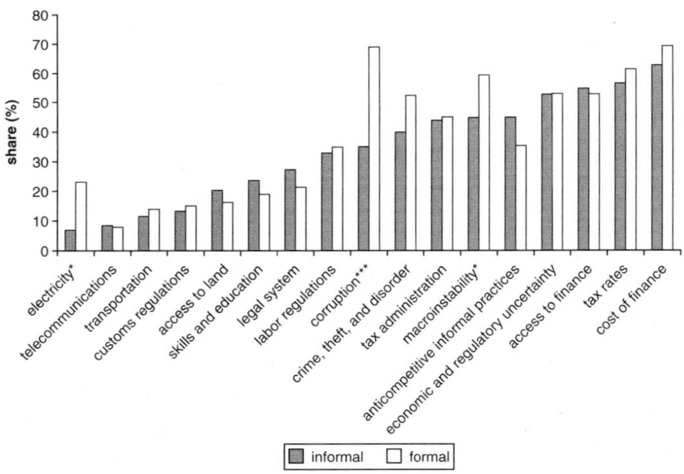

Source: World Bank Enterprise Survey for Brazil, 2003.
Note: * Indicates the difference between formal and informal firms, significant at 10 percent. ** Indicates the difference between formal and informal firms, significant at 5 percent. *** Indicates the difference between formal and informal firms, significant at 1 percent.

(continued)

Box 5.3 Informal Firms Are Less Constrained by the Investment Climate *(continued)*

Guatemala

In Guatemala, one type of firm does not systematically complain more or less than another. Interestingly, informal firms complain significantly more than formal firms about cost of and access to finance and access to land, but they also complain about economic and regulatory uncertainty. They complain less of taxes, macroeconomic instability, electricity, corruption, and anticompetitive practices.

Box figure 5.3.B Guatemala: Share of Small Firms That Report Various Elements as Major Constraints

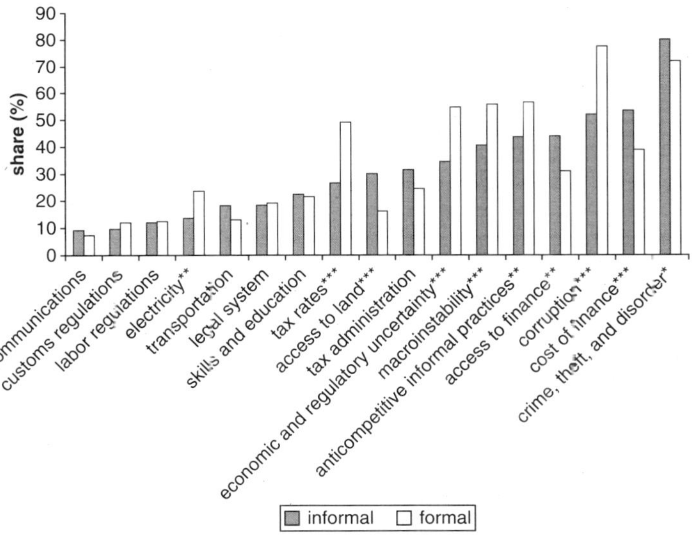

Source: World Bank Enterprise Survey for Guatemala, 2003.
Note: * Indicates the difference between formal and informal firms, significant at 10 percent. ** Indicates the difference between formal and informal firms, significant at 5 percent. *** Indicates the difference between formal and informal firms, significant at 1 percent.

Source: Authors' calculations.

Figure 5.22 Dynamic Firms Compared with Other Firms

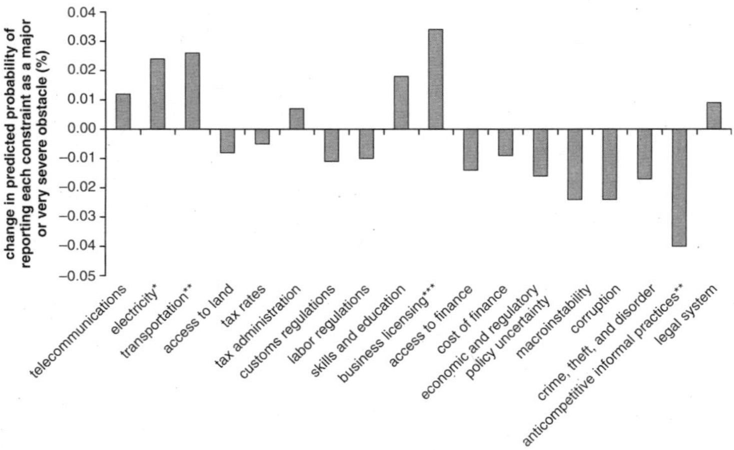

Source: World Bank Enterprise Surveys.

Note: Figure shows results from probit regressions of specifications, including the following control variables: age, size, private or public ownership, domestic or foreign ownership, exporter or nonexporter, country, innovating history, and average tendency to complain. * Indicates the difference between formal and informal firms, significant at 10 percent. ** Indicates the difference between formal and informal firms, significant at 5 percent. *** Indicates the difference between formal and informal firms, significant at 1 percent.

and in expanding their business to new areas or creating new businesses (through business licensing). Controlling for other characteristics, firms in industries that can be categorized as dynamic tend to report being more constrained than others in telecommunications, transportation, and business licensing in particular. Compared with firms in industries with low labor productivity, firms in medium-productivity industries are more constrained by customs regulations and business licensing and less constrained by electricity supply. Firms in high-productivity industries have these constraints; in addition, they are more constrained by transportation and less constrained by the skills and education among available workers and the cost of financing (figures 5.22 and 5.23).

The Relative Role of Labor Regulations

Cross-country analysis suggests that labor regulations weigh more than most other elements of the investment climate in determining the composition of employment (see annex 5.C). Given the relatively good performance

Figure 5.23 Firms in High-Productivity Sectors Compared with Firms in Low-Productivity Sectors

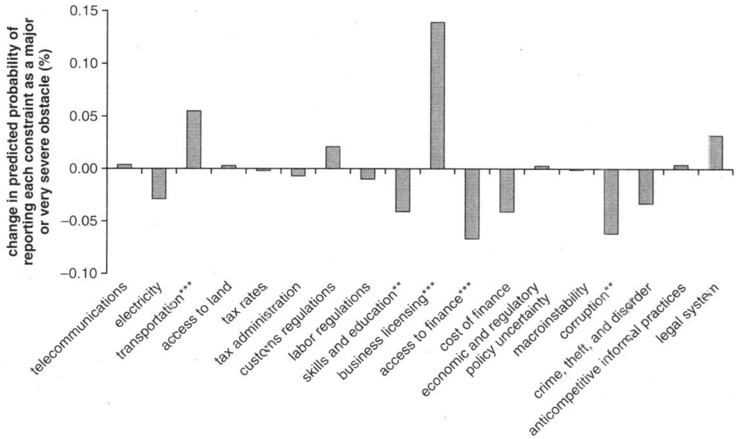

Source: World Bank Enterprise Surveys.

Note: Figure shows results from probit regressions of specifications, including the following control variables: age, size, private or public ownership, domestic or foreign ownership, exporter or nonexporter, country, innovating history, and average tendency to complain. * Indicates the difference between formal and informal firms, significant at 10 percent. ** Indicates the difference between formal and informal firms, significant at 5 percent. *** Indicates the difference between formal and informal firms, significant at 1 percent.

of employment growth in the region, this exercise examines the relationship between various components of the investment climate and the composition of employment, measured as the share of self-employed workers (data from ILO 2005). As found in other studies, the results (see annex table 5.C.2) indicate that richer countries in terms of their GDP per capita exhibit lower shares of self-employment. In terms of the business climate indicators, only hiring and firing regulations and business regulations are correlated with the share of self-employment, whereas the other components of the business climate are not. In particular, countries in which hiring and firing regulations are seen as more rigid tend to have a greater proportion of self-employed workers. Going from countries considered as the most rigid to countries considered as the least rigid (on a scale of 1–7) changes the proportion of self-employed workers by 5 percentage points. This effect is quite big given that the average proportion of self-employed workers is about 30 percent. The results also suggest that rigid business regulations tend to be associated with a lower proportion of self-employment (also a change of 5 percentage points between the least and most flexible countries). These findings do not permit any causality links to be made and should be taken with caution given the usual problems with cross-country regressions. However, in this case, hiring and firing regulations are the most important determinants.

Summing Up: Further Improvements to the Investment Climate

This chapter has shown that several investment climate constraints are important obstacles to doing business in a majority of countries: macroeconomic instability, cost of finance, corruption, and rule of law issues. At the same time, country-specific constraints exist, and no single constraint explains whether the country has jobless growth or growthless job creation.

The large and increasing population of micro and informal firms can be sourced back to the regulatory burden and lack of rule of law. Evidence for the world suggests that burdensome regulations (among which are labor regulations), combined with low enforcement and corruption, create a climate that is "favorable" in relative terms to micro firms. These findings, combined with evidence that the region shows particular difficulties in these three areas of the investment climate, partly explain the large population of smaller firms and informal firms.

These findings are important because the distortionary effect of regulations can have potentially large aggregate effects on total factor productivity and economic growth. Three broad areas of intervention can be outlined:

- *Macroeconomic instability* has been identified across Latin America and the Caribbean as among the worst obstacles to doing business. To some extent, such an issue is ongoing for most countries of the region, and maintaining sound macroeconomic policies constitutes the principal course of action.
- *Government effectiveness, rule of law, and regulatory burden* are grouped together because they are complementary. A high regulatory burden, combined with low enforcement, has led to strong distortions of the labor market and is associated with large informal sectors. These elements require an approach with two interrelated parts: (a) rationalizing regulations that are overly restrictive, especially in countries that differ strongly from the region's average, and (b) improving government effectiveness by enhancing the capacity to enforce regulations.
- *Cost of and access to finance, tax rates, and administration* for some countries reflect current policy choices that present challenges to the small and domestic firms that are most vulnerable to them and potentially prevent those firms from expanding.

Detailing specific measures in these areas is beyond the scope of this book, depending as it does on an individual country's circumstances. Some of these issues extend to labor market policies and institutions—in particular, issues of improving enforcement, choosing the appropriate regulations, and improving the effectiveness of labor market policies. These issues are reviewed in the following chapters.

Annex 5.A: Results from Estimations of Base Model

Table 5.A.1 presents the results of the base model of the determinants of investment climate complaints as described in box 5.1.

Annex Table 5.A.1 Estimations of Base Model of the Determinants of Investment Climate Complaints

	Telecommu-nications	*Electricity*	*Transport-ation*	*Access to land*	*Tax rates*	*Tax admini-stration*	*Customs regulation*	*Labor regulation*	*Skills and education*
Age 5 to 15	–0.004 (0.012)	–0.013 (0.020)	–0.034 (0.014)**	–0.022 (0.014)	0.031 (0.029)	0.079 (0.026)***	0.001 (0.020)	0.060 (0.023)***	0.019 (0.022)
Age 16+	–0.022 (0.013)*	–0.024 (0.020)	–0.054 (0.015)***	–0.050 (0.015)***	0.038 (0.029)	0.062 (0.025)**	–0.004 (0.020)	0.060 (0.023)***	0.007 (0.022)
Partly owned by government	–0.033 (0.035)	–0.028 (0.071)	0.008 (0.056)	0.027 (0.064)	0.053 (0.092)	–0.001 (0.087)	–0.028 (0.059)	–0.135 (0.050)***	0.006 (0.080)
Domestic	–0.052 (0.017)***	–0.044 (0.023)*	–0.051 (0.019)***	0.026 (0.016)	0.003 (0.030)	–0.038 (0.028)	–0.063 (0.022)***	–0.006 (0.023)	0.051 (0.022)**
Medium-size	0.008 (0.009)	0.012 (0.015)	0.014 (0.011)	–0.012 (0.010)	0.027 (0.020)	0.027 (0.018)	0.078 (0.015)***	0.041 (0.016)***	0.051 (0.016)***
Large	–0.004 (0.012)	0.041 (0.020)**	0.039 (0.016)**	–0.046 (0.012)***	0.007 (0.027)	0.022 (0.024)	0.098 (0.022)***	0.067 (0.022)***	0.038 (0.021)*
Nonexporter	–0.007 (0.011)	–0.011 (0.016)	–0.051 (0.013)***	0.022 (0.012)*	0.067 (0.023)***	0.004 (0.020)	–0.071 (0.016)***	–0.035 (0.018)*	0.003 (0.017)
Upgraded or created new product line	–0.013 (0.012)	–0.032 (0.019)*	–0.018 (0.015)	–0.009 (0.015)	0.025 (0.025)	0.056 (0.022)**	0.058 (0.017)***	0.004 (0.020)	–0.028 (0.020)
Proportion of other constraints cited as major issue	0.269 (0.018)***	0.623 (0.030)***	0.430 (0.022)***	0.369 (0.021)***	1.260 (0.045)***	1.013 (0.037)***	0.608 (0.029)***	0.830 (0.033)***	0.713 (0.032)***
Number of observations	5,294	5,297	5,297	5,274	5,281	5,268	4,721	5,288	5,294

Source: Authors' calculations.

Note: * = significant at the 10 percent level; ** = significant at the 5 percent level; *** = significant at the 1 percent level. Statistically significant results are highlighted in bold. Standard errors are in parentheses. Industry and country are controlled for. Base categories are as follows: less than 5 years old, fully private, foreign, small, exporter, and did not innovate.

Business licensing	*Access to finance*	*Cost of finance*	*Economic and regulatory policy uncertainty*	*Macro-instability*	*Corruption*	*Crime, theft, and disorder*	*Anticom-petitive informal practices*	*Legal system*
–0.011	–0.055	0.003	0.023	0.046	–0.010	–0.017	0.032	–0.018
(0.017)	(0.026)**	(0.028)	(0.029)	(0.027)*	(0.029)	(0.027)	(0.026)	(0.020)
–0.020	–0.083	–0.013	0.051	0.067	0.003	0.010	0.083	–0.005
(0.017)	(0.026)***	(0.028)	(0.029)*	(0.027)**	(0.029)	(0.027)	(0.026)***	(0.020)
0.026	–0.060	–0.073	–0.029	–0.017	–0.020	–0.130	0.059	–0.158
(0.068)	(0.095)	(0.100)	(0.101)	(0.090)	(0.099)	(0.093)	(0.090)	(0.031)***
–0.020	0.201	0.163	0.045	0.020	–0.025	0.042	0.047	–0.015
(0.020)	(0.025)***	(0.030)***	(0.031)	(0.029)	(0.031)	(0.029)	(0.027)*	(0.023)
0.014	–0.079	–0.014	0.002	–0.047	–0.067	–0.067	0.004	0.066
(0.013)	(0.018)***	(0.020)	(0.020)	(0.019)**	(0.020)***	(0.019)***	(0.018)	(0.015)***
0.015	–0.129	–0.122	0.045	–0.069	–0.142	–0.064	–0.046	0.094
(0.017)	(0.023)***	(0.027)***	(0.027)*	(0.026)***	(0.026)***	(0.025)***	(0.024)*	(0.022)***
0.002	–0.006	0.018	0.002	–0.033	0.021	0.007	0.092	–0.031
(0.014)	(0.021)	(0.022)	(0.023)	(0.021)	(0.023)	(0.021)	(0.020)***	(0.017)*
0.004	0.030	0.046	0.009	0.021	0.031	0.062	0.077	0.011
(0.016)	(0.023)	(0.025)*	(0.027)	(0.024)	(0.026)	(0.024)***	(0.023)***	(0.019)
0.663	1.039	1.215	1.538	1.239	1.551	1.292	1.090	0.992
(0.026)***	(0.041)***	(0.045)***	(0.048)***	(0.043)***	(0.049)***	(0.043)***	(0.041)***	(0.032)***
5,288	5,202	5,248	5,288	5,287	5,286	5,290	5,278	5,259

Annex 5.B: Investment Climate Constraints and Employment Growth

The results are based on Aterido, Hallward-Dreimeier, and Pagés (2007), a paper that explores the effects of the business environment on employment growth and that was prepared as background work for this report. The study is primarily based on the World Bank Enterprise Surveys, a newly available collection of firm-level data sets for a large number of developing countries and for five high-income countries. Questionnaires are administered within a framework of common guidelines in the design and implementation.[13] The data include 69,305 firms from 107 countries in six different regions, surveyed during the period from 2000 to 2006. Several countries have now conducted a second or third survey.[14] The median sample size is 350 firms, with several large countries having substantially larger samples. Brazil, China, India, Turkey, and Vietnam have samples exceeding 1,500.

The study focuses on the employment growth of permanent workers as the outcome variable of interest. The possible endogeneity of the reported business climate indicators is accounted by (a) measuring the business climate with objective rather than subjective indicators and (b) averaging the reported measures by firm location, industry, and size cells. The specification is as follows:

$$\begin{aligned} Empg_{ijs} = {} & \beta_0 small_{ijs} + \beta_1 medium_{ijs} + \beta_2 large_{ijs} + \beta_3 obstacle_{ks} \\ & + \beta_4 small_{ijs} * obstacle_{ks} + \beta_5 medium_{ijc} * obstacle_{ks} \\ & + \beta_6 large_{ks} * obstacle_{ks} + \beta_7 foreign_{ijs} + \beta_8 foreign_{ijs} * obstacle_{ks} \\ & + \beta_9 exporter_{ijs} + \beta_{10} exporter_{ijs} * obstacle_{ks} + \beta_{11} mature_{ijs} \\ & + \beta_{12} verymature_{ijs} + \beta_{13} government_{ijs} + \beta_{14} small\_noncapital_{ijs} \\ & + \beta_{15} ControlEG_{ijs} + \lambda_j + \lambda_s + \varepsilon_{ijc} \end{aligned} \qquad (5.B.1)$$

In equation 5.B.1, *small* refers to firms with between 11 and 50 employees, *medium* refers to firms with between 51 and 200 employees, and *large* refers to firms with more than 200 employees. The omitted category is microenterprises, which have between 1 and 10 employees. Age of the firm is specified in three categories: *young* is from 1 to 5 years old, *mature* is between 5 and 15 years old, and *very mature* is above 15 years old. *Obstacle* refers to an investment climate constraint, such as poor infrastructure or low enforcement of property rights. *Foreign* takes the value of 1 in firms with more than 10 percent participation of foreign capital, and *exporter* identifies firms that export more than 10 percent of their sales. *Government* identifies firms with participation of more than 10 percent from the government, and *small_noncapital* identifies firms that either are in small cities (fewer than 1 million habitants) or are not in a capital city.

The specification also controls for country and industry effects and for differences in the computation of employment growth by identifying firms for which information only for the previous year and three years ago is available, firms with information only for the previous year and two years ago, and firms with data only for the past two consecutive years. Different obstacles are interacted with selected relevant firm characteristics to assess differences in the effect of business climate indicators across different types of firms.

The results are presented in annex table 5.B.1. These results are robust to including more than one investment climate obstacle at once in the regression (plus their interactions with size and firm characteristics), to excluding one region at a time, or to running the regression separately for countries in different level of development.

Annex Table 5.B.1 Effect of Investment Climate on Employment Growth

IC variable/right-hand-side term	*IC*	*Small*IC*	*Medium*IC*	*Large*IC*	*Constant*	*Number of observations*	*R-squared*
Finance							
1 overdraft (yes/no)	0.932***	–0.111**	–0.082	–0.020	0.163		
	(0.062)	(0.046)	(0.061)	(0.078)	(0.103)	38,870	0.18
2 sh-sales-cr (%)	0.005***	–0.001	–0.002***	–0.003***	0.343***		
	(0.001)	(0.000)	(0.001)	(0.001)	(0.053)	57,252	0.12
3 sh-work.capital-fin (%)	0.013***	–0.003***	–0.005***	–0.007***	0.480***		
	(0.001)	(0.001)	(0.001)	(0.001)	(0.045)	55,895	0.13
4 sh-invest-fin (%)	0.006***	–0.000	–0.001	–0.002**	0.501***		
	(0.001)	(0.001)	(0.001)	(0.001)	(0.047)	56,065	0.12
Regulations							
5 days-license (log)	0.027*	–0.018	–0.025	–0.023	0.359***		
	(0.016)	(0.013)	(0.016)	(0.016)	(0.097)	32,049	0.13
6 management time (%)	0.013***	–0.006***	–0.006***	–0.005***	0.445***		
	(0.002)	(0.002)	(0.002)	(0.002)	(0.057)	55,923	0.12
7 days-inspections (log)	0.238***	–0.023	–0.049**	–0.064***	–0.221**		
	(0.020)	(0.015)	(0.019)	(0.024)	(0.109)	49,007	0.14

(continued)

Annex Table 5.B.1 Effect of Investment Climate on Employment Growth *(continued)*

IC variable/right-hand-side term	*IC*	*Small*IC*	*Medium*IC*	*Large*IC*	*Constant*	*Number of observations*	*R-squared*
8 days-labor-inspections (log)	0.237***	–0.101***	–0.104**	–0.136***	0.092		
	(0.034)	(0.032)	(0.041)	(0.044)	(0.098)	40,879	0.12
9 days-exports (log)	0.023**	–0.024**	–0.029**	–0.034**	0.553***		
	(0.011)	(0.010)	(0.014)	(0.015)	(0.051)	57,628	0.11
10 days imports (log)	0.017	–0.029***	–0.023	–0.018	0.552***		
	(0.011)	(0.011)	(0.014)	(0.015)	(0.051)	58,283	0.11
11 consistency of regulations	0.043***	0.025	–0.007	–0.006	0.457***		
	(0.015)	(0.015)	(0.020)	(0.020)	(0.062)	52,208	0.11
Corruption							
12 bribe (yes/no)	0.143***	–0.133***	–0.256***	–0.281***	0.533***		
	(0.044)	(0.045)	(0.057)	(0.068)	(0.061)	50,708	0.12
13 bribe (%)	–0.005	–0.011***	–0.019***	–0.019***	0.613***		
	(0.003)	(0.003)	(0.005)	(0.006)	(0.053)	50,708	0.12
14 gift to govmt (yes/no)	0.008	–0.050	0.135**	0.113*	0.573***		
	(0.041)	(0.041)	(0.054)	(0.066)	(0.055)	53,545	0.11

(continued)

Annex Table 5.B.1 Effect of Investment Climate on Employment Growth *(continued)*

IC variable/right-hand-side term	*IC*	*Small*IC*	*Medium*IC*	*Large*IC*	*Constant*	*Number of observations*	*R-squared*
15 gift (% government contract)	0.001	–0.010***	–0.017***	–0.015***	0.572***		
	(0.003)	(0.003)	(0.004)	(0.005)	(0.056)	51,369	0.11
Infrastructure							
16 days-no power (log)	0.017**	–0.008	–0.023***	–0.017**	0.519***		
	(0.009)	(0.007)	(0.008)	(0.008)	(0.055)	53,655	0.11
17 loss power (% sales)	–0.008***	–0.002	–0.005*	–0.007*	0.506***		
	(0.002)	(0.002)	(0.003)	(0.004)	(0.089)	49,482	0.11
18 days no water (log)	–0.007	–0.009	–0.018**	–0.014*	0.597***		
	(0.006)	(0.006)	(0.008)	(0.008)	(0.052)	53,993	0.11

Source: Authors' calculations.

Note: * = significant at the 10 percent level; ** = significant at the 5 percent level; *** = significant at the 1 percent level. IC variable-average country-size-industry3-city. Each row number presents the results of a regression of employment growth on one investment climate (IC) variable. Only selected coefficients are presented. Robust standard errors are in parentheses, clustered by country-size-industry3-city. Omitted variables: micro1–10, young1–5, capital&city≥1mn, textiles, Albania 2002.

Annex 5.C: Hiring and Firing Regulations and Labor Market Outcomes

Cross-country estimates of the effect of the investment climate on aggregate labor market performance have found that more rigid regulations are associated with lower labor force participation and higher unemployment (for example, Botero and others 2004; Heckman and Pagés 2004). Cross-country studies are of limited use because institutions vary little over time, and issues of endogeneity and omitted variables abound (Micco and Pagés 2006). Many institutions have been collecting data on the investment climate for several years, and the indicators provided by the Fraser Institute span several years (with gaps) dating back to 1990 and up to the present (investment climate variables are explained further in annex 5.D). The indicators show some variation (annex table 5.C.1) and can be used to document the partial correlation of several of the most important elements of the investment climate with labor market outcomes.

Given the experience of relatively good employment growth in Latin America and the Caribbean, it is more interesting to look at the correlations between investment climate and the composition of employment. In particular, longitudinal data can be obtained for the share of self-employed workers.

Results suggest that hiring and firing regulations as reported in the *Global Competitiveness Reports* are significantly correlated with self-employment (annex table 5.C.2 and annex figure 5.C.1). In particular, countries in which hiring and firing regulations are seen as more rigid tend to have a greater proportion of self-employed. Going from countries considered the most rigid to those considered the least rigid (scale of 1–7) changes the proportion of self-employed workers by 5 percentage points. This effect is quite big given that the average proportion of self-employed workers is about 30 percent. Rigid business regulations tend to be associated with lower proportions of self-employment (also a change of 5 percentage points between the least and most flexible country).

Such findings do not permit any links of causality to be made. However, it is interesting to note that hiring and firing regulation considerations are the most important determinants in both cases.

Annex Table 5.C.1 Descriptive Statistics

	Number of observations	*Mean*	*Standard deviation*	*Coefficient of variation*	*Minimum*	*Maximum*
Share of self-employed workers	59	0.30	0.07	0.25	0.19	0.43
Share of informal sector employment	57	0.49	0.08	0.16	0.36	0.67
GDP per capita (US$)	59	6,339.61	2,389.35	0.38	2,388.00	12,174.00
Investment climate indexes						
Cost of finance	59	1.09	0.27	0.24	0.68	1.71
Trade	59	6.91	0.77	0.11	4.46	8.57
Business regulations	59	4.85	1.08	0.22	1.80	7.80
Hiring and firing	59	3.95	1.36	0.34	1.00	7.20
Legal environment	59	4.15	1.37	0.33	1.43	6.87
Credit availability	59	7.19	0.94	0.13	4.70	8.73

Source: Authors' calculations based on Fraser Institute indicators and SEDLAC (see chapter 1).

Note: Legal environment: index with values from 0 to 10, where 10 represents stronger legal independence and respect of property rights. Freedom to trade internationally: index with values from 0 to 10, where 10 represents greater freedom. Credit market regulations: index with values from 0 to 10, where 10 represents more flexible regulations. Business regulations: index with values from 0 to 10, where 10 represents greater economic freedom to do business. Hiring and firing practices: index, where higher values mean greater flexibility. See annex 5.D for details.

Annex Table 5.C.2 Determinants of Self-Employment

	Share of self-employed worker
Ln(GDP per capita)	–0.752
	(0.295)**
Cost of finance	0.073
	(0.064)
Trade	0.020
	(0.025)
Business regulation	0.039
	(0.013)**
Hiring and firing	–0.041
	(0.013)***
Legal	0.025
	(0.023)
Credit availability	0.004
	(0.025)
Constant	5.257
	(2.511)**
Number of observations	59
Number of countries	18
R-squared	0.45

Source: Authors' calculations.

Note: * = significant at the 10 percent level; ** = significant at the 5 percent level; *** = significant at the 1 percent level. Standard errors are in parentheses. A fixed effects model was used.

Annex Figure 5.C.1 Share of Self-Employment in Different Contexts of Business and Labor Regulations

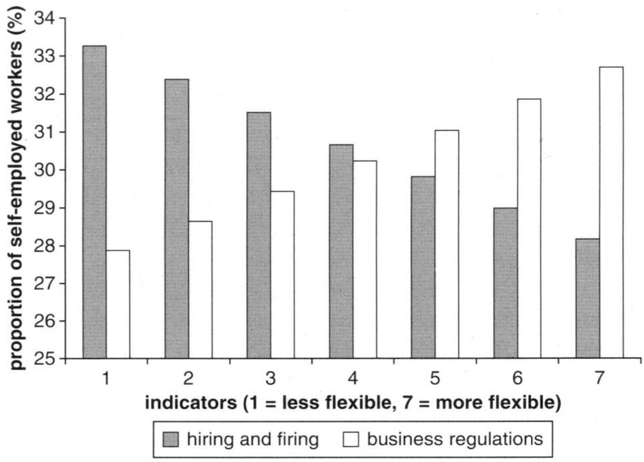

Source: Authors' calculations based on Fraser Institute indicators and SEDLAC (see chapter 1).

Annex 5.D: Explanatory Notes and Data Sources for Investment Climate Indexes

Legal Structure and Security of Property Rights

This index includes five components: judicial independence, impartial courts, protection of intellectual property, military interference in rule of law and the political process, and integrity of the legal system. Each component has been rescaled to be between 0 and 10 (or 7 in some cases), where higher values indicate stronger legal independence and respect of the property rights.

Source: Gwartney and Lawson 2005.

Freedom to Trade Internationally

This index includes five components: (a) taxes on international trade (including revenues from trade taxes, mean tariff rate, and standard deviation of tariff rates); (b) regulatory trade barriers (including nontariff trade barriers and compliance costs of importing and exporting); (c) size of the trade sector relative to expected size; (d) difference between official exchange rate and black market rate; and (e) international capital market controls (including foreign ownership and investment restrictions and capital controls). Each component has been rescaled to be between 0 and 10 (or 7 in some cases), where higher ratings indicate a greater freedom to trade.

Source: Gwartney and Lawson 2005.

Credit Market Regulations

This index includes five components: ownership of banks, competition, extension of credit, avoidance of interest rate controls and regulations that lead to negative real interest rates, and interest rate controls. Each component has been rescaled to be between 0 and 10 (or 7 in some cases), where higher values represent more flexible regulations.

Source: Gwartney and Lawson 2005.

Business Regulations

This index includes five components: price controls, administrative conditions and new businesses, time with government bureaucracy, starting of a new business, and irregular payments. Each component has been rescaled to be between 0 and 10 (or 7 in some cases), where higher ratings indicate greater economic freedom for doing business.

Source: Gwartney and Lawson 2005.

Hiring and Firing Practices

Hiring and firing practices of companies are determined by private contract. Low ratings mean higher impediments by regulations.

Sources: López-Claros, Porter, and Schwab 2005; Porter and Schwab 2008; Porter, Schwab, and López-Claros 2006; Porter and others 2004.

Cost of Finance

The cost of finance is a summary of the following variables: domestic credit provided by banking sector (percentage of GDP), interest rate spread (lending rate minus deposit rate), real interest rate (percent), and domestic credit to the private sector (percentage of GDP). The higher the index is, the higher the cost of finance will be.

Source: World Bank World Development Indicators database.

Notes

1. Institutions, policies, and regulations that affect firm entry, survival, and growth are referred to in this section as components of the investment climate. The *investment climate* is the set of location-specific factors shaping the opportunities and incentives facing firms to invest productively, create jobs, and expand. Government policies and behaviors exert a strong influence through their effect on costs, risks, and barriers to competition. See World Bank (2004e) for more details.

2. The Enterprise Surveys have been implemented in 11 Latin American countries (Bolivia, Brazil, Chile, Costa Rica, Ecuador, El Salvador, Guatemala, Guyana, Honduras, Nicaragua, and Peru). The sample sizes vary between 163 firms in Guyana and more than 1,600 firms for Brazil. The sample comprises 42 percent small firms (20 employees or fewer), 38 percent medium-size firms (21–100 employees), and 20 percent large firms (more than 100 employees). See World Bank (2001) for Bolivia, World Bank (2005a) for Brazil, World Bank (2005c) for Ecuador, World Bank (2005d) for El Salvador, World Bank (2004b) for Guatemala; World Bank (2004c) for Honduras, and World Bank (2004d) for Peru.

3. These indicators are part of the following governance indicators: voice and accountability, political stability, government effectiveness, regulatory quality, rule of law, and control of corruption. Higher numbers indicate better governance. They are calculated by World Bank staff members (Kaufmann, Kraay, and Mastruzzi 2005).

4. Intangible assets are blueprints, patents, copyrights, client lists, and trademarks.

5. *Corruption* is defined as illegal payments made by firms to influence governments' policies, laws, or regulations.

6. The latest *Global Competitiveness Report* (Porter and Schwab 2008) does not contain the updated relevant indicator. An indicator about the ethical behavior of firms (in their interactions with public officials, politicians, and other enterprises) shows similar results. The best Latin American countries are Barbados (19th out of 134 countries) and Chile (23rd); the worst are Bolivia (132nd) and Paraguay (134th). Ecuador, Uruguay, and República Bolivariana de Venezuela are respectively ranked 117th, 31st, and 127th.

7. Countries of the region comprise Argentina, Bolivia, Brazil, Chile, Colombia, Costa Rica, the Dominican Republic, Ecuador, El Salvador, Guatemala, Honduras, Jamaica, Mexico, Nicaragua, Paraguay, Peru, Trinidad and Tobago, and Uruguay. Comparator economies are Bahrain; Cyprus; the Arab Republic of Egypt; Greece; Hong Kong, China; the Republic of Korea; Malaysia; Malta; Mauritius; Morocco; Portugal; Singapore; Spain; Thailand; Tunisia; and Turkey.

8. The taxes included can be divided into five categories: profit or corporate income taxes, social security contributions and other labor taxes paid by the employer, property taxes, turnover taxes, and other small taxes (such as municipal fees and vehicle and fuel taxes).

9. This indicator has since been dropped from the *Global Competitiveness Report*, which now uses the Doing Business indicators.

10. Start-up costs are from the World Bank's Doing Business database. In this context, *informality* is defined through the responses from employers to the following question: "What percentage of sales would you estimate the typical establishment in your area of activity reports for tax purposes?" A lower proportion means greater informality.

11. See box 5.1 for description of the methodology of Aterido, Hallward-Dreimeier, and Pagés (2007).

12. The classification takes the average over the 1990s of the sectoral value added growth rate of the Group of Seven countries. The sectors are defined as "dynamic" if their growth rate was equal to or higher than the average growth rate across sectors and "less dynamic" if it was below.

13. See http://www.enterprisesurveys.org/.

14. Although efforts are shifting to building a panel data set, most repeat surveys have been additional cross-sections. Approximately 2,000 firms enter twice in the data set.

References

Aghion, P., T. Fally, and S. Scarpetta. 2007. "Credit Constraints as a Barrier to the Entry and Post-entry Growth of Firms." *Economic Policy* 22 (52): 731–79.

Aterido, R., M. Hallward-Dreimeier, and C. Pagés. 2007. "Investment Climate and Employment Growth: The Impact of Access to Finance, Corruption, and Regulations across Firms." IZA Discussion Paper 3138, Institute for the Study of Labor, Bonn, Germany.

Bartelsman, E. J., J. Haltiwanger, and S. Scarpetta. 2004. "Microeconomic Evidence of Creative Destruction in Industrial and Developing Countries." IZA Discussion Paper 1374, Institute for the Study of Labor, Bonn, Germany.

Beck, T., M. Lundberg, and G. Majnoni. 2006. "Financial Intermediary Development and Growth Volatility: Do Intermediaries Dampen or Magnify Shocks?" *Journal of International Money and Finance* 25 (7): 1146–67.

Bernanke, B., and M. Gertler. 1990. "Financial Fragility and Economic Performance." *Quarterly Journal of Economics* 105 (1): 87–114.

Botero, J., S. Djankov, R. La Porta, F. López-de-Silanes, and A. Shleifer. 2004. "The Regulation of Labor." *Quarterly Journal of Economics* 199 (4): 1339–82.

Caballero, R. J., and A. Krishnamurthy. 2001. "International Liquidity Illusion: On the Risks of Sterilization." NBER Working Paper 8141, National Bureau of Economic Research, Cambridge, MA.

Cárdenas, M., and C. Gutiérrez. 1997. "Impacto de las reformas estructurales sobre la eficiencia y la equidad." In *Empleo y distribución del ingreso en América Latina ¿Hemos avanzado?*, ed. M. Cárdenas. Bogotá: Fedesarollo-TM Editores.

Claessens, S., and L. Laeven. 2003. "Financial Development, Property Rights, and Growth." *Journal of Finance* 58 (6): 2401–35.

Demirgüç-Kunt, A., and R. Levine. 2001. "Bank-Based and Market-Based Financial Systems: Cross-Country Comparisons." In Financial Structure and Economic Growth: A Cross-Country Comparison of Banks, Markets, and Development, ed. A. Demirgüç-Kunt and R. Levine, 81–140. Cambridge, MA: MIT Press.

Fajnzylber, P., W. Maloney, and G. Montes Rojas. 2006. "Releasing Constraints to Growth or Pushing on a String? The Impact of Credit, Training, Business Associations, and Taxes on the Performance of Mexican Micro-firms." Policy Research Working Paper 3807, World Bank, Washington, DC.

Furman, J., M. Porter, and S. Stern. 2002. "The Determinants of National Innovative Capacity." *Research Policy* 31 (6): 899–933.

Gwartney, J. D., and R. Lawson. 2005. *Economic Freedom of the World: 2005 Annual Report*. Vancouver: Fraser Institute.

Heckman, J., and C. Pagés. 2004. "Introduction." In *Law and Employment: Lessons from Latin America and the Caribbean*, ed. J. Heckman and C. Pagés, 1–108. Chicago: University of Chicago Press.

Hsieh, C.-T., and P. Klenow. 2007. "Misallocation and Manufacturing TFP in China and India." NBER Working Paper 13290, National Bureau of Economic Research, Cambridge, MA.

IDB (Inter-American Development Bank). 2003. *Good Jobs Wanted: Labor Markets in Latin America—2004 Report on Economic and Social Progress in Latin America*. Washington, DC: IDB.

———. 2004. *Unlocking Credit: The Quest for Deep and Stable Bank Lending—2005 Report on Economic and Social Progress in Latin America*. Washington, DC: IDB.

ILO (International Labour Office). 2005. *2005 Labour Overview: Latin America and the Caribbean*. Lima: ILO.

Kaufmann, D., A. Kraay, and M. Mastruzzi. 2005. "Governance Matters IV: Governance Indicators for 1996–2004." Policy Research Working Paper 3630, World Bank, Washington, DC.

López-Claros, A., M. E. Porter, and K. Schwab, eds. 2005. *The Global Competitiveness Report 2005–2006*. Basingstoke, U.K.: Palgrave Macmillan.

Micco, A., and C. Pagés. 2006. "The Economic Effects of Employment Protection Laws." IZA Discussion Paper 2433, Institute for the Study of Labor, Bonn, Germany.

OECD (Organisation for Economic Co-operation and Development). 2006. *The SME Financing Gap*. Paris: OECD.

Porter, M. E., and K. Schwab, eds. 2008. *The Global Competitiveness Report 2008–2009*. New York: Palgrave Macmillan

Porter, M. E., K. Schwab, and A. López-Claros, eds. 2006. *The Global Competitiveness Report 2006–2007*. New York: Palgrave Macmillan

Porter, M. E., K. Schwab, X. Sala-i-Martin, and A. López-Claros, eds. 2004. *The Global Competitiveness Report 2004–2005*. Basingstoke, U.K.: Palgrave Macmillan.

Rajan, R., and L. Zingales. 1998. "Financial Dependence and Growth." *American Economic Review* 88 (3): 559–86.

Restuccia, D., and R. Rogerson. 2008. "Policy Distortions and Aggregate Productivity with Heterogeneous Plants." *Review of Economic Dynamics* 11 (4): 707–20.

Stein, J. C. 2003. "Agency, Information, and Corporate Investment." In *Handbook of Economics and Finance*, ed. G. Constantinides, M. Harris, and R. Stulz, 109–63. Amsterdam: North-Holland.

World Bank. 2001. *Bolivia: Microeconomic Constraints and Opportunities for Higher Growth*. Washington, DC: World Bank.

———. 2003. *Doing Business in 2004: Understanding Regulation*. Washington, DC: World Bank

———. 2004a. *Doing Business in 2005: Removing Obstacles to Growth*. Washington, DC: World Bank.

———. 2004b. *Guatemala: Investment Climate Assessment—Evidence from the Manufacturing Sector*. Washington, DC: World Bank.

———. 2004c. *Honduras: Investment Climate Assessment*. Washington, DC: World Bank.

———. 2004d. *Peru: Microeconomic Constraints to Growth—The Evidence from the Manufacturing Sector.* Washington, DC: World Bank.

———. 2004e. *World Development Report 2005: A Better Investment Climate for Everyone*. New York: Oxford University Press.

———. 2005a. *Brazil: Investment Climate Assessment*. Washington, DC: World Bank.

———. 2005b. *Doing Business in 2006: Creating Jobs*. Washington, DC: World Bank.

———. 2005c. *Ecuador Investment Climate Assessment*. Washington, DC: World Bank.

———. 2005d. *El Salvador: Investment Climate Assessment*. Washington, DC: World Bank.

———. 2006a. *Doing Business 2007: How to Reform*. Washington, DC: World Bank.

———. 2006b. *World Development Indicators 2006*. Washington, DC: World Bank.

6

Improving Protection against the Risk of Unemployment

From Job Protection to Income Support

This chapter reviews employment protection legislation and income-support schemes for the unemployed in Latin America and the Caribbean. It argues that labor market policy in the region should evolve from the logic of *protecting jobs* to that of *protecting workers* by promoting change from the current protection mechanisms based on employment protection legislation toward income-support mechanisms. The latter can provide adequate protection against the risk of unemployment while creating fewer distortions in economic activity. The chapter then discusses different alternatives for publicly funded income-support programs that can improve individuals' ability to cope with economic and social risks.

Another important barrier to protection from the risk of unemployment is that in their current form most programs cover only registered, formal sector workers. This situation creates a truncated welfare state that leaves many workers behind. This chapter argues that to face up to this challenge, governments need to develop integrated welfare states that extend coverage to all workers, for example, by funding programs from general revenues or by developing appropriate alternatives for workers who do not participate in contribution-based systems.[1]

The Risk of Unemployment

Available firm-level data indicate that almost a quarter of all jobs are created or destroyed on average in the Latin American and Caribbean countries every year (see chapter 2). Moreover, the sum of job creation and destruction rates tends to exceed those in most industrial countries. Not all jobs destroyed involve involuntary transitions out of jobs. Some of that turnover can be accommodated with attrition through retirements or quits that are not replaced. Evidence indicates, however, that job destruction tends to be more concentrated in some bad years than job creation is in good ones (Haltiwanger, Scarpetta, and Schweiger 2006). Such an uneven process of job destruction is difficult to accommodate with retirements or quits. The probability of transiting from employment to unemployment is also much higher for workers in informal jobs (not registered in social security).[2]

These findings imply that although labor reallocation is essential for an efficient redeployment of resources and productivity growth, it can impose large welfare costs on workers. How churning affects workers depends on three factors: the risk of involuntary job loss, the short-term loss associated with not receiving labor income during unemployment, and the possible long-run losses associated with accepting jobs that pay less than previous ones.

There are no direct measures of the actual short-run income loss associated with unemployment in the region. However, it is probably safe to venture that such loss is not very large, especially because the duration of unemployment is low. On average, only 11 percent of the workers who become unemployed remain so for a year or longer, compared with about 40 percent in Eastern and Western Europe (IDB 2003). At the other extreme, 36 percent of the unemployed had been in that state only one month, against a figure of 11 percent in Western Europe. In that regard, on average, the patterns of unemployment duration in Latin America and the Caribbean look quite similar to those in the United States. An exception in the region is Colombia, where during the period from 1990 to 2001, 33 percent of the unemployed remained so for a year or longer.

Although the low incidence of long-term unemployment can be seen in a favorable light, such short duration is likely to be due to the limited income-support mechanisms available in the region. Faced with a choice of no income or a bad job, workers may be forced to accept the latter. This situation implies that the long-term losses of being displaced from a job could be quite high, particularly for workers who were relatively well matched in their original job and are forced to accept a bad job after displacement.

Two recent studies measure the size of the income losses after displacement in Brazil and Mexico. The study for Brazil (Menezes-Filho forthcoming) finds substantial long-term losses from job displacement and substantial heterogeneity with respect to the size of the effects across different types of workers. Those with high tenure in their jobs suffer larger losses—wages drop by as much as 40 percent in the year after displacement and reach a level of 24 percent lower than predisplacement wages five years after displacement. In contrast, losses for short-tenure workers are lower, and wages recover the predisplacement level four years after displacement. The study also finds that high-skill workers and workers employed in large firms experience higher long-term losses than low-skill workers or workers in small firms. The study concludes that wage losses are associated with the loss of firm-specific capital and wage rents associated with working in large firms.

The study for Mexico (Kaplan, González, and Robertson 2005) suggests that the size of wage loss after displacement is associated not only with workers' characteristics (length of tenure, ability to find a job immediately after displacement, time spent out of the labor force, or changing sector), but also—and mostly—with local economic conditions. The study finds that workers who are displaced in times of economic recovery increase their wages compared with workers who remain in distressed firms, whereas workers who are displaced in times of recession not only suffer large wage losses but also take a greater amount of time to recover. Moreover, displacement in economically active regions (border and central areas) tends to be followed by quicker and better recovery than in less dynamic regions (north and south).

Role of Publicly Provided Income-Support Mechanisms

Individuals can deal with shocks in three ways: they can prevent the shock, mitigate the cost of a shock, or deal with its consequences (see De Ferranti and others 2000; Holzmann and Jorgensen 1999). Leaving individuals to deal with economic risk on their own is likely to lead to suboptimal outcomes. For example, although individuals can save, this strategy is inefficient for dealing with shocks with low probability but high costs. Insurance is a more efficient mechanism for dealing with job loss; however, around the world, moral hazard and adverse selection problems have prevented the emergence of privately provided unemployment insurance. The government can play a role in insuring workers against the risk of unemployment and improving workers' opportunities of accessing good jobs. In some instances, such as unemployment insurance, public mandating or public provision and financing are required.

Uninsured transient shocks that reduce individual consumption below a threshold needed to retain productivity can give rise to dynamic poverty traps and lead to chronic poverty. This situation occurs when families are forced to sell productive assets used to support agricultural enterprises or microenterprises or have to take children out of school so that they can work (see, for example, Ravallion 2000). Once shocks have occurred, governments can help individuals cope with them by providing social assistance—including cash transfers (with built-in work incentives), in-kind benefits, and services. Such assistance is especially important for individuals who are less able to obtain insurance against such shocks, including informal workers and the poor.

The preceding discussion indicates that the potential benefits of social risk management programs go well beyond the welfare of the unemployed or the poor. They enhance the efficiency of the allocation of resources, because social insurance schemes can stimulate the emergence of more risky—but more productive—jobs and industries (see, for example, Acemoglu and Shimer 1999). They can also prevent the emergence of socially disruptive responses, which can arise when unemployment affects a large segment of the population.

Regulating Hiring and Firing to Lower the Risk of Unemployment

In the context of the large inequalities, employment instability, and poor labor conditions that are seen in Latin America and the Caribbean, governments have used hiring and firing regulations to protect workers against the risk of unemployment by making dismissal more difficult or providing financial compensation in case of dismissal.[3] Hiring and firing regulations set basic requirements on the terms of permanent employment contracts between firms and workers.[4] However, because they affect the cost of reallocating workers, employment protection regulations strongly influence the cost of doing business—and especially the incentives and opportunities for firms to expand and exploit new technologies. Moreover, because hiring and firing regulations often do not correspond to the reality of the region's labor markets, they provide incentives for firms and workers to join or remain in the informal economy.

The controversy over hiring and firing regulations lies in their contradictory effects. On the one hand, workers and firms can benefit from minimum standards in hiring and firing procedures. Regulations mandating that firms pay severance in the event of dismissal provide income support to workers in case of job loss. In addition, regulations that reinforce job security and thereby discourage firms from lightly firing workers in downturns may enhance productivity performance, because workers may be more willing to cooperate with employers in the development of the production process (Akerlof 1984).

On the other hand, high levels of job security constrain firms' performance and job creation if workers are not willing to trade the benefits of such protection for lower wages or greater effort. When employment protection legislation is very strict, firms may become more cautious about adjusting their workforce, with the ultimate effect of reducing labor turnover (Bertola 1992). In Latin America and the Caribbean, regulations are often not fully accommodated by wages or higher productivity. For example, in the middle-income countries of Latin America, firms in the formal sector bear up to 50 percent of the nonwage labor costs (Heckman and Pagés 2004). These regulations therefore tend to raise labor costs.

Constraints of Hiring and Firing Regulations

Evidence from executive opinion surveys such as the World Economic Form's *Global Competitiveness Report* (López-Claros, Porter, and Schwab 2005; Porter, Schwab, and López-Claros 2006) shows that the region is among those where employers report to be the most impeded by hiring and firing regulations (see figure 6.1 for recent scores); over a third of firms in the sample countries of the World Bank Enterprise Surveys report labor regulations as a moderate, major, or very severe obstacle to doing business.[5] Compared with other elements of the business climate, however, labor regulations are not among the top business concerns in the region. Large differences across countries are apparent. There is a strong difference between Brazil, where 27 percent report these regulations as a

Figure 6.1 Labor Regulations

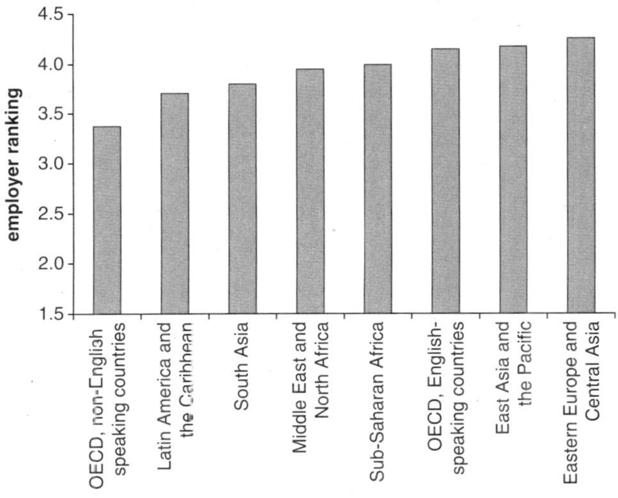

Source: Porter, Schwab, and López-Claros 2006.

Note: OECD = Organisation for Economic Co-operation and Development. Employers ranked the flexibility of regulations on a scale of 1 to 7, where 1 = regulations that impeded employers and 7 = regulations flexibly determined by employers. Thus, higher values indicate less restrictive regulations according to employers.

very severe obstacle, and the rest of the countries, where this proportion varies between 1.0 and 12.5 percent of firms (in El Salvador and Costa Rica, respectively).

Although labor market regulations are not cited among the biggest constraints to doing business, they are important for some firms. In particular, they are more binding for firms in dynamic industries and firms that are less able to accommodate or avoid regulations. Firms that are more visible to regulators, such as older firms and bigger firms, are more constrained. Firms that have expanded employment are also more constrained. In fact, firms that have attributes often associated with good performance report being more affected by labor regulations. Thus, larger, older, exporting, and partly foreign-owned firms, as well as firms that are expanding employment, report being more affected by labor regulations (Aterido, Hallward, and Pagés 2007).

Low Administrative Constraints but High Monetary Costs of Firing

Objective measures of labor regulations (from the World Bank's Doing Business database) show that from the administrative point of view, dismissing workers is quite easy in Latin America and the Caribbean, but the monetary costs of firing are higher than in many other regions. In many countries in other regions, firms need to undertake a number of administrative procedures before firing a worker or closing a firm, such as requesting the permission of officials, consulting with unions, or finding alternative placements for workers. In Latin America and the Caribbean, however, dismissal procedures are among the least rigid in the world. They rank at a similar level to those found in East Asia and the Pacific—both being more rigid than those found in English-speaking countries of the Organisation for Economic Co-operation and Development (OECD) (figure 6.2). However, firing costs, at an average of 60 weeks of wages, are among the highest.[6] Only Sub-Saharan Africa and South Asia have significantly higher costs (figure 6.3). These averages hide large differences within the region. For example, firing costs vary from around 20 weeks of wages in Belize and Nicaragua to nearly 140 weeks in Argentina and Ecuador. Similarly, some countries, such as Belize, Bolivia, Brazil, Colombia, Costa Rica, El Salvador, Guatemala, Honduras, Jamaica, Nicaragua, Uruguay, and the República Bolivariana de Venezuela, impose no procedure on the dismissal of a redundant worker, whereas others, such as Panama, Paraguay, or Peru, impose several (see table 6.1).

This combination of few administrative restrictions and high firing costs seems less problematic than the combination found in other countries in the developing world (for example, India, where mandatory severance payments are low but administrative costs of dismissal are extremely high). Unlike severance pay, although administrative costs impose large

Figure 6.2 Administrative Dismissal Procedures

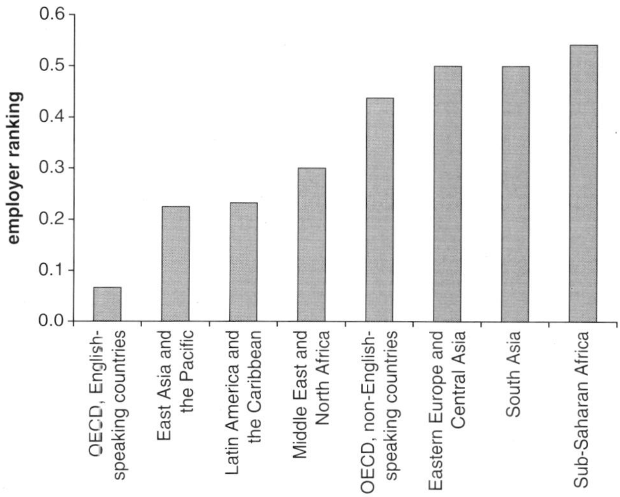

Source: Authors' calculations based on raw data from Doing Business database (2006).

Note: Higher values imply more restrictive administrative procedures.

transaction costs and reduce job turnover, they do not provide any income support for workers. Moreover, administrative costs do not protect workers against the risk of firm closure (which, as discussed in chapter 3, accounts for about one-third of total job destruction). Some early evidence indicates that administrative costs have more adverse economic effects than monetary costs (Micco and Pagés 2006).

Importance of Labor Regulations for Labor Market Performance

The effect of employment protection laws on labor market performance has sparked an ongoing debate among economists. The abundant empirical evidence has not helped settle the debate. A large body of literature assessing the effect of labor regulations on labor market variables, mostly based on analysis of data for industrial countries, has led to ambiguous results. Although some studies find that employment protection regulations have important effects on employment adjustment, worker turnover, employment, or unemployment, others find no evidence of such effects.

Figure 6.3 Costs of Firing

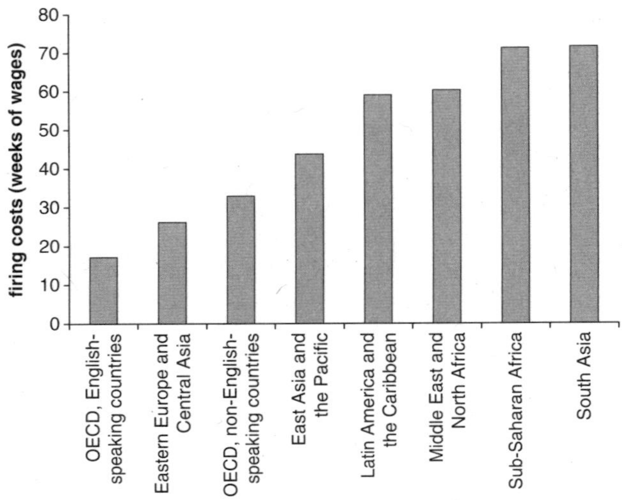

Source: Authors' calculations based on raw data from Doing Business database (2006).

Note: Higher values imply more stringent employment protection legislation.

The lack of conclusive results is partly because regulations change infrequently and tend to be applied at the national level to all workers. This situation reduces the variability available to estimate their effects. One notable exception pertains to countries in which labor regulations vary at the state level, such as India and the United States. In those two countries, researchers have exploited geographic and time variation in legislation to relate economic outcomes to regulations (for India, see Ahmad and Pagés 2007 and Besley and Burgess 2004; for the United States, see Autor, Donohue, and Schwab 2006). All these studies found negative effects of labor regulations on employment.[7] In addition, the studies for India find important negative effects of hiring and firing regulations on capital formation, wages, and output in the manufacturing sector.

Two new empirical studies (Haltiwanger, Scarpetta, and Schweiger 2006; Micco and Pagés 2006) assess the effect of regulations for a sample of OECD and developing countries (including a number of countries in the region). The studies use a new methodology that overcomes many of the problems listed previously. Both studies found that labor regulations negatively affect economic activity in important ways.

Table 6.1 Detailed Procedures for Firing a Redundant Worker, 2006

Country	*Is the termination of workers because of redundancy legally authorized?*	*Must the employer notify a third party before dismissing 1 redundant employee?*	*Does the employer need approval of a third party to dismiss 1 redundant worker?*	*Does the law mandate retraining or replacement before dismissal?*	*Do priority rules apply to dismissal or layoffs?*	*Do priority rules apply to reemployment?*	*What is the legally mandated notice period for redundancy dismissal after 20 years of continuous employment? (weeks)*
Antigua and Barbuda	Yes	No	No	Yes	Yes	No	4.3
Argentina	Yes	Yes	No	No	No	No	8.7
Belize	Yes	No	No	No	No	No	4.0
Bolivia	No	n.a.	n.a.	n.a.	n.a.	n.a.	12.9
Brazil	Yes	No	No	No	No	No	4.3
Chile	Yes	Yes	No	No	No	No	4.3
Colombia	Yes	No	No	No	No	No	0.0
Costa Rica	Yes	No	No	No	No	No	4.3
Dominica	Yes	No	No	No	Yes	Yes	8.7
Dominican Republic	Yes	Yes	No	No	Yes	No	4.0
Ecuador	Yes	No	No	Yes	Yes	Yes	4.3

(continued)

Table 6.1 Detailed Procedures for Firing a Redundant Worker, 2006 *(continued)*

Country	*Is the termination of workers because of redundancy legally authorized?*	*Must the employer notify a third party before dismissing 1 redundant employee?*	*Does the employer need approval of a third party to dismiss 1 redundant worker?*	*Does the law mandate retraining or replacement before dismissal?*	*Do priority rules apply to dismissal or layoffs?*	*Do priority rules apply to reemployment?*	*What is the legally mandated notice period for redundancy dismissal after 20 years of continuous employment? (weeks)*
El Salvador	Yes	No	No	No	No	No	0.0
Grenada	Yes	No	No	No	No	No	8.7
Guatemala	Yes	No	No	No	No	No	0.0
Guyana	Yes	Yes	No	No	No	No	4.3
Haiti	Yes	Yes	No	No	No	No	17.3
Honduras	Yes	No	No	No	No	No	8.7
Jamaica	Yes	No	No	No	No	No	12.0
Mexico	Yes	No	No	No	Yes	Yes	0.0
Nicaragua	Yes	No	No	No	No	No	2.1
Panama	Yes	Yes	Yes	No	Yes	Yes	0.0
Paraguay	Yes	Yes	Yes	No	No	Yes	12.9

(continued)

Table 6.1 Detailed Procedures for Firing a Redundant Worker, 2006 *(continued)*

Country	*Is the termination of workers because of redundancy legally authorized?*	*Must the employer notify a third party before dismissing 1 redundant employee?*	*Does the employer need approval of a third party to dismiss 1 redundant worker?*	*Does the law mandate retraining or replacement before dismissal?*	*Do priority rules apply to dismissal or layoffs?*	*Do priority rules apply to reemployment?*	*What is the legally mandated notice period for redundancy dismissal after 20 years of continuous employment? (weeks)*
Peru	Yes	Yes	Yes	Yes	Yes	Yes	0.0
St. Kitts and Nevis	Yes	No	No	No	No	Yes	8.0
St. Lucia	Yes	No	No	No	Yes	Yes	6.0
St. Vincent and the Grenadines	Yes	No	No	No	No	Yes	4.0
Suriname	Yes	Yes	Yes	No	No	No	0.0
Trinidad and Tobago	Yes	No	No	No	Yes	No	6.4
Uruguay	Yes	No	No	No	No	No	0.0
Venezuela, R.B. de	No	n.a.	n.a.	n.a.	n.a.	n.a.	13.0

Source: Doing Business database (2007).
Note: n.a. = not applicable.

Micco and Pagés (2006) estimate a difference-in-difference model to explore the effect of labor regulations across different industries with different intrinsic volatility. The hypothesis is that industries that are intrinsically more volatile will be more affected by hiring and firing regulations. Across the world, some industries (for example, the production of wood, leather, and apparel) are found to be much more volatile than other industries (for example, refineries and the production of chemical goods). Micco and Pagés (2006) find that intrinsically more volatile industries have lower levels of job turnover relative to less volatile industries in countries with more stringent labor regulations. The difference in turnover brought by labor regulations is very sizable (more than 25 percent of the mean value). Micco and Pagés (2006) also show that employment, value added, and the number of establishments (that is, firm entry) are reduced in the most volatile sectors. At the aggregate level, their findings imply that employment, value added, and firm entry are reduced in countries with very stringent hiring and firing regulations. This effect is larger if the comparative advantage of countries in the volatile industries is higher. The results also suggest that administrative firing costs may exert higher pressure on economic activity than mandatory severance pay.

Haltiwanger, Scarpetta, and Schweiger (2006) extend the methodology used by Micco and Pagés (2006) to explore the effects of labor regulations across industry or firm-size cells. Their assumption is that hiring and firing regulations are likely to be more binding on industry or firm-size cells that have the greatest propensity for reallocation. Using a different sample of countries, Haltiwanger, Scarpetta, and Schweiger (2006) confirm that industries and size classes that are intrinsically more volatile have lower job reallocation in countries with more rigid hiring and firing regulations. Moreover, they find that even though medium and large firms have lower average job flows, they are more severely affected by stringent regulations.

This evidence suggests that hiring and firing laws could have important effects for productivity growth. The finding that labor regulations impair job reallocation, combined with the evidence that the efficiency of reallocation affects the level of productivity across time, industries, and countries (Bartelsman, Scarpetta, and Haltiwanger 2004; Foster, Haltiwanger, and Krizan 2002), suggests that rigid labor regulations may adversely affect productivity level and growth. In addition, because employment protection legislation raises the cost of workforce reorganizations, it reduces firms' capacity to exploit technological opportunities. Evidence from industrial countries suggests that stricter rules are associated with lower research and development expenditure and tend to tilt specialization away from high-tech industries (Nicoletti and others 2001). Two studies for the OECD suggest that by bringing labor laws to the OECD average, countries with very strict employment regulations could reduce their productivity gap with the technological leader by about 20 percent (Scarpetta and others 2002; Scarpetta and Tressel 2004). Similar reforms in developing countries can yield even larger productivity gains, given the greater potential for adopting technologies available in international markets.

Job protection legislation also seems to affect the structure of employment. Evidence for OECD countries suggests that job security regulations reduce the share of workers in wage employment and increase self-employment (chapter 5). Hiring and firing regulations tend to promote job stability for prime-age males but to reduce job opportunities and lengthen unemployment spells for youths, women lacking work experience, and people with low skills (Addison and Teixeira 2003). Evidence from Chilean microlevel data shows that more rigid job security regulations lead to lower employment rates for youths and unskilled workers and to higher employment rates for older and skilled workers. Women and unskilled workers are also found to be more likely to be self-employed than others (Montenegro and Pagés 2004).

Finally, because severance payments are directly linked to tenure, they alter the relative costs of dismissing workers with short versus long tenure. Firms tend to lay off workers with shorter tenure first—such as women, youths, and unskilled workers. Weakening the link between severance pay and tenure, for instance, by imposing a maximum amount a worker can obtain, would reduce the bias that job security imposes against workers with less tenure (IDB 2003). Some Latin American and Caribbean countries have such caps on severance pay; for example, in Chile, Ecuador, Peru, and Uruguay, severance payments cannot be more than 11, 25, 12, and 6 months of full wages, respectively.

Recent Reforms on Fixed-Term Contracts

The preceding discussion suggests the need to move away from job protection mechanisms—particularly in countries where most of the protection takes the form of lengthy and difficult administrative procedures—toward better forms of income protection. Integral reforms have proved difficult. Some countries have attempted to shortcut political constraints by liberalizing contracts at the margin. They do so by lifting regulations on temporary contracts, which in most cases are exempt from firing regulations.[8] Although these measures please employers, they reduce the share of workers with access to unemployment risk protection, and as will be discussed, they generate considerable distortions of their own.

The region is in an intermediate position in terms of rigidity in the legislation relative to the terms of temporary employment. In fact, it ranks as the most flexible behind three groups: English-speaking OECD countries, East Asian and Pacific countries, and Middle East and North African countries (figure 6.4). There are, however, large variations across countries: some countries place no restrictions, while others, such as Brazil, Panama, and the República Bolivariana de Venezuela, place strong restrictions on the use of temporary contracts.

Figure 6.4 Restrictions on Temporary Contracts

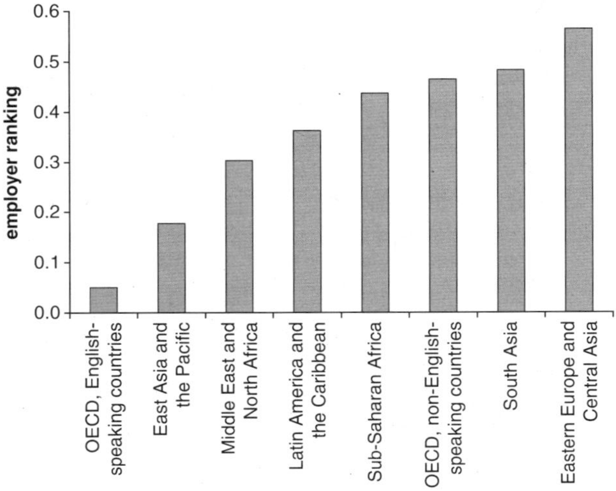

Source: Doing Business database.
Note: Relative ranking—higher values imply more restrictions.

Several countries in Latin America have tried to increase the adaptability of the labor market by liberalizing fixed-term contracts and temporary work. Argentina introduced employment promotion contracts for unemployed workers in 1991. These contracts allowed a 50 percent reduction in severance pay (Saavedra 2003). For some types of contracts, severance pay was removed entirely. Brazil, Colombia, and Peru also made the use of these types of programs easier in the late 1980s and early 1990s. The share of workers employed through these types of contracts subsequently increased significantly in these countries. For example, Peru saw the share increase from 20 percent of salaried employees in 1990 to 55 percent in 2000 (IDB 2003).

The evidence suggests that partial reforms are not necessarily better than no reforms at all. Flexible temporary contracts coupled with stringent firing laws give firms incentives to hire more workers at the entry level and to employ them for a limited period without giving them a permanent position thereafter. This situation increases job turnover but not necessarily overall employment or productivity because the additional hires will be accompanied by additional layoffs at the end of the temporary contracts; hence, little development of the internal human capital will occur. The bottom line is that countries need to equilibrate regulations for both temporary and regular workers.[9]

Toward Better Ways of Protecting Workers against Unemployment Risk

Improving the policy performance of income-support schemes in Latin America and the Caribbean requires progress toward two interrelated objectives: (a) reinforcing insurance mechanisms that help workers cope with the income losses of job dislocation and (b) extending coverage to a large share of workers in the informal sectors who generally cope with risks after they have occurred, often resorting to unproductive strategies that may perpetuate poverty. Attaining these goals requires making resources available to workers during unemployment spells; however, doing so may be problematic if the unemployment status is difficult to observe—a worker can claim to be unemployed and be working in an unregistered job or enjoying leisure. An additional problem is that income protection may reduce the search intensity of job seekers. Different income-support mechanisms address these issues in different ways.

Severance Payments

Although problematic for all the reasons stated in the previous section, mandatory severance pay is an attractive income-support mechanism in developing countries because it requires little administrative capacity to monitor the unemployment status: employers know the status of workers. Other attractive features of this mechanism are that it does not require the collection of social contributions or the payment of benefits through the social security administration. As such, this system constitutes a mandatory private exchange between workers and firms, with little intervention from the state, other than the enforcement of such payments. Enforcement is no small issue, however. Noncompliance creates a burden on labor courts and government budgets. Most of the grievances handled by labor inspection offices in Latin America are related to noncompliance with such payments (MacIsaac and Rama 2001; Rama and Maloney 2001).[10] An additional advantage is that severance payments are unlikely to negatively affect the efficiency of job search, because they are paid as a lump sum at the beginning of the unemployment spell (MacIsaac and Rama 2001; Vodopivec 2004).

Severance payments offer only limited pooling of unemployment risk; risks are pooled across workers in a firm but not across firms.[11] In addition, severance pay does not protect workers against duration risk—that is, it does not make more resources available to workers who remain unemployed longer. Another shortcoming is that workers with short tenures before termination may not receive enough funds to endure an unemployment spell (Blanchard 2004).

At the same time, many workers in regulated labor contracts may be overinsured; for example, workers may receive significantly more monthly wages upon firing than the average unemployment duration. This overinsurance, if not compensated with lower wages, raises labor costs and therefore reduces employment (IDB 2003). For example, evidence shows that severance payments may more than compensate workers for the loss in income. In Peru, consumption per capita increases by almost 7 percent when the unemployed individual gets severance (Rama and Maloney 2001).

Low levels of coverage limit the usefulness of these programs as income-support mechanisms. In Latin American and Caribbean countries, the proportion of all workers covered by such schemes varies greatly across countries and tends to be low. Workers who receive these payments tend to have formal indefinite contracts in the private sector. For example, potential recipients of severance pay are estimated to represent 8 percent of total workers in Peru, 32 percent in Argentina, 34 percent in Mexico, 35 percent in Colombia, and 44 percent in Brazil (see Jaramillo and Saavedra 2005). As a consequence, severance pay tends to cover more educated workers and may in fact be regressive (Mondino and Montoya 2004). In Peru, not only are poor workers less likely to be entitled to severance pay, but they are also less likely to receive it in case of dismissal (MacIsaac and Rama 2001; Rama and Maloney 2001).[12] Even among workers who are eligible for these payments, actual coverage may still be low. A lack of enforcement partly explains this situation. In Chile, for example, employers often avoid paying the full amount of severance payments by coming to an agreement with workers or simply by refusing to pay (Sehnbruch 2006).

Creating new schemes, such as individual unemployment savings accounts or unemployment insurance, without revising severance pay systems may lead to excessive increases in labor costs (IDB 2003). In Brazil, an existing system of severance payments was not revised when an unemployment insurance scheme was established because a review of the full system of social protection and potential interactions between schemes had not been done. The new unemployment insurance system coexists with generous severance payments,[13] effectively increasing labor costs and favoring the same workers, who are generally already better off (Chahad 2004). Similarly, in Barbados, the newly implemented unemployment insurance system initially provided much lower benefits than the existing severance payments. Only when severance payments were lowered did the unemployment insurance start to be useful (Mazza 2000). In Chile, the increase in labor costs caused by the introduction of the dual unemployment insurance scheme was partially compensated by a reduction in severance payments; employers can deduct the contributions made to the worker's individual unemployment account from the severance payments owed to the worker (Acevedo, Eskenazi, and Pagés 2005).

More generally, when introducing new income-support mechanisms, governments have to take into account their interaction with existing policies (Mazza 2000). Reviewing existing schemes may reveal gaps that can be filled by new programs, problems that can be best addressed with a different scheme, or problems that the new scheme is likely to face. This review can be part of a process of monitoring and feedback, which is a necessary component of the design of any new passive and active labor market programs (see later discussion). Moreover, existing schemes have administrative capacity and infrastructure that can be built on to implement new schemes. For example, Uruguay has an individual accounts system that finances old-age pensions. This experience in individual accounts and the accompanying infrastructure could be used to implement individual unemployment accounts (Ferrer and Riddell 2005).

To tackle the shortcomings of severance payments, some countries have introduced prefunding or have reduced the generosity of payments to bring them more in line with international experience. The following section investigates a form of prefunding: individual unemployment savings accounts.

Individual Unemployment Savings Accounts

Individual unemployment savings accounts (IUSAs) bring several advantages—and also several shortcomings—compared with severance payments. In IUSA schemes, employers (and sometimes employees) are required to deposit a monthly contribution into an individual worker's account. Distinct from severance pay, the benefits are paid whatever the reason or initiator of the separation. IUSAs are therefore expected to reduce firms' defaults on severance payments and to shift the cost of such protection onto workers in the form of lower wages (Kugler 2005). Moreover, because the payments are prepaid, they do not impede employment adjustment.

Another important advantage of IUSAs is that they do not require identifying the unemployment status and do not affect the search intensity of workers, because funds are owned by workers. This factor considerably reduces administration costs and requirements, which makes IUSAs feasible for countries with low administrative capacity.

Colombia, Panama, Peru, and the República Bolivariana de Venezuela have IUSAs in addition to mandatory severance payments. Chile and Ecuador have combined IUSAs with their unemployment insurance systems (as described later). Other countries have used the concept of IUSAs: Argentina has established them for the construction sector, and Mexico provides unemployed workers limited access to their retirement funds.[14]

IUSAs are self-insurance mechanisms because they do not pool risks across workers but rather smooth an individual's income over his or her lifetime (Blanchard 2004; Ferrer and Riddell 2005). This is especially true for individuals who experience frequent or long-lasting spells of unemployment. However, self-insurance is not an efficient way to smooth consumption in the presence of infrequent and large shocks. To improve their insurance characteristics, Chile and Ecuador mix individual accounts and unemployment insurance.[15] The worker receives a lump sum (Ecuador) or monthly payments (Chile) taken from his or her account. The adequacy of IUSAs in terms of their income-support role is currently difficult to evaluate, and further research in this area is needed (Ferrer and Riddell 2005; Vodopivec 2004).

The management of the funds is generally supervised by a government agency, and the rate of return on the funds is often regulated. The funds of the individual accounts are either managed by designated financial institutions that the workers can choose (as in Colombia and the República Bolivariana de Venezuela) or by institutions that have been awarded the role of managing the funds. In the latter case, the institutions may manage funds for a limited time (as in Chile) or permanently (as in Brazil and Ecuador). In other cases, employers (Panama) or employees (Peru) can choose among private financial institutions. In some countries, the employer can also manage the funds (for example, Peru and the República Bolivariana de Venezuela).

The volatility of returns or the knowledge that the government will compensate for negative balances sometimes motivates workers to withdraw their funds early, through collusion with firms. For example, in Brazil, hyperinflation in the 1970s made maintaining the real value of funds difficult. Only in recent years did deposits to individual accounts represent a better investment than savings accounts. The combination of volatile returns and the impossibility of withdrawing money from the fund when quitting voluntarily have led to collusive behavior between employers and workers whereby the employers label voluntary resignations as dismissals. This behavior leads to increased turnover (Ferrer and Riddell 2005).

Another problem is that in many instances funds are withdrawn for reasons other than unemployment (or resignation). Peru has, however, allowed withdrawals of the monthly deposit since 2000 (even for reasons that do not permit balance withdrawal), effectively making it part of the workers' wage and undermining the primary role of the scheme. Finally, like severance payment mechanisms, coverage of IUSAs is limited to registered workers.

Currently, no evidence is available regarding the effect of IUSAs on employment (Vodopivec 2004). As in the case of other programs, impact evaluations in individual countries are needed to understand better the circumstances under which IUSAs are successful (Ferrer and Riddell 2005).

Unemployment Insurance

Because of strong information asymmetries, as well as moral hazard and adverse selection problems, unemployment insurance cannot be handled efficiently by private providers. Moral hazard arises because unemployment insurance reduces self-protection; adverse selection arises because information problems prevent insurers from charging higher premiums for bad risks than for low risks. Correcting for these market failures calls not only for regulation in the form of obligatory membership to avoid the problem of adverse selection, but also for public provision to improve monitoring capacity and financial sustainability of the program. Public provision of social risk management programs also enhances the ability to pool resources across large groups, thereby lowering the strain on the system arising from the covariant nature of unemployment risk. However, implementing mandatory unemployment insurance schemes requires identifying the unemployment status, which in turn requires efficient monitoring and strong administrative capacity.

Unemployment insurance schemes are therefore much less developed in Latin America and the Caribbean than in industrial countries. Only eight countries in the region (Argentina, Barbados, Brazil, Chile, Colombia, Ecuador, Uruguay, and the República Bolivariana de Venezuela) have some form of unemployment insurance.[16] Apart from Barbados, which established unemployment insurance in 1982, the other systems tend to be recent; they were created or revised in the 1990s and 2000s.

In terms of level and duration of benefits, the systems are based on international standards. For Argentina, Barbados, Brazil, Uruguay, and the República Bolivariana de Venezuela, initial replacement rates are between 50 percent and 60 percent of the average wage (or best wage in Argentina) preceding unemployment. Benefits are paid for a period of 4 (Brazil) to 12 months (Argentina). In Colombia, the benefits are equal to 1.5 times the minimum wage, divided into six equal monthly payments. Unregistered workers are theoretically eligible for unemployment benefits in Colombia, but in practice they represent a small proportion of beneficiaries (World Bank 2005). In Chile, withdrawals from the individual fund are spread out in five installments; access to the unemployment insurance component of the system is limited in terms of amount and frequency (once every five years). In Ecuador, the unemployment insurance part of the system is a lump-sum payment equal to three times the insured's average wage in the past 12 months.

The costs of these unemployment insurance schemes are covered through general taxation, through social security payments, or—as is most common—through both. The government generally provides the surplus financing when the system does not finance itself. In Argentina, it is financed partly through employers' contribution and partly by the government. In Barbados and the República Bolivariana de Venezuela, it is financed through contributions from workers and employers. In Brazil and Uruguay, earmarked taxation is used. In Colombia, which created an unemployment insurance system in the labor market reform of 2002, the system is financed solely through employers' contributions.

Throughout the region, however, actual coverage tends to be low. In Brazil, 40 percent of urban workers are eligible for unemployment insurance, but only 12 percent of the unemployed actually receive it (Rama and

Maloney 2001). In Chile, only 20 percent of the unemployed are potentially entitled to full benefits (the accumulated savings in their accounts and additional funding from a solidarity fund).[17] This low coverage may be because the program is relatively new, and most new entrants are temporary workers who are not entitled to unemployment insurance (Acevedo, Eskenazi, and Pagés 2005). In Colombia, in December 2003, unemployment insurance covered about 3.4 percent of the unemployed (World Bank 2005).

Moreover, as in all systems that benefit mostly registered workers, beneficiaries are disproportionately from the richer segment of the population. For example, in Argentina, 51 percent of applicants are in the income range of Arg$300 to Arg$600 per month, and 17 percent of recipients had salaries in excess of Arg$1,000 per month, more than three times the maximum benefit level they receive from unemployment insurance (Mazza 2000). The combination of unequal coverage and funding by the state—through general revenues collected, among others, from poor workers—makes these systems highly regressive.

Unemployment insurance in the region has much simpler eligibility and benefits disbursement rules than in European benchmark countries, which tend to have strict eligibility criteria (for example, Greece and Portugal). These European countries require claimants to actively search for a job, to be involuntarily unemployed, to be available for work, and to register at employment offices. Making disbursement conditional is a way of ensuring that the beneficiaries of passive and active labor market programs have the means and incentives to go back to gainful employment. The experience of industrial countries shows that the enforcement of requirements—for example, through sanctions (such as benefits reduction)—not only leads the person sanctioned to improve his or her job search and exit unemployment more quickly, but also gives incentives to other beneficiaries to follow the rules and search actively for a job (Boone and van Ours 2006).

Such rules are difficult to implement in Latin American and Caribbean countries, where enforcement and monitoring are weak. Even in developed countries, monitoring remains an issue, and the extent of fraud in unemployment insurance is not well known (see, for example, Bajada 2005 for Australia). In Latin American and Caribbean countries, benefit fraud is particularly difficult to detect, especially given the large informal sector. The choice of requirements therefore depends principally on the capacity of the country to enforce them.

This lack of monitoring weakens the usefulness and increases the costs of these schemes. Workers who receive cash transfers without attached conditions have few incentives to look for a job. In some countries, benefit claimants may be working, sometimes in the formal sector. For example, in Brazil, evidence from household surveys suggests that a large proportion of the current unemployment benefits claimants are in fact employed (World Bank and Instituto de Pesquisa Econômico Aplicada 2002). In

Argentina, the government detected significant numbers of unemployment insurance recipients who were actually working in the formal sector while receiving unemployment benefits when it started cross-checking their social security numbers with the social security payroll (Mazza 2000). A better integration with the tax-collecting authorities can prevent workers from claiming benefits while holding jobs in the formal sector, but it does not solve the problem for unregistered workers.

Active Labor Market Programs

Another way to improve the targeting and the effectiveness of income support is to link it to active labor market programs (ALMPs). A solution currently advocated in the OECD is to develop employment services. This strategy has several advantages: only workers seeking a job are willing and able to participate in ALMPs; thus, the link with ALMPs becomes a targeting mechanism. Employment services can also collect data that can be used for analysis of the performance of the system. Moreover, employment services can provide a link with ALMPs, which can be useful for workers with specific difficulties.

Countries of the region that have unemployment insurance rarely link benefits to job intermediation or other ALMPs (Márquez 2000; Mazza 2000). For example, in Brazil, the receipt of unemployment benefits is based on a means test but does not require participating in ALMPs or using employment services. Unemployed workers can apply for benefits in three different places, including local employment service offices, but few apply through these offices because of stigma, among other reasons. In Chile, beneficiaries are registered in a national information system for job seekers.

Two main constraints are apparent when linking ALMPs and income support, especially in the context of developing countries: (a) administrative capacity and (b) quality of service. While creating demand for such services, the authorities have to ensure that the supply of service is available and of good quality. This issue is clearly illustrated by the example of the Republic of Korea, which developed an integrated approach to income support. With its early difficulties, the approach provides interesting lessons for other countries wishing to take such an approach (see box 6.1 for details). These issues are dealt with in chapter 7.

Unemployment Insurance and Labor Market Performance

Unemployment insurance schemes may have negative effects on formal employment through an increase in labor costs. As in any employment-based contributory system, contributions that are not passed on to workers may reduce employment. When social contributions are passed on to workers in the form of lower wages, some workers—especially low-skill

Box 6.1 Social Protection in the Republic of Korea: An Integrated Approach

Several Asian economies have recently come to realize that income support for the unemployed is needed. They went through crises that led to dramatic increases in unemployment.[a] The first country to implement such a system in the region was the Republic of Korea, which did so even before the financial crisis.

A Comprehensive Approach to Labor Policy

As part of an active and comprehensive human resource policy, the employment insurance system created in 1995 in Korea had two main aims: (a) to provide unemployed workers with unemployment benefits and (b) to offer workers the opportunity to upgrade their skills and thus their future employability.

The Korean system is therefore interesting because it combines passive and active measures; it explicitly encourages retraining or job search by paying employment promotion benefits (an early reemployment allowance, a vocational ability development allowance, and a transport and moving allowance) in addition to a job-seeking allowance, extended benefits, and sickness benefits. Job seekers can be disqualified if they refuse to accept job placement services provided by the public employment office, if they decline to participate in a job skills development program recommended by the public employment office, or if they attempt to receive or have received the payment of unemployment benefits by means of fraudulent or other unfair conduct. Beneficiaries who made fraudulent claims are to return all or part of the benefit, and sometimes, in addition, they are charged with a levy equivalent to the amount of the benefit paid. If the claim is fraudulent because of a false notification, report, or certification by the employer, the employer is jointly responsible with the beneficiary.

Korea provides other unemployment-related benefits in its employment insurance system. They include (a) a grant to promote employment of displaced workers, which provides subsidies for employers to hire displaced workers; (b) a grant to promote reemployment of aged workers, which provides subsidies for employers to reemploy workers between 45 and 55 years of age within two years of their job dismissal (only for dismissals for economic reasons); (c) vocational training subsidies for insured employees, which are given to an employee who is 50 years of age or over or about to be dismissed; and (d) assistance for training the unemployed, which provides a training allowance for insured employees and subsidies to training institutes to cover the costs of training unskilled youths.

(continued)

Box 6.1 Social Protection in the Republic of Korea: An Integrated Approach *(continued)*

In addition, Korea has a three-tier network of social safety protection. The first tier includes various social insurance systems, such as the Medical Insurance System and National Pension System; the second tier includes public aid and social welfare services; and the third tier is emergency aid. The Public Assistance Program, which belongs to the second tier, is a means-tested program that provides benefits to low-income people. To help poor families, livelihood assistance was introduced in October 2000. In addition, the government runs a special loan program for unemployed workers.

A Promising System That Lacked the Means to Achieve Its Objectives

The financial crisis that occurred in 1997 dramatically tested the limits of the brand-new system. Because of its relative youth and strict eligibility criteria, few workers were eligible to receive benefits. Despite subsequent relaxation of these criteria, coverage increased only marginally. The training component, which consisted of a training allowance, was often used as income support by workers who were not eligible for unemployment benefits. Training courses were not up to standard and did not fill the promise of skills upgrading. Employment services were largely understaffed, and the staff was underqualified to respond to the surge in demand.

In this context, the Korean authorities were on a steep learning curve. Several lessons can be learned from their experience. First, the integrated approach of the government clearly responded to the needs of the workforce, although the supply of services was insufficient because of lack of resources or underestimation of needs. Second and most important, this experience clearly shows that designing a comprehensive system in good times is particularly important, so the necessary laws, institutions, and structures will be in place when a crisis occurs.

Sources: Kang and others 2001; Lee, Hur, and Kim 2004; Liu 2000.

a. Three Asian economies (Korea; Taiwan, China; and Thailand) introduced unemployment insurance in recent years. Laws were passed in 1968 in Taiwan, China, and in 1990 in Thailand, but they were implemented only in 1999 in the former and in 2004 in the latter. Korea's 1993 law was first implemented in 1995 (SSA and ISSA 2005.)

workers—may value the corresponding benefits less highly and opt for work in the informal economy, trading off future insurance for immediate cash. In this regard, higher social contributions and poorly enforced regulations may exacerbate participation in the informal sector. In some countries, unemployment benefits are used as a start-up capital to set up small, unregistered firms (Chahad 2004).

Restrictions on Eligibility

Given poor targeting, the schemes in the region place a number of participation restrictions to contain spending. They require a minimum amount of contribution to the system or a minimum tenure for workers to be eligible. They restrict eligibility to formal sector employees because this system is generally contribution based. In Argentina, the government controls spending by decreasing benefits in times of greater need. Although this method solves the issue of financing, the limitation of benefits in times of need has an obvious pro-cyclical effect, reducing income support when it is most needed. This approach also goes against the experience in some developed countries, which extend benefits in times of recession (as in the United States).

Dual Systems

Two countries, Chile and Ecuador, combine unemployment insurance with IUSAs. Employers contribute to both the unemployment insurance component and the individual account component. In Chile, workers contribute to their individual accounts, while in Ecuador they contribute to unemployment insurance. In Chile, the government also contributes to the unemployment insurance system. Workers with fixed-term contracts can have an individual account, but they are not covered by the unemployment insurance system. The system costs proportionally more to workers and employers in Ecuador, where the contribution rates are much higher.

These dual systems are interesting because they combine the benefits of both types of schemes. In particular, unemployment insurance can take over when workers who face repeated unemployment spells have run down their IUSA funds and are left without income support or have to run deficits.

Extending Income Support to All Workers

In Latin American and Caribbean countries, as in other developing countries, because the described programs do not cover informal workers, they may in fact not include poorer sections of the population. In a context of low social protection, individuals who cannot afford to remain unemployed and are most likely to suffer poverty in the case of unemployment will likely end up working in the informal sector. Those individuals, who then face higher probabilities of becoming unemployed (Duryea and others 2006), are not protected by the social protection systems. Only those in persistent poverty can get support from specific programs such as public works and conditional cash transfer programs.

Of course, a significant proportion of informal sector workers—in particular the self-employed—may have freely chosen to belong to the informal sector to avoid high taxes and cumbersome regulations or because they lack better prospects (especially low-skill manual workers) (Maloney 2004). However, as in the case of registered workers, the state has a residual liability, because when workers face problems, they can still claim benefits from the state, particularly in acute recessions or economic crisis, when the government is required to intervene. Many workfare programs in Latin America and the Caribbean have resulted from the need to act in periods of crisis. Such harried responses, however, are characterized by poorly designed and implemented programs (Márquez 2000). Extending some form of social protection to unregistered workers is therefore a legitimate issue—especially in countries where the informal sector is large—but each country's circumstances need to be studied to understand the structure of informal employment so that the correct needs are addressed. Because of the nature of informal employment, the relevant systems of protection have to be noncontributory (that is, funded with general revenues). If specifically directed to informal sector workers, they need to be targeted by applying means tests or by making payments contingent on some enforceable requirements.

Unemployment assistance can potentially help formal and informal unemployed workers who are looking for a better job. It is a noncontributory form of income support in which eligibility does not require previous employment history. The level of benefits has to be low enough to avoid creating disincentive effects and attracting nonpoor individuals. For this reason, benefits are generally means tested (Atkinson and Micklewright 1991). The design has to encourage beneficiaries eventually to exit the program for a better outcome, for example, by linking benefits with current job search efforts or by limiting benefits over time. Higher-income countries have a long experience of these schemes and have embedded them in their social protection systems. When unemployment benefits have run out or when workers do not meet unemployment insurance eligibility requirements, individuals who experience financial difficulties receive these benefits. They include, for example, a lump sum in Greece or periodic payments for a specified period (depending on the age of the worker) in Portugal.

Two main issues arise concerning their implementation in developing countries. First, whether such schemes are appropriate in countries where a large proportion of workers do not contribute to social security and whether there is enough public approval to use general taxation for such benefits are arguable. Second, implementing these benefits, registering beneficiaries, and monitoring their eligibility require a good level of administrative capacity.

Several examples in the region show that, after recent economic crises, the public has expressed a willingness to support such noncontributory social protection systems (Lindert, Skoufias, and Shapiro 2006). For example, Argentina is proceeding from an emergency program designed to alleviate the poverty caused by the surge in unemployment following the economic crisis of 2001 to a more comprehensive system of "universal" social protection (box 6.2 details the evolution of the Argentine program from a cash transfer scheme to a more comprehensive social protection program).

Box 6.2 Workfare Program in Argentina: From Trabajar to Jefes de Hogar to a Comprehensive System of Social Protection?

Jefes y Jefas de Hogar (Heads of Household) is a universal program that targets unemployed household heads. It was implemented in response to the 2002 crisis and associated rise in unemployment. It expanded the Trabajar program to "universal" coverage of heads of households with dependents. Government spending on the Heads of Household program declined from 1 percent of gross domestic product in 2003 to 0.6 percent in 2005 and is likely to continue to fall in 2006 to 0.5 percent, assuming that the economy grows and beneficiaries continue to enter private employment as well as because of better enforcement of eligibility criteria.

The program consisted initially of a cash transfer to eligible individuals without requirement on the part of the beneficiary. Given early abuses of the program and to ensure that the program reached individuals in need, a requirement of 20 hours of community work, training activity, school attendance, or employment in a private company with a wage subsidy for six months was subsequently added. In practice, eligibility can be verified only through work in the formal sector. Individuals who claim to be unemployed may in fact be working in the informal sector. Moreover, the status of head of household was also difficult to verify.[a]

Although the majority of beneficiaries enrolled in the municipalities, beneficiaries were also able to enroll through civil society organizations, including organizations of the unemployed as well as unions and church groups. As a result of the economic recovery and the better governance structure of the program, enrollment has steadily declined and reached 1.42 million as of January 2006. This decline represents about a 30 percent

(continued)

Box 6.2 Workfare Program in Argentina: From Trabajar to Jefes de Hogar to a Comprehensive System of Social Protection? *(continued)*

reduction from its peak level in May 2003 when the program had close to 2 million participants, having reached 10 million people, including family members. The program's lack of targeting and the country's great need (because of the absence of alternative programs) led to participation of individuals for which the program was not suitable (about one-third of beneficiaries did not satisfy the eligibility criteria). However, the program was found to have filled its income-smoothing role; participants would have suffered significantly larger drops in income in the absence of the program. Moreover, the program was successful in reaching the poor (90 percent of participants fell below the official poverty line). The program was successful even though its implementation differed from its initial design (participation in the workfare activities never reached the target of 90 percent of beneficiaries). The program's originally specified workfare character has been eroding over time: participation in workfare activities has declined from 70 percent in 2003 to 55 percent during the first half of 2005. This change reflects the increased "pull" to other part-time employment, thanks to economic recovery, and the difficulties a number of municipalities faced enforcing the requirements.

Several reasons explain these outcomes:

- First, the larger than expected size of the program made it difficult to manage. Some municipalities (especially large ones surrounding Buenos Aires) had difficulties linking all participants to workfare activities. Moreover, during the crisis, priority was given to registering and paying people, instead of only registering a person if he or she was assigned to workfare (as had been the case in the smaller Trabajar program). This increase in scope made the enforcement of the workfare requirement more difficult.
- Second, the implementation revealed that the needs of certain vulnerable groups were not addressed adequately. Many program beneficiaries had been inactive or unable to work but were registered because the Heads of Household program was the government's main response to the crisis. Other programs that would have been expected to respond to the crisis either had very small coverage (unemployment insurance and minimum pension) or were in kind (medicine, food, soup kitchens). The program ended up serving needs for which it was not intended or designed. For example, mothers with three or more children account for nearly a third of the beneficiaries of the program. About 60 percent of these women are meeting the work requirement, but some municipalities have exempted

(continued)

Box 6.2 Workfare Program in Argentina: From Trabajar to Jefes de Hogar to a Comprehensive System of Social Protection? *(continued)*

them from the work requirement. About 5 percent of the participants of the program come from similar groups (women above 60 years of age, men above 65 years of age, people with disabilities, and parents of children with disabilities).

- Third, although a lack of compliance with the work requirement would justify suspension from the program, municipalities found dropping poor and needy beneficiaries difficult at a time when no alternative social programs were available.
- Fourth, using training and education to comply with the work requirement has only recently picked up in importance.

Argentina is now moving beyond Heads of Household to design a transition program toward a medium- to longer-term program that is integrated into the social policy framework of the country. In this context, the transition program currently discussed distinguishes between different groups of beneficiaries to better address their specific needs. On the one hand, the idea is to provide those for whom workfare is not suitable (for example, a single mother with many young children) a safety net against chronic poverty through the Familias program. On the other hand, for those who need to be helped to find a new job, the idea is to improve the active component of the current workfare program through more specific workfare activities and involvement of employment services. For example, ex-participants could be asked to actively search for a job with the assistance and under the supervision of local employment offices.

Sources: Cunningham 2006; Galasso and Ravallion 2004.

a. In this context, the setup of the program may be considered discriminatory against women, following the model of the "male breadwinner."

The administrative capacity issue is not easily solved. Program delivery can be delegated to private companies, but public services still have to be able to target individuals and monitor their eligibility. The usual requirements applied in comparator countries—to be available for work and not voluntarily unemployed—are difficult to enforce in the regional context (see SSA and ISSA 2006a, 2006b). Linking receipt of such assistance to ALMPs or job intermediation may be a better way to ensure that the beneficiaries fit the eligibility criteria and that the instrument does serve its purpose (see the example of the initial phase of Argentina's Jefes de Hogar, or Heads of Household, program, box 6.2), but it requires the presence of some form of job intermediation services. Similarly, making assistance conditional on a work requirement can improve targeting, but it requires ensuring that some form of work is available.

Valuable lessons can be learned from the countries of the region that have already implemented such assistance programs, although they have been on a small scale (that is, limited in terms of number of beneficiaries and time period). In particular, the lack of enforcement capacity may invalidate the workfare element of the programs. For example, although the public works program Heads of Household in Argentina was successful in targeting the poor, it had a large take-up by individuals who were not looking for employment (that is, they were ineligible), mostly because of a lack of enforcement of the eligibility criteria (see box 6.2 for details). In effect, the program revealed the need of a section of the population for social assistance. For those individuals, the workfare component of the program did not apply. At the same time, the services provided by the program to job seekers did not adequately support them in finding new jobs.

Before implementing unemployment assistance schemes, countries have to consider, in addition to the program's design itself, criteria such as their capacity to enforce administration of program, the adequacy of the program to address the population's urgent needs, the quality of the services to be provided, and, of course, financial constraints. These elements are found in the examples of programs that have been implemented so far in the region (public works programs are summarized in box 6.3). Social protection policy issues related to informality are analyzed in detail in the flagship regional study on the informal economy in Latin America and the Caribbean (Perry and others 2007).

Box 6.3 Programs That Untie the Link between Formal Employment History and Income Support

Public works programs are examples of already existing programs that can be used to help workers in the informal sector; no previous formal employment history is required to participate. What is the potential for extending these programs?

Helpful in Supporting Income

In many developing countries, these programs have a limited role in job creation and have so far been used only in the fight against poverty. They provide immediate employment. This role is, however, restricted because

(continued)

Box 6.3 Programs That Untie the Link between Formal Employment History and Income Support *(continued)*

their (potentially) positive effect on future employment is limited (Betcherman, Olivas, and Dar 2004). The main use for such programs is as an income-support mechanism in case of idiosyncratic shocks (Reinecke 2005; Subbarao 2003), for example through social investment funds (Siri 2000).

Public works programs do not require complex targeting mechanisms because participants in the programs are expected to self-select. A main criterion for success is to set a wage slightly below the average wage of the target population, generally the unskilled. The labor market regulations and institutions of the country have to be flexible enough to allow this. For example, the presence of a minimum wage may prevent the program's wage to be low enough.

In addition to their income-smoothing function, well-designed public works programs can help build needed infrastructure. Poor areas can benefit from financial transfers to individuals and from new or maintained infrastructure. Moreover, added indirect potential benefits of these programs include the strengthening of local government and other institutions through greater control of management of local affairs, the empowerment of women, and private sector development through involvement in public works.

Many Latin American and Caribbean countries have used these programs since the economic crises of the 1980s. Overall, their experience does not permit pinpointing of optimal designs (Reinecke 2005). A relatively successful workfare program, Trabajar, was designed in Argentina in the 1990s.[a] It entailed a tightly enforced work requirement of 30 to 40 hours, with targeting criteria to help ensure that the work was of value to residents of poor communities. This program was successful in its self-selection and has been found effective in reaching the poorest, both as workers and residents (Jalan and Ravallion 2003; Ravallion 2000). For example, 80 percent of Trabajar workers came from the poorest 20 percent of the Argentine population (Jalan and Ravallion 2003). In 2002, Bolivia implemented the National Emergency Employment Program, financed by international donors; Chile, Peru, and Uruguay have financed programs through their national budgets. These programs all involve cleaning, maintaining, and sometimes constructing infrastructure. For each program, the majority of participants appear to be from the expected groups (the unemployed or individuals from the poorest income quintiles), although a significant proportion come from inactivity or employment (Reinecke 2005).

(continued)

Box 6.3 Programs That Untie the Link between Formal Employment History and Income Support *(continued)*

Little Effect on Workers' Subsequent Employability

As previously mentioned, public employment programs create immediate employment, but they do not have a beneficial effect in terms of subsequent employment. The evidence on the latter effect is limited in developing countries, and the region is no exception. Some recent evidence finds that participants' probability of employment after the program is higher than for nonparticipants in Chile (Bravo, Contreras, and Medrano 2004) and Bolivia (Landa 2003). However, such early evaluations do not inform on the long-run employability of participants versus nonparticipants. The potential effect on future employment is likely to depend on many factors, including the design of the program. For example, small construction firms and suppliers of goods and services created through contracts with the program may sometimes survive beyond the duration of the program, or the program may lead to employment generation through higher income and spending of the local community (Siri 2000).

a. Trabajar II replaced Trabajar I in 1997. The former was replaced in 2002 by a new expanded program: Jefes y Jefas de Hogar (Heads of Household). See box 6.2.

Summing Up: A Set of Proposals for the Countries of the Region

The labor reforms that the region went through since the early 1990s have mainly aimed at reducing the restrictions from hiring and firing regulations to make labor markets more flexible. In many cases, the reforms were limited to liberalization at the margin; they focused on lifting restrictions on temporary contracts. In a few cases, such as in Colombia and Peru, reforms also reduced the amount of mandatory severance payments. Overall, the labor market policies that are currently in place protect a small proportion of workers while leaving out the majority.

As further reforms are carried out and after the recent economic difficulties, more attention will need to be paid to obtaining a greater consensus on the protection that stakeholders wish to obtain and to designing appropriate and enforceable policies.[18] The majority of individuals in the region expect comprehensive and adequate social protection: in this sense, they are closer to European populations than North American ones. The challenge is to design systems that are financially sustainable, minimize economic distortions, and provide adequate protection. As discussed in this chapter, current systems of protection do not appear to fulfill their role and are still far from achieving such goals.

At this stage of development, most Latin American and Caribbean countries can afford some level of social protection. In fact, the history of unemployment insurance in developed countries reveals that many more countries of the region could afford unemployment insurance systems (see table 6.2 for a summary of current income-support schemes in the region). On average, countries of the region are as rich as developed countries were when they first established unemployment insurance.[19]

Making labor and other regulations less constraining for firms is likely to be perceived negatively by workers. However, compensating those who may lose out on these reforms can be done through the design of income-support schemes that protect workers instead of jobs. The support of the public is necessary for the government to justify spending on the programs. In the context of employment-related income support, the willingness of workers to finance such programs will mean that their potentially distortionary effects on job creation will be reduced. Because public provision of unemployment insurance aims to pool the risk across many "players" to avoid adverse selection and account for a lack of private insurance, as many players as possible need to be brought in for the system to work.

Before a given country begins the process of reform, it would be well advised to take stock of the strengths and limitation of its current income protection systems as well as the effectiveness of its active labor policies. It should assess the nature and magnitude of uninsured unemployment risk, as well as redundancies and overlaps in protection—that is, when more than one system is protecting the same workers.

The next step is to devise ways to transit from job protection to income protection. In countries with restrictive administrative procedures for dismissal (such as Ecuador, Panama, and Peru) a reform should consider streamlining administrative procedures for dismissal. In countries where more than one program covers registered workers (for example, Brazil, where registered workers are covered by mandatory severance pay, unemployment insurance savings accounts, and unemployment insurance), reforms should envision consolidation into what should be a more efficient and better-designed system.

As discussed in this chapter, the appropriate mix of income-support policies that can replace job protection will depend on the capacity of the countries to operate and enforce administratively challenging schemes. For countries with relatively low capacity, reforms could involve adopting systems that allow firms to prepay part of the compensation for dismissal into individual or collective accounts. In countries with high capacity, reforms can entail moving toward some form of unemployment insurance. Reforms should also consider the feasibility of paying for such benefits

Table 6.2 Summary of Income-Support Systems in the Region

Severance pay only	*Severance pay + IUSA or IUSA only*	*Severance pay + unemployment insurance*	*Severance pay + unemployment insurance + IUSA*
Antigua and Barbuda	Mexico (limited IUSA)	Argentina	Chile
Belize	Peru	Barbados	Colombia
Bolivia	Panama	Brazil (severance pay is individual account)	Ecuador
Costa Rica		Uruguay	
Dominica		República Bolivariana de Venezuela	
Dominican Republic			
El Salvador			
Grenada			
Guatemala			
Guyana			
Haiti			
Honduras			
Jamaica			
Nicaragua			
Paraguay			
Trinidad and Tobago			
St. Kitts and Nevis			
St. Lucia			
St. Vincent and the Grenadines			
Suriname			

Source: SSA and ISSA 2006a.

from general revenues rather than wage contributions, because the latter lead to truncated welfare states. When that approach is not feasible, reforms should aim at facilitating the participation of unregistered workers in such schemes and should devise forms of income protection that do not act as a disincentive to registration. Finally, for income-support schemes to work, countries should also beef up their active labor market policies, which are strongly complementary to income-support mechanisms. The next chapter takes on this issue.

Notes

1. As discussed later in the chapter, the alternatives need to avoid fostering lower participation in contribution-based programs.

2. Duryea and others (2006), based on individual longitudinal data for Argentina, Mexico, and the República Bolivariana de Venezuela and a number of transition economies.

3. Botero and others (2004) find that countries with a longer history of Leftist governments have more extensive regulation of labor.

4. These regulations are generally defined through labor codes. They have several elements, including setting (a) justifiable reasons for termination, (b) severance pay obligations, (c) advance notice requirements, and (d) administrative procedures for dismissing workers (including the role of trade unions). Special requirements may apply in the case of mass layoffs.

5. These countries are Brazil, Costa Rica, Ecuador, El Salvador, Guatemala, Guyana, Honduras, Nicaragua, and Peru.

6. Firing costs include severance pay obligations, advance notice requirements, and associated penalties (see World Bank 2006).

7. In some limited occasions, reforms have applied only to some groups of workers. This situation allows researchers to implement a difference-in-difference estimation of the effects in the treated group relative to the nonaffected group of workers. See Acemoglu and Angrist (2001) and Kugler, Jimeno, and Hernanz (2003) for an application to this methodology to U.S. and Spanish data, respectively.

8. Regulations on temporary contracts generally pertain to (a) the types of work (for example, occupations) for which these forms of employment are legal and (b) the maximum duration allowed.

9. For example, in the mid 1980s, Spain saw the dramatic effects of its policy of deregulating temporary employment contracts while keeping job protection intact for permanent employment contracts. The share of temporary employment rose to 33 percent by the mid 1990s, leading to the segmentation of the labor market. Empirical evidence for Spain shows that workers with temporary contracts not only are less likely to be employed in firms that provide training but, once they are in those firms, also have a lower probability of being chosen to participate in firm-provided training (Albert, García-Serrano, and Hernanz 2005).

10. Noncompliance also has indirect costs. Payments tend to increase when financial resources are lacking because the firm is experiencing difficulties, and they may simply not be available if the firm goes bankrupt. In these circumstances, employment adjustments for economic reasons are impaired, and workers are deterred from seeking better job matches. This problem looms particularly large among small firms, which are more likely to default on their payments, and among low-skill workers, who have few alternative instruments to smooth consumption.

11. De Ferranti and others (2000) argue that when Latin American countries had little exposure to foreign competition, the effective pooling of unemployment risk offered by severance payments was spread over a greater population because consumers often subsidize potentially bankrupt firms through higher prices. However, this possibility has declined rapidly as countries have embarked on trade liberalization and reforms aimed at fostering domestic competition.

12. See Gill, Montenegro, and Domeland (2002) for a discussion of severance payment in other Latin American countries.

13. Severance payments exceed unemployment benefits.

14. In other countries, the distinction between severance pay and individual accounts sometimes becomes blurred (Parsons 2004). For example, in Brazil, the system of severance payment uses the concept of individual accounts. Workers, however, are not eligible to withdraw their funds on voluntarily quitting; they may do so only on dismissal or retirement. This restriction may void some of the advantages of IUSAs; for example, it may reduce workers' mobility.

15. Ecuador is now moving toward a system based on individual accounts only (Ferrer and Riddell 2005).

16. Mexico offers unemployment insurance only to workers 60 to 64 years of age, effectively providing an early retirement scheme. The benefit is paid under the old-age scheme (SSA and ISSA 2006a).

17. Sehnbruch (2006) suggests that about 20 percent of the total number of unemployed would be eligible.

18. This point is illustrated by the experience of several countries of the region. A proposal for a new unemployment scheme in Chile had been under discussion for several years but was never agreed on. In addition to addressing the main concerns of the social partners, the combination of a surge in unemployment, a gradual buildup of social consensus, and good political cycle timing eventually led to the approval of the reform in Congress in 2001 and to its successful implementation (Acevedo, Eskenazi, and Pagés 2005). In Brazil, although social and labor issues had been on the agenda since the 1940s, they remained low priority and untouched until the country became urbanized, with a sizable formal sector employment workforce and the emergence of cyclical economic crises. As in Chile, the unemployment insurance scheme that was approved for the first time in 1986 was the result of a debate that involved all stakeholders (from labor organizations and politicians to academics) and that looked to international experience to design a system suitable for the Brazilian economy (Chahad 2004).

19. Average per capita gross domestic product in 20 developed nations when they first enacted an unemployment insurance law was US$3,539, and the average per capita gross domestic product for 22 countries in the region was US$3,964 in 2000 (IDB 2003).

References

Acemoglu, D., and J. Angrist. 2001. "Consequences of Employment Protection? The Case of the Americans with Disabilities Act." *Journal of Political Economy* 109 (5): 915–57.

Acemoglu, D., and R. J. Shimer. 1999. "Efficient Unemployment Insurance." *Journal of Political Economy* 107 (5): 893–928.

Acevedo, G., P. Eskenazi, and C. Pagés. 2005. "Unemployment Insurance in Chile: A New Model of Income Support for Unemployed Workers." *Well-Being and Social Policy* 2 (1): 161–82.

Addison, J., and P. Teixeira. 2003. "The Economics of Employment Protection." *Journal of Labor Research* 24 (1): 85–129.

Ahmad, A., and C. Pagés. 2007. "Are All Labor Regulations Equal? Assessing the Effects of Job Security, Labor Dispute, and Contract Labor Laws in India." Policy Research Working Paper 4259, World Bank, Washington, DC.

Akerlof, G. A. 1984. "Gift Exchange and Efficiency-Wage Theory: Four Views." *American Economic Review* 74 (2): 79–83.

Albert, C., C. García-Serrano, and V. Hernanz. 2005. "Firm-Provided Training and Temporary Contracts." *Spanish Economic Review* 7 (1): 67–88.

Aterido, R., M. Hallward, and C. Pagés. 2007. "Investment Climate and Employment Growth: The Impact of Access to Finance, Corruption, and Regulations across Firms." IZA Discussion Paper 3138, Institute for the Study of Labor, Bonn, Germany.

Atkinson, A., and J. Micklewright. 1991. "Unemployment Compensation and Labor Market Transitions: A Critical Review." *Journal of Economic Literature* 29 (4): 1679–727.

Autor, D. H., J. J. Donohue, and S. J Schwab. 2006. "The Costs of Wrongful-Discharge Laws." *Review of Economics and Statistics* 88 (2): 211–31.

Bajada, C. 2005. "Unemployment and the Underground Economy in Australia." *Applied Economics* 37 (2): 177–89.

Bartelsman, E. J., S. Scarpetta, and J. Haltiwanger. 2004. "Distributed Analysis of Firm-Level Data from Industrial and Developing Countries." Institute for the Study of Labor, Bonn, Germany.

Bertola, G. 1992. "Labor Turnover Costs and Average Labor Demand." *Journal of Labor Economics* 10 (4): 389–411.

Besley, T., and R. Burgess. 2004. "Can Labor Regulation Hinder Economic Performance? Evidence from India." *Quarterly Journal of Economics* 119 (1): 91–134.

Betcherman, G., K. Olivas, and A. Dar. 2004. "Impacts of Active Labor Market Programs: New Evidence from Evaluations with Particular Attention to Developing and Transition Countries." Social Protection Discussion Paper 0402, World Bank, Washington, DC.

Blanchard, O. 2004. "Designing Labor Market Institutions." Lecture presented at the Seventh Annual Conference of the Central Bank of Chile on Labor Markets and Institutions, Santiago, March 28. http://econ-www.mit.edu/files/687.

Boone, J., and J. van Ours. 2006. "Modeling Financial Incentives to Get the Unemployed Back to Work." *Journal of Institutional and Theoretical Economics* 16 (22): 227–52.

Botero, J., S. Djankov, R. La Porta, F. López-de-Silanes, and A. Shleifer. 2004. "The Regulation of Labor." *Quarterly Journal of Economics* 199 (4): 1339–82.

Bravo, D., C. Contreras, and P. Medrano. 2004. "Evaluación de impacto: Programas de empleo con apoyo fiscal." Informe final, Universidad de Chile and Ministerio de Hacienda, Santiago.

Chahad, J. 2004. "Foreign Models in the Adoption of Unemployment Insurance in Brazil." In *Learning from Foreign Models in Latin American Policy Reform*, ed. K. Weyland, 139–65. Washington, DC: Woodrow Wilson Center Press.

Cunningham, W. 2006. *Minimum Wages in Latin America and the Caribbean: The Impact on Employment, Inequality, and Poverty*. Washington, DC: World Bank.

De Ferranti, D., G. E. Perry, I. S. Gill, and L. Servén. 2000. *Securing Our Future in a Global Economy*. Washington, DC: World Bank.

Duryea, S., G. Márquez, C. Pagés, and S. Scarpetta. 2006. "Mobility between Formal and Informal Jobs: Evidence from Transition and Latin American Countries." Inter-American Development Bank, Washington, DC.

Ferrer, A., and W. Riddell. 2005. "Unemployment Insurance Savings Accounts in Latin America: Overview and Assessment." In *Improving Severance Pay: An International Perspective*, ed. R. Holzmann and M. Vodopivec. Washington, DC: World Bank.

Foster, L., J. Haltiwanger, and C. J. Krizan. 2002. "The Link between Aggregate and Micro Productivity Growth: Evidence from Retail Trade." NBER Working Paper 9120, National Bureau of Economic Research, Cambridge, MA.

Galasso, E., and M. Ravallion. 2004. "Social Protection in a Crisis: Argentina's Plan Jefes y Jefas." *World Bank Economic Review* 18 (3): 367–99.

Gill, I. S., C. E. Montenegro, and D. Domeland, eds. 2002. *Crafting Labor Policy: Techniques and Lessons from Latin America*. Washington, DC World Bank.

Haltiwanger, J., S. Scarpetta, and H. Schweiger. 2006. "Assessing the Job Flows across Countries: The Role of Industry, Firm Size, and Regulations." IZA Discussion Paper 2450, Institute for the Study of Labor, Bonn, Germany.

Heckman, J., and C. Pagés. 2004. "Introduction." In *Law and Employment: Lessons from Latin America and the Caribbean*, ed. J. Heckman and C. Pagés, 1–108. Chicago: University of Chicago Press.

Holzmann, R., and S. Jorgensen. 1999. "Social Protection as Social Risk Management: Conceptual Underpinnings for the Social Protection Sector Strategy Paper." *Journal of International Development* 11 (7): 1005–27.

IDB (Inter-American Development Bank). 2003. *Good Jobs Wanted: Labor Markets in Latin America—2004 Report on Economic and Social Progress in Latin America*. Washington, DC: IDB.

Jalan, J., and M. Ravallion. 2003. "Estimating the Benefit Incidence of an Antipoverty Program by Propensity-Score Matching." *Journal of Business and Economic Statistics* 21 (1): 19–30.

Jaramillo, M., and J. Saavedra. 2005. "Severance Payment Programs in Latin America." *Empirica* 32 (3–4): 275–307.

Kang, S.-H., J. Keum, D.-H. Kim, and D. Shin. 2001. "Korea: Labor Market Outcomes and Policy Responses after the Crisis." In *East Asian Labor Markets and the Economic Crisis: Impacts, Responses, and Lessons*, ed. D. Betcherman, R. Islam, and A. N. Luinstra, 97–139. Washington, DC: World Bank; Geneva: International Labour Organization.

Kaplan, D., G. González, and R. Robertson. 2005. "What Happens to Wages after Displacement?" *Economía* 5 (2): 197–242.

Kugler, A. 2005. "Wage-Shifting Effects of Severance Payments Savings Accounts in Colombia." *Journal of Public Economics* 89 (2–3): 487–500.

Kugler, A., J. F. Jimeno, and V. Hernanz. 2003. "Employment Consequences of Restrictive Permanent Contracts: Evidence from Spanish Labour Market Reform." CEPR Discussion Paper 3724, Centre for Economic Policy Research, London.

Landa, F. 2003. "Transferencia de recursos hacia los más pobres: Un análisis des PLANE-I con escenarios contrafactuales." Unidad de Análisis de Políticas Sociales y Económicas, La Paz.

Lee, W.-D., J.-J. Hur, and H. Kim. 2004. "Korean Employment Insurance and Work Injury Insurance as Social Safety Nets: An Assessment." In *Modernizing the Korean Welfare State: Towards the Productive Welfare Model*, ed. R. Mishra, S. Kuhnle, N. Gilbert, and K. Hung, 133–56. London: Transaction.

Lindert, K., E. Skoufias, and J. Shapiro. 2006. "Redistributing Income to the Poor and the Rich: Public Transfers in Latin America and the Caribbean." Social Protection Discussion Paper 0605, World Bank, Washington, DC.

Liu, E. 2000. "Unemployment-Related Benefits Systems: Overall Comparison." Research and Library Services Division. Legislative Council Secretariat, Hong Kong, China.

López-Claros, A., M. E. Porter, and K. Schwab, eds. 2005. *The Global Competitiveness Report 2005–2006*. Basingstoke, U.K.: Palgrave Macmillan.

MacIsaac, D., and M. Rama. 2001. "Mandatory Severance Pay: Its Coverage and Effects in Peru." Policy Research Working Paper 2626, World Bank, Washington, DC.

Maloney, W. 2004. "Informality Revisited." *World Development* 32 (7): 1159–78.

Márquez, G. 2000. "Labor Markets and Income Support: What Did We Learn from the Crises?" Research Department Working Paper 425, Inter-American Development Bank, Washington, DC.

Mazza, J. 2000. "Unemployment Insurance: Case Studies and Lessons for Latin America and the Caribbean." Research Department Working Paper 411, Inter-American Development Bank, Washington, DC.

Menezes-Filho, N. Forthcoming, "The Earnings Losses after Displacement in Brazil." *World Development*.

Micco, A., and C. Pagés. 2006. "The Economic Effects of Employment Protection Laws." IZA Discussion Paper 2433, Institute for the Study of Labor, Bonn, Germany.

Mondino, G., and S. Montoya. 2004. "The Effects of Labor Market Regulations on Employment Decisions by Firms: Empirical Evidence from Argentina." In *Law and Employment: Lessons from Latin America and the Caribbean*, ed. J. Heckman and C. Pagés, 351–400. Chicago: University of Chicago Press.

Montenegro, C., and C. Pagés. 2004. "Who Benefits from Labor Market Regulations? Chile, 1960–1998." In *Law and Employment: Lessons from Latin America and the Caribbean*, ed. J. Heckman and C. Pagés, 401–34. Chicago: University of Chicago Press.

Nicoletti, G., A. Bassanini, E. Ernst, S. Jean, and P. Santiago. 2001. "Product and Labour Market Interactions in OECD Countries." OECD Economics Department Working Paper 312, Organisation for Economic Co-operation and Development, Paris.

Parsons, D. 2004. "Mandated Severance Pay and Savings Accounts as Job Loss Insurance: Theoretical Considerations." George Washington University, Washington, DC.

Perry, G., W. Maloney, O. Arias, P. Fajnzylber, A. Mason, and J. Saavedra-Chanduvi, eds. 2007. *Informality: Exit and Exclusion*. Washington, DC: World Bank.

Porter, M. E., K. Schwab, and A. López-Claros, eds. 2006. *The Global Competitiveness Report 2006–2007*. New York: Palgrave Macmillan.

Rama, M., and W. Maloney. 2001. "Income Support Programs for the Unemployed in Latin America." World Bank, Washington, DC.

Ravallion, M. 2000. "Monitoring Targeting Performance When Decentralized Allocations to the Poor Are Observed." *World Bank Economic Review* 14 (2): 331–46.

Reinecke, G. 2005. "Income Protection through Direct Employment Programmes: Recent Concepts and Examples from Latin America." *International Social Security Review* 58 (2–3): 163–83.

Saavedra, J. 2003. "Labor Markets during the 1990s." In *After the Washington Consensus: Restarting Growth and Reform in Latin America*, ed. P. Kuczynski and J. Williamson, 213–64. Washington, DC: Institute for International Economics.

Scarpetta, S., P. Hemmings, T. Tressel, and J. Woo. 2002. "The Role of Policy and Institutions for Productivity and Firm Dynamics: Evidence from Micro and Industry Data." Economics Department Working Paper 329, Organisation for Economic Co-operation and Development, Paris.

Scarpetta, S., and T. Tressel. 2004. "Boosting Productivity via Innovation and Adoption of New Technologies: Any Role for Labor Market Institutions?" Policy Research Working Paper Series 3273, World Bank, Washington, DC.

Sehnbruch, K. 2006. "Unemployment Insurance or Individual Savings Accounts: Can Chile's New Scheme Serve as a Model for Other Developing Countries?" *International Social Security Review* 59 (1): 27–48.

Siri, G. 2000. "Employment and Social Investment Funds in Latin America." Socio-Economic Technical Paper 7. Employment-Intensive Investment Branch, International Labour Office, Geneva.

SSA (Social Security Administration) and ISSA (International Social Security Association). 2005. *Social Security Programs throughout the World: Asia and the Pacific, 2004*. Washington, DC: SSA.

———. 2006a. *Social Security Programs throughout the World: The Americas, 2005*. Washington, DC: SSA.

———. 2006b. *Social Security Programs throughout the World: Europe, 2006*. Washington, DC: SSA.

Subbarao, K. 2003. "Systemic Shocks and Social Protection: Role and Effectiveness of Public Works Programs." Social Protection Discussion Paper 0302, World Bank, Washington, DC.

Vodopivec, M. 2004. *Income Support for the Unemployed: Issues and Options*. Washington, DC: World Bank

World Bank. 2005. *Colombia: Labor Market Adjustment, Reform, and Productivity: What Are the Factors That Matter?* Report 32068-CO. Washington, DC: World Bank.

———. 2006. *Doing Business 2007: How to Reform*. Washington, DC: World Bank.

World Bank and Instituto de Pesquisa Econômico Aplicada. 2002. *Brazil Jobs Report*. Report 24408-BR. Washington, DC: World Bank.

7

Active Labor Market Programs

Helping the Poor Find Better Jobs

Effective active labor market programs (ALMPs) are an important complementary tool to income-support policies. They actively seek to facilitate workers' job search and employers' recruitment (job intermediation), to enhance workers' skills and their employability (training), and in some cases to contribute to job creation through job subsidies and direct job creation (table 7.1 summarizes costs, benefits, and key requirements of ALMPs). When properly targeted and run efficiently, ALMPs can be cost-effective by promoting a better job match. In particular, they are expected to improve future job tenure and earnings of job seekers.

This chapter reviews the experience of ALMPs in Latin America and the Caribbean and discusses possible directions for improvement. It argues that ALMPs are generally underdeveloped in the region and have potential for scaling up. In particular, it suggests that job intermediation services can effectively help to match workers with adequate jobs and that efforts should be made to expand such services. Likewise, while acknowledging that training programs cannot replace formal education, the chapter suggests they can help to reduce skill shortages under certain circumstances. Finally, it concludes that employment subsidy programs can create employment for certain vulnerable groups or partially make up for the inefficiencies created by other policies, although at the cost of substitution effects and high fiscal outlays.

Job Intermediation

Job intermediation (JI)[1] addresses potential inefficiencies in the process of matching workers with jobs. Such inefficiencies arise because information does not flow instantly, and some workers and firms are much

Table 7.1 Theoretical Framework for Active Labor Market Programs

Schemes	*Main objectives*	*Drawbacks*	*Benefits*	*Key requirements for success*
Job intermediation services	Improve productivity of worker-job match. Link to other ALMPs. Where relevant, distribute unemployment insurance benefits and monitor eligibility.	Initial setup may require large financial investment and strong administrative capacity. Decentralized systems are more useful but more difficult to monitor.	Services are relatively cheap (in terms of costs per beneficiary) compared with those of other ALMPs.	Target to needs of unemployed workers and firms. Integrate into a "one-stop shop" approach. Consider opening to informal sector workers.
Public works programs	Provide income support, goods, and services. Empower communities.	Programs are expensive and only partially reach the poor. They do not seem to improve future employment or earning outcomes of workers.	Programs provide income to the needy. Programs provide job opportunities and address equity and insurance considerations.	Tailor to country-specific circumstances. Design program effectively. For cost-effectiveness, consider labor intensity, targeting performance, net wage gain, and indirect benefits to the poor (derived from the assets created by public works). Incorporate an insurance function.

(continued)

Table 7.1 Theoretical Framework for Active Labor Market Programs *(continued)*

Schemes	*Main objectives*	*Drawbacks*	*Benefits*	*Key requirements for success*
Training	Link income support with investment in human resources.	Training is expensive and has low coverage.	Training may improve future employability and earnings of participants.	Consider public-private partnerships, which work best (various forms exist). Monitor training quality. Target to specific groups.
Wage subsidies	Link income support with job creation.	Wage subsidies have large deadweight loss effects and substitution-displacement effects.	Subsidies allow job creation for disadvantaged workers and create jobs when other policies reduce job creation.	Target subsidies well. Assess preprogram employment levels accurately if they are to be provided only to marginal employment.
Microenterprise development	Improve productivity of microenterprises. Foster microenterprise development.	Programs may be expensive. Programs may be ineffective if not well targeted, because not all self-employed would benefit from them	Microenterprise development addresses the needs of the informal sector.	Provide services to current entrepreneurs or those with viable business ideas (ad hoc training or help does not appear successful). Link services with job intermediation and training.

Source: Authors' compilation.

better equipped to acquire information than others. When information about vacancies is difficult to obtain and JI services are not prevalent, workers fall back on personal networks of family and friends to find jobs. Similarly, when firms do not have adequate information on workers seeking jobs, they have to use expensive screening mechanisms or hire workers they know through their networks of family, friends, and current workers.

This situation creates inefficiencies and inequities. Studies (for example, Robins, Michalopoulos, and Foley 2008) have shown that supplementing income support with some form of targeted JI has enabled job seekers to obtain more secure and better-paid employment. Moreover, through its registering and coordination roles, JI can provide a basis for constructing an efficient set of ALMPs.

JI services consist of centralizing information and generally assisting individuals in their job search, expanding the pool of potential candidates for vacancies, and facilitating employers' selection of suitable candidates.[2] The services include (a) job search assistance, which provides practical help to job seekers preparing curriculum vitae and guiding workers' careers, and (b) job placement, which provides listings of job vacancies and other opportunities (for example, training programs), performs preliminary screening, and sends candidates to job interviews. Often, JI services also administer other ALMPs. In countries where unemployment insurance exists, JI services administer the payment of unemployment benefits and monitor the eligibility of beneficiaries. Effective JI services can be the central part of the whole system; they can link all the different services: job search, income support, and also training programs and other ALMPs.

As for the countries of the region, JI services need to be adapted to economies with a large concentration of poor and disadvantaged workers, where self-employment is prevalent, where a large share of the workforce is not registered, and where substantial internal and external migration is taking place (see box 7.1 for details). The problem is not that workers take too long to find jobs, but rather that they do not have the financial means to sustain themselves in unemployment and therefore cannot search long enough. In that regard, the objective of JI should be to help workers find better jobs.

The Region's Underdeveloped JI Systems

In Latin America and the Caribbean, JI services are either nonexistent or have limited coverage (Mazza 2003). The number of public employment services offices tends to be smaller than in comparator countries (table 7.2). Some countries have recently started to set up such services, but national coverage is rarely achieved. For example, Argentina currently

Box 7.1 Job Intermediation Should Take into Account the Specificities of the Region's Labor Market

Job intermediation can help identify relevant vulnerable groups. Industrial country evidence, which has focused on long-term unemployment, is not relevant for Latin American and Caribbean countries. Some countries address the "usual" vulnerable groups' needs (that is, youths, women, and those with disabilities); however, other groups may also exist, depending on the local circumstances. These groups can be identified only within countries.

JI can be a way to extend services to the specific needs of large informal sectors. The diffusion of information and other services can be extended to informal sector workers (for example, informal self-employment or microenterprises services). Some countries, such as Peru, provide information to small enterprises in a bid to give those businesses incentives to register and join the formal sector. Providing information on workers' rights and benefits as well as duties may render the formal sector more attractive to workers.

JI services have to take into account the substantial internal and external migration in the region, which is characterized by large migration flows between countries. Assisting this work-related migration also helps to improve productivity in the region by matching jobs and workers across borders. In this context, several Web sites already provide information on how to find work in other countries and supply lists of vacancies in various countries of the region.

Source: Mazza 2003.

has 50 employment offices in only 8 of 23 provinces, many of which have recently been opened or are about to be opened.[3] In Brazil in 2001, JI services registered only 23.7 percent of the unemployed (Ramos 2002). Low coverage implies that most people in the region still rely on family networks to find jobs. In Mexico, two-thirds of individuals report finding their job through networking, and 20 percent by contacting their employer directly. In Argentina, only 25 percent of the workers in the Gran Buenos Aires use public employment intermediation offices. In Brazil, only about 28 percent of unemployed workers are registered by JI services.

Moreover, JI centers tend to capture a small proportion of vacancies in the region. In Brazil, only 6.5 percent of vacancies were advertised through public employment services. Private employment services did better. Public employment services in 2001 had a ratio of vacancies to registered unemployed equal to 28 percent, whereas private employment agencies had a ratio of 43 percent (Ramos 2002).

Table 7.2 Public Employment Services Offices

Region		*Comparator countries*	
Country	*Number of public employment services offices per 100,000 habitants*	*Country*	*Number of public employment services offices per 100,000 habitants*
Brazil	0.6	Cyprus	0.78
Colombia	0.18	Mauritius	1.16
Dominican Republic	0.1	Portugal	1.17
El Salvador	0.11	Spain	1.9
Honduras	0.04	Thailand	0.13
Mexico	0.13	Tunisia	0.81
Nicaragua	0.16	Turkey	0.36
Panama	0.34		
Peru	0.14		
Venezuela, R.B. de	0.1		

Source: Survey of the World Association of Public Employment Services for 2006, http://www.ilo.org/public/english/employment/skills/empserv/public/.

Poor but Promising Performance of JIs

Little evidence exists on the effect of JI services on labor market outcomes in the region. In Brazil, public and private employment agencies direct only about two registered unemployed candidates per vacancy (with a slight advantage to public agencies). This number is lower than in countries of the Organisation for Economic Co-operation and Development (OECD).[4] In addition, public and private agencies place small numbers of job seekers. Public employment agencies appear less efficient than private ones in sending job seekers to interviews.[5] In fact, public agencies are better at placing them in jobs: 28 percent of those who were directed to vacancies by public agencies got a job offer, whereas only 19 percent of those directed by private agencies got a job offer (Ramos 2002).

Moreover, the experience of Brazil suggests that within-country disparities in terms of quality of services can be large. JI services registered 63 percent in the south but only 13.4 percent of the job seekers in the southeast in 2001. Such geographic differences are likely to occur also in other countries of the region: available evidence suggests similar geographic variations for broader ALMPs in other countries (Samaniego 2002b).

Despite their limited means and coverage, JI services appear to have some positive effects in helping the unemployed find better jobs, at least for some workers.[6] Indeed, Ramos (2002) finds that in Brazil, JI increases the probability of workers finding mainly formal jobs. Similarly, in Mexico, JI services help unemployed men find jobs more quickly, with better pay and conditions, although they seem to have little effect on women (Flores Lima 2006).

The evidence reported in this section suggests that improving JI services could significantly benefit workers and firms in the region. Moreover, using recent advances in information technologies can potentially reduce the cost of providing such services. In fact, information technologies are already enabling employment ministries of several countries—such as Argentina, Brazil, Chile, Colombia, Mexico, Peru, Uruguay, and the República Bolivariana de Venezuela—to make information more readily available to potential employers and job seekers. Such information includes workers' rights, employment regulation, availability of programs, resources for job seekers, vacancies, and links to Web sites publishing vacancies in their respective countries or in other countries of the region, as well as targeted information for vulnerable groups such as youths, women, and workers with disabilities. Although such developments are welcome, many workers do not have access to information technologies; for this reason, JI centers—which centralize such information and disseminate it among users—are still useful, particularly for low-income, less educated workers with very little direct access to the Internet.

The Need to Do More Than Provide Information

Current evidence indicates that only providing information is not enough to garner interest from employers and workers alike. Several reasons explain the lack of interest among employers. First, the perceived (and actual) quality of the services is rather low, and employers have no interest in registering their vacancies. This perception, in turn, creates a perceived lack of opportunities, which leads workers not to register, leading to an important coordination failure. In this context, current services are perceived as assisting the lower end of the labor market (IDB 2003). Second, solely publishing information about vacancies is not sufficient to improve the match between workers and employers. Services based on this assistance tend to be less efficient in placing workers (see Flores Lima 2006 for Mexico).

Better personal services to the job seekers and closer links with employers are necessary to make the system more efficient and more attractive to workers and employers. To attract employers, JI centers should demonstrate that they attract job seekers with a good range of competencies. In developed countries, JI services automatically record all job seekers but provide in-depth services only to those in greater need of help. For the Latin American and Caribbean countries that provide workfare benefits, linking the receipt of such benefits to JI and other ALMPs is likely to boost the number of registered job seekers. In turn, improvements in services will attract job seekers who do not necessarily receive benefits but who potentially need help searching for a better job. In other countries, improving access to information is the stepping-stone to enhancing help to job seekers.

To attract employers and register a greater number of vacancies, agencies should show that they can offer valuable services to employers. Experience in developed countries suggests that providing services such as managing the vacancies, helping to screen candidates, and providing information on all the subsidies available helps to boost employers' participation. Several countries of the region already publish information that employers can use. Providing extra help under the condition of registering vacancies may be a way of attracting more employers to use these services. Such help can take similar forms to what developed countries provide: for example, help lines can be established providing personalized advice on legislation, subsidies, the legal system, and the like or special services such as screening candidates.

Recent Reforms of Public Employment Services

Recent improvements of public employment services in developed and some developing countries have consisted of decentralizing, integrating, and monitoring their delivery (Mazza 2003). The aim of decentralization is to let regional and local offices tailor programs to their needs while the central administration keeps budget and funding, policy-setting, and evaluation responsibilities. The obvious advantage of being able to address local needs is balanced by the difficulties of managing such a system: it requires excellent communication between the central and local offices, the use of performance measures, and less control from the center. These issues are of particular concern in Latin America and the Caribbean, where regional differences in the quality of services abound.

Integrating services aims at ensuring efficiency by reducing the number of administrative procedures. For example, one-stop centers deliver a variety of services in one location. Another way to integrate services is to provide several levels of services by identifying the levels of job seekers' needs. For example, self-service can be developed for the majority of job seekers, while more specialized services are provided to those with more specific problems, such as youths, women, and workers with disabilities.

Monitoring can be done through the analysis of administrative data (for example, number of individuals served, types of interventions, outcomes). A step further toward raising efficiency may be to set internal performance targets. However, such targets have important disadvantages; in particular, setting specific targets may interfere with delivering services relevant to local circumstances.

Use of Public-Private Partnerships to Deliver Services

Since the 1990s, a growing consensus has emerged suggesting that the private sector has a role to play in the delivery of JI (Thuy, Hansen, and Price 2001).[7] The inclusion of the private sector has consisted of introducing market signals in the operation of public employment services[8] and encouraging the development of private employment agencies.[9] Public agencies often retain a monitoring role and are in charge of determining the eligibility of participants.

Overall, the available evidence indicates that JI can be a cost-effective way to improve productivity and better protect workers from the risks associated with labor mobility. Such schemes are currently underdeveloped and underfunded in the region. Their effectiveness needs to be improved by (a) improving registration by workers and firms, (b) improving the quality of the services, (c) extending their regional coverage, (d) developing minimum standards of performance that can be accomplished nationally but that could still be conditional on local constraints, and (e) linking them with other ALMPs and with the receipt of benefits in countries with unemployment insurance.

Training for the Unemployed

Training and retraining for the unemployed aim to provide job seekers with marketable skills that potentially increase their chances of getting a job as well as their earning capacity. In developed and developing countries alike, because of the cost of these programs, recent emphasis has been put on targeting workers in need of specific training.

If well designed, training can help job seekers improve their human capital and thus their employability. Certain groups tend to benefit more from training programs—for example, individuals who experience difficulties in securing gainful employment, either because they have experienced long-term unemployment or, more likely in the countries of the region, because they have experienced underemployment or repeated spells of unemployment.[10] Young individuals entering the labor market (in particular, disadvantaged youths) may also need training to strengthen their employability.[11] Training can equip them with skills that are closer to what is required by employers and make their early work experience, which is often characterized by frequent job changes, more productive. Finally, unemployed workers coming from sectors that are downsizing may have obsolete skills or need to find jobs in new sectors that require different skills. Retraining is particularly relevant in the case of mass layoffs where a large flow of newly unemployed reaches a local labor market.

Training Targeted at Youths: Largely Effective

The youth programs in the region have mostly targeted disadvantaged and low-income youths. These programs focus on motivating youths and fostering on-the-job training (for example, through subsidized temporary employment) of young school dropouts and other vulnerable youths who may lack the incentive to seek further qualifications.

Programs that combine training with other services, such as job readiness and job search assistance, have been developed since the early 1990s in the region. These programs follow the Jóvenes model, first implemented in Chile. Evaluations of their net effect have been carried out for several of these programs and have shown that they improve employment and earnings prospects of participants (Puerto 2007). Examples of these programs and impact evaluations include Argentina (Aedo and Núñez 2001; Elías and others 2004); Chile; Peru (Betcherman, Olivas, and Dar 2004); and Uruguay (Fawcett 2002; Naranjo Silva 2002).

Recent policy emphasis has been on improving youths' skills through training (vocational training, apprenticeship systems, life skills, and equivalency programs). In particular, the "Entra 21" programs, which started in 2002, aim to improve the employability of disadvantaged youths by providing training in information and communications technology. These programs have not been evaluated for their net effect on job creation, but they have been found to improve participants' chances of getting a job and the quality of the job found (Puerto 2007).

Interestingly, these positive findings contrast with the generally negative findings for similar programs in developed countries (Betcherman, Olivas, and Dar 2004). Rigorous evaluations of these programs have been far from the norm in the region, and when available, they have assessed only short-term results (up to a maximum of 18 months after program exit). Moreover, many evaluations do not include cost-benefit analyses, although cost per participant can be high. For example, estimates of the unit cost for the Jóvenes programs range from about US$700 to about US$2,000 per participant (Puerto 2007). Further research (impact evaluations) would therefore be useful in understanding the reasons for the differences between developed and developing countries and could bring interesting insights to the development of these programs in the region.

Training for the Unemployed and Long-Term Unemployed: A Patchwork of Contradictory Evidence

Overall, training programs have been less successful in terms of employment and earnings outcomes in developing countries than in developed countries (Betcherman, Olivas, and Dar 2004). This finding could be because the former experience specific constraints, such as weak administrative capacity and a large informal sector, which complicate the effective targeting of needs. The existing evaluations are patchy[12] but tend to suggest that women are the main beneficiaries in terms of employment and earnings. In Argentina, training provided through the Proempleo experiment from 1998 to 2000 found no effect on beneficiaries (Galasso, Ravallion, and Salvia 2004). In Colombia, training provided through the National Training Service (Servicio Nacional de Aprendizaje) in 1996 and 1997 was found to have no significant effect on earnings and a positive effect on the long-term employment prospects of women (Medina and Núñez 2005). In Mexico, the Program of Training Grants for Unemployed Workers (Programa de Becas de Capacitación para Trabajadores Desempleados) has been evaluated several times over the years (see Betcherman, Olivas, and Dar 2004; Samaniego 2002a, for an overview). Of seven reported evaluations, five showed that beneficiaries had higher earnings and employment probabilities than a control group (taken from the national urban employment survey). Moreover, although all Mexican studies found that the training program influenced different sociodemographic groups in different ways, they did not agree on whether men's or women's earnings increased because of the training.[13]

Importance of the Quality of the Curriculum and the Mode of Delivery

Despite the patchy evidence and the difficulty in finding definite conclusions on the overall effect of training programs, two elements appear crucial in ensuring their success: ensuring the quality of the programs and the mode of delivery. Not surprisingly, the quality of training is important in explaining subsequent labor market outcomes. Unfortunately, several programs—for example, the youth programs in Argentina, Chile, and Peru (see Betcherman, Olivas, and Dar 2004)—do not focus on this aspect. Moreover, the few evaluations that actually take this dimension into consideration show that it makes a big difference in the outcomes of participants. In the case of Peru, youths attending high-quality courses as opposed to lower-quality courses had greater subsequent earnings, amounting to a 32 percent difference 18 months after the program (Chong and Galdo 2006).[14]

Moreover, evidence suggests that involving private firms in the training is beneficial to trainees. The youth programs just mentioned include on-the-job training as part of their curriculum.[15] In Chile, youths who rotated classroom training with in-firm training obtained the largest effects from the program (Betcherman, Olivas, and Dar 2004). In Peru, on-the-job training tends to offset low-quality classroom training.[16] To guarantee a paid, on-the-job training experience for each trainee, the Peruvian program follows a demand-driven approach in which competing institutions must offer training for those occupations with assured labor demand. This demand-driven offer of on-the-job training appears as an important element of successful courses. The program has, in this way, been able to relocate youths—especially women—to better-paid jobs. However, the success of the program is very much related to its careful design and significant cost per trainee. Its coverage is therefore limited, and so is its overall effect on youths.

Another way to improve the quality of training is to allow private institutions to provide it.[17] In Colombia, public institutions, which tend to offer general courses as well as training in basic skills and to have greater national coverage, do not improve adult men's future earnings. Private institutions, which offer more specialized courses and are concentrated in the main cities, do improve their outcomes, especially in the long run.[18] Adult women tend to benefit from public and private training, although the gain from public training tends to be lower and less significant (Medina and Núñez 2005).

Even with private provision, the public sector retains a monitoring role. The enforcement of quality and relevant training by the authorities is necessary and useful.[19] Such control from the authorities helps workers and employers choose among providers by publishing transparent information and provides a benchmark that new providers are expected to reach. Rather than through new regulations, which create disincentives for firms to provide training, quality can be enforced through other mechanisms, such as vouchers, certification of schools and programs, and publication of information on which types of programs employers value more. In addition, significant participation and proper referral of the unemployed can be the responsibility of JI services in the ways described in the previous section.

Direct Job Creation

Until the 1980s, governments in Latin America and the Caribbean made extensive use of direct job creation in the public sector to cope with periods of high unemployment. More recently, emphasis on promoting job creation in the private sector has increased, although workfare and public works programs still play an important role in the overall ALMP expenditure in the region. The main instruments of direct job creation are (a) *public works programs*, which are self-targeted temporary job creation programs; (b) *wage and employment subsidies*, which involve reducing the payroll tax, the wages, or the severance payments of specific groups of workers to increase their employment; and (c) *microenterprise development*, which consists of giving tax incentives and business management advice to unemployed people who wish to start their own enterprises.

Public Works Programs

Public works programs provide work experience to prevent skills degradation or detachment from the labor market. Setting the program wage low enough ensures that it does not attract nonpoor individuals or create large labor market distortions. These programs, however, require strong local administrative capacity and rely on a well-structured relationship between the central government and local authorities.

In Latin America and the Caribbean, where most countries lack social protection systems, governments have often used public works programs to support the income of poor individuals in times of crisis—for example, in Argentina, Bolivia, Chile, Peru, and Uruguay (see Reinecke 2005). The available evidence shows that although these programs successfully target the poor, they often do not improve subsequent earnings or employment probabilities (see Jalan and Ravallion 2003 for Argentina).

More evidence is available from developed countries and shows that public works programs generally do not improve beneficiaries' chances of securing regular employment (Betcherman, Olivas, and Dar 2004). These results may be explained by the fact that the tasks demanded from participants often require few skills and do not have any training content; participants may become even more stigmatized by their participation in such programs. From this perspective, workfare programs may be more useful as targeting devices for income support than as ALMPs. In any case, improving the training content and linking them to JI services may improve their effect on future earnings and the probability of securing regular employment.

Hiring Subsidies

Wage and employment subsidies aim to reduce the costs of hiring for employers. They can either involve a direct wage reduction or involve a reduction in social security contributions or severance pay. Subsidies can be applied to all workers or only to new hires (marginal subsidies), although they are typically targeted at vulnerable groups of workers who are hard to place, such as the long-term unemployed, youths, workers with disabilities, or low-skill workers.

The expectation is that the subsidy covers the initial cost of training the new workers, so that by the time the subsidy ends, the productivity of the worker is high enough for the employer to have a strong incentive for keeping him or her. Theoretical analyses (for example, Phelps 1997a, 1997b) suggest that subsidies can have large positive employment effects and advocate their use. Such analyses typically assume that labor demand for the low-wage earners is very sensitive to costs, however, which may not always be the case (Dolado and others 1996; OECD 1998, 2003).

The employment effect of subsidies also depends on how much of the subsidy is transferred to workers in the form of higher wages, which in turn depends on the elasticity of labor supply. In the case where labor supply is fully inelastic, employment effects are null, and all the effect is passed onto workers through wages. In contrast, when labor supply is fully elastic or minimum wages are binding, the effect of subsidies is fully reflected in employment gains.

The available evaluations, which have mostly been carried out in developed countries, show that, in practice, subsidies lead to substantive employment creation but at the expense of large deadweight losses and substitution effects. *Deadweight losses* refer to the number of subsidized workers who would have found employment anyway; they are often estimated to be over 50 percent.[20] Such difficulty in targeting the subsidy substantially increases its costs. Evaluations also find large substitution effects, whereby subsidized individuals are employed instead of unsubsidized ones. Other effects, such as the possible displacement of some workers because of distortions in market competition, are more difficult to measure.

In Latin America and the Caribbean, wage subsidies have been much less used than have public works (Auer, Efendioglu, and Leschke 2005; IDB 2003; Márquez 2000). Apart from in Argentina, when used, wage subsidies have had a modest reach. In Argentina, the subsidy scheme Proempleo was targeted at workers displaced by retrenchment in company towns. Affected workers received a voucher that entitled a hiring employer to a wage subsidy of US$150 per month for workers age 45 and above and US$100 per month for workers younger than 45.[21] The evaluation of this program shows some positive short-term employment effect but no positive effects on future earnings. Moreover, because of the costs and administrative procedures involved for firms, take-up was quite low (Galasso, Ravallion, and Salvia 2004; Marx 2001).

In Colombia, the labor market reform of 2002 included incentives to increase employment among the following vulnerable groups: (a) poor heads of household; (b) ex-guerrillas under a state program (*reinsertados*); (c) people with disabilities; (d) people between the ages of 16 and 25 years and older than 50; and (e) former convicts. The incentives consisted of exemptions from labor taxes for firms employing individuals from these groups. Initial monitoring showed a low take-up. Employers appeared unaware of the subsidies, found them too low given the administrative burden that they necessitated, or were unwilling to employ workers from the eligible vulnerable groups. The low take-up may also have been due to a built-in conflict of interest: the subsidy actually took money away from the institution that was in charge of implementing it (World Bank 2005).

There may be an argument for using such subsidies to target vulnerable individuals; however, so far wage subsidies have not been found to improve the future earnings of beneficiaries. A case also exists for using wage subsidies to remedy the disemployment effects created by the combination of high social security taxes and binding minimum wages. Binding minimum wages prevent employers from shifting the cost of social security onto workers and therefore increase nonwage labor costs at the low end of the wage distribution. This situation, in turn, may have important employment costs for low-income workers. Of course, the best way to tackle this problem is to lower social security contributions for low-income workers or to set the minimum wage at a more appropriate level. Yet to the extent that political economy constraints prevent some of these adjustments from happening, wage subsidies given to employers can offset such effects.

Some design features could enhance wage subsidies' efficiency in improving future labor market outcomes. Combining subsidies with other ALMPs, such as training or job search programs, may improve future earnings outcomes.

Microenterprise Development

Microenterprise development consists of supporting the start-up and development of self-employment or microenterprises. These services include financial assistance (for example, through credit, allowances, or grants) as well as technical services, such as training, counseling, and assistance in business plan development. When all these elements are combined, they can successfully increase the productivity of beneficiaries and, by extension, improve the viability of microenterprises. They are also meant to increase the subsequent earnings and employment probabilities of beneficiaries. This type of intervention is important in the region, given that microenterprises employ a large proportion of the labor force (over 50 percent of the labor force in the 1990s), mostly in the informal sector (Orlando and Pollack 2000).

The evaluations that have been carried out both in developed countries and in the region tend to be encouraging. They suggest that microenterprises that have benefited from these programs have better chances of survival (see Betcherman, Olivas, and Dar 2004 for developed countries). Mexico has a program that aims to increase the productivity and competitiveness of micro, small, and medium firms through training and technical assistance. It assesses the situation of enterprises and provides support to reduce their weaknesses through consulting, training, or technology support.[22] Two evaluations found that this program positively affected different variables that are expected to increase productivity: worker training, capacity utilization, adoption of quality control, changes in logistics, and decreased turnover (Samaniego 2002b; Tan and López-Acevedo 2005). In Brazil, microenterprise development is considered to be positive overall, but several changes have been suggested—in particular, to better integrate the different services. For example, microfinance is rarely linked to training (only 23 percent of beneficiaries received a qualification), and targeting needs need to be improved (in Rio de Janeiro, 60 percent of beneficiaries had tertiary education) (Ramos 2002).

However, an important weakness of most of these evaluations is that they do not compare outcomes for beneficiaries with outcomes of a control group; they do not provide information on the net effect of these programs (see reviews of evaluation studies for developed countries in Betcherman, Olivas, and Dar 2004; for Brazil in Ramos 2002; for Mexico in Samaniego 2002a); or they poorly choose the control group.[23]

An exception is Chile, where a pilot study that defines a control group was carried out. The evaluation of the pilot found that the probability of bankruptcy is lower and the probability of expansion is higher among microenterprises that benefited from the program compared with those in the control group (Bravo, Contreras, and Crespi 2000). In particular, Bravo, Contreras, and Crespi (2000) found that the program improved the management of the businesses (management quality, strategic planning, search for business opportunities, and the like). They concluded that these improvements led to an increase in sales. As in most evaluations of such policies, however, the authors are concerned with the effect on business development rather than with individuals' outcomes, and they do not take into account displacement and substitution effects.

Overall, one can consider that microenterprises are far from having reached their potential in the region and that scope exists for the development of such intervention (as stated in Auer, Efendioglu, and Leschke 2005). At the same time, all the reviews mentioned in this section express concerns with the lack of adequate evaluation of the existing studies. They also point out that integrating services provided better outcomes. Finally, in addition to the services mentioned above, governments of the region can improve (and have done so) the regulatory framework to stimulate microenterprise creation. A particular issue is the availability of credit, as described in the literature on microfinance.[24]

Conclusion

There is potential in Latin America and the Caribbean for improving the design and performance of ALMPs, particularly job intermediation systems. These programs are going to be particularly important if income-support mechanisms to protect workers against the risk of unemployment become more important and costly. The choice of specific policies depends on country circumstances. JI has been found to have the potential not only to improve the match between workers and employers, but also to form the center point for integrating the various existing schemes and policies, for linking to income support and the disbursement of benefits where relevant, and for making the labor market more transparent by informing workers and employers about regulations and rights. Training has been implemented throughout the region with various levels of success, and the evidence shows that proper targeting and adequate design and quality improve the outcomes. This result is, in fact, true of all ALMPs that have been reviewed here. Public employment programs have been shown not to be useful in an activation role, although they are useful in their income-support role. Hiring subsidies have been shown to suffer from large costs and losses and to have little effect in terms of improving overall employment. However, they may be useful for countries that aim to correct for distortions that create disadvantages for low-income earners.

Indeed, even if labor market policies do not have strong effects on wages and employment, governments may, for a number of reasons, still want to implement them. For example, governments may want to avoid—or at least reduce—the risk of exclusion of certain groups of workers from the labor market. This chapter suggests that well-designed and properly targeted measures can have beneficial effects in this respect. However, given the dearth of evaluations, programs are advised to start small and scale up only if indications of positive outcomes are strong. Evaluations work best when embedded in the design of projects and based on an experimental design (that is, potential participants are randomly assigned to treatment and control groups).[25] In addition to the policy effect, evaluations should attempt to measure substitution and deadweight loss effects. Some countries have already established monitoring systems. For example, Brazil carries out extensive monitoring of its training system (Ramos 2002), and the youth training program of Peru has included provision for monitoring and impact evaluation from its inception. Despite these examples, progress can be made in all countries (Ramos 2002; Samaniego 2002b). In this context, evaluations of training for small and medium-size companies in Mexico have shown that if appropriate methodologies are not used, results can vary greatly even when the same data are used (Tan and López-Acevedo 2005).

Moreover, establishing labor market programs that work well in normal times is important, rather than introducing emergency programs at the time of crisis. In the past, sudden and drastic rises in unemployment rates have often triggered labor market reforms in the countries of the region. Governments have designed temporary responses to crises. The lack of preparation associated with designing programs in times of crisis and in a rush has often led to far from optimal programs that create important labor market distortions (Márquez 2000). A solution to avoid such quick-fix solutions is to establish a comprehensive social protection program in normal times with the built-in capacity to accommodate extensions of unemployment insurance or targeted short-term programs in times of need. This strategy has several advantages. It can ensure that programs are limited in time and encourage graduation of participants. Moreover, publishing information about these programs and stressing their availability in times of need may induce workers to get involved in riskier and potentially more productive employment activities (de Janvry and Sadoulet 2006; de Janvry and others 2006; Dercon 2006).

Notes

1. The term *job intermediation* refers to services provided by public employment agencies and expanding private services sectors as well as the many types of partnerships between the two.

2. Interest in these services has recently been renewed in developed countries, where they are considered to be a good value for money. The focus has been on improving them (Bucheli 2005; Mazza 2003; OECD 2000, 2005). This experience suggests that in a context of limited resources, JI may be more cost-effective than other types of ALMPs (Martin and Grubb 2001).

3. See http://www.trabajo.gov.ar/ for details.

4. A survey conducted by the OECD shows that public employment services in OECD countries send on average three or four candidates to apply for each vacancy. The survey seems to exaggerate somewhat the number of candidates for some countries, but other evidence confirms that the ratio is much higher than in Latin America and the Caribbean. Denmark reports an average of only 1.5 per vacancy in the OECD survey. More reliable estimates still suggest 3 referrals per vacancy on average for Sweden and 8 to 10 referrals for Austria. The United Kingdom regards four to eight candidates as the ideal (European Commission 2000).

5. In Brazil in 2001, public agencies directed about 53 percent of those registered toward job offers, compared with 83 percent for private agencies.

6. Limited evidence exists on the performance of JI services in the region because the focus is often on monitoring rather than on evaluating the services.

7. In the past, the provision of public employment services was reserved to the public sector. This principle, defended by the International Labour Organization, was based on an adverse selection issue: it was suggested that private provision of these services would not be universal nor serve the most vulnerable groups.

8. There are several ways to introduce competition in the provision of JI services, such as contracting out services (for example, for training provision); using vouchers, which enable the user to shop around for services; or establishing user charges, which are ethically questionable in terms of being used for unemployed workers, who lack financial resources, but can be used for employers.

9. Private employment agencies used to be banned in many countries, and the International Labour Organization had a convention advising against their use (Thuy, Hansen, and Price 2001). This tendency has been reversed, and the improvement of the regulatory environment for private and nonprofit providers has facilitated their development. See, for example, http://www.mtss.gub.uy/dinae/proyectos/agencias.htm for the case in Uruguay or http://www.mintra.gob.pe/dnfp_ape.php for the case in Peru.

10. Other potential target groups include workers with disabilities, persons displaced by violence, and the like.

11. In most countries, these difficulties are exemplified by youth unemployment rates that are much larger than adult rates.

12. The existing evaluations suffer from weaknesses, such as short evaluation periods, lack of cost-benefit analysis, or lack of focus on training quality. In some countries, such as Brazil, the monitoring of training programs is embedded in their design and is meant to provide feedback for future policies, but these evaluations do not use the latest econometric methodologies to determine the net effect of programs.

13. Revenga, Riboud, and Tan (1994) suggested that the program increased the men's earnings only. Although this finding was confirmed in a second study (STPS 1995), it was contradicted in a third study (CIESA 1998), where women's earnings increased; Calderón-Madrid and Trejo (2001) confirmed the latter results, finding that female participants' earnings were 12 percent higher than in the control group.

14. Quality is measured through quantitative and qualitative criteria: class size, expenditures per trainee, 8 teacher variables, 6 infrastructure and equipment characteristics, 19 curricular structure variables, and 9 variables characterizing the link between the content of the courses and the institution's knowledge about workers and occupational analysis of labor demand. These variables are combined into a single quality index using principal component analysis (Chong and Galdo 2006).

15. In Argentina, the program targets 16- to 29-year-olds of the lower social stratum. It has a technical knowledge phase and an internship phase. The Chilean program targets low-income 15- to 24-year-olds who are unemployed or underemployed. The training includes a six-month package aimed at attaining a semiskilled level in specific trades as well as an internship. The program in Uruguay also includes in-firm subsidized employment for youths 17 to 24 years of age.

16. Peru's Youth Training Program (Programa de Capacitación Laboral Juvenil, or PROJoven) was implemented in 1995 with the goal of increasing the employability and productivity of disadvantaged individuals 16 to 25 years of age through job-specific training in blue-collar occupations. PROJoven consists of a mix of formal and on-the-job training organized into two sequential phases. The first stage consists of 300 hours of classes at the training center locations, roughly five hours per day for three months. In the second phase, training institutions must place trainees into paid, on-the-job training experiences in private manufacturing firms for an additional period of three months.

17. From a model where the state was the main actor in providing training, systems have evolved in the face of increasing demand for skills. A large increase has occurred in the number of private providers. For example, at the beginning of the 2000s, Brazil counted 16,000 private institutions, Colombia had about 400 private training entities, and in El Salvador, some training was contracted out to a network of about 60 collaborating centers.

18. A distinction is made between short-run effects (the training took place the year before) and long-run effects (training took place over a year ago).

19. See the description of the monitoring system in Brazil in Ramos (2002).

20. Marx (2001) looks at evaluations from Australia, Belgium, Ireland, the Netherlands, the United Kingdom, and the United States.

21. The subsidy amounted to more than 50 percent of a worker's gross wage.

22. This program was created in 1987 and called the Comprehensive Quality and Modernization Program (Programa de Calidad Integral y Modernización, or CIMO). In 2001, the program changed its name to the Program to Support Training (Programa de Apoyo a la Capacitación, or PAC).

23. Tan and López-Acevedo (2005) show how results can vary with the choice of control group and empirical strategies for Mexico.

24. See, for example, a review in Bucheli (2005) and Ramírez (2004).

25. The literature on impact evaluation of programs has shown that (a) impact evaluation is useful in informing the design of new programs, and (b) to be successful, impact evaluation has to be thought of in the early stages of program design (Pierre 1999).

References

Aedo, C., and S. Núñez. 2001. "The Impact of Training Policies in Latin America and the Caribbean: The Case of 'Programa Joven.'" Graduate Program in Economics, ILADES/Georgetown University, Washington, DC.

Auer, P., U. Efendioglu, and J. Leschke. 2005. *Active Labour Market Policies around the World: Coping with the Consequences of Globalization*. Geneva: International Labour Office.

Betcherman, G., K. Olivas, and A. Dar. 2004. "Impacts of Active Labor Market Programs: New Evidence from Evaluations with Particular Attention to Developing and Transition Countries." Social Protection Discussion Paper 0402, World Bank, Washington, DC.

Bravo, D., D. Contreras, and G. Crespi. 2000. "Evaluating Training Programs for Small-Scale Entrepreneurs: A Pilot Study." Universidad de Chile, Santiago.

Bucheli, M. 2005. "Las políticas activas de mercado de trabajo: Un panorama internacional de experiencias y evaluaciones." Estudios y Perspectivas 2. Comisión Económica para América Latina y el Caribe, Montevideo.

Calderón-Madrid, A., and B. Trejo. 2001. "The Impact of the Mexican Training Program for Unemployed Workers on Re-employment Dynamics and on Earnings." Network Research Paper, Inter-American Development Bank, Washington, DC.

Chong, A., and J. Galdo. 2006. "Training Quality and Earnings: The Effects of Competition on the Provision of Public-Sponsored Training Programs." Research Department Working Paper 555, Inter-American Development Bank, Washington, DC.

CIESA. 1998. "Estudio de evaluación de la modalidad mixta del PROBECAT 1998." Final report for the Secretariat of Labor and Social Welfare, CIESA, Mexico City.

de Janvry, A., F. Finan, E. Sadoulet, and R. Vakis. 2006. "Can Conditional Cash Transfer Programs Serve as Safety Nets in Keeping Children at School and from Working When Exposed to Shock?" *Journal of Development Economics* 79 (2): 349–73.

de Janvry, A., and E. Sadoulet. 2006. "Making Conditional Cash Transfer Programs More Efficient: Designing for Maximum Effect of the Conditionality." *World Bank Economic Review* 20 (1): 1–29.

Dercon, S. 2006. "Risk, Growth, and Poverty: What Do We Know, What Do We Need to Know?" Department of Economics, Oxford University, Oxford, U.K.

Dolado, J., F. Kramarz, S. Machin, A. Manning, D. Margolis, and C. Teulings. 1996. "The Economic Impact of Minimum Wages in Europe." *Economic Policy* 11 (23): 317–57.

Elías, V., F. Ruiz Núñez, R. Cossa, and D. Bravo. 2004. "An Econometric Cost-Benefit Analysis of Argentina's Youth Training Program." Research Network Working Paper 482, Inter-American Development Bank, Washington, DC.

European Commission, Employment and Social Affairs DG. 2000. "The Service Model of Public Employment Services (PES) to Support the Fight against Long-Term Unemployment." Working paper, Commission Services, European Commission, Brussels.

Fawcett, C. 2002. "Latin American Youth in Transition: A Policy Paper on Youth Unemployment in Latin America." Labor Market Policy Brief, School of International Service, American. http://www.eldis.org/static/DOC11803.htm.

Flores Lima, R. 2006. "El Servicio de Intermediación Laboral como instrumento para promover la inclusión social y de género en el mercado laboral en México." Centro de Investigaciones sobre Economía Laboral y Gestión del Conocimiento, Mexico City.

Galasso, E., M. Ravallion, and A. Salvia. 2004. "Assisting the Transition from Workfare to Work: A Randomized Experiment." *Industrial and Labor Relations Review* 58 (1): 128–42.

IDB (Inter-American Development Bank). 2003. *Good Jobs Wanted: Labor Markets in Latin America—2004 Report on Economic and Social Progress in Latin America*. Washington, DC: IDB.

Jalan, J., and M. Ravallion. 2003. "Estimating the Benefit Incidence of an Antipoverty Program by Propensity-Score Matching." *Journal of Business and Economic Statistics* 21 (1): 19–30.

Márquez, G. 2000. "Labor Markets and Income Support: What Did We Learn from the Crises?" Research Department Working Paper 425, Inter-American Development Bank, Washington, DC.

Martin, J., and D. Grubb. 2001. "What Works and for Whom: A Review of OECD Countries' Experiences with Active Labour Market Policies." *Swedish Economic Policy Review* 8 (2): 9–56.

Marx, I. 2001. "Job Subsidies and Cuts in Employers' Social Security Contributions: The Verdict of Empirical Evaluation Studies." *International Labour Review* 140 (1): 69–83.

Mazza, J. 2003. "Labour Intermediation Services: Lessons from Latin America and the Caribbean." *CEPAL Review* 80 (August): 159–75.

Medina, C., and J. Núñez. 2005. "The Impact of Public and Private Job Training in Colombia." Research Network Working Paper 484, Inter-American Development Bank, Washington, DC.

Naranjo Silva, A. 2002. *Capacitación y formación profesional para jóvenes en Uruguay*. Montevideo: Cinterfor.

OECD (Organisation for Economic Co-operation and Development). 1998. *OECD Employment Outlook*. Paris: OECD.

———. 2000. *Labour Market Policies and the Public Employment Service*. Paris: OECD.

———. 2003. *OECD Employment Outlook*. Paris: OECD.

———. 2005. *OECD Employment Outlook*. Paris: OECD.

Orlando, M. B., and M. Pollack. 2000. *Microenterprises and Poverty: Evidence from Latin America*. Washington, DC: Inter-American Development Bank.

Phelps, E. S. 1997a. *Rewarding Work: How to Restore Participation and Self-Support to Free Enterprise*. Cambridge, MA: Harvard University Press.

———. 1997b. "Wage Subsidy Programmes: Alternative Designs." In *Unemployment Policy: Government Options for the Labour Market*, ed. D. J. Snower and G. de la Dehesa, 206–43. Cambridge, U.K.: Cambridge University Press.

Pierre, G. 1999. "A Framework for Active Labour Market Policy Evaluation." Employment and Training Paper 49, International Labour Organization, Geneva.

Puerto, O. 2007. "Interventions to Support Young Workers in Latin America and the Caribbean: Regional Report for the Youth Employment Inventory." World Bank, Washington, DC.

Ramírez, Á. 2004. "The Microfinance Experience in Latin America and the Caribbean." Paper presented at the Workshop on Modalities of Microfinance Delivery in Asia: Latin America Economics and Business Association Research Conference on Microfinance in Latin America and Asia, Asian Development Bank Institute, Manila, October 4–8. http://www.ruralfinance.org/servlet/BinaryDownloaderServlet?filename=1126101177627_Microfinance_experience_in_LAC.pdf.

Ramos, C. 2002. "Las políticas del mercado de trabajo y su evaluación en Brasil." Macroeconomía del Desarrollo 16, Economic Commission for Latin America and the Caribbean, United Nations, Santiago.

Reinecke, G. 2005. "Income Protection through Direct Employment Programmes: Recent Concepts and Examples from Latin America." *International Social Security Review* 58 (2–3): 163–83.

Revenga, A., M. Riboud, and H. Tan. 1994. "The Impact of Mexico's Retraining Program on Employment and Wages." *World Bank Economic Review* 8 (2): 247–77.

Robins, P., C. Michalopoulos, and K. Foley. 2008. "Are Two Carrots Better Than One? The Effects of Adding Employment Services to Financial Incentive Programs for Welfare Recipients." *Industrial and Labor Relations Review* 61 (3): 410–23.

Samaniego, N. 2002a. "Las políticas de mercado de trabajo en México y su evaluación." Macroeconomía del Desarrollo 18, Economic Commission for Latin America and the Caribbean, United Nations, Santiago.

———. 2002b. "Las políticas de mercado de trabajo y su evaluación en América Latina." Macroeconomía del Desarrollo 19, Economic Commission for Latin America and the Caribbean, United Nations, Santiago.

STPS (Secretaría de Trabajo y Previsión Social). 1995. "Evaluación del Programa de Becas de Capacitación para Desempleados." Dirección General de Empleo, STPS, Mexico City.

Tan, H., and G. López-Acevedo. 2005. "Evaluating Training Programs for Small and Medium Enterprises: Lessons from Mexico." Policy Research Working Paper 3760, World Bank, Washington, DC.

Thuy, P., E. Hansen, and D. Price. 2001. *The Public Employment Service in a Changing Labour Market.* Geneva: International Labour Organization.

World Bank. 2005. *Colombia: Labor Market Adjustment, Reform, and Productivity: What Are the Factors That Matter?* Report 32068-CO. Washington, DC: World Bank.

8

Improving the Quality of Jobs

From Legislation to Productivity Growth

Policies aimed at improving the quality and productivity of jobs assume a central role in ensuring equitable and efficient outcomes in the labor market. Governments may intervene in different ways:

- Imposing standards on workplace practices
- Promoting risk pooling to diversify sickness, disability, and old-age risks across a large number of workers
- Promoting collective bargaining
- Setting minimum wages to limit the risk of poverty while at jobs
- Fostering upgrading of skills through on-the-job training.

Although advances in mandatory benefits tend to be viewed as advances in workers' welfare, excessive and burdensome regulations may also lead to poor job creation, particularly in higher-paying firms (see chapter 5). For this reason, governments need to walk a fine line between legislating better work conditions and assessing whether such conditions are appropriate given a country's level of development and labor productivity. This balancing act is particularly necessary when enforcement capabilities are weak and inappropriate regulations lead firms or workers to opt out of such higher standards and work under informal or substandard conditions.

This chapter shows that Latin America and the Caribbean is within international standards with respect to workplace regulations and mandatory benefits, such as working hours and social contributions, although important differences occur across countries. Nonetheless, the evidence suggests that the costs of such provisions are only partially passed onto workers and that high levels of benefits tend to be associated with disemployment effects for low-income workers, particularly in countries with high minimum wages. This finding implies that in some countries decreases in employer contribution for low-wage workers could provide an important stimulus for registered employment, particularly in countries where minimum wages are binding.

Countries have attempted to improve workers' earnings by setting minimum wages. The evidence suggests that despite low compliance, the minimum wage is binding in the formal sector of several countries of the region and operates as a strong pay signal for the informal sector in many countries. It contributes to increasing wages but at the cost of employment losses for workers around the minimum wage in some countries.

This finding suggests that increasing the quality of jobs through legislated benefits has to be considered carefully. Other policies may be more promising to improve the quality of jobs. One of these might be to improve job training as an engine of productivity growth and higher earnings. Although many countries in Latin America and the Caribbean have made important advances in providing training, important deficiencies and inequities remain, and governments need to improve the incentives for firms and workers to seek training. Another area that holds promise for improving job quality is improving social dialogue, which is seriously lacking in the region and can have beneficial effects in terms of improved enforcement and public acceptance of often unpopular labor market reforms.

An important issue in most countries of the region is the lack of capacity to enforce laws. Because enforcement significantly influences the final effect and effectiveness of regulations, such as those described in this report, the penultimate section of the chapter is devoted to this issue. It reviews the evidence regarding the role and effect of the three main institutions that enforce laws and regulations (the administration, the unions, and the judiciary).

Regulating Working Conditions: Adding Flexibility, Improving Enforcement, and Protecting Workers

Promoting better health and safety conditions in firms, regulating working time, and encouraging paid annual leave have been major achievements in all societies that protect workers against abusive working conditions. As in most other areas of public policy, improvements in working conditions in industrial countries have evolved gradually, hand in hand with more general economic progress. By contrast, many low- and middle-income countries have skipped the intermediate steps and directly adopted far-reaching workplace regulations, sometimes going beyond the protection that exists in many industrial countries.

Latin American and Caribbean countries tend to regulate hours and holidays similarly to industrial countries (figure 8.1).[1] However, within the region, large variations exist, even in countries of similar levels of

Figure 8.1 Working Hours, by Region

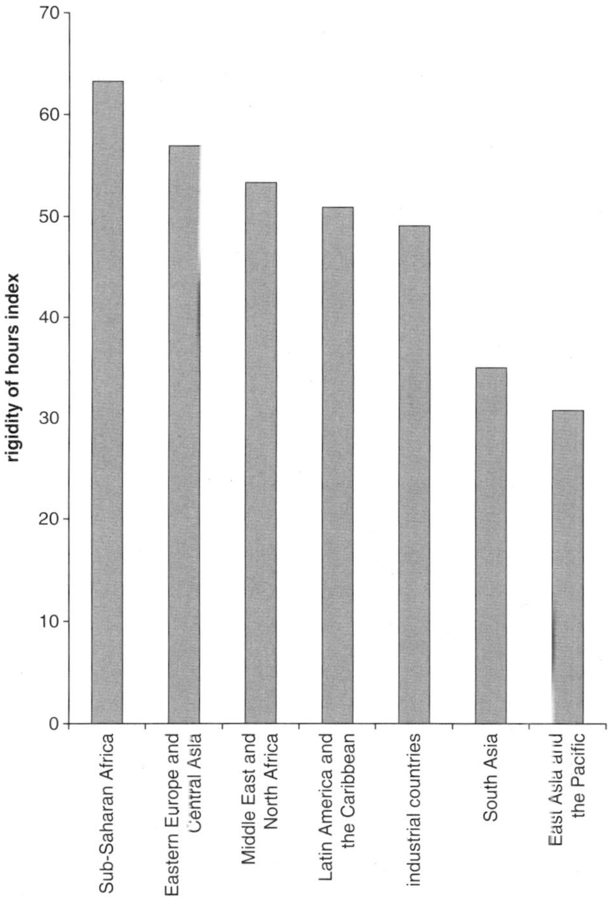

Source: World Bank Doing Business database.

development (figure 8.2). Moreover, the actual coverage of such regulations is likely to be quite low because workers in the informal sector, which represented about 47 percent of nonagricultural employment in the region in the mid 2000s (ILO 2005), are not likely to benefit from them. Even in the formal sector, enforcement can be low.

Figure 8.2 Working Hours, by Country

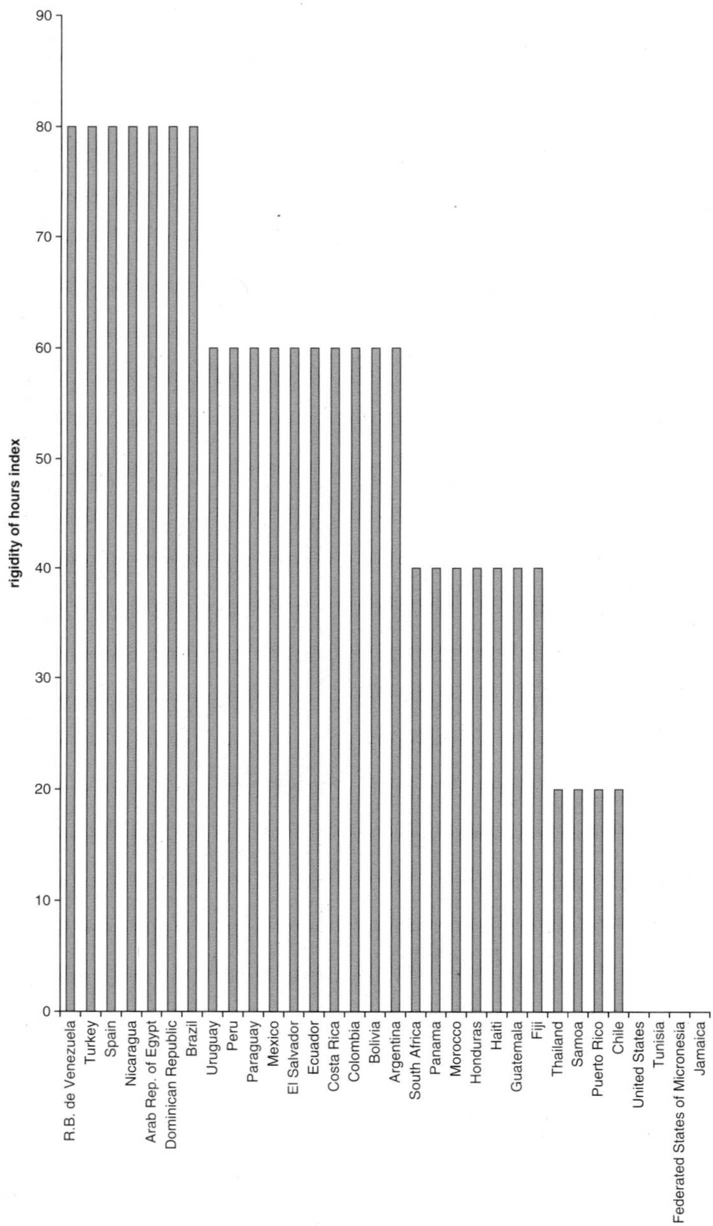

Source: World Bank Doing Business database.

Like hiring and firing regulations, workplace regulations potentially can significantly affect labor costs and the ability of firms to accommodate fluctuations in demand. The size of the effect depends on firms' ability to pass costs onto workers. Governments' strategy to protect specific vulnerable groups of workers, such as women, may backfire because such regulations make them more costly to employers. In the region, such regulations may become an additional incentive for firms to be in the informal economy. Some countries of the region have recently introduced reforms that make hours of work regulations more flexible (for example, Colombia[2]).

An interesting and promising effort to make regulations on working hours more flexible while keeping workers protected comes from European countries. Many have started to make possible the calculation of the weekly limit on working hours imposed by labor law as an average over a period of time (six months or one year). The purpose of this approach is to allow firms to adjust to peak and slack periods in the production schedule. Hence, in a given period, employees may work for more than the stipulated maximum weekly working hours (peak period), while in other periods they may work for fewer hours (slack periods). This type of working arrangement is relatively recent in contrast to more traditional forms of working time, such as overtime, shift work, and the like. No countries regulate in explicit terms the annualization of hours worked. Most countries allow working time limits on normal working time (daily, weekly, or both) to be exceeded as long as the normal limits are maintained on average over a certain reference period. The maximum length of this period is often one year but can be shorter. The organization of working time is generally done at the company level, often through collective agreements. Remuneration is generally a fixed sum that corresponds to remuneration for a standard working week or for a fixed amount of hours over the reference period.

Making Social Security Contributions a Value for the Money

Protection against health risk and old-age poverty and, to a lesser extent, compensation for life events such as birth of children and the disability or death of household members are provided in most countries around the world. In Latin America and the Caribbean, they are part of a tradition of formally providing social security that dates to the beginning of the 20th century. In recent years, in the face of a growing issue of financial sustainability of the systems, many countries of the region have reformed their social security and, in particular, the pension system (Gill, Packard, and Yermo 2005).

A common issue is financing these benefits. They are generally financed through payroll taxes in the form of mandatory contributions by employers and employees (social security contributions). Higher payroll taxes may lead to higher labor costs. In particular, firms will not be able to pass the full cost of these contributions onto workers who do not want these benefits or who perceive that they are not value for money. Empirical evidence at the country level is therefore necessary to decide whether particular levels of contributions are appropriate for the country's circumstances.

How Do Social Security Contributions Compare with International Standards?

Looking at total social security contributions (figure 8.3) shows that, on average, the region does not have especially high rates compared with those of other regions. However, a lot of variation occurs within the region.

Figure 8.3 Social Security Contribution Rates, by Country

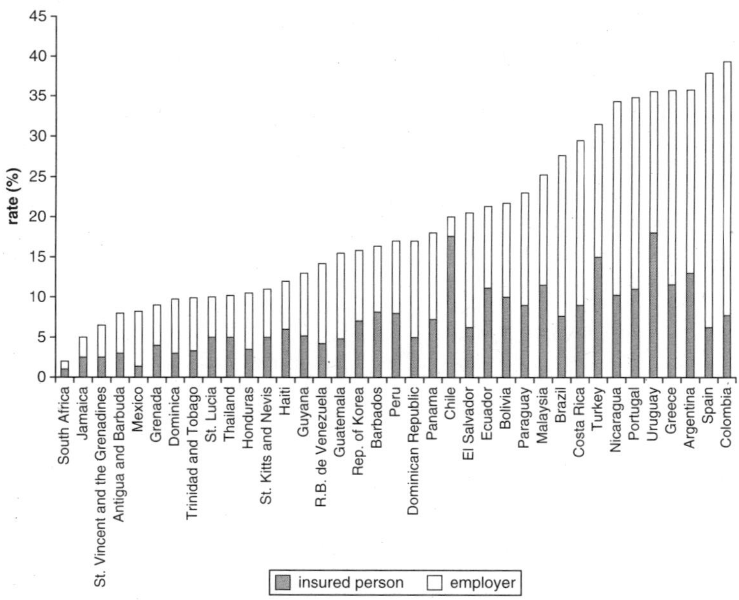

Sources: SSA and ISSA 2006a, 2006b, 2007a, 2007b.

South American countries have the highest contribution rates, followed by Central American countries. Caribbean countries, in contrast, have the lowest rates by far.

What Do Contributors Get for These Rates?

On average, the higher the contribution rates, the greater the number of programs. Five countries (Argentina, Brazil, Chile, Colombia, and the República Bolivariana de Venezuela) cover all types of risks; eight other countries cover all except unemployment (Bolivia, Costa Rica, the Dominican Republic, Mexico, Nicaragua, Trinidad and Tobago, and Uruguay) or family allowances (Ecuador). Most Caribbean countries provide only old-age benefits, disability coverage, cash benefits for sickness and maternity, and work injury coverage.[3]

Looking at the level of benefits provided under the available programs, according to this measure, one notes that social security regulations in the region appear to offer less protection to workers than those in developed countries and countries in Eastern Europe and Central Asia, but they offer more protection than regulations in East Asia (IDB 2003). Large variations exist across the region, with Bolivia, Jamaica, and Peru having the lowest benefits, and Argentina, Colombia, and Panama having the highest levels of protection, similar to the levels observed in developed countries. However, recent evidence suggests that the benefits are often not valued to the full amount of the associated social security contributions (Heckman and Pagés 2004; Perry and others 2007).

Who Ultimately Assumes the Burden?

In the economics literature, the effects of labor costs—including wages and nonwage costs such as social security contributions—on employment are generally assessed by estimating the change in employment in response to a 1 percent change in labor costs (that is, the elasticity of labor demand). However, this approach assumes that the whole burden of the tax is borne by employers—and, therefore, any change in social security implies a one-to-one change in labor costs. In reality, which party bears the burden of the tax depends on how much the supply and demand of labor adjust with a change in the price of labor.

The existing empirical literature offers some guidance on the plausible range of labor demand elasticity estimates. Heckman and Pagés (2004) review the available estimates and suggest that most lie between –0.30 and –0.50 (that is, a 10 percent increase in the cost of labor would cause employment to decline between 3 percent and 5 percent).[4] Taymaz (2006) summarizes additional studies for transition and other middle-income countries, such as Turkey, and also reports that most of the (long-run) elasticities estimates are in the –0.20 to –0.40 range.[5]

As noted, labor demand elasticities do not fully capture the employment effects of changes in labor taxes because those effects also depend on the tax incidence. The available evidence in the region shows that the shift of the cost of contributions onto wages is only partial (see the cross-country analysis in Heckman and Pagés 2004). Such results have been confirmed by individual country studies, for example, in Argentina (Mondino and Montoya 2004); Chile (Edwards and Cox Edwards 2002); Colombia (Kugler and Kugler 2003); Ecuador (MacIsaac and Rama 1997); and Mexico (Marrufo 2001, as reported in Auerbach, Genoni, and Pagés 2005), although at least one study (Gruber 1997) finds evidence of a full shift of taxes onto workers in Chile.

Payroll taxation therefore leads to lower formal employment and higher unemployment. Heckman and Pagés (2004) estimate that a 10 percentage point increase in taxes reduces employment by about 4 percent. A similar conclusion is reached by Nickell (2003), who assembles the results of a number of studies, albeit only from countries of the Organisation for Economic Co-operation and Development (OECD). Nickell (2003: 8) concludes that a 10 percentage point change in the tax wedge can be expected to affect employment by between 1 and 3 percent, "a relatively small but by no means insignificant effect."

An important issue is that the cost of social security contributions is less likely to be transferred to workers when minimum wages are binding. In this case, employers necessarily pay all increases in social security contributions for low-income workers. In fact, high and binding minimum wages may explain why the pass-through of contributions to wages is low in Colombia, where minimum wages are known to be high and binding, but high in the United States, where minimum wages are low and according to many studies not binding.[6] A World Bank (2005a) study for Colombia confirms that there is an important relationship between increasing social security contributions and rising unemployment and informal employment. Figures 8.4 and 8.5 strongly suggest the links between these variables. Figure 8.4 suggests that unemployment increased shortly after an important hike in nonlabor costs brought by the social security reform of 1993. Figure 8.5 confirms that the share of salaried employment relative to self-employment initiates an important downward trend shortly after the same event. Statistical analysis confirms a negative relationship between social security contributions and formal employment and a positive relation between contributions and unemployment.[7]

In sum, although on average a good part of social security contributions may be shifted onto workers in the form of lower wages, that shift is far from total, and it is likely to be particularly low for workers with earnings around the minimum, implying large disemployment effects among low-wage workers.

Figure 8.4 Nonwage Costs and Unemployment in Colombia

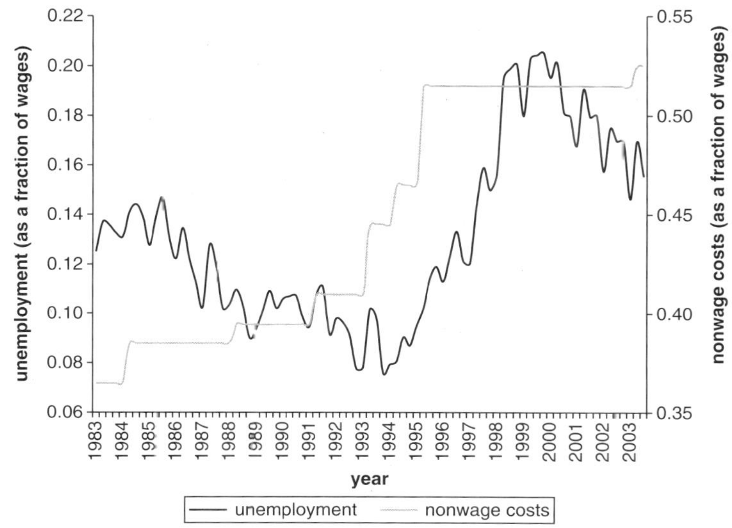

Source: World Bank 2005a.
Note: Data are for the fourth quarter of each year.

What Is the Coverage?

Another important issue regarding social security contributions is that although they have the potential to create important distortions in the labor market, their actual coverage can be quite low, particularly for low-income workers. Depending on the country, the coverage rate of salaried workers varies from about 30 percent (for example, Bolivia and Paraguay) to 77 percent (for example, Chile); on average, only about 40 percent of salaried workers are covered (see Auerbach, Genoni, and Pagés 2005; Rofman 2005). The numbers imply large inequities also; those who are not covered tend to belong to more disadvantaged groups of workers (Perry and others 2007).

A number of factors help explain the low social security coverage in the region. Some evidence shows that although some workers prefer to avoid contributing, disadvantaged workers may actually be rationed out (Auerbach, Genoni, and Pagés 2005). Comparing social security take-up of salaried with self-employed workers,[8] who are similar in other ways,

Figure 8.5 Evolution of Relative Sector Sizes and Wages (Salaried and Self-Employed) in Colombia, 1984–2004

Source: World Bank 2005a.
Note: Data are for the fourth quarter of each year.

Auerbach, Genoni, and Pagés (2005) find that low contribution rates are mostly explained by the low willingness of workers to contribute. Because enforcement is lacking in the region, even salaried workers, for whom contribution ought to be mandatory, are able to evade contributing. However, Auerbach, Genoni, and Pagés (2005) also find evidence that at least some low-wage and part-time workers are rationed out of social security: although they would like to contribute, their employers do not register them (Perry and others 2007).

Rethinking the Provision of Social Security in Latin America and the Caribbean

As discussed, financing social security from labor income is likely to generate important distortions in the labor market and to imply low coverage; countries can consider various options to improve their system.[9] Tax rebates for low-wage workers could provide an important stimulus for registered employment, particularly in countries where minimum wages are binding. The shortfall in revenues could be financed by slightly higher value added taxes. A recent feasibility study for Turkey (Betcherman,

Daysal, and Pagés 2008) suggests that this route may be promising (see box 8.1).

Beyond tinkering with the contribution rate, other reforms can be considered to improve coverage and reduce labor market distortions. Unbundling of contributions for different types of benefits could be an option, for example. Providing basic benefits that are most valued by less affluent workers and allowing higher contributions (and possibly higher benefits) for higher-income workers could bring in the less affluent. Finally, countries should consider the feasibility of financing social security benefits (or

Box 8.1 Employment and Fiscal Effects of Reducing Social Security Contributions in Turkey

Despite strong economic performance, Turkey shows poor employment performance and high labor taxes (World Bank 2006). At the request of the government, the World Bank initiated a study on the employment and fiscal effects of reducing labor taxes. The estimates on the employment effects and the fiscal analysis are summarized in Betcherman and Pagés (2007). Estimates based on establishment-level data for manufacturing and construction reveal that labor demand elasticity in Turkey is quite high (on the order of 0.41 and 0.64, depending on the industries). However, the study also finds evidence of a large wage pass-through at the average wage level, although a much lower one at the minimum wage level. This finding indicates a much higher cost-effectiveness of a tax cut targeted for low-wage workers.

Fiscal simulations show that a 5 percentage point pension contribution reduction coupled with a reduction of 2 percentage points in the unemployment insurance fund contribution for all new hires would increase registered employment by about 1.1 percent, or 85,000 jobs; would reduce the unemployment rate by about 0.35 percentage points; and would increase the social security deficit by 0.75 percent of gross domestic product (GDP) in the first period after the reforms, with a somewhat higher gap over much of the period of the simulation. In contrast, a tax cut that implied the same reduction in social security and unemployment insurance contributions, but targeted only to new hires under 30 years of age, would create almost as many new jobs (70,000) as the across-the-board tax reduction but with only a relatively small effect on the balance of the pension fund (about 0.2 percent of GDP). The estimation of the employment effect does not take into account possible substitutions of subsidized young workers for unsubsidized older ones. Similarly, the estimates of the fiscal effects do not include possible deadweight loss effects (see chapter 7), which, as suggested by Betcherman, Daysal, and Pagés (2008), could be sizable and could increase the estimated fiscal costs by a substantial amount.

some subcomponents) through general revenues. Delinking social security provision from the labor market would eliminate perverse incentives toward informal employment.

Improving Working Conditions through Collective Bargaining

Three main features of collective bargaining affect the flexibility of wages and the performance of firms: (a) the degree of bargaining power of unions together with the monopoly rent that can be shared between firms and workers, (b) the level of negotiation and the coordination between employers' and workers' organizations, and (c) the extent to which direct government intervention influences their behavior and representation.[10]

Decline of Union Influence

Economic and political factors have led to the weakening of unions in many Latin American and Caribbean countries. For example, the drop in unionization in Peru from 40 to 30 percent in the second half of the 1980s was largely due to the decline in government employment and the expansion of temporary employment. In addition, after 1992, the diminished protection granted to labor unions in Peru was the main reason behind the even sharper decline in unionization (Saavedra and Torero 2004).[11]

The weakness of the region's unions is demonstrated in the following three characteristics. First, union membership, which partly determines unions' power, varies across the region, but it has mostly been declining (IDB 2003). This decline occurred largely because union membership was often concentrated in manufacturing and public services, both downsized substantially in many countries. Moreover, the increasing competition, the expansion of small firms in services, the development of temporary contracts, and the expansion of the informal economy have contributed to reduce unionization. For example, even in countries where all workers with written contracts are covered under collective agreements, the small proportion of workers who actually have written contracts means that only a small share of all salaried workers are covered by collective bargaining. This share is about 25 percent in Jamaica, according to unions, and 5 percent in Honduras, according to government sources.[12]

Second, except in a few countries such as Brazil, Honduras, and Jamaica, the coverage of collective agreements typically does not extend to nonmembers in the region (such as can be the case in some European countries). Unions' influence is therefore not boosted in this way.

Finally, the state controls participation at the bargaining table and legitimizes agreements (O'Connell 1999). The state also defines what type of unions can organize and in some cases requires state authorization for a union to form. For example, in Brazil, only one union may exist in a given occupational category, and it has a monopoly in representing the corresponding workers. In Mexico, more than one union can exist, but only certified union leaders can engage in collective bargaining or call a strike. Certification requires that unions be registered by the state.

Little Influence of Unions on Labor Market Performance

One of the ways in which unions affect employment is through their wage demands. In Latin America and the Caribbean, wage premiums for union members are between 5 and 10 percent (IDB 2003). This level is low by international standards; for example, in Malaysia, premiums are 15 to 20 percent, and in South Africa, they are 10 to 24 percent. Within the region, other factors are more important in determining wage differentials: for example, the returns to education in the region are greater (that is, every year of secondary education increases earnings by 11 percent relative to the earnings of workers with primary education).

The effects of unions on productivity depend on market conditions and industrial relations. Unions tend to be firm or sector based, rather than national or sector based, as in non-English-speaking OECD countries. Under certain circumstances and depending on the coordination between employers' and workers' organizations, such arrangements can lead to efficient wage setting. In Mexico, unions have attempted to protect low-skill jobs at the expense of higher productivity (Maloney and Ribeiro 2001), and in Guatemala, unionization is associated with lower productivity of coffee farmers (Urizar and Lee 2003). In other countries, the opposite has happened. In Brazil, greater participation of workers in certain aspects of company management contributed to better productivity and profitability. The effect was greater in unionized companies because unions facilitated communication between management and workers (Menezes-Filho and others 2008). An unstable political environment also tends to reduce incentives for unions to "invest" in wage restraint in exchange for better expected economic outcomes in the future (see Aidt and Tzannatos 2002; Forteza and Rama 2006). Higher union wage premiums and bigger drags on productivity are found in countries and sectors lacking competitive pressure. Investment climate improvements that enhance competition in output markets and economic stability are therefore likely to discipline union behavior so that it is more conducive to better outcomes for the economy (Calmfors 1993). However, as illustrated in some countries of the region, increased market liberalization may also lead to a decline in unionization.

Evolving Role of Unions in a Globalized World

Since the 1990s, many unions in the region have taken on new roles and adapted to new economic realities. For example, unions in Mexico participated in the design of adjustment programs, including actions in the labor market, and agreed on social pacts that facilitated macrostabilization. Some reforms of collective bargaining were also carried out. For example, the wage bargaining system in Peru was reformed in 1992. The reform increased direct negotiation by relaxing the collective negotiation process, introducing voluntary arbitration as an alternative to state administrative decision, and eliminating state approval of agreements. The reform also increased collective autonomy by protecting unions' right to registration—and union pluralism by allowing more than one union to exist in a firm (Eslava and others 2004). In other countries, unions have expanded their intervention by helping informal workers to get credit, improve their human capital, and obtain health support. For example, the Argentinian Union of Rural Workers and Stevedores (Unión Argentina de Trabajadores Rurales y Estibadores) operates a health insurance and unemployment fund that includes a large number of unregistered and unprotected agricultural workers, many of whom are from neighboring countries such as Bolivia, Paraguay, and Uruguay.

Overall, unions do not appear to have a strong effect on labor market outcomes in the region, mostly because they have little bargaining power. However, in a globalized world, unions have taken on important new roles, such as extending help to informal sector workers. Moreover, in a context of labor market reforms, unions have a role to play and have a place in voicing the concerns of workers. Such an inclusive process can help obtain buy-in for generally unpopular reforms. These issues are explored in more detail later.

Applying Wage Floors

Minimum wages are controversial because, although they may protect individuals from becoming working poor, they may negatively affect employment. Moreover, when enforcement is weak, a hike in the minimum wage provides incentives for firms and workers to underreport wages or for firms and jobs to remain in the informal economy. The minimum wage makes firms and jobs with low productivity levels unviable, at least in the formal sector. In fact, noncompliance with the minimum wage is concentrated among the most vulnerable workers because the minimum wage represents a higher proportion of their available wage than for other types of workers. They are therefore likely to be overrepresented in informal activities, where they work for only a fraction of the mandated minimum wage.

Compliance decreases with the level of minimum wage. In Latin America and the Caribbean, the largest proportions of workers who earn less than the minimum wage are found in countries where it is comparatively high—as in Paraguay (where the majority of workers earn less than two-thirds of the minimum wage), Nicaragua (40 percent of workers earn below the minimum), and Colombia (25 percent earn below the minimum). At the same time, other countries of the region, such as Argentina, Jamaica, Mexico, and Uruguay, see very small proportions of individuals working at subminimal wages, likely because of the very low level of the minimum wage rather than because of good enforcement (Cunningham 2006; see also ILO 2004, figure 1.d).

Despite low compliance, the minimum wage is binding in the formal sector of several countries of the region[13] and operates as a strong pay signal for the informal sector in many countries. This finding implies that hikes in the minimum wage can have distributional implications that go beyond the formal sector: the income of the low paid might increase in both segments of the economy, but their employment prospects might decline (Cunningham 2006; Gindling and Terrell 2005; Maloney and Núñez 2004).

Overall, increases in the minimum wage have resulted in somewhat higher unemployment and lower employment (Cunningham 2006). The size of the effect is, on average, a job loss of 2 percent for a 10 percent increase in the minimum wage. Mexico is an exception, perhaps because of the very low level of the minimum wage. As could be expected, these effects concern mostly jobs in the formal economy, and vulnerable groups of workers such as women, youths, and low-skill workers. To evaluate the significance of such an effect, one finds it useful to compare these findings with those of developed countries. For example, in the United States, although a 10 percent increase in the minimum wage was found to reduce teenage employment by 1 to 3 percent by Brown, Gilroy, and Kohen (1982), subsequent studies found smaller and even insignificant effects (Brown 1999; Card and Krueger 1995). Because the Latin American and Caribbean findings concern overall employment rather than a subsection of the workforce, they point to a larger impact in the region (although the reduction of employment is concentrated in the lower end of the wage distribution). However, as suggested in Gindling and Terrell (2007), the overall employment effect tends to be small.

Minimum wages can help governments protect the income of workers. However, they should be set at levels that, while guaranteeing a basic minimum, do not create large distortions. They should be adapted to the structure of national labor markets. Countries of the region can follow the experience of several countries that have reduced the minimum wage relative to the average wage, largely by reducing its indexation and applying a subminimum wage to some groups (young workers) or for subnational labor markets. The effects can be marked. For example, the erosion of the minimum wage in Mexico in the 1990s is estimated to have boosted female employment (Feliciano 1998). Subminimum apprenticeship wages are available in many industrial countries (such as Belgium, Canada, New Zealand, Portugal, and Spain) and are being used in several countries of Latin America and the Caribbean, including Chile and Colombia. They are estimated to have significantly increased job opportunities for young graduates in Chile.[14] In the 2002 reform of the labor market, Colombia further allowed remunerations to be lower than the minimum wage for apprenticeship contracts: 50 percent in the learning phase, and 75 percent in the practical one (Cunningham 2006).

Improving Workers' Skills

A way to increase the income of workers is to enhance their earning potential by improving their skills. Formal education plays a central role in giving workers the skills necessary for future employment, and evidence in industrial, transition, and developing countries shows that formal education cannot be substituted for training.[15] However, empirical evidence also suggests that training can bridge the gap between skills learned at school and skills that firms need to adopt new technologies and innovations (De Ferranti and others 2003; Gill, Montenegro, and Domeland 2002).

In fact, most countries of the region have developed vocational training that is accessible to all in parallel with their education system (Bucheli 2005).[16] In recent years, training policies have evolved to accommodate the increased demand for skills in most countries of the region. In particular, they have focused on involving private training suppliers and on giving incentives for firms to provide formal training.

The region has the same level, if not more, of formal training provision by firms as found in other regions. Data from the Enterprise Surveys reveal that firms of Latin America and the Caribbean are, on average, more likely to offer formal training than those of Eastern Europe and Central Asia, those of a sample of European countries, and those of the Middle East and North Africa. If one controls for firms' characteristics, Latin American and Caribbean firms have an average probability of providing formal training of 63.6 percent, compared with 24.1 percent in the Middle East and North Africa, 35.3 percent in European countries, and 39 percent in Eastern Europe and Central Asia.

Latin America and the Caribbean differs from other regions in several respects, however. In particular, small firms, which have been singled out in this book as being at a particular disadvantage in the region, are found to be even less likely to provide training relative to large firms in Latin America and the Caribbean than in the rest of the world (see figure 8.6). This result, combined with the earlier findings that these firms tend

Figure 8.6 Determinants of Firms' Provision of Formal Training

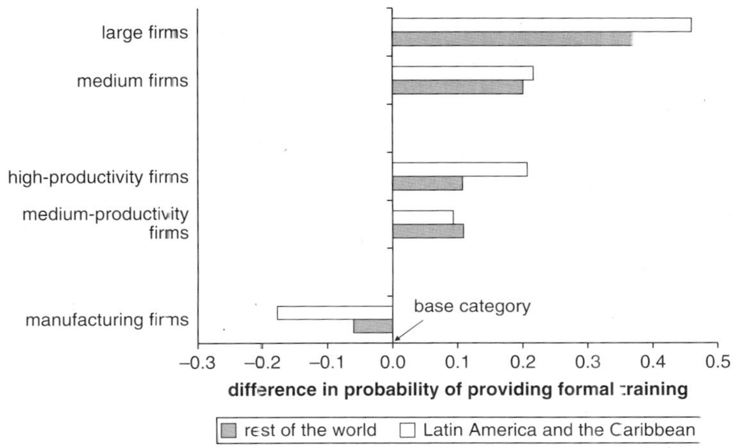

Source: Authors' calculations based on World Bank Enterprise Surveys.

Note: Marginal effects from probit models estimating the provision of formal training as a function of firms' characteristics, interacted with a Latin America and Caribbean region dummy. Marginal effects are statistically significant at 1 percent for large firms, high-productivity firms, and manufacturing firms.

not to be constrained by skills mismatch of labor supply, indicates that small firms in the region have fewer incentives to invest in and adapt new technologies than small firms in other regions. They may therefore be less likely to grow and become more productive. Similarly, firms in manufacturing are found to provide even less training than firms in other sectors relative to other regions. As can be expected, firms in high-productivity sectors are more likely to provide training. Interestingly, firms in high-productivity sectors in the region are even more likely to provide formal training than those in other sectors relative to other regions.

Although training for formal employees is best provided at the level of the firm, governments have a role to play in making sure firms provide enough training. Human capital theory views training, together with formal education, as an investment that raises future productivity at a cost (Becker 1964). Becker's analysis suggests that training provided by firms includes a general and a specific component: the former includes skills that are easily transferable to all firms, and the latter includes skills that are specific to the firms providing the training. Becker's theory suggests that firms provide training in specific skills, whereas workers invest in general skills. Consequently, only in cases where workers are severely credit constrained would government intervention be needed—and not in training itself, but in the credit market. Recent developments in the theoretical literature (Acemoglu and Pischke 1999; extended in Booth and Zoega 2004) have taken into account that firms do provide general training to their workers. They postulate that firms do so because the increase in productivity resulting from any type of training is likely to be higher than the associated increase in wage, thus enabling firms to recoup their investment. This theory does not require relative wage compression, only absolute wage compression. In particular, Booth and Zoega (2004) show that this finding means that firms can have incentives to train under many institutional arrangements, even under piece rates.

In this context, government intervention is desirable because the amount of training provided by the market is unlikely to be sufficient (Acemoglu and Pischke 1999; Booth and Zoega 2004). Such intervention can take two main forms: on-the-job training or classroom training. Various providers exist. Classroom training can be implemented by unions, private agents, and nongovernmental organizations, among other agents, as has occurred in Argentina, Brazil, Mexico, and Uruguay. Training has also developed within sectors—for example, construction in Chile and Mexico, the graphic industry in Argentina, plastics in Colombia, and transportation in Brazil.

Governments either tax firms to provide training or give tax incentives to firms that provide training. Classroom training has been financed through payroll taxes applied to private and sometimes public enterprises (the percentages in the region vary between 0.5 and 2.0 percent). On-the-job training, which can be carried out by the firm itself or through a training provider, has been financed by tax breaks. For example, the Colombian labor market reform allowed refunds of labor taxes to firms that carry out on-site training.[17]

Although the government may relinquish its role as a provider of training, it has to monitor the quality of training actually taking place. There is indeed a risk that firms may carry out some form of (potentially low-quality) training just to recover their fee or that "on-the-job" training may be equivalent to no training at all. Moreover, classroom training provided outside the workplace may be out of touch with the needs of the private sector.

However, monitoring the quality of on-the-job training is very difficult. Using additional regulations or restrictions to guarantee quality tends to be inefficient because it, in turn, creates additional regulatory burdens and leads to low take-up by firms. A way to help improve the quality is to enable workers to vote with their feet (demand-driven approach): giving workers vouchers allows them to choose for themselves relevant training courses. Of course, information about training courses still needs to be centralized and made available to workers: this is the role of the training agencies, which are already in place in the region.

As has happened for the provision of training to the unemployed (chapter 7), provision has been moving from state-led, centralized, supply-driven systems toward more flexible, demand-driven public-private partnerships that are decentralized at the local and sectoral levels. In such systems, governments focus on creating legal frameworks and financial incentives to advance private sector and individual investment in training. The most common include levy grant schemes (compulsory or voluntary taxes on payroll or outcome); levy rebate schemes, as have been implemented in Malaysia, Nigeria, the Netherlands, and many Latin American countries, in which employers are partially reimbursed for approved training; levy exemption schemes, as have been implemented in France, the Republic of Korea, and Morocco, where employers are exempt from levy payments if they spend a percentage (upper bounded) of their payroll in training; tax incentives for approved training, as exist in Chile; and training credits, training awards, and individual training accounts (Aterido 2007).

Chile's system, which relies on a direct tax credit to firms, has been successful. Three main reasons lie behind this success: (a) a decentralized approach, whereby corporations were able to manage public vocational schools, which introduced flexible curricula that matched local labor market needs; (b) the removal of entry barriers to new providers; and (c) the effective allocation of tax credits, which covered not only the cost of training but also the salaries of trainees and contributions to training schools. By contrast, the Brazilian and Nicaraguan tax rebate schemes have been less effective, mostly because of lack of consistency, inefficiency, complicated procedures, and information failures (Aterido 2007).

Improving Enforcement of Labor Regulations and Policies

The effect of labor regulations and policies, such as those described in this chapter and the two previous chapters, on employment and productivity depends significantly on the capacity of countries of the region to enforce the law. Although such effects are well known and commonsense, their effect on employment and productivity is hard to estimate. This section shows that although the countries of the region have made great progress in terms of government accountability, they are still lagging countries of a similar income level in terms of rule of law and government effectiveness. This environment of low governance complicates enforcement of labor (and other) regulations at all levels. Some quantitative estimates of these effects show that the negative impact on labor market performance is statistically significant. However, a lack of data makes assessing the aggregate employment and productivity loss difficult.

Influence of Enforcement on Labor Market Outcomes

Whether the objectives that rules and regulations are meant to achieve ultimately prevail depends on the way they are implemented on the ground. For example, in the context of labor regulations, developing countries often have detailed labor codes, which provide substantial protection—at least on paper. In practice, they generally protect a minority of workers in a subset of activities, often in the public sector, and are largely ignored by the majority of employers. At the same time, however, trying to enforce excessively stringent regulations may be costly for the public authorities and have a negative impact on labor market outcomes. The best strategy is to strengthen enforcement while pursuing regulatory reform to reduce the stringency of such regulations, if excessive.

Empirical evidence shows that better enforcement that increases compliance is associated with higher labor costs, which, in turn, lead to some disemployment effects (see Mondino and Montoya 2004, for Argentina; MacIsaac and Rama 1997, for Ecuador). Better administrative enforcement is also found to lead to lower wages, productivity, and investment. One explanation is that firms' ability to tap into the flexible informal labor market is impeded (see Almeida and Carneiro 2005, for Brazil).

Three Levels of Enforcement: Government, Unions, and Judiciary

Enforcement of labor regulations occurs at several levels. The first level is through public authorities: they are in charge of implementing regulations. Countries that lack administrative capacity will not be able to require economic agents to comply with regulations.[18] Moreover, economic agents will be less inclined to comply with regulations if they perceive the returns to respecting these regulations to be low. This result is especially common when governments and public services are deemed inefficient. Second, within the workplace, unions provide another level of enforcement of regulations. Again, public authorities have a role to play because they set the rules of the game for collective bargaining and influence the potential roles of unions. Finally, the judicial system may be called on to settle industrial and other business-related disputes. The actual or perceived imbalance of bargaining power between employers and employees leads to the assumption that tribunals and courts have social policy responsibilities independent of the legislature. Judiciary decisions come in addition to labor codes and collective agreements, when such legislation and agreements fail, or when there are disputes over them. Depending on judicial direction and scope, this intervention may significantly affect industrial relations and the business environment—and eventually job creation.

Low Administrative Capacity

Employers in Latin America and the Caribbean tend to have little trust in the government's effectiveness and are negatively affected by weak rule of law (chapter 5). The level of enforcement affects the way firms view labor regulations. Surveys of employers reveal that firms that find labor regulations to be a major or very severe obstacle to doing business are less likely than others to find that their government is efficient in delivering services and slightly less likely to find that interpretations of regulations are consistent and predictable.[19] These results tend to hold for all other elements of the business climate. To employers, inefficient governments are associated with greater obstacles to doing business. For example, excessive inspections have a negative effect on employment (see chapter 5). Moreover, these surveys show that employers who report being at their optimum employment level are significantly more likely to report efficient governments than others (figure 8.7). This finding hints that employers who are not satisfied with their government's intervention are not able to adjust employment as freely as they would like, although such analysis does not permit a conclusion on any causality link.

Figure 8.7 Employers' Confidence in the Government and Optimal Employment Level

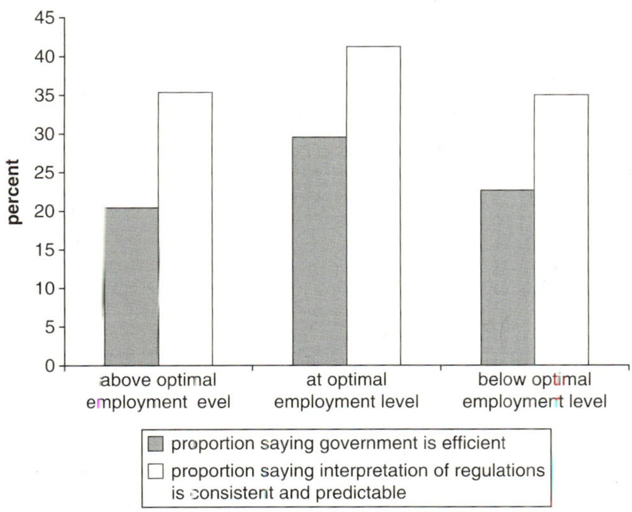

Source: World Bank Enterprise Surveys.

Solutions for Improving the Administration of Services

Involving the private sector and using technological advances can make program administration more efficient. Countries of Latin America and the Caribbean can improve the quality and delivery of social services at relatively low costs by applying technological advances. New products and technologies include magnetic or electronic cards, mobile computing, automated teller machines, and solar technology. A major issue is the initial cost entailed in implementing them. They should therefore be used selectively and in combination with more traditional solutions, depending on the country's need and existing capacity (see Gallaher 2005). For example, smart cards were used to transfer a universal social pension in Namibia. Thanks to this technology, the government was able to make the transfers on time, reliably, and conveniently to beneficiaries; the pension was successful in reaching the poor (van Ginneken 2003). Governments in several countries of the region (Argentina, Brazil, Chile, the Dominican Republic, Mexico, Panama, Peru, Uruguay, and the República Bolivariana de Venezuela) are using private international companies to deliver social services, such as meal and food vouchers or conditional cash transfers, to the population. Governments or public institutions generally buy vouchers (or smart cards) issued by the private company and distribute them to the beneficiaries of the public program. The users spend the vouchers at their face value (or the units of the card) in affiliated networks such as food stores. The private company then refunds the stores. In Chile, the government uses an electronic and voucher-based system to help unemployed people to establish small businesses. Services include providing nonmonetary support for the acquisition of equipment and training for successful creation of small enterprises.

Role of Unions in Enforcement

As well as participating in bargaining over wages, unions can facilitate and monitor the implementation of labor regulations. In the formal sector, unions rely on labor codes and other labor market policies to guarantee their members' rights. For example, U.S. evidence shows that occupational safety and health regulations tend to be better implemented in firms that have unions because these establishments tend to receive more inspections and bigger fines than others (Weil 1991, 1999). More recently, formal and informal unions have emerged and represent the interests of certain groups of workers in Latin America and the Caribbean. Such institutions may push through new standards even for informal workers. For example, the Argentinian Union of Rural Workers and Stevedores, which has created an unemployment fund, provides advanced insurance protection to otherwise ineligible workers.

Nevertheless, labor relations in the region are overall confrontational and marred by lack of trust (IDB 2003). Evidence from World Economic Forum opinion surveys (López-Claros, Porter, and Schwab, 2005; Porter and others 2004a, 2004b) shows that the region is among those where labor relations are generally the most confrontational (figure 8.8). This finding holds true for most countries of the region, except Costa Rica, the Dominican Republic, and El Salvador, where employers and labor tend to be relatively cooperative. A lack of productive cooperation may, in turn, lead to additional costs for employers. For example, disputes may occur more often, and unions may use regulations as a confrontation tool instead of a means to protect unfair treatment of workers. In countries such as Brazil and Peru, a large proportion of workers took part in strikes and labor disputes. Moreover, the countries of the region tend to lose more days to labor disputes than do other regions (IDB 2003).

Figure 8.8 Labor-Employer Relations, 2006

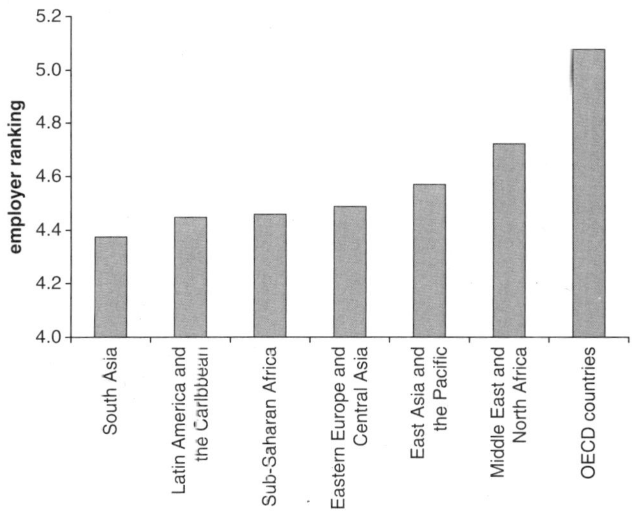

Source: Porter, Schwab, and López-Claros 2006.

Note: Employers ranked the level of cooperation in labor-employer relations on a scale of 1 to 7, where 1 = generally confrontational and 7 = generally cooperative. The Latin American and Caribbean ranking is unchanged from a year earlier (López-Claros, Porter, and Schwab 2005).

Need for Consensus in Improving Labor Regulations

As suggested above, improving enforcement is likely to be associated with an increase in the effect of labor regulations. Therefore, countries also need to revise their regulations and make them more in tune with the requirements of their now-open economies. As the preceding example of the number of hours worked shows, making regulations more flexible does not always mean decreasing protection. New ways of providing flexibility to workers and employers can be found that accommodate all involved. Even if some workers may lose out, the compensating effect of extended coverage may leave aggregate social welfare similar or better. Improved enforcement can be synonymous with improved transparency of procedures and better diffusion of information to workers and employers alike (for example, through the publication on the Internet of labor legislation, as in Peru), thereby improving workers' information set and bargaining power.

In this context, a framework for social dialogue that brings in all the interested stakeholders and responds to the needs of the economy and its stakeholders could be developed. Such a fruitful social dialogue remains a challenge in many countries. However, examples of successful dialogue between government, employer, and workers' representatives exist, some of which are in the region—for example, Barbados and Panama (see Fashoyin 2004).

Role of the Judiciary in Enforcement

The importance of the judiciary in affecting economic outcomes has recently become the focus of empirical research (Besley and Payne 2003; La Porta and others 2004). The judiciary's functions of conflict resolution and rule enforcement are a crucial part of government intervention. With more recognition comes more responsibility and scrutiny, however, and the contributions of the judiciary to economic development have not all been viewed in a positive light. Thus, stakeholders have increasingly demanded institutional changes (World Bank 2003). The region has known several decades of judicial reforms, including in the labor courts. From these changes, some evidence on the way the latter work and affect labor market outcomes has emerged.

The implementation of labor law in courts is likely to affect the impact of labor regulations such as severance payments or notice periods on labor outcomes. Evidence for countries of the region (Argentina, Brazil, and the Dominican Republic) suggests that the majority of claims related to labor matters pertain to payment disputes, generally after a dismissal (World Bank 2003).

The empirical and theoretical evidence currently available on this topic is based on court case studies. They identify several types of issues that can arise when the judiciary is involved in labor relations, all of which affect its eventual effect on labor market outcomes. First, judges may make idiosyncratic decisions that have wider impacts. For example, a U.S. Supreme Court ruling held that the fines imposed by a union on members who—in violation of the union constitution—resigned during a strike constituted an unfair labor practice. This decision weakened the ability of unions to rely on the support of their membership in industrial actions (Morgenstern 1991).

Second is an issue of judicial independence and accountability. Judges' decisions may be influenced by external factors that lead them to make judgments biased toward one of the parties. In an environment of comparatively low rule of law, such as Latin America and the Caribbean, this phenomenon may be exacerbated. However, these issues may arise even in countries with strong governance (for example, in federal countries where implementation varies by state and in countries that allow greater discretionary power to judges). In most countries of the region, except The Bahamas, Honduras, and Trinidad and Tobago, judges have very limited or no discretionary power over the amount of the award that workers receive when they win a case.[20] In most cases, the bias that judges may have, therefore, comes through the choice of the winning party. Other delays may appear even when this bias does not exist. For example, in Argentina, where awards are on the whole evenly shared between employers and employees, appeal rates are high: cases that could, in principle, be solved quickly end up being drawn out, often because of the parties (mostly employers), not the judicial system (World Bank 2003). Moreover, enforcement of judicial decisions may become a source of conflict itself, and even when it does not, the steps are multiple, onerous, and costly (Hammergren 2002).

Third, excessive judicial intervention in labor relations may lead to increases in caseloads and eventually to delays. In Brazil, employer surveys indicate that when workers contest dismissals in a tribunal, the full process, from notification of dismissal to court decision, takes, on average, nearly two years. Evidence for Brazil indicates that labor court procedures may become a significant part of the total budget for the judiciary. Evidence from several countries of the region shows that conciliation is generally cheaper and less time consuming; however, conciliation is not often emphasized. A small majority of countries of the region have no built-in official conciliation system, whether administrative or as part of the judicial procedure. In only a few countries (Argentina, Haiti, Trinidad and Tobago, and Uruguay) is conciliation required as a first step in a labor dispute. Case analysis (for example, in Argentina) indeed reveals that delays can be reduced when judges emphasize conciliation (World Bank 2003). In other countries (such as Bolivia, Costa Rica, Ecuador, and Panama), some form of administrative proceeding or optional conciliation exists. The recourse to the courts also depends on the cost that workers expect to incur. For example, in Argentina, the amount in dispute is often larger in labor cases than in civil cases.[21] Probably this result is because, unlike civil courts, labor courts do not require the accusing parties to pay a deposit based on a percentage of the amount in dispute (World Bank 2003).

Finally, as previously mentioned, the overall effect on labor market outcomes is difficult to assess. Because of a relatively small number of cases,[22] judgments themselves are unlikely to have a direct effect on employment and productivity. They may increase labor costs (by interpretation of regulations more in favor of workers, delays, and legal costs) for the firms involved in the court action. In this context, the effects of the judicial system may be more of an issue for certain types of firms. World Bank Enterprise Surveys for Brazil suggest that, among firms that have fired workers in the year preceding the survey, large firms are more likely to see laid-off workers contest the firing through a tribunal. Moreover, once started, court procedures last longer for large firms than for other firms.[23] Finally, suggesting that unions could have a beneficial role in conciliation, the correlation between the proportion of laid-off workers who go to court and union density (controlling for firm size) in the firm is negative but statistically insignificant.

The perceived action of the labor courts likely influences the behavior of firms in the economy at large, however.[24] This type of effect is to some extent captured in business climate indicators that have been discussed in chapter 5—in particular those pertaining to the legal environments of the countries and the associated uncertainty about the interpretation of the law. Direct evidence of such effects exists for the United States. For example, states in which judges are appointed rather than elected have fewer cases of race, age, and gender discrimination brought to court. In other words, judges whose position does not depend on popular accountability are more likely to make pro-employer judgments. These effects are likely attributable to a reputation effect (Besley and Payne 2003).

Conclusion

Similarly to other countries around the world, the countries of the Latin American and Caribbean region have designed policies that aim to improve the quality of jobs. Some progress has been achieved in a number of countries (for example, the training system in Chile and the youth training programs in a number of countries). Apart from the case of collective bargaining, for which it has been shown that most countries of the region need to foster better industrial relations, the main issue that has been identified is the lack of effectiveness of these policies. There are two reasons for this problem: (a) enforcement has been lacking, and

(b) government effectiveness, given limited resources and regulatory quality, has been lacking, thereby depressing the incentives for workers and firms to abide by the regulations and take advantage of the services. Resolving these problems are priorities for most countries of the region.

Notes

1. The rigidity of hours index has five components: (a) whether night work is unrestricted; (b) whether weekend work is allowed; (c) whether the workweek can consist of 5.5 days; (d) whether the workday can extend to 12 hours or more, including overtime; and (e) whether the annual paid vacation days are 21 or fewer. For each of these questions, if the answer is "no," the country is assigned a score of 1; otherwise a score of 0 is assigned. See http://www.doingbusiness.org.

2. In the Colombian 2002 reform, the diurnal shift was extended from 12 hours to 14 hours (from 6 a.m. to 10 p.m. instead of from 6 a.m. to 6 p.m.). This measure reduced the premium paid for nocturnal work (40 percent over the regular wage). The new law also allows flexible working hours for the commerce and service sectors. For these sectors, daily working hours can vary from 4 to 10 hours, with a maximum of 48 hours per week; work can be completed at any time of the day and any day of the week. Moreover, extra payments for work on Sundays and holidays were slightly reduced.

3. See SSA and ISSA (2006a, table 1) for a detailed list of the programs for each country.

4. This range is based on the literature review in Vroman and Brusentsev (2005), who rely heavily on Hamermesh (1993). Heckman and Pagés (2004) present these estimates with some caution, because of the lack of empirical evidence from middle-income countries. A more recent study of the eight new European Union countries (Czech Republic, Estonia, Hungary, Latvia, Lithuania, Poland, Slovak Republic, and Slovenia) finds a higher elasticity of employment of between 0.5 and 0.8 (World Bank 2005b). However, some possibility of bias exists in these estimates, which rely on macrodata, although which direction any bias might go is not clear.

5. For a list of these studies, see Taymaz (2006).

6. See Gruber (1994) for an analysis of the effect of mandatory maternity leave on employment and wages in the United States.

7. In particular, the study found that formal employment and unemployment is cointegrated with social security contributions and that the sign of the cointegration relationship confirms the stated relationships.

8. Because contributions are generally voluntary for the self-employed, their decisions are likely closer to their preferences.

9. See Perry and others (2007) on informality for a more elaborated discussion on social security reforms.

10. Industrial relations between freely elected (and representative) associations of workers and employers can improve firms' performance by reducing uncertainty and transaction costs and improving information flows. However, under certain circumstances, unions may act as monopolists, improving wages and working conditions for their members at the expense of nonunionized workers and the economy.

11. See also Zegarra and Ravina (2003) for a discussion of the declined union density among teachers in Peru.

12. These numbers come from a questionnaire administered by the Inter-American Development Bank in 2003.

13. A World Bank study (Cunningham 2006) finds that the wage distribution in the formal economy shows a spike at the minimum wage in Brazil, Chile, Colombia, Ecuador, Nicaragua, Panama, Paraguay, Peru, and the República Bolivariana de Venezuela. Spikes are also present in the wage distribution of the informal economy in Brazil, Chile, Colombia, Ecuador, El Salvador, Mexico, Nicaragua, Panama, Paraguay, Peru, and the República Bolivariana de Venezuela.

14. See Feliciano (1998) for Mexico and Gill, Montenegro, and Domeland (2002) for the experience of Latin American countries that have introduced apprentice wages in the 1990s.

15. The evaluation of vocational and academic education provided as part of the basic curriculum is beyond the scope of this report. See De Ferranti and others (2003) for a review of the ways to close the education and technology gaps in the region.

16. See Cinterfor (2001) for a description of the main organizational arrangements in the region.

17. The region has seen a dramatic increase in training provision that has been financed through other means, such as international cooperation, international organizations, and application of user fees (that is, participants in the programs pay a fee) to those who can afford it. As well as financing training, this method can help in formalization, especially if services are geared toward informal workers.

18. For example, interviews reveal that sanctions against firms that do not comply with minimum wage regulations are often not enforced because of lack of resources—ranging from lack of vehicles to perform inspections to lack of telephones to receive complaints (Kristensen and Cunningham 2006).

19. About 16 percent of firms that report labor regulations to be a major or very severe obstacle to doing business find their government efficient, against 30 percent for other firms. Similarly, about 34 percent of firms that report labor regulations to be a major or very severe obstacle to doing business agree that interpretations of regulations are consistent and predictable, against 43 percent of other firms. All mean differences are statistically different.

20. Data collected by Inter-American Development Bank in 1999 and 2000.

21. The amounts in dispute tend to be relatively small in civil and labor courts; 60 percent of cases are under US$15,352 for labor.

22. Data for Brazil indicate about 25 labor cases filed per 100,000 economically active persons (World Bank 2004).

23. Interestingly, there is no difference across firms' sizes in the proportion of workers who contest layoffs in courts.

24. An empirical study for Italy reveals that the same company may adopt different personnel policy and strategies for workforce adjustment depending on the perceived orientation of judges, which, in turn, is influenced by local labor market conditions (see Ichino, Polo, and Rettore 2003).

References

Acemoglu, D., and J.-S. Pischke. 1999. "The Structure of Wages and Investment in General Training." *Journal of Political Economy* 107 (3): 539–72.

Aidt, T., and Z. Tzannatos. 2002. *Unions and Collective Bargaining: Economic Effects in a Global Environment*. Washington, DC: World Bank.

Almeida, R., and P. Carneiro. 2005. "Enforcement of Labor Regulations, Informal Labor, and Firm Performance." Policy Research Working Paper 3756, World Bank, Washington, DC.

Aterido, R. 2007. "If On-the-Job Training Is So Important to Competitiveness, Why Isn't There a Better Market for It?" Employment Policy Primer 8, World Bank, Washington, DC.

Auerbach, P., M.-E. Genoni, and C. Pagés. 2005. "Social Security Coverage and the Labor Market in Developing Countries." Research Department Working Paper 537, Inter-American Development Bank, Washington, DC.

Becker, G. 1964. *Human Capital*. Chicago: University of Chicago Press.

Besley, T., and A. Payne. 2003. "Judicial Accountability and Economic Policy Outcomes: Evidence from Employment Discrimination Charges." Working Paper 03/11, Institute for Fiscal Studies, London.

Betcherman G., N. M. Daysal, and C. Pagés. 2008. "Do Employment Subsidies Work? Evidence from Regionally Targeted Subsidies in Turkey." IZA Discussion Paper 3508, Institute for the Study of Labor, Bonn.

Betcherman, G., and C. Pagés. 2007. "Estimating the Impact of Labor Taxes on Employment and the Balances of the Social Insurance Funds in Turkey." World Bank, Washington, DC.

Booth, A., and G. Zoega. 2004. "Is Wage Compression a Necessary Condition for Firm-Financed General Training?" *Oxford Economic Papers* 56 (1): 88–97.

Brown, C. 1999. "Minimum Wages, Employment, and the Distribution of Income." In *Handbook of Labor Economics*, ed. O. Ashenfelter, 2101–53. Amsterdam: North-Holland.

Brown, C., C. Gilroy, and A. Kohen. 1982. "The Effect of Minimum Wage on Employment and Unemployment." *Journal of Economic Literature* 20 (2): 487–528.

Bucheli, M. 2005. "Las políticas activas de mercado de trabajo: Un panorama internacional de experiencias y evaluaciones." Estudios y Perspectivas 2, Comisión Económica para América Latina y el Caribe, Montevideo.

Calmfors, L. 1993. "Centralisation of Wage Bargaining and Macroeconomic Performance: A Survey." *OECD Economic Studies* 21 (Winter): 161–91.

Card, D., and A. B. Krueger. 1995. *Myth and Measurement: The New Economics of the Minimum Wage*. Princeton, NJ: Princeton University Press.

Cinterfor (Inter-American Centre for Knowledge Development in Vocational Training). 2001. *Modernization in Vocational Education and Training in the Latin American and the Caribbean Region*. Montevideo: Cinterfor, ILO.

Cunningham, W. 2006. *Minimum Wages in Latin America and the Caribbean: The Impact on Employment, Inequality, and Poverty*. Washington, DC: World Bank.

De Ferranti, D., G. E. Perry, I. S. Gill, J. L. Guasch, W. Maloney, C. Sánchez-Páramo, and N. Schady. 2003. *Closing the Gap in Education and Technology*. Washington, DC: World Bank.

Edwards, S., and A. Cox Edwards. 2002. "Social Security Privatization and Labor Markets: The Case of Chile." *Economic Development and Cultural Change* 50 (3): 465–89.

Eslava, M., J. Haltiwanger, A. Kugler, and M. Kugler. 2004. "The Effects of Structural Reforms on Productivity and Profitability Enhancing Reallocation: Evidence from Colombia." *Journal of Development Economics* 75 (2): 333–72

Fashoyin, T. 2004. "Tripartite Cooperation, Social Dialogue, and National Development." *International Labour Review* 143 (4): 342–71.

Feliciano, Z. M. 1998. "Does Minimum Wage Affect Employment in Mexico?" *Eastern Economic Journal* 24 (2): 165–80.

Forteza, A., and M. Rama. 2006. "Labor Market 'Rigidity' and the Success of Economic Reforms across More Than 100 Countries." *Journal of Policy Reform* 9 (1): 75–105.

Gallaher, M. 2005. "A Technology White Paper on Improving the Efficiency of Social Safety Net Program Delivery in Low Income Countries: An Introduction to Available and Emerging Mobile Technologies." Social Protection Discussion Paper 0522, World Bank, Washington, DC.

Gill, I. S., C. E. Montenegro, and D. Domeland, eds. 2002. *Crafting Labor Policy: Techniques and Lessons from Latin America*. Washington, DC: World Bank.

Gill, I. S., T. Packard, and J. Yermo. 2005. *Keeping the Promise of Social Security in Latin America*. Palo Alto, CA: Stanford University Press.

Gindling, T. H., and K. Terrell. 2005. "The Effect of Minimum Wages on Actual Wages in Formal and Informal Sectors in Costa Rica." *World Development* 33 (11): 1905–21.

———. 2007. "The Effects of Multiple Minimum Wages throughout the Labor Market: The Case of Costa Rica." *Labor Economics* 14 (3): 485–511.

Gruber, J. 1994. "The Incidence of Mandated Maternity Benefits." *American Economic Review* 84 (3): 622–41.

———. 1997. "Consumption Smoothing Effects of Unemployment Insurance." *American Economic Review* 87 (1): 192–205.

Hamermesh, D. S. 1993. *Labor Demand*. Princeton, NJ: Princeton University Press.

Hammergren, L. 2002. "Uses of Empirical Research in Refocusing Judicial Reforms: Lessons from Five Countries." World Bank, Washington, DC. http://siteresources.worldbank.org/INTLAWJUSTINST/Resources/usesOfER.pdf.

Heckman, J., and C. Pagés. 2004. "Introduction." In *Law and Employment: Lessons from Latin America and the Caribbean*, ed. J. Heckman and C. Pagés, 1–108. Chicago: University of Chicago Press.

Ichino, A., M. Polo, and E. Rettore. 2003. "Are Judges Biased by Labor Market Conditions?" *European Economic Review* 47 (5): 913–44.

IDB (Inter-American Development Bank). 2003. *Good Jobs Wanted: Labor Markets in Latin America—2004 Report on Economic and Social Progress in Latin America*. Washington, DC: IDB.

ILO (International Labour Office). 2004. *2004 Labour Overview: Latin America and the Caribbean*. Lima: ILO.

———. 2005. *2005 Labour Overview: Latin America and the Caribbean*. Lima: ILO.

Kristensen, N., and W. Cunningham. 2006. "Do Minimum Wages in Latin America and the Caribbean Matter? Evidence from 19 Countries." Policy Research Working Paper 3870, World Bank, Washington, DC.

Kugler, A., and M. Kugler. 2003. "The Labor Market Effects of Payroll Taxes in a Middle-Income Country: Evidence from Colombia." IZA Discussion Paper 852, Institute for the Study of Labor, Bonn, Germany.

La Porta, R., F. López-de-Silanes, C. Pop-Eleches, and A. Shleifer. 2004. "Judicial Checks and Balances." *Journal of Political Economy* 112 (2): 445–70.

López-Claros, A., M. E. Porter, and K. Schwab, eds. 2005. *The Global Competitiveness Report 2005–2006*. Basingstoke, U.K.: Palgrave Macmillan.

MacIsaac, D., and M. Rama. 1997. "Determinants of Hourly Earnings in Ecuador: The Role of Labor Market Regulations." *Journal of Labor Economics* 15 (3): S126–65.

Maloney, W., and J. Núñez. 2004. "Measuring the Impact of Minimum Wages: Evidence from Latin America." In *Law and Employment: Lessons from Latin America and the Caribbean*, ed. J. Heckman and C. Pagés, 109–30. Chicago: University of Chicago Press.

Maloney, W., and E. P. Ribeiro. 2001. "Employment and Wage Effects of Mexican Unions: A Case of Extreme Efficient Bargaining." World Bank, Washington, DC.

Marrufo, G. 2001. "The Incidence of Social Security Regulation in Economies with Partial Compliance: Evidence from the Reform in Mexico." Ph.D. diss., University of Chicago, Chicago.

Menezes-Filho, N., J. Chahad, H. Zylberstajn, and E. Pazello. 2008. "Trade Unions and the Economic Performance of Brazilian Establishments." *Estudios Económicos* 38 (1): 55–72.

Mondino, G., and S. Montoya. 2004. "The Effects of Labor Market Regulations on Employment Decisions by Firms: Empirical Evidence from Argentina." In *Law and Employment: Lessons from Latin America and the Caribbean*, ed. J. Heckman and C. Pagés, 351–400. Chicago: University of Chicago Press.

Morgenstern, F. 1991. "From the Particular to the General: Limitations to the Judicial Treatment of Social Policy Issues." *International Labour Review* 130 (5–6): 559.

Nickell, S. J. 2003. "Employment and Taxes." CESifo Working Paper 1109, Center for Economic Studies and Ifo Institute for Economic Research, Munich, Germany.

O'Connell, L. D. 1999. "Collective Bargaining Systems in Six Latin American Countries: Degrees of Autonomy and Decentralization." Working Paper 399, Office of the Chief Economist, Inter-American Development Bank, Washington, DC.

Perry, G., W. Maloney, O. Arias, P. Fajnzylber, A. Mason, and J. Saavedra-Chanduvi, eds. 2007. *Informality: Exit and Exclusion*. Washington, DC: World Bank.

Porter, M. E., K. Schwab, and A. López-Claros, eds. 2006. *The Global Competitiveness Report 2006–2007*. New York: Palgrave Macmillan.

Porter, M. E., K. Schwab, X. Sala-i-Martin, and A. López-Claros, eds. 2004a. *The Global Competitiveness Report 2003–2004*. New York: Oxford University Press.

———. 2004b. *The Global Competitiveness Report 2004–2005*. Basingstoke, U.K.: Palgrave Macmillan.

Rofman, R. 2005. "Social Security Coverage in Latin America." Social Protection Discussion Paper Series 0523, World Bank, Washington, DC.

Saavedra, J., and M. Torero. 2004. "Labor Market Reforms and Their Impact on Formal Employment and Job Turnover." In *Law and Employment: Lessons from Latin America and the Caribbean*, ed. J. Heckman and C. Pagés, 131–82. Chicago: University of Chicago Press.

SSA (Social Security Administration) and ISSA (International Social Security Association). 2006a. *Social Security Programs throughout the World: The Americas, 2005*. Washington, DC: SSA.

———. 2006b. *Social Security Programs throughout the World: Europe, 2006*. Washington, DC: SSA.

———. 2007a. *Social Security Programs throughout the World: Africa, 2007*. Washington, DC: SSA.

———. 2007b. *Social Security Programs throughout the World: Asia and the Pacific, 2006*. Washington, DC: SSA.

Taymaz, E. 2006. "Labor Demand in Turkey." World Bank, Washington, DC.

Urizar, H. C., and S. Lee. 2003. "The Effects of Unions on Productivity: Evidence from Large Coffee Producers in Guatemala." Research Network Working Paper R-473, Inter-American Development Bank, Washington, DC.

van Ginneken, W. 2003. "Extending Social Security: Policies for Developing Countries." *International Labour Review* 142 (3): 277–94.

Vroman, W. and V. Brusentsev. 2005. *Unemployment Compensation throughout the World: A Comparative Analysis*. Kalamazoo, MI: W.E. Upjohn Institute.

Weil, D. 1991. "Enforcing OSHA: The Role of Labor Unions." *Industrial Relations* 30 (1): 20–36.

———. 1999. "Are Mandated Health and Safety Committees Substitutes for or Supplements to Labor Unions?" *Industrial Relations* 52 (3): 339–60.

World Bank. 2003. *Regional Research Project: An Analysis of Court Users and Uses in Two Latin American Countries*. Washington, DC: World Bank.

———. 2004. *Brazil: Making Justice Count—Measuring and Improving Judicial Performance in Brazil*. Washington, DC: World Bank.

———. 2005a. *Colombia: Labor Market Adjustment, Reform, and Productivity: What Are the Factors That Matter?* Report 32068-CO. Washington, DC: World Bank.

———. 2005b. "EU-8 Quarterly Economic Report, April 2005, Part II." World Bank, Warsaw.

———. 2006. *Turkey Country Economic Memorandum: Promoting Sustained Growth and Convergence with the European Union*. Washington, DC: World Bank.

Zegarra, E., and R. Ravina. 2003. "Teacher Unionization and the Quality of Education in Peru: An Empirical Evaluation Using Survey Data." Research Network Working Paper R-474, Inter-American Development Bank, Washington, DC.

Index

Boxes, figures, notes, and tables are indicated by b, f, n, and t following page numbers.

C

D

J

K

N

Y

Z

ECO-AUDIT

Environmental Benefits Statement

The World Bank is committed to preserving endangered forests and natural resources. The Office of the Publisher has chosen to print ***Job Creation in Latin America and the Caribbean*** on recycled paper with 30 percent post-consumer waste, in accordance with the recommended standards for paper usage set by the Green Press Initiative, a nonprofit program supporting publishers in using fiber that is not sourced from endangered forests. For more information, visit www.greenpressinitiative.org.

Saved:
- 15 trees
- 11 million British thermal units of energy
- 1,360 pounds of greenhouse gases
- 5,644 gallons of water
- 725 pounds of solid waste

green press INITIATIVE